OXFORD WORLD'S CLASSICS

SELECTED LETTERS

JOHN KEATS was born in London in 1795. Orphaned early, he studied medicine at Guy's Hospital and, in 1816, became one of a new generation of qualified apothecaries. Medicine remained for him a standard of effective action against suffering, but he soon abandoned the profession in order to live for and by his poetry. He published three volumes during his lifetime and, while many of his contemporaries were prompt to recognize his greatness, snobbery and political hostility led the Tory press to vilify and patronize him as a 'Cockney poet'. He died of TB at the age of twenty-five. Financial anxieties and the loss of those he loved most had tried him persistently, yet he dismissed the concept of life as a vale of tears and substituted the concept of a 'vale of Soul-making'. His poetry and his remarkable letters reveal a spirit of questioning vitality and profound understanding and his final volume, which contains the great odes and the unfinished *Hyperion*, attests to an astonishing maturity and power.

ROBERT GITTINGS was a poet, biographer, and playwright. His many publications include *John Keats: The Living Years* (1954), *The Mask of Keats* (1956), *The Keats Inheritance* (1964), and *The Odes of Keats* (1970). He died in 1992.

JON MEE is Margaret Candfield Fellow in English at University College, Oxford. He writes on Romantic Period and Post-Colonial literature, and is co-editor of *An Oxford Companion to the Romantic Age* (1999).

OXFORD WORLD'S CLASSICS

JOHN KEATS

Selected Letters

Edited by
ROBERT GITTINGS

Revised, with a new Introduction and Notes, by
JON MEE

OXFORD
UNIVERSITY PRESS

OXFORD
UNIVERSITY PRESS

Great Clarendon Street, Oxford OX2 6DP

Oxford University Press is a department of the University of Oxford.
It furthers the University's objective of excellence in research, scholarship,
and education by publishing worldwide in

Oxford New York

Auckland Bangkok Buenos Aires Cape Town Chennai
Dar es Salaam Delhi Hong Kong Istanbul Karachi Kolkata
Kuala Lumpur Madrid Melbourne Mexico City Mumbai Nairobi
São Paulo Shanghai Singapore Taipei Tokyo Toronto

and an associated company in Berlin

Published in the United States
by Oxford University Press Inc., New York

First published as an Oxford World's Classics paperback 2002

British Library Cataloguing in Publication Data

Data available

Library of Congress Cataloging in Publication Data

Data available

ISBN 0–19–284053–3

1 3 5 7 9 10 8 6 4 2

Typeset in Ehrhardt
by RefineCatch Limited, Bungay, Suffolk
Printed in Great Britain by
Cox & Wyman Ltd.
Reading, Berkshire

CONTENTS

1818

CONTENTS

CONTENTS

1820

ix

CONTENTS

ACKNOWLEDGEMENTS TO THE
FIRST EDITION

Acknowledgement is due to the following institutions holding the originals of manuscript letters: the Berg Collection of the New York Public Library, the British Museum, Haverford College, the Houghton Library of Harvard University, the Indiana University Library, the Keats Museum of the Hampstead Public Library, the Maine Historical Society, the Pierpont Morgan Library, the Historical Society of Pennsylvania, the Princeton University Library, the University of Texas Library, and the Yale University Library; also to the following individual owners of letters: Mr Archibald S. Alexander, Bernardsville, New Jersey; Mr Roger Barrett, Chicago; Mr C. H. Pforzheimer, Jr., New York City; Dr Dallas Pratt, New York City; and Mr Robert H. Taylor, Princeton, New Jersey. A detailed list of sources of manuscript letters appears at page 419.

R.G.

ACKNOWLEDGEMENTS TO THE
SECOND EDITION

I would like to thank Sarah Lodge and Porscha Fermanis without whose valuable assistance this volume would not have been possible. Thanks are also due to Kevin Gilmartin, Andrew King, Helen Moore, Christopher Pelling, Mark Philp, Gillian Russell, and Fiona Stafford for their help. Also, to the Humanities Research Centre of the Australian National University and to everyone who helped in Australia: Judy Buchanan, Leena Messina, and David Free. Finally, I would like to record my deep thanks to Leila Jordan and Sharmila Jordan-Mee for their patience and support while I was preparing this edition.

J.M.

INTRODUCTION

Keats the Letter Writer

'Do you not see how necessary a World of Pains and troubles is to school an Intelligence and make it a soul?' (to George and Georgiana Keats, 14 February–3 May 1819, p. 233). Keats's letters have long been regarded as an extraordinary record of the creation of a soul. But his interest in soul-making is not exclusively bound up with poetic development. Nor is the relationship between these letters and the poetry the only reason that readers today might still find them compelling. For all that Keats was extraordinarily devoted to his aspiration of being 'among the English Poets after my death' (to George and Georgiana Keats, 14–31 October 1818, p. 151), his correspondence is also a lively record of the responses of a particularly sensitive individual to the events and ideas of his contemporary world. London is everywhere in these letters. Its politics, its theatres, its newspapers, the cant language of its literary circles, even its imperial aspirations; these and other threads of London life are woven into the dazzling tapestry of the letters. But Keats is not simply an outside observer. The letters are in a sense written *by* the social life that went on around him. The ideas and language of early nineteenth-century London provide the discourse in which he wrote, but Keats is also participating in a more specific series of ongoing and intersecting conversations between various individuals and groups living in the city and its suburbs. He tells his brothers (23, 24 January 1818, p. 55): 'I am in the habit of taking my papers to Dilkes & copying there; so I chat & proceed at the same time.' There is a strong sense of the correspondence being part of an ongoing 'chat': its digressions, punning, speculations, exaggerations, and teasing extend the sociable culture of the capital's middle classes from the drawing-room to the page. Some letters were literally joint productions—Charles Brown and Keats sometimes interrupt and mock each other as they struggle on the same page for the attention of their recipients (to C. W. Dilke, 31 July 1819, p. 255)—but they are also alert to the fact that their recipients play a part in their creation. He even addresses J. H. Reynolds in one letter as his 'Coscribbler' (3 February 1818, p. 59). Both manner and matter are fitted to his correspondents. Keats tells his brother, for instance, that 'though I am writing *to* you I am all the while writing *at* your Wife' (to George and Georgiana, 17–27 September 1819, p. 296). Treating the ideas expressed in them as formal aesthetic declarations, as critics have traditionally done, is to ignore the fact that he was writing *letters*. Their conversational form is an essential part of their epistolary nature, but what makes them particularly distinctive is Keats's self-consciousness about letter-writing as an activity. At one stage he even jokingly floats the idea of 'a dissertation on letter writing' (to Dilke, 20, 21 September 1818, p. 142). That Keats thought it such a 'pregnant subject' in itself suggests that his letters should be read more carefully in their own right than is often the case. Even if criticism is only just beginning to develop the tools to think about such a complex and unstable genre, Keats's letters deserve to rank as an 'achievement' with the poetry rather than simply be taken as a commentary on it.

Keats and his Age

Keats was the eldest of three brothers; George was born in 1797 and Tom in 1799; as this selection of letters shows, they were very close and kept in constant contact. Keats was also particularly solicitous of the welfare of his younger sister Fanny. The children were born into a family that ran a prosperous livery business from an inn called the Swan and Hoop in Moorgate, London, but the early death of their father in 1804, followed by their mother in 1810, compounded by the uneasy relationship with the tea-broker Richard Abbey, their guardian from 1814, meant that financial problems dogged the lives of all the Keats siblings. Keats himself was born in 1795, a year that witnessed serious economic and political unrest. Britain had been at war with revolutionary France since 1793. Food shortages and the poor progress of the war encouraged the spread of radical ideas that manifested themselves in the mass meetings held by the London Corresponding Society, the capital's main popular radical organization, but despite the fears of the ruling classes about the spread of Thomas Paine's republican ideas among the masses there was no English revolution. By the end of 1795 William Pitt's government had moved to clamp down on radical activity with repressive legislation that played a major part in stifling calls for political reform over the next decade. Throughout Keats's life it remained the case that only those with substantial property were allowed the vote, and many areas, such as the new industrial towns and cities in the north, were completely without parliamentary representation.

Apart from the brief lull of the Peace of Amiens in 1802-3, Keats's entire childhood and early adulthood were spent in a nation at war with the France of the Revolution and then Napoleon. The nation suffered severe economic recessions as a consequence of the burden in 1795-7, 1806-9, and 1810-12. The general sense of commercial, intellectual, and political progress shared by many in the eighteenth century was severely challenged by these twin experiences of war and political repression. Keats's ideas on progress, a constant theme of the letters, consequently had to accommodate the French Revolution as a problem case for his more general sense of a history as a story of continual development for the better. Yet for all these obstacles, industrialization continued apace through the war, and together with the strength of its trading empire this industrial power seemed to many to have been the ultimate cause of British victory in 1815. Indeed Britain emerged from the Napoleonic Wars with its Empire much expanded. The cultural exoticism and sense of national destiny that went with this process of imperial expansion is echoed in Keats's poetry and letters as it is more obviously in Lord Byron's 'Turkish Tales' of 1813-14. Apart from the growth of Empire, Britain was witnessing massive social transformations on the domestic front. Although the most spectacular effects were seen in the rapid growth in the northern cities, such as Birmingham and Manchester, London continued to expand at a rapid pace. From a mid-century population of three-quarters of a million, nearly a million people lived there by 1801. By 1830 this figure had doubled. The result was an uneven mix of new wealth and extreme poverty. By 1807 parts of Pall Mall and the West End were illuminated by gas light, but the environment of other parts of the the city was increasingly polluted by smog and the stench of the river. In between the extremes of what William Cobbett called 'the Great Wen' Keats and his brothers, like many other middle-class families, struggled to maintain and improve their precarious social standing.

Although the letters are very much the record of a writer trying to make a name for himself in the competitive world of literary London over 1816–20, Keats was educated outside the capital itself at a school in Enfield that continued to propound Enlightenment ideas of social and political progress through the dark years of the war. Under the guidance of its headmaster John Clarke, the syllabus at Enfield Academy mixed the Classics with newer scientific subjects and promoted the educational value of questioning and curiosity. The principles instilled by Clarke's school provide a bedrock for much of Keats's writing. Not least because he first became a regular reader of Hunt's weekly paper the *Examiner* there, Enfield prepared Keats perfectly for his involvement with Leigh Hunt and what hostile reviewers were to attack as the 'Cockney School' of young progressive poets. After his education in Enfield, Keats was apprenticed to the apothecary-surgeon Thomas Hammond at Edmonton in 1810. Medicine was a profession undergoing profound changes at the time. Not only were scientific advances making revolutionary changes to the treatment of patients, but medicine was also becoming a regulated profession, a change that was enshrined in the Apothecary Act of July 1815. In the eighteenth century there had been three ranks in the medical profession: apothecaries (who were officially only allowed to dispense drugs, but often acted as doctors to the poor); surgeons (licensed by the Royal College with something of the role of general practitioners); and physicians (expensive, university-trained, healers for the élite). By Keats's time these distinctions were becoming blurred as demand increased. The 1815 legislation was designed to calm the tensions with regard to status between the different kinds of medical practitioners and more specifically to provide proper qualifications for apothecaries. When Keats graduated from his apprenticeship to begin studying at Guy's Hospital, London, in 1815, he was entering what must have looked like a newly respectable profession. Prior to the 1815 Act he would have been free to practise as an apothecary without any further training. Now he had to work in a hospital to gain the minimum qualifications needed to gain an apothecary's licence, but Guy's was an environment which Keats would have found welcoming to the kind of principles he would have imbibed at Enfield. It had a reputation as a centre for modern medical research, but also for liberal sentiments in political and cultural matters.

If his education at Enfield had instilled in him the idea of public service reflected in his choice of a medical career, it also equipped him with a respect for the Arts as an improving human endeavour. Of course the expanding metropolis to which Keats moved in 1815 was full of opportunities for those with any kind of disposable income. Theatres, galleries, and concerts contributed to the capital's rich and varied cultural life. Despite reservations about the relationship between the Arts and commerce shared by Hunt and others of his correspondents, Keats retained a keen interest in drama, music, and painting throughout his life. Not the least interesting aspect of the letters is the commentary they provide on developments in the Arts contemporary with Keats. The continuing expansion of print culture was among the most notable of these developments. Books were relatively expensive, but there were plenty of eager readers. New publishers, such as Taylor and Hessey, who eventually published Keats's *Endymion* and the *Lamia* volumes, sprang up to feed the demand. Of the poets, Sir Walter Scott (whose career as a novelist did not begin until 1814) and Lord Byron were the most successful in terms of sales. Keats envied both their commercial success. In a congested market-place, a new breed of reviewers was deeply influential in directing the traffic of taste, often desperately seeking to school an expanding consumer society's aesthetics of pleasure towards more traditional principles. The *Edinburgh*, founded in 1802, and its Tory opponent the *Quarterly*, founded in 1809, were chief among them, but their authority was hotly contested. The hostile notices Keats received from *Blackwood*'s in 1818 were from a new publication ideologically opposed to the values of the Hunt circle but also eager to make a name for itself in a fiercely competitive book trade.

Hunt's *Examiner* had been founded in 1808 as an organ for more liberal opinion. The year may be significant as it was around this time, with the possibility of defeat in the war with Napoleon receding, that more open criticism of the government began to appear in the press. Byron succeeded Scott as the period's most popular poet at much the same juncture, a development that may also indicate a certain loosening of the restraints of wartime consensus. Certainly

Hunt, Shelley, and to a lesser extent Keats always regarded Byron as a sympathetic figure, even if he was their social superior. In 1811 the Prime Minister Spencer Perceval was assassinated and replaced by Lord Liverpool who presided over a cabinet that set its face against domestic reform until 1827; 1811 also saw the final lapse of George III into insanity and the elevation of the future George IV to the Regency. The *Examiner* reviled the Prince Regent as the chief sign of the corruption of the political times, earning Leigh and his brother John a sentence of two years in prison for libel in February 1813. After the final defeat of Napoleon at Waterloo, peace increased the variety and volume of opposition to the old political order. The *Examiner* viewed the re-establishment of the *ancien régime* by the victorious allies at the Congress of Vienna as a betrayal of the aspirations of their people for peacetime liberty. In Britain, 1816–17 saw a period of machine breaking, riots, and popular disturbances. The Corn Laws introduced to protect the profits of landowners by fixing a minimum price were a major source of discontent. Populist leaders such as Henry Hunt provided a focus for the reform movement. Journalists such as William Cobbett, Richard Carlile, and T. J. Wooller wrote directly for a new lower-class readership beyond the more polite circles reached by the *Examiner*. Middle-class intellectuals such as Keats were forced to take sides on the future prospects of the nation. By 1816 the field of culture was more obviously defined by ideological differences than it had been for almost two decades. Although by 1815 Hunt, Keats, and others in their circle had come to admire the poet of the *Lyrical Ballads* (1798), Wordsworth was more immediately known to them through his great commemoration of national victory, *The Excursion* (1814). Coleridge emerged as a major spokesman for Anglican and conservative values in the *Lay Sermons* (1816–17) and the *Biographia Literaria* (1817). The latter-day conservatism of the Lake School was regarded, as it is in these letters, as a betrayal by the *Examiner* and many of its readers. Keats's thoughts on 'the vale of Soul-making', for instance, should be judged as a part of a group attempt to rebut the conservative Christian values of the older poets. When the legal and military defenders of Church and State threatened the liberty of the press or perpertuated even more overt acts of repression, such as the Peterloo Massacre of 1819, the *Examiner* and its readers could make common cause with Cobbett and others, but more generally liberal middle-class opinion was nervous about political change. It was in these turbulent post-war years that Keats became a poet, and his letters participate vigorously in the political and poetic debates of Regency England over 1816–20. Not that the political and poetic dominate or are even separable from the personal in the letters. For they are always mediated by the individual anxieties of a young man trying to make a name for himself in the new literary market-place. Once he was engaged, as he was eventually to Fanny Brawne by the end of 1819, this need became acute for Keats and adds a particular desperation to those passionate and sometimes painful letters of the final year before his death.

Leigh Hunt and the Examiner

At the centre of the social life in which these letters circulated was a mix of young writers and artists associated as readers and often contributors with the *Examiner*. Keats gleaned much of his information about contemporary public life from the paper's heady blend of politics and commentary on the arts. Before they had even met, its editor Leigh Hunt was already a hero for Keats. The end of his sentence for having libelled the Prince Regent is commemorated in the early sonnet 'Written on the Day That Mr. Leigh Hunt Left Prison'. Until recently champions of Keats have often tried to dissociate Keats from what they perceive as Hunt's mawkish sentimentality and vanity, but Hunt remained a loyal friend and important influence throughout Keats's career. Although Keats sometimes expressed a desire for solitude, for the most part his letters express a delight in the urban sociability he discovered through Hunt and his friends. They buzz with the excitement of William Hazlitt's crowded lecture hall at the Surrey Institution and revel in the gossip and spectacle of London's theatre world. These more public places of leisure are complemented by a polite, middle-class domain of domestic entertainments, comprising sonnet-writing competitions, laurel crowns, literary and political arguments, and musical evenings. The letters themselves seem to have been passed around in these sociable settings: 'I know you will interread one another,' he tells J. H. Reynolds and Richard Woodhouse (to Woodhouse, 21, 22 September 1819, p. 276). To the disgust of the élite literary reviewers, whose opinions of 'Cockney' social life merged with their reviews of the poetry of Hunt, Keats, and others in their circle, this culture seemed both far too open and much too feminine. Of course the radical aspects of middle-class sociability should not be exaggerated or idealized. It was in the political interest of the conservative reviews to represent the Cockney phenomenon as a degrading spectacle of female and plebeian insubordination. The truth was rather more circumscribed. Yet women such as Jane and Marianne Reynolds (the sisters of J. H. Reynolds) and the mysterious Isabella Jones clearly did influence Keats's ideas and opinions, even if the chat took a distinctly bawdier turn once the women had withdrawn. Within the limits set by such gender boundaries and evolving ideas of middle-class taste and politeness that excluded the 'vulgar', Keats moved in a relatively meritocratic world whose emergence was feared by the reviewers who attacked his poetry.

By no means all of Keats's friends were close to Hunt, although most of them seem to have been at least readers of the *Examiner*. Nor was the Hunt circle itself anything like a homogeneous grouping or its influence uniformly felt through Keats's life. There were deep tensions, reflected in these letters, even between those at the heart of this federation of friends. Keats himself offers some sharp criticisms of Hunt in the letters, but the contexts of the criticisms need to be understood. Letters to Benjamin Haydon often reflect the fact that the painter conceived of himself as involved in something of a struggle with Hunt over the possession of Keats's soul (even though Haydon himself was very much part of Hunt's social circle). Religion played a large part in these disputes, which came to a head over the winter of 1816–17 with Shelley's arrival on the scene. Perhaps jealous of the greater attention that Hunt paid to Shelley, Keats often agrees with Haydon and others about Hunt's vanity (see the letter of 10, 11 May 1817, p. 14), but in another letter written on the same day he congratulates Hunt on the fact that 'The last Examiner was Battering Ram against Christianity' (p. 10). Criticisms made of Hunt in the correspondence with J. H. Reynolds (see the letter of 3 February 1818) are given some of their piquancy by the fact that the two young poets were well aware they had much in common with the object of their criticism. To an extent, Keats and Reynolds were competing with Hunt for space on the same platform. What was the topography of the shared landscape on which the three of them stood? It comprised, among other things, a sense that they were participating in something new happening in English poetry. This involved the demise of what Hunt called 'the French school'. The 'Preface' to Hunt's collection of poetry *Foliage* (1818) provides a handy statement of the principles behind the February 1818 letter to Reynolds. Fundamental to those principles was the idea that the 'cold and artificial compositions' of Pope and the Augustans were to be replaced by what was construed as the purer and more manly example of earlier English writers such as Chaucer, Spenser, Milton, and above all Shakespeare. These poets were valued by Hunt, Keats, and Reynolds for their imaginative expansiveness and 'sensativeness to the beauty of the external world'.[1] William Wordsworth they regarded as the contemporary poet who above all others had managed to capture this spirit. For Keats, Hunt, and the circle's great critic, William Hazlitt (whose influence on the letters merits a section of its own in this introduction), Wordsworth had rediscovered 'the human heart' as the defining subject of true poetry. Although Keats came to share the concerns of Hunt and Hazlitt that Wordsworth made his own feelings too narrowly the index of humanity's as a whole, he never abandoned the idea that in 'Tintern Abbey' and other poems Wordsworth had at least begun the exploration of the 'Burden of the Mystery' essential to a modern renaissance in poetry (to J. H. Reynolds, 3 May 1818, p. 87).

The doubts about Wordsworth in the Hunt circle concerned religion and politics as well as poetics. Keats initially responded to Wordsworth's poetry as a manifestation of a general trend in history. Indeed, he claimed in the 3 May letter to Reynolds that this historical progress was the cause of Wordsworth's superiority over Milton: 'Here I must think Wordsworth is deeper than Milton—though I think it has depended more upon the general and gregarious advance of intellect, than individual greatness of Mind' (p. 90). Increasingly, however, Keats came to see the moral depth of *The Excursion* as compromised by what Hazlitt called its 'Sunday school morality'.[2]

---

[1] Leigh Hunt, 'Preface, including Cursory Observations on Poetry and Cheerfulness', *Foliage* (1818), 9 and 11.

[2] William Hazlitt, 'On Manner', *The Round Table*, in *Complete Works*, ed. P. P. Howe, 21 vols. (1930–4), iv. 46.

Whatever he thought of the latent spirit of the poetry, from the spring of 1818 Keats became more and more willing to see its manifest intention as an attempt to shore up the existing social order. Discovering that Wordsworth was an agent for a Tory candidate when he visited the Lake District later that summer, Keats reports the fact to his brother with the resignation of someone who has had his growing suspicions confirmed: 'I enquired of the waiter for Wordsworth—he said he knew him, and that he had been here a few days ago, canvassing for the Lowthers. What think you of that—Wordsworth versus Brougham!! Sad—sad—sad' (to Tom Keats, 25–7 June 1818, p. 95). Implicitly Keats, like others in the Hunt circle, saw his own liberal doctrine of 'cheerfulness' and its optimistic faith in the progressive advance of history, as the next step in the exploration of the chambers of thought that Wordsworth could not or would not take.

Keats and Politics

Politics was part of the common ground on which Keats stood with the *Examiner*. Enfield had educated him in the progressive ideas of the Enlightenment, whose triumph, he was later—in the heady days of unity among reformers after Peterloo—to suggest, had only been deflected rather than denied by the unhappy course of the French Revolution (to George and Georgiana Keats, 17–27 September 1819, p. 290). It was at Enfield too, probably through Charles Cowden Clarke, before he ever actually met Hunt in person, that he first encountered the *Examiner*. The politics of Hunt's paper were broadly reformist; strongly in favour of parliamentary reform; suspicious of the Whig party's principles in opposition; and contemptuous of the contemporary Tory government, but they were also aloof—'independent' would have been Hunt's preferred term—from the mass platform politics that dominated the revival of the radical movement after 1815. Popular figures such as William Cobbett and Henry 'Orator' Hunt, who Leigh Hunt was keen to stress was no relation of his, were often placed at a distance by the *Examiner*. In the aftermath of Peterloo, for instance, such differences within radical opinion could be elided beneath the general revulsion against 'Old Corruption', but at other times middle-class concerns about public order and good taste clearly distinguished the *Examiner*'s position. One must be careful of reading too much consistency into the use of the word 'liberal', favoured by both Hunt and Keats when discussing such matters, but the *Examiner*'s stress on 'independence' from party—its motto was 'Party is the madness of many for the gain of a few'—often translated into a disengagement from the plebeian politics of mass assembly. When Keats describes his neighbour Lewis 'going on as usual among his favorite democrat papers' (to George and Georgiana, 14 February–3 May 1819, p. 200), he seems to be distancing himself from Lewis in a way that echoes the strategies of the *Examiner*'s rhetoric of independence. Yet the point should not be exaggerated. Issues such as the liberty of the press could always be relied upon to unite opposition opinion. Hence Keats's unconfined joy at the acquittals of Wooler and Hone in 1817, and his sympathy with Carlile's plight in 1819.

The question of the role of these political opinions in Keats's poetry has increasingly exercised critics. There is no doubt that some of his poems, such as the 1815 prison sonnet to Hunt, are explicitly political statements. Whether other later poems should be understood as covertly so, as has recently been suggested of 'To Autumn', is another matter. What cannot be doubted is that the letters display a continuing interest in political matters. Towards the end of his life, Keats announced the ambition of contributing something to 'the Liberal side of the Question before I die' (to C. W. Dilke, 22 September 1819, p. 282). The example of Leigh Hunt and William Hazlitt as cultural and political commentators in the periodical press was continuously before him. Some of the his correspondence suggests that he believed pursuing their examples meant abandoning a career in poetry. Hunt sometimes presented himself as a poet who had been reluctantly, temporarily, but necessarily distracted from poetry at a time of national crisis. Partly this was an aspect of the politics of taste that Hunt used to distinguish himself from what he regarded as the vulgarity of Cobbett and other plebeian radicals. When Keats advised Shelley to 'curb your magnanimity' (to Shelley, 16 August 1820, p. 361), he might also have been asserting the primary role of poetry as a concern with the 'beautiful' rather than the political. But it is also true that this aesthetics of pleasure was itself politically inflected as part of the struggle against what both Hunt and Keats perceived as the gloomy Christianity of the old order. The question of the relation of politics to poetry in his thinking, like many others, was left unresolved by his death. Had he lived to take up Shelley's invitation to join him in Italy, debates over this question would almost certainly have been at the heart of their relationship.

Hazlitt's 'depth of Taste'

William Hazlitt provided a complex example in regard to these issues, and one which provided ambivalences of its own about the relationship between politics and art. Whether writing on theatre, literature, painting, or politics, all spheres in which Keats learnt from him, Hazlitt was one of the great journalists of the age, but he also had serious ambitions as a metaphysician. Both journalism and metaphysics were subjects on which, on two specific different occasions, Keats proposed to seek advice from him, but his influence on Keats was pervasive and more enduring than any other single writer's. Whole passages from Hazlitt's prose are quoted in the letters, sometimes over several pages, while his ideas provide the framework at least for most of Keats's best known opinions. Although Keats did not always agree with specific critical judgements—he thought Hazlitt too harsh on Chatterton, for instance, an opinion of which Hazlitt seems to have taken notice—his early sense of Hazlitt's 'depth of Taste' (to George and Tom, 13, 19 January 1818, p. 47) as one of the three finest things of the age never seriously wavered. When Keats discovers that Hazlitt had quoted him in one of his lectures, the thrill leaps off the page of the letter. As a metaphysician, Hazlitt's reputation rested on the little known *Essay on the Principle of Human Action* (1805), a book Keats seems to have first read with Benjamin Bailey in 1818, and owned at his death. Developing out of the British tradition of psychological empiricism, Hazlitt's dissertation took the *basis* of knowledge to be the impressions created on our minds by external objects, but these 'sensations'—a key word for Keats no less than Hazlitt—were framed into ideas by the active powers of the mind itself. The Keatsian principle that 'axioms in philosophy are not axioms until they are proved upon our pulses' (to J. H. Reynolds, 3 May 1818, p. 88) reverberates with Hazlitt's emphasis on the importance of the warmth and vivacity of ideas in convincing us of their truth. Against the position of the perfectibilarian philosopher William Godwin, a veteran of the radicalism of the 1790s to whose ideas Keats's friend Charles Dilke was devoted, and its stress on rational judgement based on the principle of utility—what Keats called 'consequitive reasoning' (to Benjamin Bailey, 22 November 1817, p. 36)—Hazlitt saw human knowledge as the product of 'habit, sense, association, local and personal attachment, natural affection, &c.'[3] Yet beneath the labyrinthine relations that made up its everyday experience, Hazlitt believed the mind to be naturally 'disinterested' (another key term in the vocabulary of Keats's letters). Primarily pitted against the writings of Hobbes, Mandeville, and others who argued that the basis of human action was self-interest, Hazlitt's essay claimed that our ability to think about our future selves depended on a power of self-projection no different from that required to think ourselves into the lives of others. This power of sympathetic identification he considered the domain of the imagination. Hazlitt's emphasis on this imaginative power lies beneath Keats's various reflections on the idea of '*Negative Capability*' (to George and Tom Keats, 21, 27 December 1817, p. 41). Not that Hazlitt believed that natural dis-interestedness was easy to maintain. Nor did it necessarily lead to a benevolent concern for others. The latter was a quality that had to be cultivated in the teeth of the egotism inculcated in us by worldly experience. He saw in Wordsworth, for instance, a great power of imaginative sympathy, but frequently accused him of too often let-ting it lead him back to a gloomy brooding on his own feelings. When Keats raises the idea of the mind as a 'Mansion of Many Apart-ments' in the 3 May letter to Reynolds, he also raises the question of whether the Lake Poet had been able to carry forward the explor-ation he began in 'Tintern Abbey'. Several of the letters suggest that Keats increasingly thought of himself, like Cortez in 'On First Look-ing into Chapman's Homer', as the next to extend the empire of the human heart. Throughout the letters Keats displays a fondness for presenting his own 'gradual ripening of the intellectual powers' as part of a natural process; a process he frequently correlated with parallel developments in the history of taste and politics.

[3] William Hazlitt, 'On the English Novelists', in *Complete Works*, vi. 132.

'A gradual ripening'?

Although Hazlitt himself was often more sceptical about progress than Keats, his ideas about disinterestedness offered one way of conceiving the 'grand march of intellect' (to J. H. Reynolds, 3 May 1818, p. 90). Under Hunt's influence, Keats had been encouraged to work out a liberal aesthetics of pleasure of which Pan was the tutelary deity. For the Hunt circle, as Robert Ryan has shown, the simplicity of Greek religion was superior to the gloomy Christianity they found in Wordsworth's *Excursion* and Coleridge's *Lay Sermons*.[4] The early Keats sonnet 'Written in Disgust at Vulgar Superstition' shares in J. H. Reynolds's perception that 'Religion should be dressed in smiles, not frowns'.[5] When at their first meeting in mid-December 1817 Wordsworth described Keats's 'Hymn to Pan' as a 'very pretty piece of Paganism', he was disapproving of this aspect of his young disciple's thinking.[6] The meeting was a staging post in his disillusionment with Wordsworth, although they continued to meet afterwards during Wordsworth's stay in London. The letters show that in the months prior to Wordsworth's London visit, Keats had been putting pressure on the optimistic philosophy of Hunt by questioning the role of suffering in human experience. His friendship with Benjamin Bailey, who was about to embark on a career in the Church, directed him both to Hazlitt's writing and the consolatory Christian poetry of *The Excursion*. Keats responds earnestly in the letters to the disinterestedness of Bailey, but resists his Christian doctrine: 'You know my ideas about Religion', he tells him quietly but firmly on 13 March. Keats had been gradually loosening himself from the influence of Bailey, and at the same time developing his scepticism about whether Wordsworth's Christian consolations really provided a proper religion of the human heart. Wordsworth's egotistical conduct in London and Hazlitt's lectures that began in January must have hastened the process. Bailey distanced himself from what he took to be the poet's inclination towards 'that

---

[4] 'The Politics of Greek Religion', in Hermione de Almeida (ed.), *Critical Essays on John Keats* (1990).

[5] *Selected Prose of John Hamilton Reynolds*, ed. L. M. Jones (1966), 219.

[6] The details from Haydon's diary are given at *KC* ii. 144. Ironically Keats's hymn was indebted to a passage in *The Excursion*, IV. 925-40.

abominable principle of *Shelley's*—that Sensual Love is the principle of things'.[7] When Keats declares his desire for 'a Life of Sensations rather than of Thoughts' in the letter to Bailey of 22 November 1817 (p. 36), he is making these inclinations clear to Bailey. Over 1818 and 1819 Keats looked to triangulate his interest in the world of sensations, his ideas on suffering (intensified by the experience of nursing his dying brother Tom), and his thinking about cultural and historical progress. Critics have often charted a development in Keats's thinking towards the disinterested notion of the buffetings of circumstance as part of a process of soul-making, frequently taken to be expressed above all in the philosophical equanimity of the ode 'To Autumn'. Certainly in the famous soul-making letter of May 1819, he presents himself as the acolyte of a religion of the human heart that is historically superseding Christianity. Like Shelley, though with less prophetic fanfare, he often seems to present himself as the harbinger of 'futurity'. This idea is reiterated in the 'Ode to Psyche', copied a few pages later (pp. 236–8), where Keats appears as a 'Priest' to a new religion of the 'untrodden region of my Mind'. Yet one has to be careful of accepting Keats's self-representations as simple truth. He is trying to persuade his brother and sister-in-law, and perhaps himself, that his personal development is in line with a historical process that furthers the exploration of the mind of man begun in Wordsworth. If this idea seems to underpin the achievement of the great Odes, 'Lamia', and 'The Fall of Hyperion' that Keats was writing at this time, it is well to remember that he also continued to write letters with a very different tone for another year. The reassurances of the doctrine of soul-making should be read as part of an ongoing debate with himself and his correspondents about the vicissitudes of human experience. The perfection of 'To Autumn' is not often echoed in the later letters. The correspondence with Fanny Brawne—which so appalled Victorian critics in its feverish lack of self-control, and is usually glossed over by more recent commentators—reveals a much more unquiet mind.

[7] Letter from Bailey to John Taylor, 29 Aug. 1818, *KC* i. 35.

Keats and Social Insecurity

The provisionality of the correspondence might be taken as a triumphant demonstration of negative capability, recording Keats's ability to project himself into different roles and live in a state of creative uncertainty, but these letters also seem to express a deep sense of insecurity, which frequently took the form of a desire to escape the fever and the fret of the life around him. While Keats sometimes articulates a robust sense that 'uproar's your only musick' (to George and Tom, 13, 19 January 1818, p. 47), he was far from experiencing social life as an endless whirligig of pleasurable sensation. He was acutely aware of what he took to be his physical and social inadequacies, perhaps most memorably captured in his comparison of himself with Lord Byron: 'You see what it is to be under six foot and not a lord' (to George and Georgiana, 14 February–3 May 1819, p. 198). Keats was part of an urban middle class that was self-conscious about the breadth and treachery of the terrain it occupied in society. While many of those in the Hunt circle were trying to make a career in writing for themselves on the basis of their own talents, the reviewers in *Blackwood's* and the *Quarterly* who mocked 'Cockney' social pretensions were attempting to draw up a cultural barrier against these self-made men. Against the emergence of a literary market-place, the reviews still tended to offer a defensive model of the virtues of a Classical university education and independent means. Articulating a different idea of independence, based on a meritocratic notion of freedom of thought, rather than property or birth, the Cockney circle itself did not find the market a kind master. Keats and his friend J. H. Reynolds both swapped the prospect of entering the professional classes for a literary career. Without altogether crushing his literary aspirations, the realities of middle-class life soon forced Reynolds into taking up a legal training. Keats seems to have found the example ominous for his own case, and was not able to be certain that he might not have to return to medicine (even entertaining the prospect of serving as a surgeon on an East India Company ship).

Moreover the letters offer some very different conceptions of what a literary career might be. Most often the 'independence' of literature is precisely figured in terms of its separation from the market-place, and privileges posterity over the reading public—usually for Keats gendered as perniciously female—who bought books. But over a crucial period June to September 1819, when some of his greatest poetry was being written, Keats seems to have thrown himself with a new zeal into the idea of being a professional writer, explicitly looking, as he did in many things, to the example of Hazlitt.[8] Over this period words such as 'diligence' and 'industry' become key terms in the letters; 'indolence', a state of being previously represented as a precondition of poetic composition, is to be conquered. Exacerbated by his guardian's less than frank dealings over money matters and his own perhaps culpable ignorance of another source of money held for him in Chancery, his precarious financial situation feeds into the social attitudes expressed in the letters.[9] (His awkward relationship with Shelley, for instance, seems to have been coloured by the contrast with the latter's aristocratic background.) Part of the pain caused to Keats, but also to Hunt himself, by the hostile 'Cockney School' reviews lay in their tactic of collapsing the middle-class context of the Hunt circle into the social classes beneath them. There is an element of snobbery in Keats's discomfort at being confused with a 'weaver boy' (to George and Georgiana, 17–27 September 1819, p. 284) correlative to Hunt's eagerness to distinguish himself from Cobbett on the grounds of taste. The doctrine of beauty espoused by the Hunt circle may have been intended as a liberation from the conventionality of an élite education, but it was also an almost copybook attempt to distinguish middle-class politeness from the classes beneath them. This double-edged attitude can be seen in various other aspects of Cockney discourse. The frequent attacks on Methodism and popular religious enthusiasm in the pages of the *Examiner*, echoed in Keats's various comments about 'the pious frauds of Religion' (to George and Georgiana, 14 February–3 May 1819, p. 214), may have been primarily part of a campaign against repressive Christian moralism, but they are also a class-based judgement on the populace's lack of taste for beauty. As early as his 1808 *Letters on the Folly and Dangers*

---

[8] There is an excellent discussion of this period in Andrew Bennett's chapter on the letters.

[9] The situation is set out very clearly by Andrew Motion, *Keats* (1997), 121.

of Methodism, Hunt was disparaging the idea that matters of religion might be left to the judgement of those better off attending two-penny peep shows. Such opinions find an echo in the Keats sonnet 'On Vulgar Superstition'. Keats may have delighted in many aspects of the popular culture of his time; the pantomimes, the panoramas, and plays of London life; he may even have sometimes preferred low company to what he saw as the mannered and affected sociability of Horace Smith and his friends, but he was also protective of his own fragile middle-class social identity in the face of the crowd. At the beginning of 1820, under pressure from financial and other anxieties, he is as capable as Wordsworth in Book VII of *The Prelude* of distancing himself from London's crowds and 'the dull processes of their every day Lives' (to Georgiana Keats, 13–28 January 1820, p. 324). When Keats yearns for a world of sensation in this mood, he is seeking oblivion for a sensibility, to coin a phrase of Coleridge's, '*sore* from excess of stimulation'.[10]

Keats and Women

There is a similarly complex, often defensive, attitude towards women in the letters. Keats seems at once to have a gloriously porous sense of his masculine identity, which some feminist critics have read as a positive aspect of his negative capability, and at other times to be deeply threatened by an idea of feminine otherness. The correspondence is full of frank admissions of desire. He flirted with the Reynolds sisters from early on. Jane Cox and Isabella Jones both clearly excited and fascinated him. His passionate and jealous relationship with Fanny Brawne is ardently recorded in the letters of the final year, perhaps never more despairingly than in that last crude but desperate cry to Charles Brown that 'I should have had her when I was in health' (to Charles Brown, 1 November 1820, p. 368). Moreover, attraction often seems to topple over into identification in his sympathetic nature. He frequently casts himself as a ravished victim in his letters to Fanny. A parallel might be found in his gendering of the poet's negative capability in terms of feminine sexuality: 'It has been an old Comparison for our urging on—the Bee hive—however

---

[10] *Collected Letters*, ed. E. L. Griggs (1956–71), v. 24.

it seems to me that we should rather be the flower than the Bee—for it is a false notion that more is gained by receiving than giving—no the receiver and the giver are equal in their benefits—The f[l]ower I doubt not receives a fair guerdon from the Bee—its leaves blush deeper in the next spring—and who shall say between Man and Woman which is the most delighted?' (to J. H. Reynolds, 19 February 1818, p. 63). Passages such as this one sharply distinguish his ideas of negative capability from the more masculinist discourse of Hazlitt from which it was derived. The indolence in which Keats delights is very different from Hazlitt's idea of Shakespeare as a masculine hero throwing himself into the lives of his characters. Hazlitt himself seemed to insist on the gendered distinction when after Keats's death he suggested the main fault in the poetry was 'a deficiency in masculine energy of style'.[11] Nor was Keats unaware of the difference between this aspect of his own personality and the ideal he learnt from Hazlitt. Running through the letters is a fear of the feminine as a honeytrap that might sap his true manly identity away: 'I equally dislike the favour of the public with the love of a woman—they are both a cloying treacle to the wings of independence' (to John Taylor, 23 August 1819, p. 261). Love and marriage often figure in this respect as a prospect that will force him away from the independence necessary to a poet and towards conformity with middle-class domestic values. The conflation of the 'public' and 'the love of a woman' in this letter to his publisher was characteristic. A 'manly' independence usually seems to depend on deploring the women who actually bought and read his work. Perhaps provoked by the reviews suggesting his Cockney stress on beauty and luxury was effeminate, he objects in several letters to becoming the 'versifying Pet-lamb' (to Miss Jeffery, 9 June 1819, p. 241) of his female readers and later talks of writing a play that will shock them. Moreover, although clearly influenced by a number of the period's women writers, he often tries to deny their role in his development. Or, to put it another way, his emphasis on his 'natural' development frequently presents his correspondents with the idea that he has progressed beyond his early feminine influences. Mary Tighe, for

---

[11] William Hazlitt, 'Effeminacy of Character', *Table Talk*, in *Complete Works*, viii. 254.

instance, whom he praised directly in one early lyric, is dismissed in
1819 as an outworn creed, yet the influence of her popular Spenserian poem *Psyche* (1805/1811) is well attested in both 'The Eve of St
Agnes' and 'Ode to Psyche'.[12] Perhaps the organic metaphors of
development that Keats habitually uses are meant to suggest a progressive subsuming of the past into the future in a way which also
provides for the male incorporation of the female on a higher plane.
Certainly in his letter to Reynolds of 19 February he seems to try to
fold his feminine comparison into a larger masculine identity when
he interrupts it with the question: 'Now it is more noble to sit like
Jove [than] to fly like Mercury' (p. 63). Whatever his personal disposition towards passivity and indolence, the idea that they may
have been judged effeminate by his contemporaries caused him
some discomfort. Yet his attempts to assert a masculine authority,
not least in the letters to Fanny Brawne, where he oscillates between
demanding obedience from her and presenting himself as a martyr
to love, usually only betray the painful insecurities they are meant to
mask.

'An Awkward Bow'

The letters are a fascinating record of these vicissitudes of opinion,
but for all their extempory manner they are not simply unmediated
expressions of feeling. Their extemporaneity, like the punning that
runs through the letters, is a bravura entertainment with an audience
in mind. Frequently his correspondence self-consciously attempts to
portray Keats in a particular light. With Reynolds he is often playful
and punning as well as forthcoming about the politics of literature
and his literary career. With Charles Brown the playfulness often
turns into bawdiness. With Bailey he strives to present himself as
serious minded and philosophically inclined, but refuses to sacrifice
the doctrine of beauty to a clergyman's idea of Christian disinterestedness. To the attentive Woodhouse, axioms are delivered to
someone who he knows regards him seriously as a poet. Nichola
Deane has drawn attention to the way he 'plays the lover' with
Fanny; dramatizing his feelings with literary allusions to Rousseau

[12] See E. V. Weller (ed.), *Keats and Mary Tighe* (1928).

and quotations from Shakespeare.[13] This kind of awareness of himself as a writer addressing a particular reader or group of readers is integral to the drama of the correspondence. Take the wonderful scene he presented to his brother and sister-in-law of himself at his table as he is writing:

the fire is at its last click—I am sitting with my back to it with one foot rather askew upon the rug and the other with the heel a little elevated from the carpet . . . These are trifles—but . . . Could I see the same thing done of any great Man long since dead it would be a great delight: as to know in what position Shakespeare sat when he began 'To be or not to be' (to George and Georgiana, 14 February–3 May 1819, p. 208).

Out of the kind of domestic familarity one might expect of a fraternal letter, Keats suddenly casts himself as a character in the pageant of literary history for his own contemplation. Keats may have fashioned himself in his letters, but the process is an open-ended and unstable one. What begins as a family letter can end with a consideration of himself before posterity as a 'great Man long since dead'. Just as he seems to put ideas forward so as to explore and test them out in the letters, so he puts on different kinds of identity as if rehearsing different ideas of himself. His love of London's theatre life permeates his correspondence. Even the language of that last moving communication to Charles Brown invokes the idea of his life as an improperly concluded series of performances: 'I always made an awkward bow.' So the ultimate buffet of circumstance brought to an end perhaps the most brilliant sequence of dramatic improvisations in literary history. The poems and the life have often been understood in terms of a ripening towards a 'mellow fruitfulness'. Reading the letters—which continue for a year after the composition of 'To Autumn'—reveals the more painful spectacle of a brilliant tragi-comedian forced from the stage before his time. Nowhere perhaps is there a better example of what Hazlitt called 'our imperfect, and mixed being'.[14]

[13] Nichola Deane, 'Keats's Lover's Discourse and the Letters to Fanny Brawne', *Keats-Shelley Review*, 13 (1999), 105–14.

[14] William Hazlitt, 'On the English Novelists', in *Complete Works*, vi. 132.

NOTE ON THE TEXT

The original edition of this selection was published under the editor-ship of Robert Gittings in 1970. The present edition has been re-edited to bring the volume into the Oxford World's Classics series. The selection of letters has been retained, but the notes and other supporting material have been substantially revised to reflect the developments in Keats criticism since 1970. These changes have primarily involved a closer scrutiny of Keats's social and political context, and in particular his relationship with the circle of writers associated with Leigh Hunt.

The standard edition of the letters remains Hyder E. Rollins's *Letters of John Keats, 1814–1821* (1958). The short appendix to the present edition explains those variations from Rollins introduced by Gittings. Those letters of which neither Gittings nor I have seen either the original or a photocopy are marked [R] to indicate an entire reliance on the Rollins reading. One important new letter, not included here, has been discovered since Robert Gittings originally edited this volume. For details, and a transcription of this letter, see Deaning Lewis, 'A John Keats Letter Rediscovered', *Keats-Shelley Journal*, 47 (1998), 14–17. The original copy of the letter to Rey-nolds that Gittings dates 10 April 1818 on the basis of the text in Richard Woodhouse's letterbook has been rediscovered and is now held at Harvard University. Examination has shown that it was in fact dated 17 April 1818. Other minor faults in Woodhouse's version have been corrected on the basis on the transcript supplied in W. H. Bond, *Keats-Shelley Journal*, 20 (1971), 17–19. There is an excellent update on the manuscripts of Keats's letters by Jack Stillinger, *Keats-Shelley Journal*, 36 (1987), 16–19. I have accepted Stillinger's point that there is no good reason to suppose that Mary-Ann rather than Sarah Jeffery was the recipient of the letters of 31 May and 9 June. The letters are now simply described here as written to Miss Jeffery.

Where Keats is simply repeating a passage in one letter already reproduced elsewhere to another correspondent, this passage has been omitted with a note to that effect. The notes attempt to extend the principle Gittings adopted of explaining anything that might prevent the reader's understanding and full enjoyment of these unique letters. I have also maintained Gittings's practice of excluding the texts of the better known poems from some of the letters on the principle that these can easily be consulted in editions readily to hand. Where the eccentricities of Keats's handwriting have made his sense obscure, the missing word, letter, or intended spelling has been inserted in square brackets, as have any other editorial interpolations. Rounded brackets are Keats's own. Where the letter is torn, or there is any other gap, editorial conjectures have been added in shaped brackets (⟨ ⟩). With the poet's crossings-out, if they seem to reveal some aspect of his thinking that might usefully be indicated to the reader, they are printed with a rule through. Slips of the pen have simply been left in the form amended by the poet.

What a printed edition cannot do is reproduce those material aspects of the handwritten originals that seem to bring us so close to the poet and his times. His penmanship reveals much about his energy and the pressures under which he wrote. The urgent hand-writing of the originals makes his speed and spontaneity very clear. Wide gaps between words as he jumps from left to right create a sense of intense purpose. Certain characteristic slips soon become familiar to readers. He habitually omits certain letters; 'r' was a particular difficulty for him. On the other hand, his 'you' for 'your' may reveal an aspect of his spoken English, possibly reflecting the West Country origins of his father. Yet it would be misleading to suggest that his mis-spellings show how he spoke habitually. Some words are simply written in haste: he was apt to reverse the middle letters of any word. The various editorial devices explained above are all intended to create an impression for the modern reader of how the letters were written by Keats.

SELECT BIBLIOGRAPHY

The literature on Keats is very large and this note can only give an indication of the scholarly resources and critical works that will be of particular interest to readers of the letters. A useful brief guide to scholarly resources, biographies, and criticism can be found in Greg Kucich's essay on Keats in Michael O' Neill (ed.), *Literature of the Romantic Period: A Bibliographical Guide* (1998).

Editions

The standard edition of the letters remains *The Letters of John Keats 1814–21* edited by Hyder E. Rollins, 2 vols. (1958). Various letters to and about Keats are published in the invaluable *The Keats Circle: Letters and Papers 1816–1878*, ed. H. E. Rollins, 2 vols. (1948) (abbreviated as *KC* throughout this volume) and *More Letters and Poems of the Circle*, ed. A. E. Rollins (1955).

The standard edition of the poems is now *John Keats: Complete Poems*, ed. Jack Stillinger (1982). A useful selection of the poetry, prose, and letters is *John Keats*, ed. Elizabeth Cook (1990).

Biography

Three important biographies of Keats written in the 1960s have become standard: Walter Jackson Bate, *John Keats* (1963); Robert Gittings, *John Keats* (1968); Aileen Ward, *John Keats: The Making of a Poet* (1963). These have more recently been supplemented by Andrew Motion's readable *Keats* (1997).

Criticism

Most discussions of Keats deal with the letters somewhere, usually as a commentary on the development of the poems, but his letters are increasingly the subject of scholarly work in their own right. Some of the most useful works that involve extended discussions of the letters or their immediate contexts are listed below:

Barnard, John, *John Keats* (1987).
—— 'Keats's "Robin Hood", John Hamilton Reynolds and the "Old Poets"', *Proceedings of the British Academy*, 75 (1989), 181–200.
Bate, W. J., *Negative Capability: The Intuitive Approach in Keats* (1939).

Bennett, Andrew, *Keats, Narrative and Audience: The Posthumous Life of Writing* (1994).

—— '"Fragment of Castle Builder" and Keats's Use of Sexual Slang', *English Language Notes*, 28 (1990), 39–50.

Bromwich, David, *Hazlitt: The Mind of a Critic* (1983).

—— 'Keats's Radicalism', *Studies in Romanticism*, 25 (1986), 197–210.

Chandler, James, *England in 1819: The Politics of Literary Culture and the Case of Romantic Historicism* (1998).

Cox, Jeffrey N., *Poetry and Politics in the Cockney School: Keats, Shelley, Hunt and their Circle* (1998).

De Almeida, Hermione, *Romantic Medicine and John Keats* (1991).

Deane, Nichola, 'Keats's Lover's Discourse and the Letters to Fanny Brawne', *Keats-Shelley Review*, 13 (1999), 105–14.

Dickstein, Morris, 'Keats and Politics', *Studies in Romanticism*, 25 (1986), 175–81.

Gilmartin, Kevin, *Print Politics: The Press and Radical Opposition in Early Nineteenth-Century England* (1996).

Hughes-Hallett, Penelope, *The Immortal Dinner: A Famous Evening of Genius & Laughter in Literary London, 1817* (2000).

Homans, Margaret, 'Keats Reading Women: Women Reading Keats', *Studies in Romanticism*, 34 (1995), 343–64.

Jack, Ian, *Keats and the Mirror of Art* (1967).

Jones, Leonidas, *The Life of John Hamilton Reynolds* (1984).

Kucich, Greg, 'The Poetry of Mind in Keats's Letters', *Style*, 21 (1987), 76–94.

—— 'Gender Crossings: Keats and Tighe', *Keats-Shelley Journal*, 44 (1995), 29–39.

Lamont, Claire, 'Meg the Gipsy in Scott and Keats', *English*, 36 (1987), 137–45.

Lau, Beth, *Keats's Reading of the Romantic Poets* (1991).

Levinson, Marjorie, *Keats's Life of Allegory* (1988).

Luke, David, 'Keats's Letters: Fragments of an Aesthetic of Fragments', *Genre*, 11 (1978) 209–26.

Mellor, Anne K., *Romanticism and Gender* (1993).

Michael, Jennifer Davis, 'Pectoriloquy: The Narrative of Consumption in the Letters of Keats', *European Romantic Review*, 6 (1995), 38–56.

Mizukoshi, Ayumi, *Keats, Hunt, and the Aesthetics of Pleasure* (2001).

Muir, Kenneth (ed.), *John Keats: A Reassessment* (1969).

Perkins, David, 'Keats's Odes and Letters: Recurrent Diction and Imagery', *Keats-Shelley Journal*, 2 (1953), 51–60.

Ricks, Christopher, *Keats and Embarrassment* (1974).

Roe, Nicholas (ed.), *Keats and History* (1995).

—— *John Keats and the Culture of Dissent* (1997).

Ross, Marlon B., *The Contours of Masculine Desire: Romanticism and the Rise of Women's Poetry* (1989).

Ryan, Robert, *Keats: The Religious Sense* (1976).

—— 'The Politics of Greek Religion', in Hermione de Almeida (ed.), *Critical Essays on John Keats* (1990).

Sperry, Stuart M., 'Keats's Skepticism and Voltaire', *Keats-Shelley Journal*, 28 (1979), 35–8.

Stillinger, Jack, 'Wordsworth and Keats', in Kenneth R. Johnston and Gene W. Ruoff (eds.), *The Age of William Wordsworth: Critical Essays on the Romantic Tradition* (1987), 173–95.

—— *John Keats: Letters from a Walking Tour* (1995).

Vendler, Helen, *The Odes of John Keats* (1983).

Webb, Timothy, '"Cutting Figures": Rhetorical Strategies in Keats's Letters', in Michael O'Neill (ed.), *Keats: Bicentenary Readings* (1987), 145–69.

White, R. S., *Keats as a Reader of Shakespeare* (1987).

Wolfson, Susan, 'Keats the Letter-Writer: Epistolary Poetics', *Romanticism Past and Present*, 6 (1982), 43–61.

Further Reading in Oxford World's Classics

Byron, Lord, *Selected Poetry*, ed. Jerome J. McGann.

Five Romantic Plays 1768–1821, ed. Paul Baines and Edward Burns.

Keats, John, *The Major Works*, ed. Elizabeth Cook.

—— *Selected Poetry*, ed. Elizabeth Cook.

Wordsworth, William, *Selected Poetry*, ed. Stephen Gill and Duncan Wu.

A CHRONOLOGY OF
JOHN KEATS

Life	*Historical and Cultural Background*
1795 Keats born in London (31 October) to Thomas and Frances Keats (née Jennings).	Government passes repressive 'Two Acts' in a year of poor harvest and great political unrest.
1797 George Keats born (28 February).	Mutinies in British fleet. Edmund Burke dies; Mary Wollstonecraft dies.
1798	Wordsworth and Coleridge, *Lyrical Ballads*
1799 Tom Keats born (18 November).	London Corresponding Society declared illegal; Combination Acts against trade unions; Bonaparte becomes First Consul. Brockden Brown, *Ormond* Godwin, *St. Leon*
1801 Edward Keats born (28 April).	Resignation of Pitt over Catholic Emancipation; Addington becomes PM; Nelson victorious at Copenhagen. Southey, *Thalaba*
1802 Edward Keats dies (28 April).	
1802–3	Peace of Amiens, March 1802–May 1803.
1803 Frances (Fanny) Keats born (3 June). Keats and George start to attend John Clarke's school at Enfield (joined by Tom later).	Fears of French invasion dominate public opinion.
1804 Keats's father has a fatal riding accident (16 April). His mother marries William Rawlings (June). The children move in with their maternal grandparents, John and Alice Jennings, at Enfield.	Addington resigns; Pitt becomes PM; Napoleon becomes Emperor. Ann and Jane Taylor, *Original Poems for Infant Minds* Jane Porter, *The Scottish Chiefs*
1805 John Jennings dies (8 March); lawsuit over will. Family moved to Lower Edmonton.	Battle of Trafalgar. Mary Tighe's *Psyche* privately printed Hazlitt, *Essay on the Principles of Human Action*

Life	*Historical and Cultural Background*
1806 Mother leaves husband; lives apart from children until 1809.	Death of Pitt.
1807	Wordsworth, *Poems in Two Volumes*
1808	Hunt brothers start the *Examiner*.
1809	Perceval becomes Prime Minister.
1810 Keats's mother returns to children but dies (10 March). Keats is apprenticed to the surgeon Thomas Hammond of Edmonton.	Coleridge lectures on Shakespeare.
1811	Prince of Wales becomes Regent; Luddite riots. Leigh Hunt, *The Feast of the Poets* Posthumous edition of Tighe's *Psyche, with Other Poems* P. Shelley, *Necessity of Atheism*
1812	Perceval assassinated; Lord Liverpool becomes PM; Castlereagh becomes Foreign Secretary; Napoleon invades Russia. Byron, *Childe Harold*, i and ii Horace and James Smith, *Rejected Addresses*
1813	Leigh Hunt and his brother John imprisoned for libelling the Regent; Southey becomes Poet Laureate. Shelley, *Queen Mab*
1814 Keats writes his earliest known poems. Death of Alice Jennings (19 December); Richard Abbey becomes official guardian of the Keats children.	Napoleon abdicates. Kean establishes himself with his reinterpretation of Shylock at Drury Lane. Wordsworth, *The Excursion* Cary's trans. of Dante's *Divine Comedy* completed Scott, *Waverley*
1815 Keats enters Guy's Hospital (October) as a student; a few weeks later he becomes a dresser.	Hazlitt starts to write regularly for the *Examiner*. Leigh Hunt released; Napoleon's 'Hundred Days'; Battle of Waterloo; 'Holy Alliance' of European monarchs. Scott, *Guy Mannering* Wordsworth, *Poems*

Life	*Historical and Cultural Background*
1816 'To Solitude' appears in the *Examiner*. Keats passes his qualifying examinations to practise as apothecary. Holidays in Margate (meets Isabella Jones). Meets Hunt, Haydon, and Reynolds. Mid-November living in Cheapside with Tom and George. Named with Reynolds and Shelley in Hunt's 'Young Poets' review in *Examiner*. Meets Shelley through Hunt.	Economic depression and political discontent; mass meeting at Spa Fields followed by rioting (December). Byron, *Childe Harold*, iii Coleridge, *Christabel, Statesman's Manual* Hunt, *The Story of Rimini* J. H. Reynolds, *The Naiad* Scott, *The Antiquary* P. Shelley, *Alastor* Jane Taylor, *Essays in Rhyme*
1817 *Poems* published by the Olliers (3 March). Brothers move to Hampstead (March). Keats at work on *Endymion* between April and late November. Meets Bailey, Brown, Dilke. Theatrical reviewing for *Champion* while Reynolds is away. Meets Wordsworth in mid-December.	Suspension of Habeas Corpus (March); William Cobbett flees to America; trials and acquittals of T. J. Wooler (June) and William Hone (December); Princess Charlotte dies; *Blackwood's* founded. Byron, *Manfred* Coleridge, *Sibylline Leaves, Lay Sermons*, ii Godwin, *Mandeville* Hazlitt, *Characters of Shakespeare's Plays, The Round Table*
1818 Revises *Endymion*. Attends Hazlitt's lectures on the English poets (January–March). Sonnet competition on Egyptian theme with Hunt and Shelley (February); Haydon takes him to see Elgin marbles (March). With Tom in Devon (March–April); George marries Georgiana Wylie (May). *Endymion* published by Taylor and Hessey; scathingly reviewed in *Blackwood's* (May), *British Critic* (June), and *Quarterly* (September). George and Georgiana depart for the United States (23 June). Keats leaves for his tour of the North with Charles	Congress of European powers attended by Castlereagh; Habeas Corpus restored. Byron, *Childe Harold*, iv Hunt, *Foliage* P. Shelley, *The Revolt of Islam* Mary Shelley, *Frankenstein*

Life   *Historical and Cultural Background*

Brown; returns to London
due to ill health (8 August).
Discovers Tom is very ill.
Meets Fanny Brawne. Begins
Hyperion (November). Tom
dies (1 December). Keats
becomes Brown's tenant at
Wentworth Place.

1819   Writes 'Eve of St Agnes'   Arrest of radical publisher Richard Carlile
       (January); gives up *Hyperion*.   (February, not tried until October);
       Financial difficulties lead to   Peterloo Massacre (16 August); Six Acts
       thoughts of becoming ship's   restricting rights to hold meetings and
       surgeon; meets and walks with   press freedom. Hazlitt lecturing on the
       Coleridge. Composes the   Elizabethans (November–December).
       great odes; with James Rice on   Byron, *Don Juan*, i and ii
       the Isle of Wight (late June).   Barry Cornwall, *Dramatic Scenes*
       'Ode to Nightingale' appears   Hazlitt, *Lectures on the English Comic*
       in *Annals of Fine Arts* (July). *Writers, Letter to William Gifford*
       Begins work on 'Lamia' and   Hunt, *Hero and Leander, Poetical Works*
       with Brown *Otho the Great*;   Reynolds, *Peter Bell, A Lyrical Ballad*
       with Brown to Winchester.   Wordsworth, *Peter Bell*
       Witnesses Henry Hunt's
       triumphal entry into London
       (13 September). Composes
       'Ode to Autumn'; begins and
       abandons 'Fall of Hyperion'.
       Back in Winchester.
       Considers writing for the
       press. Hazlitt quotes him in
       public lecture (November).
       He is engaged to Fanny
       Brawne by the end of the year.

1820   George returns to London   George III dies; John Wolcot (Peter
       to raise funds (departs   Pindar) dies. Arrest of Cato St
       28 January). Severe   conspirators (February); Thistlewood
       haemorrhage (3 February);   hanged for treason (May). Public attention
       moves to Kentish Town for   dominated by 'Queen Caroline Affair' for
       the summer; joins Hunt's   much of the year.
       household (23 June); *Lamia,*   Barry Cornwall, *A Sicilian Story*
       Isabella, Eve of St Agnes and   Hunt, *Amyntas*
       Other Poems published by   Shelley, *The Cenci, Prometheus Unbound*
       Taylor and Hessey. Doctors
       recommend going to Italy.
       Leaves Hunt's house and
       moves in with the Brawnes

Life	*Historical and Cultural Background*
(12 August). *Lamia* volume positively reviewed. Keats and Joseph Severn sail from Gravesend (18 September); reach Naples (21 October); kept in quarantine for ten days. Arrive in Rome (15 November).	
1821 Keats dies (23 February). Buried at Protestant cemetery (26 February).	Napoleon dies; Queen Caroline dies; Greek War of Liberation begins. John Scott killed in duel. Hazlitt, *Table Talk* Reynolds, *Garden of Florence* Shelley, *Adonais* Horace Smith, *Amarynthus the Nympholept*

SELECTED LETTERS

1816–1817

To C. C. Clarke, 9 October 1816

Wednesday Octr 9th—

My dear Sir,

The busy time has just gone by, and I can now devote any time you may mention to the pleasure of seeing Mr Hunt—'t will be an Era in my existence—I am anxious too to see the Author of the Sonnet to the Sun,* for it is no mean gratification to become acquainted with Men who in their admiration of Poetry do not jumble together Shakespeare and Darwin*—I have coppied out a sheet or two of Verses which I composed some time ago, and find so much to blame

worst

in them that the best part will go into the fire—those to G. Mathew* I will suffer to meet the eye of Mr H. notwithstanding that the Muse is so frequently mentioned. I here sinned in the face of Heaven even while remembering what, I think, Horace says, "never presume to make a God appear but for an Action worthy of a God.* From a few Words of yours when last I saw you, I have no doubt but that you have something in your Portfolio which I should by rights see—I will put you in Mind of it—Although the Borough is a beastly place in dirt, turnings and windings; yet No 8 Dean Street is not difficult to find; and if you would run the Gauntlet over London Bridge, take the first turning to the left and then the first to the right and more-over knock at my door which is nearly opposite a Meeting, you would do one a Charity which as St Paul saith is the father of all the Virtues—At all events let me hear from you soon—I say at all events not excepting the Gout in your fingers—   Your's Sincerely

John Keats—

[R]   *To C. C. Clarke, 31 October 1816*

My daintie Davie,*

I will be as punctual as the Bee to the Clover—Very glad am I at the thoughts of seeing so soon this glorious Haydon and all his Creation.* I pray thee let me know when you go to Ollier's* and where he resides—this I forgot to ask you—and tell me also when you will help me waste a sullen day—God 'ield you—

J—K—

To B. R. Haydon, 20 November 1816

My dear Sir—   Novr 20th

Last Evening wrought me up, and I cannot forbear sending you the following*—Your's unfeignedly John Keats—

> Great Spirits now on Earth are sojourning
>   He of the Cloud, the Cataract the Lake
>   Who on Helvellyn's summit wide awake
> Catches his freshness from Archangel's wing
> He of the Rose, the Violet, the Spring
>   The social Smile, the Chain for freedom's sake:
>   And lo!—whose stedfastness would never take
> A Meaner Sound than Raphael's Whispering.
> And other Spirits are there standing apart
>   Upon the Forehead of the Age to come;
> These, These will give the World another heart
>   And other pulses—hear ye not the hum
> Of mighty Workings in a distant Mart?
> Listen awhile ye Nations, and be dumb.!

Novr 20—

Removed to 76. Cheapside

To J. H. Reynolds, 17 March 1817

My dear Reynolds,

My Brothers are anxious that I sho^d go by myself into the country—they have always been extremely fond of me; and now that

4

Haydon has pointed out how necessary it is that I sho^d be alone to improve myself, they give up the temporary pleasure of living with me continually for a great good which I hope will follow—So I shall soon be out of Town—You must soon bring all your present troubles to a close, and so must I; but we must, like the Fox, prepare for a fresh swarm of flies.* Banish money—Banish sofas—Banish Wine—Banish Music—But right Jack Health—honest Jack Health, true Jack Health—banish health and banish all the world. I must   myself* I come this Evening I shall horribly commit myself elsewhere. So I will send my excuses to them & Mrs Dilk by my Brothers

Y^r sincere friend John Keats

[R]   *To George and Tom Keats, 15 April 1817*

Tuesday Morn—

My dear Brothers,

   I am safe at Southampton—after having ridden three stages out-side and the rest in for it began to be very cold. I did not know the Names of any of the Towns I passed through—all I can tell you is that sometimes I saw dusty Hedges—sometimes Ponds—then nothing—then a little Wood with trees look you like Launce's Sister "as white as a Lilly and as small as a Wand"*—then came houses which died away into a few straggling Barns—then came hedge trees aforesaid again. As the Lamplight crept along the following things were discovered—"long heath broom furze"*—Hurdles here and there half a Mile—Park palings when the Windows of a House were always discovered by reflection—One Nymph of Fountain—*N.B. Stone*—lopped Trees—Cow ruminating—ditto Donkey—Man and Woman going gingerly along—William seeing his Sisters over the Heath—John waiting with a Lanthen for his Mistress—Barber's Pole—Doctor's Shop—However after having had my fill of these I popped my Head out just as it began to Dawn—*N.B. this tuesday Morn saw the Sun rise*—of which I shall say nothing at present. I felt rather lonely this Morning at breakfast so I went and unbox'd a Shakspeare—"There's my Comfort"*—I went immediately after Breakfast to Southampton Water where I enquired for the Boat to the Isle of Wight as I intend seeing that place before I settle—it will go at 3, so shall I after having taken a Chop—I know nothing of this place but that it is long—tolerably broad—has bye streets—two or three Churches—a very respectable old Gate with two Lions to guard it—the Men and Women do not materially differ from those I have been in the Habit of seeing—I forgot to say that from dawn till half past six I went through a most delightful Country—some open Down but for the most part thickly wooded. What surprised me most was an immense quantity of blooming Furze on each side the road cutting a most rural dash. The Southampton water when I saw it just now was no better than a low Water Water which did no more than answer my expectations—it will have mended its Manners by 3. From the Warf are seen the shores on each side stretching to the isle of Wight. You, Haydon, Reynolds &c. have been pushing each other out of my Brain by turns—I have conned over every Head in Haydon's Picture*—you must warn them not to be afraid should my Ghost visit them on Wednesday—tell Haydon to Kiss his Hand at Betty over the Way for me yea and to spy at her for me. I hope one of you will be competent to take part in a Trio while I am away—you need only agravate your voices a little and mind not to speak Cues and all—when you have said Rum-ti-ti—you must not rum any more or else another will take up the ti-ti alone and then he might be taken God shield us for little better than a Titmouse. By the by talking of Titmouse Remember me particularly to all my Friends— give my Love to the Miss Reynoldses and to Fanny who I hope you will soon see. Write to me soon about them all—and you George particularly how you get on with Wilkinson's plan.* What could I have done without my Plaid? I don't feel inclined to write any more at present for I feel rather muzzy—you must be content with this fac simile of the rough plan of Aunt Dinah's Counterpane.

Your most affectionate Brother

John Keats

Reynolds shall hear from me soon.

To J. H. Reynolds, 17, 18 April 1817

Carisbrooke April 17th

My dear Reynolds,

Ever since I wrote to my Brothers from Southampton I have been in a taking, and at this moment I am about to become settled, for I have unpacked my books, put them into a snug corner—pinned up Haydon—Mary Queen of Scotts, and Milton with his daughters in a row. In the passage I found a head of Shakspeare which I had not before seen—It is most likely the same that George spoke so well of; for I like it extremely—Well—this head I have hung over my Books, just above the three in a row, having first discarded a French Ambassador—Now this alone is a good morning's work—Yesterday I went to Shanklin, which occasioned a great debate in my mind whether I should live there or at Carisbrooke. Shanklin is a most beautiful place—sloping wood and meadow ground reaches round the Chine, which is a cleft between the Cliffs of the depth of nearly 300 feet at least. This cleft is filled with trees & bushes in the narrow part; and as it widens becomes bare, if it were not for primroses on one side, which spread to the very verge of the Sea, and some fishermen's huts on the other, perched midway in the Ballustrades of beautiful green Hedges along their steps down to the sands.—But the sea, Jack, the sea—the little waterfall—then the white cliff—then St Catherine's Hill—"the sheep in the meadows, the cows in the corn."—Then, why are you at Carisbrooke? say you—Because, in the first place, I sho^d be at twice the Expense, and three times the inconvenience—next that from here I can see your continent—from a little hill close by, the whole north Angle of the Isle of Wight, with the water between us. In the 3^d place, I see Carisbrooke Castle from my window, and have found several delightful wood-alleys, and copses, and quick freshes—As for Primroses—the Island ought to be called Primrose Island: that is, if the nation of Cowslips agree thereto, of which there are diverse Clans just beginning to lift up their heads and if an how the Rain holds whereby that is Birds eyes abate*—another reason of my fixing is that I am more in reach of the places around me—I intend to walk over the island east—West—North South—I have not seen many specimens of Ruins—I dont think however I shall ever see one to surpass Carisbrooke Castle. The trench is o'ergrown with the smoothest turf, and the walls with ivy—The Keep within side is one Bower of ivy—a Colony of Jackdaws have been there many years—I dare say I have seen many a descendant of some old cawer who peeped through the Bars at Charles the first, when he was there in Confinement. On the road from Cowes to Newport I saw some extensive Barracks which disgusted me extremely with Government for placing such a Nest of Debauchery in so beautiful a place—I asked a man on the Coach about this—and he said that the people had been spoiled—In the room where I slept at Newport I found this on the Window "O Isle spoilt by the Milatary"—I must in honesty however confess that I did not feel very sorry at the idea of the Women being a little profligate—The Wind is in a sulky fit, and I feel that it would be no bad thing to be the favorite of some Fairy, who would give one the power of seeing how our Friends got on, at a Distance—I should like, of all Loves, a sketch of you and Tom and George in ink which Haydon will do if you tell him how I want them—From want of regular rest, I have been rather *narvus*—and the passage in Lear—"Do you not hear the Sea?"*—has haunted me intensely.

On the Sea.

It keeps eternal Whisperings around
   Desolate shores, and with its mighty swell
   Gluts twice ten thousand Caverns; till the spell
Of Hecate leaves them their old shadowy sound.
often 'tis in such gentle temper found
   That scarcely will the very smallest shell
   Be moved for days from whence it sometime fell
When last the winds of Heaven were unbound.
O ye who have your eyeballs vext and tir'd
   Feast them upon the wideness of the Sea
O ye whose Ears are dinned with uproar rude
   Or fed too much with cloying melody—
Sit ye near some old Cavern's Mouth and brood
   Until ye start as if the Sea Nymphs quired—

April 18th
Will you have the goodness to do this? Borrow a Botanical
Dictionary—turn to the words Laurel and Prunus show the explanations to your sisters* and Mrs Dilk and without more ado let them
send me the Cups Basket and Books they trifled and put off and off
while I was in Town—ask them what they can say for themselves—
ask Mrs Dilk wherefore she does so distress me—Let me know how
Jane has her health—the Weather is unfavorable for her—Tell
George and Tom to write.—I'll tell you what—On the 23rd was
Shakespeare born—now If I should receive a Letter from you and
another from my Brothers on that day 'twould be a parlous good
thing—Whenever you write say a Word or two on some Passage in
Shakespeare that may have come rather new to you: which must be
continually happening, notwithstandg that we read the same Play
forty times—for instance, the following, from the Tempest, never
struck me so forcibly as at present,

> "Urchins
> *Shall, for that vast of Night that they may work,*
> All exercise on thee—"

How can I help bringing to your mind the Line—

> *In the dark backward and abysm of time—**

I find that I cannot exist without poetry—without eternal poetry—
half the day will not do—the whole of it—I began with a little, but
habit has made me a Leviathan—I had become all in a Tremble from
not having written any thing of late—the Sonnet over leaf did me
some good. I slept the better last night for it—this Morning, however, I am nearly as bad again—Just now I opened Spencer, and the
first Lines I saw were these.—

> "The noble Heart that harbors vertuous thought,
> And is with Child of glorious great intent,
> Can never rest, until it forth have brought
> Th' eternal Brood of Glory excellent*—"

Let me know particularly about Haydon: ask him to write to me
about Hunt, if it be only ten lines—I hope all is well—I shall forthwith begin my Endymion,* which I hope I shall have got some way

into by the time you come, when we will read our verses in a delightful place I have set my heart upon near the Castle—Give my Love to your Sisters severally—To George and Tom—Remember me to Rice M^r & Mrs Dilk and all we know.——

Your sincere Friend
John Keats.

Direct J. Keats Mrs Cook's new Village

Carisbrooke

To Leigh Hunt, *10 May 1817*

Margate May 10th

My dear Hunt,

The little Gentleman that sometimes lurks in a gossips bowl ought to have come in very likeness of a *coasted* crab* and choaked me outright for not having answered your Letter ere this—however you must not suppose that I was in Town to receive it; no, it followed me to the isle of Wight and I got it just as I was going to pack up for Margate, for reasons which you anon shall hear. On arriving at this treeless affair I wrote to my Brother George to request C. C. C. to do the thing you wot of respecting Rimini; and George tells me he has undertaken it with great Pleasure; so I hope there has been an understanding between you for many Proofs—C. C. C. is well acquainted with Bensley.* Now why did you not send the key of your Cupboard which I know was full of Papers? We would have lock'd them all in a trunk together with those you told me to destroy: which indeed I did not do for fear of demolishing Receipts. There not b[e]ing a more unpleasant thing in the world (saving a thousand and one others) than to pay a Bill twice. Mind you—Old Wood's* a very Varmant—sharded in Covetousness—And now I am upon a horrid subject—what a horrid one you were upon last Sunday and well you handled it. The last Examiner was Battering Ram against Christianity—Blasphemy—Tertullian—Erasmus—Sr Philip Sidney. And then the dreadful Petzelians and their expiation by Blood—and do Christians shudder at the same thing in a Newspaper which the attribute to their God in its most aggravated form? What is to be the end of this?—I must mention Hazlitt's Southey*—O that he had left out

the grey hairs!—Or that they had been in any other Paper not con-
cluding with such a Thunderclap—that sentence about making a
Page of the feelings of a whole life appears to me like a Whale's back
in the Sea of Prose. I ought to have said a word on Shakspeare's
Christianity—there are two, which I have not looked over with you,
touching the thing: the one for, the other against: That in favor is in
Measure for Measure Act. 2. S. 2 Isab. Alas! Alas!

> Why all the Souls that were; were forfeit once
> And he that might the vantage best have took,
> Found out the Remedy—

That against is in Twelfth Night. Act. 3. S 2. Maria—for there is no
Christian, that means to be saved by believing rightly, can ever
believe such impossible Passages of grossness!' Before I come to the
Nymphs* I must get through all disagreeables—I went to the Isle of
Wight—thought so much about Poetry so long together that I could
not get to sleep at night—and moreover, I know not how it was, I
could not get wholesome food—By this means in a Week or so I
became not over capable in my upper Stories, and set off pell mell for
Margate, at least 150 Miles—because forsooth I fancied that I should
like my old Lodging here, and could contrive to do without Trees.
Another thing I was too much in Solitude, and consequently was
obliged to be in continual burning of thought as an only resource.
However Tom is with me at present and we are very comfortable. We
intend though to get among some Trees. How have you got on
among them? How are the Nymphs? I suppose they have led you a
fine dance—Where are you now—In Judea, Cappadocia, or the Parts
of Lybia about Cyrene, Strangers from "Heaven, Hues and
Prototypes—I wager you have given given several new turns to the
~~whole~~ old saying "Now the Maid was fair and pleasant to look on" as
well as mad[e] a little variation in "once upon a time" perhaps too
you have rather varied "thus endeth the first Lesson" I hope you
have made a Horse shoe business of—"unsuperfluous lift" "faint
Bowers" and fibrous roots. I vow that I have been down in the Mouth
lately at this Work. These last two day however I have felt more
confident—I have asked myself so often why I should be a Poet
more than other Men,—seeing how great a thing it is,—how great
things are to be gained by it—What a thing to be in the Mouth of

Fame—that at last the Idea has grown so monstrously beyond my seeming Power of attainment that the other day I nearly consented with myself to drop into a Phæton—yet 't is a disgrace to fail even in a huge attempt, and at this moment I drive the thought from me. I began my Poem about a Fortnight since and have done some every day except travelling ones—Perhaps I may have done a good deal for the time but it appears such a Pin's Point to me that I will not coppy any out—When I consider that so many of these Pin points go to form a Bodkin point (God send I end not my Life with a bare Bodkin, in its modern sense)* and that it requ[i]res a thousand bodkins to make a Spear bright enough to throw any light to posterity—I see that nothing but continual uphill Journeying? Now is there any thing more unpleasant (it may come among the thousand and one) than to be so journeying and miss the Goal at last—But I intend to whistle all these cogitations into the Sea where I hope they will breed Storms violent enough to block up all exit from Russia. Does Shelley* go on telling strange Stories of the Death of kings? Tell him there are stran⟨ge⟩ Stories of the death of Poets—some have died before they were conceived "how do you make that out Master Vellum"* Does Mrs S—cut Bread and Butter as neatly as ever? Tell her to procure some fatal Scissars and cut the th[r]ead of Life of all to be disappointed Poets. Does Mrs Hunt tear linen in half as straight as ever? Tell her to tear from the book of Life all blank Leaves. Remember me to them all—to Miss Kent* and the little ones all—

Your sincere friend
John Keats alias Junkets—

You shall know where we move—

To B. R. Haydon, *10, 11 May 1817*

Margate Saturday Eve

My dear Haydon,

> Let Fame, which all hunt after in their Lives,
> Live register'd upon our brazen tombs,
> And so grace us in the disgrace of death:
> When spite of cormorant devouring time

> The endeavour of this present breath may buy
> That Honor which shall bate his Scythe's keen edge
> And make us heirs of all eternity.*

To think that I have no right to couple myself with you in this speech would be death to me so I have e'en written it—and I pray God that our brazen Tombs be nigh neighbors. It cannot be long first the endeavor of this present breath will soon be over—and yet it is as well to breathe freely during our sojourn—it is as well if you have not been teased with that Money affair—that bill-pestilence.* However I must think that difficulties nerve the Spirit of a Man—they make our Prime Objects a Refuge as well as a Passion. The Trumpet of Fame is as a tower of Strength the ambitious bloweth it and is safe—I suppose by your telling me not to give way to forebodings George has mentioned to you what I have lately said in my Letters to him—truth is I have been in such a state of Mind as to read over my Lines and hate them. I am "one that gathers Samphire dreadful trade"* the Cliff of Poesy Towers above me—yet when, Tom who meets with some of Pope's Homer in Plutarch's Lives reads some of those to me they seem like Mice to mine.* I read and write about eight hours a day. There is an old saying well begun is half done"—'t is a bad one. I would use instead—Not begun at all 'till half done" so according to that I have not begun my Poem and consequently (a priori) can say nothing about it. Thank God! I do begin arduously where I leave off, notwithstanding occasional depressions: and I hope for the support of a High Power while I clime this little eminence and especially in my Years of more momentous Labor. I remember your saying that you had notions of a good Genius presiding over you—I have of late had the same thought for things which [I] do half at Random are afterwards confirmed by my judgment in a dozen features of Propriety—Is it too daring to Fancy Shakspeare this Presider? When in the Isle of Wight I met with a Shakspeare in the Passage of the House at which I lodged—it comes nearer to my idea of him than any I have seen—I was but there a Week yet the old Woman made me take it with me though I went off in a hurry—Do you not think this is ominous of good? I am glad you say every Man of great Views is at times tormented as I am—

Sunday Aft. This Morning I received a letter from George by which it appears that Money Troubles are to follow us up for some time to come perhaps for always—these vexations are a great hindrance to one—they are not like Envy and detraction stimulants to further exertion as being immediately relative and reflected on at the same time with the prime object—but rather like a nettle leaf or two in your bed. So now I revoke my Promise of finishing my Poem by the Autumn which I should have done had I gone on as I have done—but I cannot write while my spirit is fevered in a contrary direction and I am now sure of having plenty of it this Summer—At this moment I am in no enviable Situation—I feel that I am not in a Mood to write any to day; and it appears that the loss of it is the beginning of all sorts of irregularities. I am extremely glad that a time must come when every thing will leave not a wrack behind. You tell me never to despair—I wish it was as easy for me to observe the saying—truth is I have a horrid Morbidity of Temperament which has shown itself at intervals—it is I have no doubt the greatest Enemy and stumbling block I have to fear—I may even say that it is likely to be the cause of my disappointment. How ever every ill has its share of good—this very bane would at any time enable me to look with an obstinate eye on the Devil Himself—ay to be as proud of being the lowest of the human race as Alfred could be in being of the highest. I feel confident I should have been a rebel Angel had the opportunity been mine. I am very sure that you do love me as your own Brother—I have seen it in your continual anxiety for me—and I assure you that your welfare and fame is and will be a chief pleasure to me all my Life. I know no one but you who can be fully sensible of the turmoil and anxiety, the sacrifice of all what is called comfort the readiness to Measure time by what is done and to die in 6 hours could plans be brought to conclusions.—the looking upon the Sun the Moon the Stars, the Earth and its contents as materials to form greater things—that is to say ethereal things——but here I am talking like a Madman greater things that our Creator himself made!! I wrote to Hunt yesterday—scar[c]ely know what I said in it—I could not talk about Poetry in the way I should have liked for I was not in humor with either his or mine. His self delusions are very lamentable they have inticed him into a Situation which I should be less eager after than that of a galley Slave—what you observe thereon is very true must be in time. Perhaps it is a self delusion to say so—but I think I could not be deceived in the Manner that Hunt is—may I die tomorrow if I am to be. There is no greater Sin after the 7 deadly than to flatter oneself into an idea of being a great Poet—or one of those beings who are privileged to wear out their Lives in the pursuit of Honor—how comfortable a feel it is that such a Crime must bring its heavy Penalty? That if one be a Selfdeluder accounts will be balanced? I am glad you are hard at Work—'t will now soon be done—I long to see Wordsworth's as well as to have mine in:* but I would rather not show my face in Town till the end of the Year—if that will be time enough—if not I shall be disappointed if you do not write for me even when you think best—I never quite despair and I read Shakspeare—indeed I shall I think never read any other Book much—Now this might lead me into a long Confab but I desist. I am very near Agreeing with Hazlit that Shakspeare is enough* for us—By the by what a tremendous Southean Article his last was—I wish he had left out "grey hairs" It was very gratifying to meet your remarks of the Manuscript*—I was reading Anthony and Cleopat[ra]* when I got the Paper and there are several Passages applicable to the events you commentate. You say that he arrived by degrees, and not by any single Struggle to the height of his ambition—and that his Life had been as common in particulars as other Mens—Shakspeare makes Enobarb say—Where's Antony Eros—He's walking in the garden—thus: *and spurns the rush that lies* before him, cries fool, Lepidus! In the same scene we find: "let determined things to destiny hold unbewailed their way". Dolabella says of Antony's Messenger

"An argument that he is pluck'd when hither
He sends so poor a pinion of his wing"—Then again,
      Eno—"I see Men's Judgments are
    A parcel of their fortunes; and things outward
    Do draw the inward quality after them,
    To suffer all alike"—The following applies well to Bertram*
      "Yet he that can endure
To follow with allegience a fallen Lord,
Does conquer him that did his Master conquer,
And earns a place i' the story"

But how differently does Buonap bear his fate from Antony!

'T is good too that the Duke of Wellington has a good Word or so in the Examiner A Man ought to have the Fame he deserves—and I begin to think that detracting from him as well as from Wordsworth is the same thing. I wish he had a little more taste—and did not in that respect "deal in Lieutenantry"* You should have heard from me before this—but in the first place I did not like to do so before I had got a little way in the 1st Book and in the next as G.* told me you were going to write I delayed till I had hea[r]d from you—Give my Respects the next time you write to the North* and also to John Hunt*—Remember me to Reynolds and tell him to write, Ay, and when you sent Westward tell your Sister that I mentioned her in this—So now in the Name of Shakespeare Raphael and all our Saints I commend you to the care of heaven!

Your everlasting friend
John Keats

To Taylor and Hessey, 16 May 1817

Margate May 16—

My dear Sirs,

I am extremely indebted to you for your liberality in the Shape of manufactu[r]ed rag value £20 and shall immediately proceed to destroy some of the Minor Heads of that spr[i]ng-headed Hydra the Dun—To conquer which the knight need have no Sword. Shield Cuirass Cuisses Herbadgeon spear Casque, Greves, Pauldrons Spurs Chevron or any other scaly commodity: but he need only take the Bank Note of Faith and Cash of Salvation, and set out against the Monster invoking the aid of no Archimago or Urganda*—and finger me the Paper light as the Sybils Leaves in Virgil* whereat the Fiend skulks off with his tail between his Legs. Touch him with this enchanted Paper and he whips you his head away as fast as a Snail's Horn—but then the horrid Propensity he has to put it up again has discouraged many very valliant Knights—He is such a never ending still beginning sort of a Body—like my Landlady of the Bell—I should conjecture that the very Spright that the "g[r]een sour ringlets makes [w]hereof the Ewe not bites"* had manufactured it of the dew fallen on said sour ringlets—I think I could make a nice little

Alegorical Poem called "the Dun" Where we wold have the Castle of Carelessness—the Draw Bridge of Credit—Sir Novelty Fashion'⟨s⟩* expedition against the City of Taylors—&c &c——I went day by day at my Poem for a Month at the end of which time the other day I found my Brain so overwrought that I had neither Rhyme nor reason in it—so was obliged to give up for a few days—I hope soon to be able to resume my Work—I have endeavoured to do so once or twice but to no Purpose—instead of Poetry I have a swimming in my head—And feel all the effects of a Mental Debauch—lowness of Spirits—anxiety to go on without the Power to do so which does not at all tend to my ultimate Progression—However tomorrow I will begin my next Month—This Evening I go to Cantrerbury—having got tired of Margate—I was not right in my head when I came—At Cant^y I hope the Remembrance of Chaucer will set me forward like a Billiard-Ball—I am gald to hear of M^r T's health and of the Wellfare of the In-town-stayers" and think Reynolds will like his trip—I have some idea of seeing the Continent some time in the summer—

In repeating how sensible I am of your kindness I remain

Your Obedient Servt and Friend

John Keats—

I shall be very happy to hear any little intelligence in the literary or friendly way when you have time to scribble—

To J. H. Reynolds, September 1817

. . . Wordsworth sometimes, though in a fine way, gives us sentences in the Style of School exercises—for Instance

> The lake doth glitter
> Small birds twitter &c.*

Now I think this is an excellent method of giving a very clear description of an interesting place such as Oxford is—

> The Gothic looks solemn,—
> The plain Doric column
> Supports an old Bishop & crosier;
> The mouldering arch,

Shaded o'er by a larch,
Lives next door to Wilson the hosier

———

Vicè—that is, by turns—
O'er pale visages mourns
The black-tassel trencher, or common-hat:
The Chauntry boy sings,
The steeple bell rings,
And as for the Chancellor—dominat.

———

There are plenty of trees,
And plenty of ease,
And plenty of fat deer for parsons;
And when it is venison,
Short is the benison,—
Then each on a leg or thigh fastens.

To Fanny Keats, 10 September 1817

Oxford Septr 10th

My dear Fanny,

Let us now begin a regular question and answer—a little pro and con; letting it interfere as a pleasant method of my coming at your favorite little wants and enjoyments, that I may meet them in a way befitting a brother.

We have been so little together since you have been able to reflect on things that I know not whether you prefer the History of King Pepin to Bunyan's Pilgrims Progress—or Cinderella and her glass slipper to Moor's Almanack. However in a few Letters I hope I shall be able to come at that and adapt my Scribblings to your Pleasure— You must tell me about all you read if it be only six Pages in a Week—and this transmitted to me every now and then will procue you full sheets of Writing from me pretty frequently—This this I feel as a necessity: for we ought to become intimately acquainted, in order that I may not only, as you grow up love your [*for* you] as my only Sister, but confide in you as my dearest friend. When I saw you last I told you of my intention of going to Oxford and 't is now a

Week since I disembark'd from his Whipship's Coach the Defiance
in this place. I am living in Magdalen Hall on a visit to a young Man*
with whom I have not been long acquainted, but whom I like very
much—we lead very industrious lives he in general Studies and I in
proceeding at a pretty good rate with a Poem which I hope you will
see early in the next year—Perhaps you might like to know what I am
writing about—I will tell you—

Many Years ago there was a young handsome Shepherd who fed
his flocks on a Mountain's Side called Latmus—he was a very con-
templative sort of a Person and lived solitary among the trees and
Plains little thinking—that such a beautiful Creature as the Moon
was growing mad in Love with him—However so it was; and when
he was asleep on the Grass, she used to come down from heaven and
admire him excessively from a long time; and at last could not refrain
from carying him away in her arms to the top of that high Mountain
Latmus while he was a dreaming—but I dare say [you] have read this
and all the other beautiful Tales which have come down from the
ancient times of that beautiful Greece. If you have not let me know
and I will tell you more at large of others quite as delightful—

This Oxford I have no doubt is the finest City in the world—it is
full of old Gothic buildings—Spires—towers—Quadrangles—
Cloisters Groves & and is surrounded with more Clear streams than
ever I saw together—I take a Walk by the Side of one of them every
Evening and thank God, we have not had a drop of rain these many
days—I had a long and interesting Letter from George, cross lines
by a short one from Tom yesterday dated Paris—They both send
their loves to you—Like most Englishmen they feel a mighty preference for every thing English—the french Meadows the trees the
People the Towns the Churches, the Books the every thing—
although they may be in themselves good: yet when put in comparison with our green Island they all vanish like Swallows in October. They have seen Cathedrals Manuscripts. Fountains, Pictures,
Tragedy Comedy,—with other things you may by chance meet with
in this Country such a[s] Washerwomen, Lamplighters, Turnpike-
men Fish kettles, Dancing Masters, kettle drums, Sentry Boxes,
Rocking Horses &c and, now they have taken them over a set of
boxing gloves—I have written to George and requested him, as you
wish I shou⟨ld,⟩ to write to you. I have been writing very hard

lately even till an utter incapacity came on, and I feel it now about my head: so you must not mind a little out of the way sayings—though bye the bye where my brain as clear as a bell I think I should have a little propensity thereto. I shall stop here till I have finished the 3ʳᵈ Book of my Story; which I hope will be accomplish'd in at most three Weeks from to day—about which time you shall see me. How do you like Miss Taylor's essays in Rhyme—I just look'd into the Book and it appeared to me suitable to you—especially since I remember your liking for those pleasant little things the Original Poems*—the essays are the more mature production of the same hand. While I was speaking about france it occurred to me to speak a few Words on their Language—it is perhaps the poorest one ever spoken since the jabbering in the Tower of Ba⟨bel⟩ and when you come to know that the real use and greatness of a Tongue is to be referred to its Literature—you will be astonished to find how very inferior it is to our native Speech—I wish the Italian would supersede french in every School throughout the Country for that is full of real Poetry and Romance of a kind more fitted for the Pleasure of Ladies than perhaps our own—It seems that the only end to be gained in acquiring french—is the immense accomplishment of speaking it—it is none at all—a most lamentable mistake indeed—Italian indeed would sound most musically from Lips which had b[e]gan to pronounce it as early as french is cramme'd down our Mouths, as if we were young Jack daws at the mercy of an overfeeding Schoolboy.*

Now Fanny you must write soon—and write all you think about, never mind what—only let me have a good deal of your writing—You need not do it all at once—be two or three or four day about it, and let it be a diary of your little life. You will preserve all my Letters and I will secure yours—and thus in the course of time we shall each of us have a good Bundle—which, hereafter, when things may have strangely altered and god knows what happened, we may read over together and look with pleasure on times past—that now are to come—Give my Respects to the Ladies—and so my dear Fanny I am ever

Your most affectionate Brother

John.

If you direct—Post Office Oxford—your Letter
    will be brought to me—

To J. H. Reynolds, 21 September 1817

My dear Reynolds.   Oxford Sunday Morn

So you are determined to be my moral foe—draw a Sword at me, and I will forgive—Put a Bullet in my Brain, and I will shake it out as a dewdrop from the Lion's Mane;—put me on a Gridiron, and I will fry with great complancency—but, oh horror! to come upon me in the shape of a Dun! Send me Bills! as I say to my Taylor send me Bills and I'll never employ you more—However, needs must when the devil drives: and for fear of "before and behind Mr Honey-comb"* I'll proceed—I have not time to elucidate the forms and shapes of the grass and trees; for, rot it! I forgot to bring my math-ematical case with me; which unfortunately contained my triangular Prism so that the hues of the grass cannot be dissected for you—

For these last five or six days, we have had regularly a Boat on the Isis, and explored all the streams about, which are more in number than your eye lashes. We sometimes skim into a Bed of rushes, and there become naturalized riverfolks,—there is one particularly nice nest which we have christened "Reynolds's Cove"—in which we have read Wordsworth and talked as may be. I think I see you and Hunt meeting in the Pit.—What a very pleasant fellow he is, if he would give up the sovereignty of a Room pro bono—What Evenings we might pass with him, could we have him from M^rs H—Failings I am always rather rejoiced to find in a Man than sorry for; for they bring us to a Level—He has them,—but then his makes-up are very good. He agrees with the Northe[r]n Poet in this, "He is not one of those who much delight to season their fireside with personal talk"*—I must confess however having a little itch that way, and at this present I have a few neighbourly remarks to make—The world, and especially our England, has within the last thirty year's been vexed and teased by a set of Devils, whom I detest so much that I almost hunger after an acherontic* promotion to a Torturer, pur-posely for their accomodation; These Devils are a set of Women, who having taken a snack or Luncheon of Literary scraps, set them-selves up for towers of Babel in Languages Sapphos in Poetry—Euclids in Geometry—and everything in nothing. Among such the Name of Montague* has been preeminent. The thing has made a very uncomfortable impression on me.—I had longed for some real feminine Modesty in these things, and was therefore gladdened in the extreme on opening the other day one of Bayley's Books—a Book of Poetry written by one beautiful Mrs Philips, a friend of Jeremy Taylor's, and called "the matchless Orinda"*—You must have heard of her, and most likely read her Poetry—I wish you have not, that I may have the pleasure of treating you with a few stanzas—I do it at a venture:—You will not regret reading them once more. The following to her friend Mrs M. A. at parting you will Judge of.

−1−

I have examined and do find
   of all that favour me
There's none I grieve to leave behind
   But only, only thee
To part with thee I needs must die
Could parting sep'rate thee and I.

−2−

But neither chance nor Compliment
   Did *element* our Love;
'Twas sacred sympathy was lent
.   Us from the Quire above.
That friendship fortune did create,
Still fears a wound from time or fate.

3

Our chang'd and mingled souls are grown
   To such acquaintance now,
That if each would resume her own
   Alas! we know not how.
We have each other so engrost
That each is in the union lost

−4−

And thus we can no absence know
   Nor shall we be confin'd;

Our active souls will daily go
    To learn each others mind.
Nay should we never meet to sense
Our souls would hold intelligence.

5

Inspired with a flame divine
    I scorn to court a stay;
For from that noble soul of thine
    I ne'er can be away.
But I shall weep when thou dost grieve
Nor can I die whilst thou dost live

6

By my own temper I shall guess
    At thy felicity,
And only like my happiness
    Because it pleaseth thee.
Our hearts at any time will tell
If thou, or I be sick or well.

—7—

All honour sure I must pretend,
    All that is good or great;
She that would be Rosania's friend,
    Must be at least compleat,†
If I have any Bravery,
'Tis cause I have so much of thee.

---

† A compleat friend—this Line sounded very oddly to me at first.

8

Thy Leiger Soul in me shall lie,
    And all thy thoughts reveal;
Then back again with mine shall flie
    And thence to me shall steal.
Thus still to one another tend;
Such is the sacred name of friend.

9—

Thus our twin souls in one shall grow,
   And teach the world new Love,
Redeem the age and sex, and show
   A Flame Fate dares not move:
And courting death to be our friend,
Our Lives together too shall end

10

A Dew shall dwell upon our Tomb
   of such a Quality
That fighting Armies thither come
   Shall reconciled be
We'll ask no epitaph but say
Orinda and Rosannia.

========

In other of her Poems there is a most delicate fancy of the Fletcher Kind*—which we will con over together: So Haydon is in Town—I had a letter from him yesterday—We will contrive as the Winter comes on—but that [is] neither here nor there. Have you heard from Rice? Has Martin met with the Cumberland Beggar or been wondering at the old Leech gatherer?* Has he a turn for fossils? that is, is he capable of sinking up to his Middle in a Morass?—I have longed to peep in and see him at supper after some tolerable fatigue. How is Hazlitt? We were reading his Table* last night—I know he thinks himself not estimated by ten People in the World—I wishe he knew he is—I am getting on famous with my third Book—have written 800 lines thereof, and hope to finish it next week—Bailey likes what I have done very much—Believe me, my Dear Reynolds, one of my chief layings-up is the pleasure I shall have in showing it to you; I may now say, in a few days—I have heard twice from my Brothers, they are going on very well, and send their Remembrances to you. We expected to have had notices from little Hampton* this Morning—we must wait till Tuesday. I am glad of their Days with the Dilks. You are I know very much teased in that precious London, and want all the rest possible; so shall be content with as brief a scrall—a word or two—till there comes a pat hour.—

    Send us a few of your Stanzas to read in "Reynolds's cove" Give

my Love and respects to your Mother and remember me kindly to all
at home.   Yours faithfully

John Keats

I have left the doublings for Bailey who is going to say that he will
write to you to Morrow

To B. R. Haydon, 28 September 1817

Oxford Septr 28th—

My dear Haydon,

I read your last to the young Man whose Name is Crips.* He
seemed more than ever anxious to avail himself of your offer. I think
I told you we asked him to ascertain his Means. He does not possess
the Philosophers stone—nor Fortunatus' purse, nor Cyges' ring—
but at Bailey's suggestion, whom I assure you is a very capital fellow,
we have stummed up a kind of contrivance whereby he will be
enabled to do himself the benefits you will lay in his Path—I have a
great Idea that he will be a tolerable neat brush. 'T is perhaps the
finest thing that will befal him this many a year: for he is just of an
age to get grounded in bad habits from which you will pluck him. He
brought a Copy of Mary Queen of Scotts. it appears to me that he
has coppied the bad style of the painting as well as couloured the
eyebals yellow like the original. He has also the fault that you pointed
out to me in Hazlitt—on the constringing and diffusing of sub-
stance. However I really believe that he will take fire at the sight of
your Picture—and set about things. If he can get ready in time to
return to Town with me which will be in a few days—I will bring
[him] to you. You will be glad to hear that within these last three
weeks I have written 1000 lines—which are the third Book of my
Poem. My Ideas with respect to it I assure you are very low—and I
would write the subject thoroughly again. but I am tired of it and
think the time would be better spent in writing a new Romance
which I have in my eye for next summer—Rome was not built in a
Day. and all the good I expect from my employment this summer is
the fruit of Experience which I hope to gather in my next Poem.
Bailey's kindest wishes and my vow of being

Yours eternally.

John Keats—

To Benjamin Bailey, 8 October 1817

Hamps[t]ead Octr Wednesday

My dear Bailey,

After a tolerable journey I went from Coach to Coach to as far as
Hampstead where I found my Brothers—the next Morning finding
myself tolerably well I went to Lambs Conduit Street and delivered
your Parcel—Jane and Marianne were greatly improved Marianne
especially she has no unhealthy plumpness in the face—but she
comes me healthy and angular to the Chin—I did not see John I was
extrem(e)ly sorry to hear that poor Rice after having had capital
Health During his tour, was very ill. I dare say you have heard from
him. From No. 19 I went to Hunt's and Haydon's who live now
neighbours. Shelley was there—I know nothing about any thing in
this part of the world—every Body seems at Loggerheads. There's
Hunt infatuated—theres Haydon's Picture in statu quo. There's
Hunt walks up and down his painting room criticising every head
most unmercifully—There's Horace Smith* tired of Hunt. The web
of our Life is of mingled Yarn"* Haydon having removed entirely
from Marlborough street Crips must direct his Letter to Lisson
Grove North Paddington. Yesterday Morning while I was at
Brown's in came Reynolds—he was pretty bobbish we had a pleasant
day—but he would walk home at night that cursed cold distance.
Mrs Bentley's children* are making a horrid row—whereby I regret I
cannot be transported to your Room to write to you. I am quite
disgusted with literary Men and will never know another except
Wordsworth—no not even Byron—Here is an instance of the friend-
ships of such—Haydon and Hunt have known each other many
years—now they live pour ainsi dire jealous Neighbours. Haydon
says to me Keats dont show your Lines to Hunt on any account
or he will have done half for you—so it appears Hunt wishes it
to be thought. When he met Reynolds in the Theatre John told
him that I was getting on to the completion of 4000 Lines. Ah! says
Hunt, had it not been for me they would have been 7000! If
he will say this to Reynolds what would he to other People?
Haydon received a Letter a little while back on this subject from
some Lady—which contains a caution to me through him on this
subject—Now is not all this a most paultry thing to think about?

You may see the whole of the case by the following extract from a
Letter I wrote to George in the spring* "As to what you say
"about my being a poet, I can retu[r]n no answer but by saying
"that the high Idea I have of poetical fame makes me think I
"see it towering to high above me. At any rate I have no right to
"talk until Endymion is finished—it will be a test, a trial of my
"Powers of Imagination and chiefly of my invention which is a
"rare thing indeed—by which I must make 4000 Lines of one
"bare circumstance and fill them with Poetry; and when I con-
"sider that this is a great task, and that when done it will take
"me but a dozen paces towards the Temple of Fame—It makes
"me say—God forbid that I should be without such a task! I
"have heard Hunt say and may be asked—why endeavour after
"a long Poem? To which I should answer—Do not the Lovers
"of Poetry like to have a little Region to wander in where they
"may pick and choose, and in which the images are so numerous
"that many are forgotten and found new in a second Reading:
"which may be food for a Week's stroll in the Summer? Do not
"they like this better than what they can read through before
"Mʳˢ Williams* comes down stairs? a Morning work at most.
"Besides a long Poem is a test of Invention which I take to be the
"Polar Star of Poetry, as Fancy is the Sails, and Imagination the
"Rudder. Did our great Poets ever write short Pieces? I mean in
"the shape of Tales—This same invention seems i⟨n⟩deed of late
"Years to have been forgotten as a Poetical excellence⟨.⟩ But
"enough of this, I put on no Laurels till I shall have finished
"Endymion, and I hope Apollo is ⟨not⟩ angered at my having
"made a Mockery at him at Hunts"* You see Bailey how independant my writing has been—Hunts dissuasion was of no avail—I
refused to visit Shelley, that I might have my own unfetterd scope—
and after all I shall have the Reputation of Hunt's elevé—His corrections and amputations will by the knowing ones be trased in the
Poem—This is to be sure the vexation of a day—nor would I say so
many Words about it to any but those whom I know to have my
wellfare and Reputation at Heart—Haydon promised to give directions for those Casts* and you may expect to see them soon—with as
many Letters You will soon hear the dinning of Bells—never mind
you and Gleg* will defy the foul fiend—But do not sacrifice your

heal[t]h to Books do take it kindly and not so voraciously. I am
certain if you are your own Physician your stomach will resume its
proper strength and then what great Benefits will follow. My Sister
wrote a Letter to me which I think must be at $\frac{e}{y}$ post office Ax Will*
to see. My Brothers kindest remembrances to you—we are going to
dine at Brown's where I have some hopes of meeting Reynolds. The
little Mercury I have taken has corrected the Poison and improved
my Health*—though I feel from my employment that I shall never
be again secure in Robustness—would that you were as well as

> your sincere friend & brother
>
> John Keats

The Dilks are expected to day—

To Benjamin Bailey, 28–30 October 1817

My dear Bailey,

So you have got a Curacy! good—but I suppose you will be
obliged to stop among your Oxford favorites during term-time—
never mind. When do you p[r]each your first sermon tell me—for I
shall propose to the two R s* to hear it so dont look into any of the
old corner oaken pews for fear of being put out by us—Poor Johnny
Martin cant be there He is ill—I suspect—but that's neither here
nor there—all I can say I wish him as well through it as I am like to
be. For this fortnight I have been confined at Hampstead—Saturday
evening was my first day in town—when I went to Rices as we intend
to do every Saturday till we know not when—Rice had some business at Highgate yesterday—so he came over to me and I detained
him for the first time of I hope 24860 times. We hit upon an old
Gent.* we had known some few years ago and had a veray pleausante
daye, In this World there is no quiet nothing but teasing and snub-
bing and vexation—my Brother Tom look'd very unwell yesterday
and I am for shipping him off to Lisbon, perpaps I ship there with
him. I have not seen Mrs Reynolds since I left you—wherefore my
conscience smites me—I think of seeing her tomorrow have you any
Message? I hope Gleg came soon after I left. I dont suppose I've
w[r]itten as many Lines as you have read Volumes or at least Chap-
ters since I saw you. However, I am in a fair way now to come to a

conclusion in at least three Weeks when I assure you I shall be glad to dismount for a Month or two—although I'll keep as tight a reign as possible till then nor suffer myself to sleep. I will copy for you the opening of the 4 Book—in which you will see from the Manner I had not an opportunity of mentioning any Poets, for fear of spoiling the effect of the passage by particularising them!

Muse of my Native Land. Loftiest Muse!
O First born of the Mountains, by the hues
Of Heaven on the spiritual air begot—
Long didst thou sit alone in northern grot
While yet our England was a wolfish den;
Before our forests heard the talk of Men;
Before the first of Druids was a child.—
Long didst thou sit amid our regions wild
Wrapt in a deep, prophetic Solitude.
There came a hebrew voice of solemn Mood
Yet wast thou patient: then sang forth the Nine
Apollo's Garland; yet didst thou divine
Such homebred Glory, that they cry'd in vain
"Come hither Sister of the Island." Plain
Spake fair Ausonia, and once more she spake
A higher Summons—still didst thou betake
     darling
Thee to thy ~~self and to thy~~ hopes. O thou has won
A full accomplishment—the thing is done
Which undone these our latter days had risen
On barren Souls. O Muse thou Knowst what prison
Of flesh and bone curbs and confines and frets
Our Spirits Wings: despondency besets
Our Pillows and the fresh tomorrow morn
Seems to give ⟨forth⟩ its light in very scorn
Of our dull uni⟨nspired⟩ snail paced lives.
Long have I said "how happy he who shrive⟨s⟩
To thee"—but then I thought on Poets gone
And could not pray—nor can I now—so on
I move to the end in Humbleness of Heart..—

Thus far had I written when I received your last which made me at the sight of the direction caper for despair—but for one thing I am glad that I have been neglectful—and that is, therefrom I have received a proof of your utmost kindness which at this present I feel very much—and I wish I had a heart always open to such sensations—but there is no altering a Man's nature and mine must be radically wrong for it will lie dormant a whole Month—This leads me to suppose that there are no Men thouroughly wicked—so as never to be self spiritualized into a kind of sublime Misery—but alas! 't is but for an Hour—he is the only Man "who has kept watch on Man's Mortality"* who has philantrophy enough to overcome the disposition [to] an indolent enjoyment of intellect—who is brave enough to volunteer for uncomfortable hours.

You must forgive although I have only written 300 Lines[1]—they would have been five but I have been obliged to go to town. yesterday I called at Lambs—St   Jane look'd very flush when I first went in but was much better before I left.

You remember in Hazlit's essay on commonplace people—He says they read the Edinburgh and Quarterly and think as they do" Now with respect to Wordsworth's Gipseys I think he is right and yet I think Hazlitt is right* and yet I think Wordsworth is rightest. Wordsworth had not been idle he had not been without his task—nor had they Gipseys—they in the visible world had been as picturesque an object as he in the invisible. The Smoke of their fire—their attitudes—their Voices were all in harmony with the Evenings—It is a bold thing to say and I would not say it in print—but it seems to me that if Wordsworth had though[t] a little deeper at that Moment he would not have written the Poem at all—I should judge it to have been written in one of the most comfortable Moods of his Life—it is a kind of sketchy intellectual Landscape—not a search after Truth—nor is it fair to attack him on such a subject—for it is with the Critic as with the poet had Hazlitt thought a little deeper and been in a good temper he would never have spied an imaginary fault there. The Sunday before last I asked Haydon to dine with me, when I thought of settling all Matters with him in regard to Crips and let you know about it—now although I engaged him a Fortnight before—he sent illness as an excuse—he never will come—I have not

---

[1] See Appendix, note 1.

been well enough to stand the chance of a Wet night, and so have not seen him nor been able to expurgatorize those Masks* for you—but I will not spaek: your speakers are never dooers—then Reynolds—every time I see him and mention you he puts his hand to his head and looks like a son of Niobe's—but he'll write soon. Rome you know was not built in a day—I shall be able, by a little perseverance to read your Letters off hand. I am affraid your health will suffer from over study before your examination—I think you might regulate the thing according to your own Pleasure—and I would too—They were talking of your being up at Christmas—will it be before you have passed? There is nothing my dear Bailey I should rejoice at more that [*for* than] to see you comfortable with a little Pæòna* Wife—an affectionate Wife I have a sort of confidence would do you a great happiness May that be one of the many blessings I wish you—Let me be but [t]he 1/10 of one to you and I shall think it great—My Brother Georges kindest wishes to you. My dear Bailey I am

> your affectionate friend.
>
> John Keats

I should not like to be Pages in your way when in a tolerable hungry mood—you have no Mercy—your teeth are the Rock tarpeian* down which you capsise Epic Poems like Mad—I would not for 40 shillings be Coleridge's Lays* in your way. I hope you will soon get through this abominable writing in the schools—and be able to keep the terms with more comfort in the hope of retu[r]ning to a comfortable and quiet home out of the way of all Hopkinses and black beetles*—When you are settled I will comes and take a peep at your Church—your house—try whether I shall have grow[n] two lusty for my chair—by the fire side—and take a peep at my cordials Bower[1]—A Question is the best beacon towards a little Speculation. You ask me after my health and spirits—This Question ratifies in my Mind what I have said above—Health and Spirits can only belong unalloyed to the selfish Man—the Man who thinks much of his fellows can never be in Spirits—when I am not suffering for vicious beastliness I am the greater part of the week in spirits.

---

[1] See Appendix, note 2.

To Benjamin Bailey, 3 November 1817

Monday—Hampstead

My dear Bailey,

Before I received your Letter I had heard of your disappointment*—an unlook'd for piece of villainy. I am glad to hear there was an hindrance to your speaking your Mind to the Bishop: for all may go straight yet—as to being ordained—but the disgust consequent cannot pass away in a hurry—it must be shocking to find in a sacred Profession such barefaced oppression and impertinence—The Stations and Grandeurs of the World have taken it into their heads that they cannot commit themselves towards and inferior in rank—but is not the impertinence from one above to one below more wretchedly mean than from the low to the high? There is something so nauseous in self-willed yawning impudence in the shape of conscience—it sinks the Bishop of Lincoln into a smashed frog putrifying: that a rebel against common decency should escape the Pillory! That a mitre should cover a Man guilty of the most coxcombical, tyranical and indolent impertinence! I repeat this word for the offence appears to me most especially *impertinent*— and a very serious return would be the Rod—Yet doth he sit in his Palace. Such is this World—and we live—you have surely in a continual struggle against the suffocation of accidents—we must bear (and my Spleen is mad at the thought thereof) the Proud Mans Contumely*—O for a recourse somewhat human independant of the great Consolations of Religion and undepraved Sensations, of the Beautiful, the poetical in all things—O for a Remedy against such wrongs within the pale of the World! Should not those things be pure enjoymen⟨t⟩ should they stand the chance of being contaminated by being called in as antagonists to Bishops? Would not earthly things do? By Heavens my dear Bailey, I know you have a spice of what I mean—you can set me and have set it in all the rubs that may befal me you have I know a sort of Pride which would kick the Devil on the Jaw Bone and make him drunk with the kick— There is nothing so balmy to a soul imbittered as yours must be, as Pride—When we look at the Heavens we cannot be proud—but shall stocks and stones be impertinent and say it does not become us to kick them? At this Moment I take your hand let us walk up yon

Mountain of common sense now if our Pride be vainglorious such a support woud fail—yet you feel firm footing—now look beneath at that parcel of knaves and fools. Many a Mitre is moving among them. I cannot express how I despise the Man who would wrong or be impertinent to you—The thought that we are mortal makes us groan I will speak of something else or my Spleen will get higher and higher—and I am not a bearer of the two egded Sword. I hope you will recieve an answer from Haydon soon—if not Pride! Pride! Pride! I have received no more subscription*—but shall soon have a full health Liberty and leisure to give a good part of my time to him—I will certainly be in time for him—We have promised him one year let that have elapsed and then do as we think proper. If I did not know how impossible it is, I should say 'do not at this time of disappointments disturb yourself about others'—There has been a flaming attack upon Hunt in the Endinburgh Magazine*—I never read any thing so virulent—accusing him of the greatest Crimes—dep[r]eciating his Wife his Poetry—his Habits—his company, his Conversation—These Philipics are to come out in Numbers—calld 'the Cockney School of Poetry' There has been but one Number published—that on Hunt to which they have prefixed a Motto from one Cornelius Webb Poetaster*—who unfortunately was of our Party occasionally at Hampstead and took it into his head to write the following—something about—"we'll talk on Wordsworth Byron—a theme we never tire on and so forth till he comes to Hunt and Keats. In the Motto they have put Hunt and Keats in large Letters—I have no doubt that the second Number was intended for me: but have hopes of its non appearance from the following advertisement in last Sunday's Examiner. "To Z. The writer of the Article signed Z in Blackwood's Ed[i]nburgh magazine for October 1817 is invited to send his address to the printer of the Examiner, in order that Justice may be executed of the proper person" I dont mind the thing much—but if he should go to such lenghts with me as he has done with Hunt I mu[s]t infalibly call him to an account—if he be a human being and appears in Squares and Theatres where we might possibly meet—I dont relish his abuse Yesterday Rice and I were at Reynolds—John was to be articled tom[or]row I suppose by this time it is done.* Jane was much better—At one time or other I will do you a Pleasure and the Poets

a little Justice—but it ought to be in a Poem of greater moment
than Endymion—I will do it some day—I have seen two Letters of
a little Story Reynolds is writing—I wish he would keep at it—
Here is the song I enclosed to Jane if you can make it out in this
cross wise writing.

> O Sorrow
>   Why dost borrow
> The natural hue of health from vermil Lips?
>   To give maiden blushes
>   To the white Rose bushes
> Or ist thy dewy hand the daisy tips?

> O Sorrow
>   Why dost borrow
> The Lustrous Passion from an orbed eye?
>   To give the glow worm Light?
>   Or on a moonless night
> To tinge on syren shores the salt sea spry?

> O Sorrow
>   Why dost borrow
> The tender ditties from a mourning tongue?
>   To give at Evening pale
>   Unto the Nightingal
> That thou mayest listen the cold dews among?

> O Sorrow
>   Why dost borrow
> Heart's lightness from the Merriment of May?
>   A Lover would not tread
>   A Cowslip on the head
> Though he should dance from eve till peep of day;
>   Nor any drooping flower
>   Held sacred to thy bower
> Wherever he may sport himself and play.

> To Sorrow
>   I bade ⟨good morrow,⟩
> And thought to leave her far away behind

> But cheerly, cheerly,
> She loves me dearly—
> She is to me so constant, and so kind—
> I would deceive her
> And so leave her
> But ah! she is too constant and too kind.

O that I had Orpheus lute—and was able to cha[r]m away all your Griefs and Cares—but all my power is a Mite—amid all you troubles I shall ever be—

your sincere and affectionate friend

John Keats

My brothers remembrances to you
Give my respects to Gleig and Whitehead*

To Benjamin Bailey, 22 November 1817

My dear Bailey,

I will get over the first part of this (*un*said) Letter as soon as possible for it relates to the affair of poor Crips—To a Man of your nature, such a Letter as Haydon's must have been extremely cutting—What occasions the greater part of the World's Quarrels? simply this, two Minds meet and do not understand each other time enough to p[r]aevent any shock or surprise at the conduct of either party—As soon as I had known Haydon three days I had got enough of his character not to have been surp[r]ised at such a Letter as he has hurt you with. Nor when I knew it was it a principle with me to drop his acquaintance although with you it would have been an imperious feeling. I wish you knew all that I think about Genius and the Heart—and yet I think you are thoroughly acquainted with my innermost breast in that respect or you could not have known me even thus long and still hold me worthy to be your dear friend. In passing however I must say of one thing that has pressed upon me lately and encreased my Humility and capability of submission* and that is this truth—Men of Genius* are great as certain ethereal Chemicals operating on the Mass of neutral intellect—by [*for* but] they have not any individuality, any determined Character. I would call the top and head of those who have a proper self Men of Power—

But I am running my head into a Subject which I am certain I could not do justice to under five years s[t]udy and 3 vols octavo— and moreover long to be talking about the Imagination—so my dear Bailey do not think of this unpleasant affair if possible—do not—I defy any ha[r]m to come of it—I defy—I'll shall write to Crips this Week and reque[s]t him to tell me all his goings on from time to time by Letter wherever I may be—it will all go on well—so dont because you have suddenly discover'd a Coldness in Haydon suffer yourself to be teased. Do not my dear fellow. O I wish I was as certain of the end of all your troubles as that of your momentary start about the authenticity of the Imagination. I am certain of nothing but of the holiness of the Heart's affections and the truth of Imagination*— What the imagination seizes as Beauty must be truth—whether it existed before or not—for I have the same Idea of all our Passions as of Love they are all in their sublime, creative of essential Beauty—In a Word, you may know my favorite Speculation by my first Book and the little song I sent in my last*—which is a representation from the fancy of the probable mode of operating in these Matters—The Imagination may be compared to Adam's dream*—he awoke and found it truth. I am the more zealous in this affair, because I have never yet been able to perceive how any thing can be known for truth by consequitive reasoning—and yet it must be—Can it be that even the greatest Philosopher ever arrived at his goal without putting aside numerous objections—However it may be, O for a Life of Sensations rather than of Thoughts!* It is 'a Vision in the form of Youth' a Shadow of reality to come—and this consideration has further conv[i]nced me for it has come as auxiliary to another favor-ite Speculation of mine, that we shall enjoy ourselves here after by having what we called happiness on Earth repeated in a finer tone and so repeated*—And yet such a fate can only befall those who delight in sensation rather than hunger as you do after Truth— Adam's dream will do here and seems to be a conviction that Imagination and its empyreal reflection is the same as human Life and its spiritual repetition. But as I was saying—the simple imagina-tive Mind may have its rewards in the repeti[ti]on of its own silent Working coming continually on the spirit with a fine suddenness—to compare great things with small—have you never by being surprised with an old Melody—in a delicious place—by a delicious voice, fe[l]t over again your very speculations and surmises at the time it first operated on your soul—do you not remember forming to yourself the singer's face more beautiful that [*for* than] it was possible and yet with the elevation of the Moment you did not think so—even then you were mounted on the Wings of Imagination so high—that the Prototype must be here after—that delicious face you will see— What a time! I am continually running away from the subject—sure this cannot be exactly the case with a complex Mind—one that is imaginative and at the same time careful of its fruits—who would exist partly on sensation partly on thought—to whom it is necessary that years should bring the philosophic Mind—such an one I con- sider your's and therefore it is necessary to your eternal Happiness that you not only ~~have~~ drink this old Wine of Heaven which I shall call the redigestion of our most ethereal Musings on Earth; but also increase in knowledge and know all things. I am glad to hear you are in a fair Way for Easter—you will soon get through your unpleasant reading and then!—but the world is full of troubles and I have not much reason to think myself pesterd with many—I think Jane or Marianne has a better opinion of me than I deserve—for really and truly I do not think my Brothers illness connected with mine—you know more of the real Cause than they do—nor have I any chance of being rack'd as you have been—you perhaps at one time thought there was such a thing as Worldly Happiness to be arrived at, at certain periods of time marked out—you have of necessity from your disposition been thus led away—I scarcely remember counting upon any Happiness—I look not for it if it be not in the present hour— nothing startles me beyond the Moment. The setting sun will always set me to rights—or if a Sparrow come before my Window I take part in its existince and pick about the Gravel. The first thing that strikes me on hea[r]ing a Misfortune having befalled another is this. 'Well it cannot be helped.—he will have the pleasure of trying the resources of his spirit, and I beg now my dear Bailey that hereafter should you observe any thing cold in me not to but [*for* put] it to the account of heartlessness but abstraction—for I assure you I some- times feel not the influence of a Passion or Affection during a whole week—and so long this sometimes continues I begin to suspect myself and the genuiness of my feelings at other times—thinking them a few barren Tragedy-tears—My Brother Tom is much

37

improved—he is going to Devonshire—whither I shall follow him—
at present I am just arrived at Dorking to change the Scene—change
the Air and give me a spur to wind up my Poem, of which there are
wanting 500 Lines. I should have been here a day sooner but the
Reynoldses persuaded me to spop in Town to meet your friend
Christie*—There were Rice and Martin—we talked about Ghosts—
I will have some talk with Taylor and let you know—when please
God I come down a[t] Christmas—I will find that Examiner if pos-
sible. My best regards to Gleig—My Brothers to you and M^rs
Bentley

Your affectionate friend
John Keats

I want to say much more to you—a few hints will set me going
Direct Burford Bridge near dorking

To J. H. Reynolds, 22 November 1817

Saturday

My Dear Reynolds,

There are two things which tease me here—one of them Crips—
and the other that I cannot go with Tom into Devonshire—however
I hope to do my duty to myself in a week or so; and then Ill try what I
can do for my neighbour—now is not this virtuous? on returning to
Town—Ill damn all Idleness—indeed, in superabundance of
employment, I must not be content to run here and there on little
two penny errands—but turn Rakehell* i e go a *making* or Bailey will
think me just as great a Promise keeper as *he* thinks you—for my self
I do not,—and do not remember above one Complaint against you
for matter o' that—Bailey writes so abominable a hand, to give his
Letter a fair reading requires a little time; so I had not seen when I
saw you last, his invitation to Oxford at Christmas—I'll go with
you—You know how poorly Rice was—I do not think it was all
corporeal—bodily pain was not used to keep him silent. Ill tell you
what; he was hurt at what your Sisters said about his joking with
your Mother he was, soothly to sain—It will all blow over. God
knows, my Dear Reynolds, I should not talk any sorrow to you—you
must have enough vexations—so I won't any more. If I ever start a

rueful subject in a Letter to you—blow me! Why dont you—Now I was a going to ask a very silly Question neither you nor any body else could answer, under a folio, or at least a Pamphlet—you shall judge—Why dont you, as I do, look unconcerned at what may be called more particularly Heart-vexations? They never surprize me—lord! a man should have the fine point of his soul taken off to become fit for this world—I like this place very much—There is Hill & Dale and a little River—I went up Box hill this Evening after the Moon—you a' seen the Moon—came down—and wrote some lines. Whenever I am separated from you, and not engaged in a continued Poem—every Letter shall bring you a lyric—but I am too anxious for you to enjoy the whole, to send you a particle. One of the three Books I have with me is Shakespear's Poems:* I neer found so many beauties in the sonnets—they seem to be full of fine things said unintentionally—in the intensity of working out conceits—Is this to be borne? Hark ye!

> When lofty trees I see barren of leaves
> Which erst from heat did canopy the herd,
> And Summer's green all girded up in sheaves,
> Borne on the bier with white and bristly beard.

He has left nothing to say about nothing or any thing: for look at Snails, you know what he says about Snails, you know where he talks about "cockled snails"—well, in one of these sonnets, he says—the chap slips into—no! I lie! this is in the Venus and Adonis: the Simile brought it to my Mind.

> Audi—As the snail, whose tender horns being hit,
>   Shrinks back into his shelly cave with pain,
>   And there all smothered up in shade doth sit,
>   Long after fearing to put forth again:
>   So at his blody view her eyes are fled,
>   Into the deep dark Cabins of her head.

He overwhelms a genuine Lover of Poesy with all manner of abuse, talking about—

> "a poets rage
> And stretched metre of an antique song"—

Which by the by will be a capital Motto for my Poem—wont it?—He speaks too of "Time's antique pen"—and "aprils first born flowers"—and "deaths eternal cold"—By the Whim King! I'll give you a Stanza, because it is not material in connection and when I wrote it I wanted you to——give your vote, pro or con.—

> Christalline Brother of the Belt of Heaven,
> Aquarius! to whom King Jove ha'th given
> Two liquid pulse streams! s'tead of feather'd wings—
> Two fan like fountains—thine illuminings
> For Dian play:
> Dissolve the frozen purity of air;
> Let thy white shoulders silvery and bare
> Show cold through watery pinions: make more bright
> The Star-Queen's Crescent on her marriage night:
> Haste Haste away!—

Now I hope I shall not fall off in the winding up,—as the Woman said to the rounce*—I mean up and down. I see there is an advertizement in the chronicle to Poets—he is so overloaded with poems on the late Princess.*—I suppose you do not lack—send me a few—lend me thy hand to laugh a little—send me a little pullet sperm, a few finch eggs*—and remember me to each of our Card playing Club—when you die you will all be turned into Dice, and be put in pawn with the Devil—for Cards they crumple up like any King—I mean John in the stage play what pertains Prince Arthur*—I rest

Your affectionate friend
John Keats

Give my love to both houses—hinc atque illinc.*

To George and Tom Keats, 21, 27 (?) December 1817

Hampstead Sunday
22 December 1818

My dear Brothers

I must crave your pardon for not having written ere this & &* I saw Kean* return to the public in Richard III, & finely he did it, & at the request of Reynolds I went to criticise his Luke in Riches*—the critique is in todays champion, which I send you with the Examiner in which you will find very proper lamentation on the obsoletion of christmas Gambols & pastimes:* but it was mixed up with so much egotism of that drivelling nature that pleasure is entirely lost. Hone the publisher's trial, you must find very amusing; & as Englishmen very encouraging—his *Not Guilty* is a thing, which not to have been, would have dulled still more Liberty's Emblazoning—Lord Ellenborough has been paid in his own coin—Wooler & Hone have done us an essential service*—I have had two very pleasant evenings with Dilke yesterday & today; & am at this moment just come from him & feel in the humour to go on with this, began in the morning, & from which he came to fetch me. I spent Friday evening with Wells* & went the next morning to see *Death on the Pale horse*. It is a wonderful picture, when West's age is considered; But there is nothing to be intense upon; no women one feels mad to kiss; no face swelling into reality. the excellence of every Art is its intensity, capable of making all disagreeables evaporate, from their being in close relationship with Beauty & Truth—Examine King Lear & you will find this examplified throughout; but in this picture we have unpleasantness without any momentous depth of speculation excited, in which to bury its repulsiveness—The picture is larger than Christ rejected*—I dined with Haydon the sunday after you left, & had a very pleasant day, I dined too (for I have been out too much lately) with Horace Smith & met his two brothers with Hill & Kingston & one Du Bois,* they only served to convince me, how superior humour is to wit in respect to enjoyment—These men say things which make one start, without making one feel, they are all alike; their manners are alike; they all know fashionables; they have a mannerism in their very eating & drinking, in their mere handling a Decanter—They talked of Kean & his low company—Would I were with that company instead of yours said I to myself! I know such like acquaintance will never do for me & yet I am going to Reynolds, on wednesday—Brown & Dilke walked with me & back from the Christmas pantomime. I had not a dispute but a disquisition with Dilke, on various subjects; several things dovetailed in my mind, & at once it struck me, what quality went to form a Man of Achievement especially in Literature & which Shakespeare posessed so enormously—I mean *Negative Capability*,* that is when man is capable of being in uncertainties, Mysteries, doubts, without any irritable reaching after fact & reason*—Coleridge, for instance, would let go by a fine isolated verisimilitude caught from the Penetralium* of mystery, from being incapable of remaining content with half knowledge. This pursued through Volumes would perhaps take us no further than this, that with a great poet the sense of Beauty overcomes every other consideration, or rather obliterates all consideration.*

Shelley's poem is out & there are words about its being objected too, as much as Queen Mab was.* Poor Shelley I think he has his Quota of good qualities, in sooth la!! Write soon to your most sincere friend & affectionate Brother

John

[R]   *To George and Tom Keats, 5 January 1818*

Featherstone Buildgs Monday

My dear Brothers,

I ought to have written before, and you should have had a long
Letter last week; but I undertook the Champion for Reynolds who is
at Exeter. I wrote two articles, one on the Drury Lane Pantomime,
the other on the Covent Garden New Tragedy, which they have not
put in.* The one they have inserrted is so badly punc[t]uated* that,
you perceive, I am determined never to write more without some
care in that particular. Wells tells me, that you are licking your Chops
Tom, in expectation of my Book coming out; I am sorry to say I have
not began my corrections yet: tomorrow I set out. I called on Sawrey* this morning. He did not seem to be at all out at any thing I said
and the enquiries I made with regard to your spitting of Blood: and
moreover desired me to ask you to send him a correct accou[n]t of all
your sensations and symptoms concerning the Palpitation and the
spitting and the Cough—if you have any. Your last Letter gave me at
[*for* a] great Pleasure for I think the Invalid is in a better spirit there
along the Edge*—and as for George I must immediately, now I think
of it, correct a little misconception of a part of my last Letter. The
Miss Reynolds have never said one word against me about you, or by
any means endeavoured to lessen you in my estimation. That is not
what I referred to: but the manner and thoughts which I knew they
internally had towards you—time will show. Wells and Severn dined
with me yesterday: we had a very pleasant day—I pitched upon
another bottle of claret—Port—we enjoyed ourselves very much
were all very witty and full of Rhyme—we played a Concert* from
4 o'clock till 10—drank your Healths the Hunts and N. B. Severn
Peter Pindars.* I said on that day the only good thing I was ever
guilty of—we were talking about Stephens* and the Is Gallery. I said

I wondered that careful Folks would go there for although it was but a Shilling still you had to pay through the Nose.* I saw the Peachey family* in a Box at Drury one Night. I have got such a curious—or rather I had such, now I am in my own hand. I have had a great deal of pleasant time with Rice lately, and am getting initiated into a little Cant—they call dr[i]nking deep dying scarlet, and when you breathe in your wartering they bid you cry hem and play it off*—they call good Wine a pretty tipple, and call getting a Child knocking out an apple stopping at a Tave[r]n they call hanging out—Where do you sup? is where do you hang out? This day I promised to dine with Wordsworth and the Weather is so bad that I am undecided for he lives at Mortimer street I had an invitation to meet him at Kingstons—but not liking that place I sent my excuse—What I think of doing to day is to dine in Mortimer Street (words^th) and sup here in Feathers^ne Buildg^s as Mr Wells has invited me—On Saturday I called on Wordsworth before he went to Kingston's and was sur-p[r]ised to find him with a stiff Collar. I saw his Spouse and I think his Daughter—I forget whether I had written my last before my Sunday Evening at Haydon's*—no I did n⟨o⟩t or I should have told you Tom of a y⟨oung⟩ Man you met at Paris at Scott's of the n⟨ame of⟩ Richer* I think—he is going to Fezan in Africa there to proceed if possible like Mungo Park—he was very polite to me and enquired very particularly after you—then there was Wordsworth, Lamb,* Monkhouse,* Landseer,* Kingston and your humble Sarvant. Lamb got tipsey and blew up Kingston—proceeding so far as to take the Candle across the Room hold it to his face and show us wh-a-at sort-fello he-waas I astonished Kingston at supper with a pertinacity in favour of drinking—keeping my two glasses at work in a knowing way—I have seen Fanny twice lately—she enquired par-ticularly af[t]er you and wants a Co-partnership Letter from you—she has been unwell but is improving—I think she will be quick—Mrs Abbey* was saying that the Keatses were ever indolent—that they would ever be so and that it was born in them—Well whispered fanny to me 'If it is born with us how can we help it—She seems very anxious for a Letter—I asked her what I should get for her, she said a Medal of the Princess. I called on Haslam*—we dined very snugly together—he sent me a Hare last Week which I sent to Mrs Dilk. Brown is not come back—I and Dilk are getting capital

Friends—he is going to take the Champion—he has sent his farce to Covent Garden—I met Bob Harris in the Slips* at Covent Garden—we had a good deal of curious chat—he came out with his old humble Opinion—The Covent Garden Pantonine is a very nice one—but they have a middling Harlequin, a bad Pantaloon, a worse Clown and a shocking Columbine who is one of the Miss Dennets. I suppose you will see my Critique on the new Tragedy in the next Weeks Champion—It is a shocking bad one. I have not seen Hunt, he was out when I called—Mrs Hunt looks as well as ever I saw her after her Confinement—There is an article in the sennight Examiner—on Godwin's Mandeville signed E. K. I think it Miss Kents*—I will send it. There are fine Subscriptions going on for Hone. You ask me what degrees there are between Scotts Novels and those of Smollet—They appear to me to be quite distinct in every particular—more especially in their Aim—Scott endeavours to th[r]ow so interesting and ramantic a colouring into common and low Characters as to give them a touch of the Sublime—Smollet on the contrary pulls down and levels what with other Men would continue Romance. The Grand parts of Scott are willing [*for* within] the reach of more Minds that [*for* than] the finest humours in Humphrey Climker—I forget whether that fine thing of the Sargeant is Fielding's or Smollets but it gives me more pleasure that [*for* than] the whole Novel of the Antiquary—you must remember what I mean. Some one says to the Sargeant "thats a non sequiter," "if you come to that" replies the Sargeant "you're another."* I see by Wells Letter, Mr Abbey does not overstock you with Money—you must insist—I have not seen Loveless yet—but expect it on Wednesday— I am affraid it is gone. Severn tells me he has an order for some drawings for the Emperor of Russia I was at a Dance at Redhall's and passed a pl[e]asant time enough—drank deep and won 10.6 at cutting for Half Guinies there was a younger Brother of the Squibs made him self very conspicuous after the Ladies had retired from the supper table by giving Mater Omnium—Mr Redhall* said he did not understand any thing but plain english—where at Rice egged the young fool on to say the World plainly out. After which there was an enquirey about the derivation of the Word C—t when while two parsons and Grammarians were setting together and settling the matter Wm Squibs interrupting them said a very good thing*—

'Gentleman says he I have always understood it to be a Root and not
a Derivitive.' On proceeding to the Pot in the Cupboard it soon
became full on which the Court door was opened Frank Floodgate
bawls out, Hoollo! here's an opposition pot—Ay, says Rice in one
you have a Yard for your pot, and in the other a pot for your Yard—
Bailey was there and seemed to enjoy the Evening Rice said he cared
less about the hour than any one and the p[r]oof is his dancing—he
cares not for time, dancing as if he was deaf. Old Redall not being
used to give parties had no idea of the Quantity of wine that would
be drank and he acually put in readiness on the kitchen Stairs 8
dozen—E[v]ery one enquires after you—an⟨d every⟩ one desires
their remembrances to you You must get well Tom and then I shall
feel 'Whole and general as the casing Air.'* Give me as many Letters
as you like and write to Sawrey soon—I received a short Letter from
Bailey about Crips and one from Haydon ditto—Haydon thinks he
improves very much Here a happy twelveth days to you and may we
pass the next together—Mrs Wells desires particularly to Tom and
her respects to George—and I desire no better than to be ever your
most affectionate

Brother John—
I had not opened the Champion before—I find both my articles
in it—

To B. R. Haydon, 10 January 1818

Saturday Morn—
My dear Haydon,
    I should have seen you ere this, but on account of my sister being
in Town: so that when I have sometimes made ten paces towards
you, Fanny has called me into the City; and the Xmas Holyday[s] are
your only time to see Sisters, that is if they are so situated as mine. I
will be with you early next week—to night it should be, but we have a
sort of a Club every Saturday evening—to morrow—but I have on
that day an insuperable engagement—Crips has been down to me,
and appears sensible that a binding to you would be of the greatest
advantage to him—if such a thing be done it cannot be before £150

or £200 are secured in subscriptions to him—I will write to Bailey about it, give a Copy of the Subscribers names to every one I know who is likely to get a £5 for him. I will leave a Copy at Taylor and Hesseys, Rodwell and Martin and will ask Kingston and Cº to cash up. Your friendship fo⟨r⟩ me is now getting into its teens—and I feel the past. Also evey day older I get—the greater is my idea of your atchievements in Art: and I am convinced that there are three things to rejoice at in this Age—The Excursion Your Pictures, and Hazlitt's depth of Taste.*

> Your's affectionately
> John Keats

To George and Tom Keats, *13, 19 January 1818*

> Tuesday Hampstead 1818

My dear Brothers

I am certain I think of having a letter tomorrow morning for I expected one so much this morning, having been in town two days, at the end of which my expectations began to get up a little, I found two on the table, one from Bailey & one from Haydon, I am quite perplexed in a world of doubts & fancies—there is nothing stable in the world—uproar's your only musick, I do not mean to include Bailey in this & so I dismiss him from this, with all the oprobrium he deserves, that is in so many words, he is one of the noblest men alive at the present day. In a note to Haydon about a week ago, (which I wrote with a full sense of what he had done, and how he had never manifested any little mean drawback in his value of me) I said if there were three things superior in the modern world, they were "the Excursion." "Haydon's pictures" & "Hazlitts depth of Taste" So I do believe—Not thus speaking with any poor vanity that works of genius were the first things in this world. No! for that sort of probity & disinterestedness* which such men as Bailey possess, does hold & grasp the tip top of any spiritual honours, that can be paid to any thing in this world—And moreover having this feeling at this pres-ent come over me in its full force, I sat down to write to you with a grateful heart, in that I had not a Brother, who did not feel & credit me, for a deeper feeling & devotion for his uprightness, than for any marks of genius however splendid I was speaking about doubts & fancies—I Mean there has been a quarrel of a severe nature between Haydon & Reynolds & another ("the Devil rides upon a fiddle stick"*) between Hunt & Haydon—the first grew from the sunday* on which Haydon invited some friends to meet Wordsworth. Reynolds never went, & never sent any Notice about it, this offended Haydon more than it ought to have done—he wrote a very sharp & high note to Reynolds & then another in palliation—but which Reynolds feels as an aggravation of the first—Considering all things—Haydons frequent neglect of his Appointments &c. his notes were bad enough to put Reynolds on the right side of the question but then Reynolds has no powers of sufferance; no idea of having the thing against him; so he answered Haydon in one of the most cutting letters I ever read; exposing to himself all his own weaknesses, & going on to an excess, which whether it is just or no, is what I would fain have unsaid, the fact is they are both in the right & both in the wrong.

The quarrel with Hunt I understand thus far. Mrs H. was in the habit of borrowing silver of Haydon, the last time she did so, Haydon asked her to return it at a certain time—She did not—Haydon sent for it; Hunt went to expostulate on the indelicacy &c. they got to words & parted for ever—All I hope is at some time to bring them all together again—Lawk! Molly there's been such doings—Yesterday evening I made an appointment with Wells, to go to a private theatre & it being in the neighbourhood of Drury Lane, & thinking we might be fatigued with sitting the whole evening in one dirty hole; I got the Drury Lane ticket & therewith we divided the evening with a Spice of Richard III—Good Lord,! I began this letter nearly a week ago, what have I been doing since—I have been—I mean not been sending last sunday's paper* to you I believe because it was not near me—for I cannot find it, & my conscience presses heavy on me for not sending it; You would have had one last thursday but I was called away, & have been about somewhere ever since. Where. What. well I rejoice almost that I have not heard from you, because no news is good news.—I cannot for the world recollect why I was called away, all I know is, that there has been a dance at Dilke's & another at the London Coffee House; to both of which I went. But I must tell you in another letter the circumstances thereof—for though a week should have passed since I wrote on the other side it quite appalls me—I can only write in scraps & patches, Brown is returned from Hampstead*—Haydon has returned an answer in the same style— they are all dreadfully irritated against each other. On sunday I saw Hunt & dined with Haydon, met Hazlitt & Bewick* there; & took Haslam with me—forgot to speak about Crips though I broke my engagement to Haslams on purpose—Mem. Haslam came to meet me, found me at Breakfast, had the goodness to go with me my way—I have just finished the revision of my first book,* & shall take it to Taylor's tomorrow—intend to persevere—Do not let me see many days pass without hearing from you

Your most affectionate Brother

John

To B. R. Haydon, 23 January 1818

Friday 23rd

My dear Haydon,

I have a complete fellow-feeling with you in this business*—so much so that it would be as well to wait for a choice out of *Hyperion*—when that Poem is done there will be a wide range for you—in Endymion I think you may have many bits of the deep and sentimental cast—the nature of *Hyperion* will lead me to treat it in a more naked and grecian Manner—and the march of passion and endeavour will be undeviating—and one great contrast between them will be—that the Hero of the written tale* being mortal is led on, like Buonaparte, by circumstance; whereas the Apollo in Hyperion being a fore-seeing God will shape his actions like one. But I am counting &c.

Your proposal pleases me—and, believe me, I would not have my Head in the shop windows from any hand but yours—no by Apelles! I will write Taylor and you shall hear from me

Your's ever John Keats

To John Taylor, 23 January 1818

Friday 23rd

My dear Taylor,

I have spoken to Haydon about the Drawing—he would do it with all his Art and Heart too if so I will it—however he has written thus to me—but I must tell you first, he intends painting a finished picture from the Poem—thus he writes

"When I do any thing for your poem, it must be effectual—an honor to both of us—to hurry up a sketch for the season won't do. I think an engraving from your head, from a Chalk drawing of mine—done with all my might—to which I would put my name, would answer Taylor's Idea more than the other indeed I am sure of it—this will do & this will be effectual and as I have not done it for any other human being—it will have an effect"

What think you of this? Let me hear—I shall have my second book in readiness forthwith—

Your's most sincerely

John Keats—

If Reynolds calls tell him three lines would be acceptable for I am squat at Hampstead

To Benjamin Bailey, 23 January 1818

My dear Bailey,   Friday Jany 23rd

Twelve days have pass'd since your last reached me—what has gone through the myriads of human Minds since the 12th we talk of the immense number of Books, the Volumes ranged thousands by thousands—but perhaps more goes through the human intelligence in 12 days than ever was written.* How has that unfortunate Family lived through the twelve?* One saying of your's I shall never forget—you may not recollect it—it being perhaps said when you were looking on the surface and seeming of Humanity alone, without a thought of the past or the future—or the deeps of good and evil—you were at the moment estranged from speculation and I think you have arguments ready for the Man who would utter it to you—this is a formidable preface for a simple thing—merely you said; "*Why*

should Woman suffer?" Aye. Why should she? 'By heavens I'd coin my
very Soul and drop my Blood for Drachmas."! These things are, and
he who feels how incompetent the most skyey Knight errantry its
[*for* is] to heal this bruised fairness is like a sensitive leaf on the hot
hand of thought. Your tearing, my dear friend, a spiritless and
gloomy Letter up to rewrite to me is what I shall never forget—it
was to me a real thing. Things have happen'd lately of great
Perplexity—You must have heard of them—Reynolds and Haydon
retorting and recrimminating—and parting for ever—the same
thing has happened between Haydon and Hunt—It is unfortunate—
Men should bear with each other—there lives not the Man who may
not be cut up, aye hashed to pieces on his weakest side. The best of
Men have but a portion of good in them—a kind of spiritual yeast in
their frames which creates the ferment of existence—by which a
Man is propell'd to act and strive and buffet with Circumstance. The
sure way Bailey, is first to know a Man's faults, and then be passive, if
after that he insensibly draws you towards him then you have no
Power to break the link. Before I felt interested in either Reynolds or
Haydon—I was well read in their faults yet knowing them I have
been cementing gradually with both—I have an affection for them
both for reasons almost opposite—and to both must I of necessity
cling—supported always by the hope that when a little time—a few
years shall have tried me more fully in their esteem I may be able to
bring them together—the time must come because they have both
hearts—and they will recollect the best parts of each other when
this gust is overblown. I had a Message from you through a Letter to
Jane* I think about Cripps—there can be no idea of binding* till a
sufficient sum is sure for him—and even then the thing should be
maturely consider'd by all his helpers. I shall try my luck upon as
many fat-purses as I can meet with—Cripps is improving very
fast—I have the greater hopes of him because he is so slow in
devellopment—a Man of great executing Powers at 20—with a look
and a speech almost stupid is sure to do something. I have just look'd
th[r]ough the second side of your Letter—I feel a great content at it.
I was at Hunt's the other day, and he surprised me with a real
authenticated Lock of *Milton's Hair*. I know you would like what I
wrote thereon—so here it is—*as they say of a Sheep in a Nur*sery
Book

On seeing a Lock of Milton's Hair—

Ode.

Chief of organic Numbers!
　Old scholar of the spheres!
Thy spirit never slumbers,
　But rolls about our ears
For ever and for ever.
O, what a mad endeavour
　　Worketh he
Who, to thy sacred and ennobled hearse,
Would offer a burnt sacrifice of verse
　　And Melody!

How heavenward thou soundedst
　Live Temple of sweet noise;
And discord unconfoundedst:
　Giving delight new joys,
And Pleasure nobler pinions—
O where are thy Dominions!
　　Lend thine ear
To a young delian oath—aye, by thy soul,
By all that from thy mortal Lips did roll;
And by the kernel of thine earthly Love,
Beauty, in things on earth and things above,
　When every childish fashion
　　Has vanish'd from my rhyme
　Will I grey-gone in passion,
　　Give to an after-time
　　Hymning and harmony
Of thee, and of thy Works and of thy Life:
But vain is now the burning and the strife—
Pangs are in vain—until I grow high-rife
　　With Old Philosophy
And mad with glimpses at futurity!
For many years my offerings must be hush'd:
When I do speak I'll think upon this hour,
Because I feel my forehead hot and flush'⟨d,⟩

> Even at the simplest vassal of thy Po⟨wer—⟩
>   A Lock of thy bright hair!
>   Sudden it came,
>   And I was startled when I heard thy name
>   Coupled so unaware—
>   Yet, at the moment, temperate was my blood:
>   Methought I had beheld it from the flood.
>
> Jany 21st

This I did at Hunt's at his request—perhaps I should have done something better alone and at home—I have sent my first book to the Press—and this afternoon shall begin preparing the second—my visit to you will be a great spur to quicken the Proceeding—I have not had your Sermon returned—I long to make it the subject of a Letter* to you—What do they say at Oxford?

I trust you and Gleig pass much fine time together. Remember me to him and Whitehead. My Brother Tom is getting stronger but his Spitting of blood continues—I sat down to read King Lear yesterday, and felt the greatness of the thing up to the writing of a Sonnet preparatory thereto—in my next you shall have it There were some miserable reports of Rice's health—I went and lo! Master Jemmy had been to the play the night before and was out at the time—he always comes on his Legs like a Cat—I have seen a good deal of Wordsworth. Hazlitt is lectu[r]ing on Poetry at the Surry institution*—I shall be there next Tuesday.

> Your most affectionate Friend
> John Keats—

To George and Tom Keats, 23, 24 January 1818

Friday, 23^d January 1818

My dear Brothers.

I was thinking what hindered me from writing so long, for I have many things to say to you & know not where to begin. It shall be upon a thing most interesting to you my Poem. Well! I have given the 1st book to Taylor; he seemed more than satisfied with it, & to my surprise proposed publishing it in Quarto if Haydon would make a drawing of some event therein, for a Frontispeice. I called on

Haydon, he said he would do anything I liked, but said he would rather paint a finished picture, from it, which he seems eager to do; this in a year or two will be a glorious thing for us; & it will be, for Haydon is struck with the 1st Book. I left Haydon & the next day received a letter from him, proposing to make, as he says, with all his might, a finished chalk sketch of my head, to be engraved in the first style & put at the head of my Poem, saying at the same time he had never done the thing for any human being, & that it must have considerable effect as he will put the name to it—I begin to day to copy my 2nd Book "thus far into the bowels of the Land"*—You shall hear whether it will be Quarto or non Quarto, picture or non Picture. Leigh Hunt I showed my 1st Book to, he allows it not much merit as a whole; says it is unnatural & made ten objections to it in the mere skimming over. He says the conversation is unnatural & too high-flown for the Brother & Sister. Says it should be simple forgetting do ye mind, that they are both overshadowed by a Supernatural Power, & of force could not speak like Franchesca in the Rimini. He must first prove that Caliban's poetry is unnatural,—This with me completely overturns his objections—the fact is he & Shelley are hurt & perhaps justly, at my not having showed them the affair officiously & from several hints I have had they appear much disposed to dissect & anatomize, any trip or slip I may have made.*— But whose afraid Ay! Tom! demme if I am.* I went last tuesday, an hour too late, to Hazlitt's Lecture on poetry, got there just as they were coming out, when all these pounced upon me. Hazlitt, John Hunt & son, Wells, Bewick, all the Landseers, Bob Harris, Rox* of the Burrough Aye & more; the Landseers enquired after you particularly—I know not whether Wordsworth has left town—But sunday I dined with Hazlitt & Haydon, also that I took Haslam with me—I dined with Brown lately. Dilke having taken the Champion, Theatricals was obliged to be in Town. Fanny has returned to Walthamstow—Mr Abbey appeared very glum, the last time I went [to] see her, & said in an indirect way, that I had no business there— Rice has been ill, but has been mending much lately—I think a little change has taken place in my intellect lately—I cannot bear to be uninterested or unemployed, I, who for so long a time, have been addicted to passiveness—Nothing is finer for the purposes of great productions, than a very gradual ripening of the intellectual powers*—As an instance of this—observe—I sat down yesterday to read King Lear once again the thing appeared to demand the pro-logue of a Sonnet, I wrote it & began to read—(I know you would like to see it)

> ### "On sitting down to King Lear once Again"
>
> O golden tongued Romance with serene Lute!
> Fair plumed syren! Queen! if* far away!
> Leave melodizing on this wintry day,
> Shut up thine olden volume & be mute.
> Adieu! for once again the fierce dispute,
> Betwixt Hell torment & impassioned Clay
> Must I burn through; once more assay
> The bitter sweet of this Shakespeareian fruit
> Cheif Poet! & ye clouds of Albion.
> Begettors of our deep eternal theme,
> When I am through the old oak forest gone
> Let me not wander in a barren dream
> But when I am consumed with the Fire
> Give me new Pheonix-wings to fly at my desire

So you see I am getting at it, with a sort of determination & strength, though verily I do not feel it at this moment—this is my fourth letter this morning & feel rather tired & my head rather swimming—so I will leave it open till tomorrow's post.——

I am in the habit of taking my papers to Dilkes & copying there; so I chat & proceed at the same time. I have been there at my work this evening, & the walk over the Heath takes off all sleep, so I will even proceed with you—I left off short in my last, just as I began an account of a private theatrical—Well it was of the lowest order, all greasy & oily, insomuch that if they had lived in olden times, when signs were hung over the doors; the only appropriate one for that oily place would have been—a guttered Candle—they played John Bull The Review. & it was to conclude with Bombastes Furioso*—I saw from a Box the 1st Act of John Bull, then I went to Drury & did not return till it was over; when by Wells' interest we got behind the scenes. there was not a yard wide all the way round for actors, scene shifters & interlopers to move in; for 'Note Bene' the Green Room was under the stage & there was I threatened over & over again to be turned out by the oily scene shifters—there did I hear a little painted Trollop own, very candidly, that she had failed in Mary, with a "damned if she'd play a serious part again, as long as she lived," & at the same time she was habited as the Quaker in the Review—there was a quarrel & a fat good natured looking girl in soldiers Clothes wished she had only been a man for Tom's sake*—One fellow began a song but an unlucky finger-point from the Gallery sent him off like a shot, One chap was dressed to kill for the King in Bombastes. & he stood at the edge of the scene in the very sweat of anxiety to show himself, but Alas the thing was not played. the sweetest morsel of the night moreover was, that the musicians began pegging & fagging away at an overture—never did you see faces more in earnest, three times did they play it over, dropping all kinds of correctness & still did not the curtain draw up—Well then they went into a country-dance then into a region they well knew, into their old boonsome Pothouse. & then to see how pompous o' the sudden they turned; how they looked about, & chatted; how they did not care a Damn; was a great treat—I hope I have not tired you by this filling up of the dash in my last,—Constable the Bookseller has offered Reynolds ten gineas a sheet to write for his magazine,* it is an Edinburgh one which, Blackwoods started up in opposition to. Hunt said he was nearly sure that the 'Cockney School' was written by Scott,* so you are right Tom!—There are no more little bits of news I can remember at present I remain

My dear Brothers Your very affectionate Brother

John

To John Taylor, 30 January 1818

My dear Taylor,   Friday
    These Lines, as they now stand, about Happiness have rung in my ears like a 'chime a mending'. see here,

Behold
Wherein Lies happiness Pœona? fold—

This appears to me the very contrary of blessed. I hope this will appear to you more elegible.

> Wherein lies Happiness? In that which becks
> Our ready Minds to fellowship divine;
> A fellowship with essence, till we shine
> Full alchymized and free of space. Behold
> The clear Religion of heaven—fold &c—*

You must indulge me by putting this in for setting aside the badness of the other, such a preface is necessary to the Subject. The whole thing must I think have appeared to you, who are a consequitive Man, as a thing almost of mere words—but I assure you that when I wrote it, it was a regular stepping of the Imagination towards a Truth. My having written that ~~Passage~~ Argument will perhaps be of the greatest Service to me of any thing I ever did—It set before me at once the gradations of Happiness even like a kind of Pleasure Thermometer*—and is my first Step towards the chief Attempt in the Drama—the playing of different Natures with Joy and Sorrow.

Do me this favor and believe Me, Your sincere friend

John Keats

I hope your next Work will be of a more general Interest—
I s[u]ppose you cogitate a little about it now and then.

To J. H. Reynolds, 3 February 1818

Hampstead Tuesday.

My dear Reynolds,

I thank you for your dish of Filberts—Would I could get a basket of them by way of desert every day for the sum of two pence—* Would we were a sort of ethereal Pigs, & turn'd loose to feed upon spiritual Mast & Acorns—which would be merely being a squirrel & feed upon filberts. for what is a squirrel but an airy pig, or a filbert but a sort of archangelical acorn. About the nuts being worth cracking, all I can say is that where there are a throng of delightful Images ready drawn simplicity is the only thing. the first is the best on account of the first line, and the "arrow—foil'd of its antler'd food"—and moreover (and this is the only word or two I find fault with, the more because I have had so much reason to shun it as a quicksand) the last has "tender and true"—We must cut this, and not be rattlesnaked into any more of the like—It may be said that we ought to read our Contemporaries. that Wordsworth &c should have their due from us. but for the sake of a few fine imaginative or domestic passages, are we to be bullied into a certain Philosophy engendered in the whims of an Egotist*—Every man has his speculations, but every man does not brood and peacock over them till he makes a false coinage and deceives himself—Many a man can travel to the very bourne of Heaven, and yet want confidence to put down his halfseeing. Sancho will invent a Journey heavenward as well as any body. We hate poetry that has a palpable design upon us—and if we do not agree, seems to put its hand in its breeches pocket. Poetry should be great & unobtrusive, a thing which enters into one's soul, and does not startle it or amaze it with itself but with its subject.— How beautiful are the retired flowers! how would they lose their beauty were they to throng into the highway crying out, "admire me I am a violet! dote upon me I am a primrose! Modern poets differ from the Elizabethans in this. Each of the moderns like an Elector of Hanover governs his petty state, & knows how many straws are swept daily from the Causeways in all his dominions & has a continual itching that all the Housewives should have their coppers well scoured: the antients were Emperors of vast Provinces, they had only heard of the remote ones and scarcely cared to visit them.—I will cut all this—I will have no more of Wordsworth or Hunt in particular*—Why should we be of the tribe of Manasseh* when we can wander with Esau? Why should we kick against the Pricks, when we can walk on Roses? Why should we be owls, when we can be Eagles? Why be teased with "nice Eyed wagtails,"* when we have in sight "the Cherub Contemplation"?*—Why with Wordsworths "Matthew with a bough of wilding in his hand"* when we can have Jacques "under an oak &c"*—The secret of the Bough of Wilding will run through your head faster than I can write it—Old Matthew spoke to him some years ago on some nothing, & because he happens in an Evening Walk to imagine the figure of the old man—he must stamp it down in black & white, and it is henceforth sacred—I don't mean to deny Wordsworth's grandeur & Hunt's merit, but I mean to say we need not be teazed with grandeur & merit—when we can have them uncontaminated & unobtrusive. Let us have the old Poets, & robin Hood Your letter and its sonnets gave me more pleasure than will the 4th Book of Childe Harold* & the whole of any body's life &

opinions. In return for your dish of filberts, I have gathered a few Catkins.* I hope they'll look pretty.

To J. H. R. In answer to his Robin Hood Sonnets.

"No those days are gone away &c"—*

I hope you will like them they are at least written in the Spirit of Outlawry.—Here are the Mermaid lines

"Souls of Poets dead & gone, &c"—*

I will call on you at 4 tomorrow, and we will trudge together for it is not the thing to be a stranger in the Land of Harpsicols.* I hope also to bring you my 2ᵈ book—In the hope that these Scribblings will be some amusement for you this Evening—I remain copying on the Hill

Yʳ sincere friend and Coscribbler

John Keats.

To George and Tom Keats, *14 February 1818*

Hampstead Saturday Night

My dear Brothers

When once a man delays a letter beyond the proper time, he delays it longer for one or two reasons; first because he must begin in a very commonplace style, that is to say, with an excuse; & secondly things & circumstances become so jumbled in his mind, that he knows not what, or what not, he has said in his last—I shall visit you as soon as I have copied my poem all out, I am now much beforehand with the printer, they have done none yet, & I am half afraid they will let half the season by before the printing, I am determined they shall not trouble me when I have copied it all.—Horace Smith has lent me his manuscript called "Nehemiah Muggs, an exposure of the Methodists" perhaps I may send you a few extracts—Hazlitts last Lecture was on Thompson, Cowper & Crabbe,* he praised Cowper & Thompson but he gave Crabbe an unmerciful licking—I think Hunts article of Fazio—no it was not, but I saw Fazio the first night,* it hung rather heavily on me—I am in the high way of being introduced to a squad of people, Peter Pindar, Mʳˢ Opie.* Mʳˢ

Scott*—Mr Robinson a great friend of Coleridges called on me*—
Richards tell[s] me that my Poems are known in the west country &
that he saw a very clever copy of verses, headed with a Motto from
my Sonnet to George—Honors rush so thickly upon me that I shall
not be able to bear up against them. What think you, am I to be
crowned in the Capitol, am I to be made a Mandarin—No! I am to
be invited, Mrs Hunt tells me, to a party at Ollier's to keep Shake-
speares birthday Shakespeare would stare to see me there—The
Wednesday before last Shelley, Hunt & I wrote each a Sonnet on the
River Nile, some day you shall read them all.* I saw a sheet of
Endymion & have all reason to suppose they will soon get it done.
there shall be nothing wanting on my part. I have been writing at
intervals many songs & Sonnets, & I long to be at Teignmouth, to
read them over to you: however I think I had better wait till this Book
is off my mind; it will not be long first,

Reynolds has been writing two very capital articles in the Yellow
Dwarf on popular Preachers*—All the talk here is about Dr Croft
the Duke of Devon &c*

Your most affectionate Brother
John.

Nehemiah Muggs—An Exposure of the Methodists——

Muggs had long wished to be a father
And told his wish without succeeding
At length Rose brought him two together
And there I think she show'd her breeding

Behold them in the Holy place
With others all agog for Grace
Where a perspiring preacher vexes
Sundry old women of both sexes
Thumping as though his zeal were pushing
To make a convert of the cushion

But in their hurry to proceed
Each reached the door at the same minute
Where as the[y] scuffled for the lead
Both struggling stuck together in it

Shouting rampant amorous hymns
Under pretext of singing Psalms

———

He shudder'd & withdrew his eye
Perk'd up his head some inches higher
Drew his chair nearer to the fire
And hummed as if he would have said
Pooh! Nonsense! damme! who's afraid
Or sought by bustling up his frame
To make his courage do the same
Thus would some blushing trembling Elves
Conceal their terrors from themselves
By their own cheering wax the bolder
And pat themselves upon the shoulder

A Saints' a sort of human Mill
That labours when the body's still
And gathers grist with inward groans
And creaking melancholy moans
By waving heavenward o'er his head
His arms & working them for bread

———

Is it that addled brains perchance
When the skull's dark with ignorance
Like rotten eggs surveyed at night
Emit a temporary light?
Or is it that a heated brain
When it is rubbed against the grain,
Like a Cats' back though black as charcoal
Will in the gloom appear to sparkle

———

New Missions sent
To make the Antipodes relent
Turn the Anthropophagetic race
To sucking lambs & babes of grace
Or tempt the hairy Hebrew rogues
To cut their beards & Synagogues

———

> This grave advertisement was seen
> "Wanted a serious Shopman, who
> To Gospel principles is true
> Whose voice for Hymns is not too gruff
> Who can grind brick dust, mix up snuff
> And has an undisputed Nack in
> Fearing the Lord & making Blacking

[R]   *To J. H. Reynolds, 19 February 1818*

My dear Reynolds,

I have an idea that a Man might pass a very pleasant life in this manner—let him on any certain day read a certain Page of full Poesy or distilled Prose and let him wander with it, and muse upon it, and reflect from it, and bring home to it, and prophesy upon it, and dream upon it—untill it becomes stale—but when will it do so? Never—When Man has arrived at a certain ripeness in intellect any one grand and spiritual passage serves him as a starting post towards all "the two-and thirty Pallaces"* How happy is such a "voyage of conception,' what delicious diligent Indolence!* A doze upon a Sofa does not hinder it, and a nap upon Clover engenders ethereal finger-pointings—the prattle of a child gives it wings, and the converse of middle age a strength to beat them—a strain of musick conducts to 'an odd angle of the Isle' and when the leaves whisper it puts a 'girdle round the earth. Nor will this sparing touch of noble Books be any irreverance to their Writers—for perhaps the honors paid by Man to Man are trifles in comparison to the Benefit done by great Works to the 'Spirit and pulse of good' by their mere passive existence. Memory should not be called knowledge—Many have original Minds who do not think it—they are led away by Custom—Now it appears to me that almost any Man may like the Spider spin from his own inwards his own airy Citadel—the points of leaves and twigs on which the Spider begins her work are few and she fills the Air with a beautiful circuiting: man should be content with as few points to tip with the fine Webb of his Soul and weave a tapestry empyrean—full of Symbols for his spiritual eye, of softness for his spiritual touch, of space for his wandering of distinctness for his Luxury—But the Minds of Mortals are so different and bent on such diverse Journeys

that it may at first appear impossible for any common taste and
fellowship to exist between two or three under these suppositions—
It is however quite the contrary—Minds would leave each other in
contrary directions, traverse each other in Numberless points, and
all [*for* at] last greet each other at the Journeys end—A old Man and
a child would talk together and the old Man be led on his Path, and
the child left thinking—Man should not dispute or assert but whisper results to his neighbour, and thus by every germ of Spirit sucking the Sap from mould ethereal every human might become great,
and Humanity instead of being a wide heath of Furse and Briars
with here and there a remote Oak or Pine, would become a grand
democracy of Forest Trees.* It has been an old Comparison for our
urging on—the Bee hive—however it seems to me that we should
rather be the flower than the Bee—for it is a false notion that more is
gained by receiving than giving—no the receiver and the giver are
equal in their benefits—The f[l]ower I doubt not receives a fair
guerdon from the Bee—its leaves blush deeper in the next spring—
and who shall say between Man and Woman which is the most
delighted? Now it is more noble to sit like Jove that [*for* than] to fly
like Mercury—let us not therefore go hurrying about and collecting
honey-bee like, buzzing here and there impatiently from a knowledge of what is to be arrived at: but let us open our leaves like a
flower and be passive and receptive—budding patiently under the
eye of Apollo and taking hints from every noble insect that favors us
with a visit—sap will be given us for Meat and dew for drink—I was
led into these thoughts, my dear Reynolds, by the beauty of the
morning operating on a sense of Idleness—I have not read any
Books—the Morning said I was right—I had no Idea but of the
Morning and the Thrush said I was right—seeming to say—

> 'O thou whose face hath felt the Winter's wind;
>   Whose eye has seen the Snow clouds hung in Mist
> And the black-elm tops 'mong the freezing Stars
> To thee the Spring will be a harvest-time—
> O thou whose only book has been the light
> Of supreme darkness which thou feddest on
> Night after night, when Phœbus was away
> To thee the Spring shall be a tripple morn—

> O fret not after knowledge—I have none
> And yet my song comes native with the warmth
> O fret not after knowledge—I have none
> And yet the Evening listens—He who saddens
> At thought of Idleness cannot be idle,
> And he's awake who thinks himself asleep.'

Now I am sensible all this is a mere sophistication, however it may neighbour to any truths, to excuse my own indolence—so I will not deceive myself that Man should be equal with jove—but think himself very well off as a sort of scullion-Mercury or even a humble Bee—It is not [*for* no] matter whether I am right or wrong either one way or another, if there is sufficient to lift a little time from your Shoulders.   Your affectionate friend
                                            John Keats—

To George and Tom Keats, 21 February 1818

                                     Hampstead Saturday—
My dear Brothers,

   I am extremely sorry to have given you so much uneasiness by not writing: however you know good news is no news or vice versa—I do not like to write a short Letter to you—or you would have had one long before—The Weather although boisterous to day has been very much milder—and I think Devonshire is no[t] the last place to receive a temperate change—The occasion of my writing to day is the enclosed Letter by the Post Mark from Miss Wylie*—does she expect you in town George? I have been abominably id[l]e since you left—but have just turned over a new leaf—and used as a marker a Letter of excuse to an invitation from Horace Smith. I received a Letter from Haydon the other day in which he says, his essays on the elgin Marbles* are being translated into italian—the which he superintends. I did not mention that I had seen the British Gallery—there are some nice things by Stark and Bathsheba by Wilkie which is condemned—I could not bear Leslie's Uriel*—Reynolds has been very ill for some time—confined to the house—and had Leeches applied to the chest—When I saw him on Wednesday he was much the same—and he is in the worst place in the world for amendment—among the strife of womens tongues in a hot and parch'd room—I wish he would move to Butler's* for a short time. The Thrushes and Blackbirds have been singing me into an idea that it was spring, and almost that Leaves were on the trees—so that black clouds and boisterous winds seem to have muster'd and collected to full Divan for the purpose of convincing me to the contrary—I have not been to Edmonton all this While, and there is not a day but Le Mesurier's image reproaches me for it—and I suppose the Haughtons think us dead—I will shortly go and set matters to rights thereabouts* Taylor says my Poem shall be out in a Month. I think he'll be out before it—The Thrushes are singing now—af it [*for* as if] they would speak to the Winds because their big brother Jack, the spring was'nt far off—I am reading Voltaire and Gibbon,* although I wrote to Reynolds the other day to prove reading of no use—I have not seen Hunt since. I am a good deal with Dilke and Brown—we are very thick—they are very kind to me—they are well—I don't think I could stop in Hampstead but for their neighbourhood. I hear Hazlitt's Lectures regularly—his last was on Grey Collins, Young &c and he gave a very f⟨ine⟩ piece of discriminating criticism on Swift, Vo⟨ltaire⟩ And Rabelais—I was very disappointed at his treatment of Chatterton—I generally meet with many I know there.* Lord Byron's 4th Canto* is expected out—and I heard somewhere that Walter Scott has a new Poem in readiness—I am sorry that Wordsworth has left a bad impression where-ever he visited in Town—by his egotism, Vanity and bigotry*—yet he is a great Poet if not a Philosopher. I have not yet read Shelly's Poem—I don't suppose you have it at the Teignmouth Libraries—These double Letters must come rather heavy—I hope you have a moderate portion of Cash—but dont fret at all if you have not—Lord I intend to play at cut and run as well as Falstaff—that is to say before he got so lusty—I have not time to chequer work this Letter for I should like to be sure of the 4 o Clock Post—So I remain praying for your hea[l]th; my dear Brothers, your affectionate Brother—

John—

To John Taylor, 27 February 1818

Hampstead 27 Feby—

My dear Taylor,

Your alteration strikes me as being a great improvement—the page looks much better. And now I will attend to the Punctuations you speak of—the comma should be at *soberly*, and in the other passage the comma should follow *quiet*, .* I am extremely indebted to you for this attention and also for your after admonitions—It is a sorry thing for me that any one should have to overcome Prejudices in reading my Verses—that affects me more than any hypercriticism on any particular Passage. In *Endymion* I have most likely but moved into the Go-cart from the leading strings. In Poetry I have a few Axioms,* and you will see how far I am from their Centre. 1st I think Poetry should surprise by a fine excess and not by Singularity—it should strike the Reader as a wording of his own highest thoughts, and appear-almost a Remembrance—2nd Its touches of Beauty should never be half way therby making the reader breathless instead of content: the rise, the progress, the setting of imagery should like the Sun come natural natural too him—shine over him and set soberly although in magnificence leaving him in the Luxury of twilight—but it is easier to think what Poetry should be than to write it—and this leads me on to another axiom. That if Poetry comes not as naturally as the leaves to a tree it had better not come at all. However it may be with me I cannot help looking into new countries with 'O for a Muse of fire to ascend!'*—If Endymion serves me as a Pioneer perhaps I ought to be content. I have great reason to be content, for thank God I can read and perhaps understand Shakspeare to his depths, and I have I am sure many friends, who, if I fail, will attribute any change in my Life and Temper to Humbleness rather than to Pride—to a cowering under the Wings of great Poets rather than to a Bitterness that I am not appreciated. I am anxious to get Endymion printed that I may forget it and proceed. I have coppied the 3rd Book and have begun the 4th. On running my Eye over the Proofs—I saw one Mistake I will notice it presently and also any others if there be any—There should be no comma in 'the raft branch down sweeping from a tall Ash top'*—I have besides made one or two alteration⟨s⟩ and also altered the 13 Line Page 32 to make sense of it as you will see. I will take care the Printer shall not trip up my Heels—There should be no dash after Dryope in the Line 'Dryope's lone lulling of her Child. Remember me to Percy Street.*

Your sincere and oblig^d friend
John Keats—

P.S. You shall have a sho[r]t *Preface* in good time—

To Benjamin Bailey, *13 March 1818*

My dear Bailey,   Teignmouth Friday

When a poor devil is drowning, it is said he comes thrice to the surface, ere he makes his final sink if however, even at the third rise, he can manage to catch hold of a piece of weed or rock, he stands a fair chance,—as I hope I do now, of being saved. I have sunk twice in our Correspondence, have risen twice and been too idle, or something worse, to extricate myself—I have sunk the third time and just now risen again at this two of the Clock P.M. and saved myself from utter perdition—by beginning this, all drench'd as I am and fresh from the Water—and I would rather endure the present inconvenience of a Wet Jacket, than you should keep a laced one in store for me. Why did I not stop at Oxford in my Way?—How can you ask such a Question? Why did I not promise to do so? Did I not in a Letter to you make a promise to do so? Then how can you be so unreasonable as to ask me why I did not? This is the thing—(for I have been rubbing up my invention; trying several sleights—I first polish'd a cold, felt it in my fingers tried it on the table, but could not pocket it: I tried Chilblains, Rheumatism, Gout, tight Boots, nothing of that sort would do, so this is, as I was going to say, the thing.—I had a Letter from Tom saying how much better he had got, and thinking he had better stop—I went down to prevent his coming up—Will not this do? Turn it which way you like—it is selvaged all round—I have used it these three last days to keep out the abominable Devonshire Weather—by the by you may say what you will of devonshire: the thuth [*for* truth] is, it is a splashy, rainy, misty snowy, foggy, haily floody, muddy, slipshod County—the hills are very beautiful, when you get a sight of 'em—the Primroses are out, but then you are in—the Cliffs are of a fine deep Colour, but then the

Clouds are continually vieing with them—The Women like your London People in a sort of negative way—because the native men are the poorest creatures in England—because Government never have thought it worth while to send a recruiting party among them. When I think of Wordswo[r]th's Sonnet 'Vanguard of Liberty! ye Men of Kent!' the degenerated race about me are Pulvis Ipecac. Simplex* a strong dose—Were I a Corsair I'd make a descent on the South Coast of Devon, if I did not run the chance of having Cowardice imputed to me: as for the Men they'd run away into the methodist meeting houses, and the Women would be glad of it— Had England been a large devonshire we should not have won the Battle of Waterloo—There are knotted oaks—there are lusty rivulets there are Meadows such as are not—there are vallies of femminine Climate—but there are no thews and Sinews—Moor's Almanack is here a curiosity—A[r]ms Neck and shoulders may at least be seen there, and The Ladies read it as some out of the way romance— Such a quelling Power have these thoughts over me, that I fancy the very Air of a deteriorating quality—I fancy the flowers, all preco- cious, have an Acrasian* spell about them—I feel able to beat off the devonshire waves like soap froth—I think it well for the honor of Brittain that Julius Cæsar did not first land in this County—A Dev- onshirer standing on his native hills is not a distinct object—he does not show against the light—a wolf or two would dispossess him. I like, I love England, I like its strong Men—Give me a "long brown plain" for my Morning so I may meet with some of Edmond Iron side's desendants—Give me a barren mould so I may meet with some shadowing of Alfred in the shape of a Gipsey, a Huntsman or as [*for* a] Shepherd. Scenery is fine—but human nature is finer— The Sward is richer for the tread of a real, nervous, english foot— the eagles nest is finer for the Mountaineer has look'd into it—Are these facts or prejudices? Whatever they are, for them I shall never be able to relish entirely any devonshire scenery—Homer is very fine, Achilles is fine, Diomed is fine, Shakspeare is fine, Hamlet is fine, Lear is fine, but dwindled englishmen are not fine—Where too the Women are so passable, and have such english names, such as Ophelia, Cordelia &—that they should have such Paramours or rather Imparamours—As for them I cannot, in thought help wishing as did the cruel Emperour, that they had but one head and I might cut it off to deliver them from any horrible Courtesy they may do their undeserving Countrymen—I wonder I meet with no born Monsters—O Devonshire, last night I thought the Moon had dwindled in heaven—I have never had your Sermon from Wordsworth but Mrs Dilke lent it me—You know my ideas about Religion*—I do not think myself more in the right than other people and that nothing in this world is proveable. I wish I could enter into all your feelings on the subject merely for one short 10 Minutes and give you a Page or two to your liking. I am sometimes so very sceptical as to think Poetry itself a mere Jack a lanthern to amuse whoever may chance to be struck with its brilliance—As Tradesmen say every thing is worth what it will fetch, so probably every mental pursuit takes its reality and worth from the ardour of the pursuer*—being in itself a nothing—Ethereal thing[s] may at least be thus real, divided under three heads—Things real—things semireal—and no things—Things real—such as existences of Sun Moon & Stars and passages of Shakspeare—Things semireal such as Love, the Clouds &c which require a greeting of the Spirit to make them wholly exist—and Nothings which are made Great and dignified by an ardent pursuit—Which by the by stamps the burgundy mark on the bottles of our Minds, insomuch as they are able to "*consec[r]ate whate'er they look upon*" I have written a Sonnet here of a somewhat collateral nature—so don't imagine it an a propos des bottes.

Four Seasons fill the Measure of the year;
  Four Seasons are there in the mind of Man.
He hath his lusty spring when fancy clear
  Takes in all beauty with an easy span:
He hath his Summer, when luxuriously
  He chews the honied cud of fair spring thoughts,
Till, in his Soul dissolv'd they come to be
  Part of himself. He hath his Autumn ports
And Havens of repose, when his tired wings
  Are folded up, and he content to look
On Mists in idleness: to let fair things
  Pass by unheeded as a threshhold brook.
    He hath his Winter too of pale Misfeature,
    Or else he would forget his mortal nature.

Aye this may be carried—but what am I talking of—it is an old maxim of mine and of course must be well known that every point of thought is the centre of an intellectual world—the two uppermost thoughts in a Man's mind are the two poles of his World he revolves on them and every thing is southward or northward to him through their means—We take but three steps from feathers to iron. Now my dear fellow I must once for all tell you I have not one Idea of the truth of any of my speculations—I shall never be a Reasoner because I care not to be in the right, when retired from bickering and in a proper philosophical temper—So you must not stare if in any future letter I endeavour to prove that Apollo as he had a cat gut string to his Lyre used a cats' paw as a Pecten*—and further from said Pecten's reiterated and continual teasing came the term Hen peck'd. My Brother Tom desires to be remember'd to you—he has just this moment had a spitting of blood poor fellow—Remember me to Greig [*for* Gleig] and Whitehed—

Your affectionate friend
John Keats—

To J. H. Reynolds, *14 March 1818*

Teignmouth Saturday

Dear Reynolds.

I escaped being blown over and blown under & trees & house[s] being toppled on me.—I have since hearing of Brown's accident had an aversion to a dose of parapet. and being also a lover of antiquities I would sooner have a harmless piece of herculaneum sent me quietly as a present, than ever so modern a chimney pot tumbled onto my head—Being agog to see some Devonshire, I would have taken a walk the first day, but the rain wo^d not let me; and the second, but the rain wo^d not let me; and the third; but the rain forbade it— Ditto 4 ditto 5—So I made up my Mind to stop in doors, and catch a sight flying between the showers; and behold I saw a pretty valley— pretty cliffs, pretty Brooks, pretty Meadows, pretty trees, both standing as they were created, and blown down as they are uncreated— The green is beautiful, as they say, and pity it is that it is amphibious—mais! but alas! the flowers here wait as naturally for the rain twice a day as the Muscles do for the Tide.—so we look upon a brook in these parts as you look upon a dash in your Country—there must be something to support this, aye fog, hail, snow rain—Mist—blanketing up three parts of the year—This devonshire is like Lydia Languish,* very entertaining when at smiles, but cursedly subject to sympathetic moisture. You have the sensation of walking under one great Lamplighter: and you cant go on the other side of the ladder to keep your frock clean, and cosset your superstition. Buy a girdle—put a pebble in your Mouth—loosen your Braces—for I am going among Scenery whence I intend to tip you the Damosel Radcliffe*—I'll cavern you, and grotto you, and waterfall you, and wood you, and water you, and immense-rock you, and tremendous sound you, and solitude you. Ill make a lodgment on your glacis by a row of Pines, and storm your covered way with bramble Bushes.* Ill have at you with hip and haw smallshot, and cannonade you with Shingles—Ill be witty upon salt fish, and impede your cavalry with clotted cream. But ah Coward! to talk at this rate to a sick man, or I hope to one that was sick—for I hope by this you stand on your right foot.—If you are not—that's all,—I intend to cut all sick people if they do not make up their minds to cut sickness—a fellow to whom I have a complete aversion, and who strange to say is harboured and countenanced in several houses where I visit—he is sitting now quite impudent between me and Tom—He insults me at poor Jem Rice's—and you have seated him before now between us at the Theatre—where I thought he look'd with a longing eye at poor Kean. I shall say, once for all, to my friends generally and severally, cut that fellow, or I cut you—I went to the Theatre here the other night, which I forgot to tell George, and got insulted, which I ought to remember to forget to tell any Body; for I did not fight, and as yet have had no redress—"Lie thou there, sweetheart!"* I wrote to Bailey yesterday, obliged to speak in a high way, and a damme who's affraid—for I had owed him so long; however, he shall see I will be better in future. Is he in Town yet? I have directed to Oxford as the better chance. I have copied my fourth Book, and shall write the preface soon. I wish it was all done; for I want to forget it and make my mind free for something new—Atkins the Coachman, Bartlet the Surgeon, Simmons the Barber, and the Girls over at the Bonnet shop say we shall now have a Month of seasonable Weather. warm, witty, and full of invention—Write to me and tell me you are well or

thereabouts, or by the holy Beaucœur,—which I suppose is the
virgin Mary, or the repented Magdalen, (beautiful name, that
Magdalen) Ill take to my Wings and fly away to any where but old or
Nova Scotia—I wish I had a little innocent bit of Metaphysic in my
head, to criss-cross this letter: but you know a favorite tune is hardest
to be remembered when one wants it most and you, I know, have
long ere this taken it for granted that I never have any speculations
without assoc[i]ating you in them, where they are of a pleasant
nature and you know enough to [*for of*] me to tell the places where
I haunt most, so that if you think for five minutes after having
read this you will find it a long letter and see written in the Air
above you,

> Your most affectionate friend
> John Keats.

Remember me to all. Tom's remembrances to you.

To James Rice, 24 March 1818

> Teignmouth Tuesday,

My dear Rice,

Being in the midst of your favorite Devon, I should not by
rights, pen one word but it should contain a vast portion of Wit,
Wisdom, and learning—for I have heard that Milton ere he wrote
his Answer to Salmasius* came into these parts. and for on[e]
whole Month, rolled himself, for three whole hours in a certain
meadow hard by us—where the mark of his nose at equidistances
is still shown. The exhibitor of said Meadow further saith that
after these rollings, not a nettle sprang up in all the seven acres
for seven years and that from said time a new sort of plant was
made from the white thorn, of a thornless nature very much used
by the Bucks of the present day to rap their Boots withall—This
accou[n]t made me very naturally suppose that the nettles and
thorns etherealized by the Scholars rotatory motion and gardner'd
in his head, thence flew after a ⟨n⟩ew fermentation against the
luckless Salmasius and accasioned his well known and unhappy
end. What a happy thing it would be if we could settle our
thoughts, make our minds up on any matter in five Minutes and

remain content—that is to build a sort of mental Cottage of feelings quiet and pleasant—to have a sort of Philosophical Back Garden, and cheerful holiday-keeping front one—but Alas! this never can be: for as the material Cottager knows there are such places as france and Italy and the Andes and the Burning Mountains—so the spiritual Cottager has knowledge of the terra semi incognita of things unearthly; and cannot for his Life, keep in the check rein—Or I should stop here quiet and comfortable in my theory of Nettles. You will see however I am obliged to run wild, being attracted by the Loadstone Concatenation. No sooner had I settle[d] the [k]notty point of Salmasius that [*for* than] the Devil put this whim into my head in the likeness of one of Pythagora's questionings 'Did Milton do more good or ha[r]m to the world? He wrote let me info[r]m you (for I have it from a friend, who had it of—) he wrote Lycidas, Comus, Paradise Lost and other Poems, with much delectable prose—he was moreover an active friend to Man all his Life and has been since his death. Very good—but my dear fellow I must let you know that as there is ever the same quantity of matter constituting this habitable globe—as the ocean notwithstanding the enormous changes and revolutions taking place in some or other of its demesnes—notwithstanding Waterspouts whirlpools and mighty Rivers emptying themselves into it, it still is made up of the same bulk—nor ever varies the number of its Atoms—And as a certain bulk of Water was instituted at the Creation—so very likely a certain portion of intellect was spun forth into the thin Air for the Brains of Man to prey upon it—You will see my drift without any unnecessary parenthesis. That which is contained in the Pacific and [*for* can't] lie in the hollow of the Caspian—that which was in Miltons head could not find Room in Charles the seconds—he like a Moon attracted Intellect to its flow—it has not ebbd yet—but has left the shore pebble all bare—I mean all Bucks* Authors of Hengist* and Castlereaghs* of the present day—who without Miltons gormandizing might have been all wise Men—Now for as much as—I was very peedisposed to a Country I had heard you speak so highly of, I took particular notice of every thing during my journey and have bought some folio asses skin for Memorandums—I have seen every thing but the wind—and that they say becomes visible by taking a dose of Acorns or sleeping on[e] night in a hog trough with your tail to the Sow Sow west. Some of the little Barmaids look'd at me as if I knew Jem Rice—but when I took ⟨a glass of⟩ Brandy they were quite convinced. One asked whether ⟨you pres-⟩er⟨v⟩ed a secret she gave you on the nail—another how m[an]y buttons of your Coat were buttoned in general—I ⟨told⟩ her it used to be four—but since you had become acqu⟨ain⟩ted with one Martin you had reduced it to three and had been turning this third one in your Mind—and would do so with finger and thumb only you had taken to snuff—I have met with a Brace or twain of little Long heads—not a kit o' the german[1]—all in the neatest little dresses, and avoiding all the pudd[l]es—but very fond of peppermint drops, laming ducks, and seeing little Girls affairs.* Well I cant tell! I hope you are showing poor Reynolds the way to get well—send me a good account of him and if I can I'll send you one of Tom—Oh! for a day and all well! I went yesterday to dawlish fair—

> Over the hill and over the dale,
> And over the bourn to Dawlish—
> Where Gingerbread Wives have a scanty sale
> And gingerbred nuts are smallish—
>
> Rantipole Betty she ran down a hill
> And ki[c]k'ed up her pettic[o]ats fairly
> Says I I'll be Jack if you will be Gill—
> So she sat on the Grass debonnairly—
>
> Here's somebody coming, here's somebody coming!
>   Says I 't is the Wind at a parley
> So without any fuss any hawing and humming
>   She lay on the grass debonnai[r]ly—
>
> Here's somebody here and here's somebody *there!*
>   Say's I hold your tongue you young Gipsey.
> So she held her tongue and lay plump and fair
>   And dead as a venus tipsy—

---

[1] See Appendix, note 3.

O who would'nt hie to Dawlish fair
  O who would'nt stop in a Meadow
O [who] would not rumple the daisies there
  And make the wild fern for a bed do—

Tom's Remembrances and mine to all—

                              Your sincere friend
                              John Keats

To J. H. Reynolds, 25 March 1818

Dear Reynolds, as last night I lay in bed,
There came before my eyes that wonted thread
Of Shapes, and Shadows and Remembrances,
That every other minute vex and please:
Things all disjointed come from North and south,
Two witch's eyes above a cherub's mouth,
Voltaire with casque and shield and Habergeon,
And Alexander with his night-cap on—
Old Socrates a tying his cravat;
And Hazlitt playing with Miss Edgworth's cat;
And Junius Brutus pretty well so, so,*
Making the best of 's way towards Soho.
    Few are there who escape these visitings—
P'erhaps one or two, whose lives have patent wings;
And through whose curtains peeps no hellish nose.
No wild boar tushes, and no Mermaid's toes:
But flowers bursting out with lusty pride;
And young Æolian harps personified,
Some, Titian colours touch'd into real life.—
The sacrifice goes on; the pontif knife
Gloams in the sun, the milk-white heifer lows,
The pipes go shrilly, the libation flows:
A white sail shews above the green-head cliff
Moves round the point, and throws her anchor stiff.
The Mariners join hymn with those on land.—
You know the Enchanted Castle it doth stand
Upon a Rock on the Border of a Lake

Nested in Trees, which all do seem to shake
From some old Magic like Urganda's sword.
O Phœbus that I had thy sacred word
To shew this Castle in fair dreaming wise
Unto my friend, while sick and ill he lies.

    You know it well enough, where it doth seem
A mossy place, a Merlin's Hall, a dream.
You know the clear lake, and the little Isles,
The Mountains blue, and cold near neighbour rills—
All which elsewhere are but half animate
Here do they look alive to love and hate;
To smiles and frowns; they seem a lifted mound
Above some giant, pulsing underground.

    Part of the building was a chosen See
Built by a banish'd santon of Chaldee:
~~Poor Man he left the Terrace Walls of Ur~~
The other part two thousand years from him
Was built by Cuthbert de Saint Aldebrim;
Then there's a little wing, far from the sun,
Built by a Lapland Witch turn'd maudlin nun—
And many other juts of aged stone
Founded with many a mason-devil's groan.

    The doors all look as if they oped themselves,
The windows as if latch'd by fays & elves—
And from them comes a silver flash of light
As from the Westward of a summer's night;
Or like a beauteous woman's large blue eyes
Gone mad through olden songs and Poesies—

    See what is coming from the distance dim!
A golden galley all in silken trim!
Three rows of oars are lightening moment-whiles
Into the verdurous bosoms of those Isles.
Towards the shade under the Castle Wall
It comes in silence—now tis hidden all.
The clarion sounds; and from a postern grate
An echo of sweet music doth create
A fear in the poor herdsman who doth bring
His beasts to trouble the enchanted spring:

He tells of the sweet music and the spot
To all his friends, and they believe him not.
    O that our dreamings all of sleep or wake
Would all their colours from the sunset take:
From something of material sublime.
Rather than shadow our own Soul's daytime
In the dark void of Night. For in the world
We jostle—but my flag is not unfurl'd
On the Admiral staff—and to philosophize
I dare not yet!—Oh never will the prize,
High reason, and the lore of good and ill
Be my award. Things cannot to the will
Be settled, but they tease us out of thought.*
Or is it that Imagination brought
Beyond its proper bound, yet still confined,—
Lost in a sort of Purgatory blind,
Cannot refer to any standard law
Of either earth or heaven?—It is a flaw
In happiness to see beyond our bourn—
It forces us in Summer skies to mourn:
It spoils the singing of the Nightingale.
    Dear Reynolds. I have a mysterious tale
And cannot speak it. The first page I read
Upon a Lampit Rock of green sea weed
Among the breakers—'Twas a quiet Eve;
The rocks were silent—the wide sea did weave
An untumultuous fringe of silver foam
Along the flat brown sand. I was at home,
And should have been most happy—but I saw
Too far into the sea; where every maw
The greater on the less feeds evermore:—
But I saw too distinct into the core
Of an eternal fierce destruction,
And so from Happiness I far was gone.
Still am I sick of it: and though to day
I've gathered young spring-leaves, and flowers gay
Of Periwinkle and wild strawberry,
Still do I that most fierce destruction see,

> The shark at savage prey—the hawk at pounce,
> The gentle Robin, like a pard or ounce,
> Ravening a worm—Away ye horrid moods,
> Moods of one's mind!* You know I hate them well,
> You know I'd sooner be a clapping bell
> To some Kamschatkan missionary church,
> Than with these horrid moods be left in lurch—
> Do you get health—and Tom the same—I'll dance,
> And from detested moods in new Romance
> Take refuge—Of bad lines a Centaine dose
> Is sure enough—and so "here follows prose."

My Dear Reynolds.

In hopes of cheering you through a Minute or two I was determined nill he will he to send you some lines so you will excuse the unconnected subject, and careless verse—You know, I am sure, Claude's Enchanted Castle* and I wish you may be pleased with my remembrance of it—The Rain is Come on again—I think with me Devonshire stands a very poor chance, I shall damn it up hill and down dale, if it keeps up to the average of 6 fine days in three weeks. Let me have better news of you.

Your affectionate friend
John Keats.

Toms Rememb^s to you. Rem^r
us to all—

To B. R. Haydon, 8 April 1818

Wednesday—

My dear Haydon,

I am glad you were pleased with my nonsense* and if it so happen that the humour takes me when I have set down to prose to you I will not gainsay it. I should be (god forgive me) ready to swear because I cannot make use of you assistance in going through Devon if I was not in my own Mind determined to visit it thoroughly at some more favorable time of the year. But now Tom (who is getting greatly better) is anxious to be in Town therefore I put off my threading the County. I purpose within a Month to put my knapsack at my back and make a pedestrian tour through the North of England, and part of Scotland—to make a sort of Prologue to the Life I intend to pursue—that is to write, to study and to see all Europe at the lowest expence. I will clamber through the Clouds and exist. I will get such an accumulation of stupendous recollolections that as I walk through the suburbs of London I may not see them—I will stand upon Mount Blanc and remember this coming Summer when I intend to straddle ben Lomond—with my Soul!—galligaskins* are out of the Question—I am nearer myself to hear your Christ is being tinted into immortality—Believe me Haydon your picture is a part of myself—I have ever been too sensible of the labyrinthian path to eminence in Art (judging from Poetry) ever to think I understood the emphasis of Painting. The innumerable compositions and decompositions which take place between the intellect and its thousand materials before it arrives at that trembling delicate and snail-horn* perception of Beauty—I know not you many havens of intenseness—nor ever can know them—but for this I hope not [*for* nought] you atchieve is lost upon me: for when a Schoolboy the abstract Idea I had of an heroic painting—was what I cannot describe I saw it somewhat sideways large prominent round and colour'd with magnificence—somewhat like the feel I have of Anthony and Cleopatra. Or of Alcibiades, leaning on his Crimson Couch in his Galley, his broad shoulders imperceptibly heaving with the Sea*—That [*for* What] passage in Shakspeare is finer than this

'See how the surly Warwick mans the Wall'*

I like your consignment of Corneille—that's the humor of it—They shall be called your Posthumous Works. I don't understand you bit of Italian.* I hope she will awake from her dream and flourish fair— my respects to her—The Hedges by this time are beginn[in]g to leaf—Cats are becoming more vociferous—young Ladies that wear Watches are always looking at them—Women about forty five think the Season very back ward—Lady's Mares have but half an allowance of food—It rains here again, has been doing so for three days— however as I told you I'll take a trial in June July or August next year—

I am affraid Wordsworth went rather huff'd out of Town—I am sorry for it. he cannot expect his fireside Divan to be infallible he cannot expect but that every Man of worth is as proud as himself. O that he had not fit with a Warrener that is din'd at Kingston's.* I shall be in town in about a fortnight and then we will have a day or so now and then before I set out on my northern expedition—we will have no more abominable Rows—for they leave one is [*for* in] a fearful silence having settled the Methodists let us be rational—not upon compulsion—no if it will out let it—but I will not play the Basoon any more delibe[r]ately—Remember me to Hazlitt, and Bewick—Your affectionate friend

John Keats

To J. H. Reynolds, 9 April 1818

My Dear Reynolds.   Th^y Morn^g

Since you all agree that the thing* is bad, it must be so—though I am not aware there is any thing like Hunt in it, (and if there is, it is my natural way, and I have something in common with Hunt) look it over again and examine into the motives, the seeds from which any one sentence sprung—I have not the slightest feel of humility towards the Public—or to any thing in existence,—but the eternal Being, the Principle of Beauty,—and the Memory of great Men— When I am writing for myself for the mere sake of the Moment's enjoyment, perhaps nature has its course with me—but a Preface is written to the Public; a thing I cannot help looking upon as an Enemy, and which I cannot address without feelings of Hostility—If I write a Preface in a supple or subdued style, it will not be in character with me as a public speaker—I wo^d be subdued before my friends, and thank them for subduing me—but among Multitudes of Men—I have no feel of stooping, I hate the idea of humility to them—

I never wrote one single Line of Poetry with the least Shadow of public thought.

Forgive me for vexing you and making a Trojan Horse of such a Trifle, both with respect to the matter in Question, and myself—but it eases me to tell you—I could not live without the love of my friends—I would jump down Ætna for any great Public good—but I hate a Mawkish Popularity.—I cannot be subdued before them—My glory would be to daunt and dazzle the thousand jabberers about

Pictures and Books—I see swarms of Porcupines with their Quills erect "like lime-twigs set to catch my Winged Book" and I would fright 'em away with a torch—You will say my preface is not much of a Torch. It would have been too insulting "to begin from Jove" and I could not [set] a golden head upon a thing of clay—if there is any fault in the preface it is not affectation: but an undersong of disrespect to the Public.—if I write another preface. it must be done without a thought of those people—I will think about it. If it should not reach you in four—or five days—tell Taylor to publish it without a preface, and let the dedication simply stand "inscribed to the memory of Thomas Chatterton." I had resolved last night to write to you this morning—I wish it had been about something else—something to greet you towards the close of your long illness—I have had one or two intimations of your going to Hampstead for a space; and I regret to see your confounded Rheumatism keeps you in Little Brittain where I am sure the air is too confined—Devonshire continues rainy. As the drops beat against the window, they give me the same sensation as a quart of cold water offered to revive a half drowned devil—No feel of the clouds dropping fatness; but as if the roots of the Earth were rotten cold and drench'd—I have not been able to go to Kents' Ca[ve] at Babbicun—however on one very beautiful day I had a fine clamber over the rocks all along as far as that place: I shall be in Town in about Ten days.—We go by way of Bath on purpose to call on Bailey. I hope soon to be writing to you about the things of the north, purposing to wayfare all over those parts. I have settled my accoutrements in my own mind, and will go to gorge wonders: However we'll have some days together before I set out—

I have many reasons for going wonder-ways: to make my winter chair free from spleen—to enlarge my vision—to escape disquisitions on Poetry and Kingston Criticism,*—to promote digestion and economise shoe leather—I'll have leather buttons and belt; and if Brown holds his mind, over the Hills we go.—If my Books will help me to it,—thus will I take all Europe in turn, and see the Kingdoms of the Earth and the glory of them—Tom is getting better he hopes you may meet him at the top o' the hill—My Love to your nurses. I am ever

> Your affectionate Friend,
> John Keats.

To J. H. Reynolds, 17 April 1818

Friday

My dear Reynolds

I am anxious you should find this Preface* tolerable—if there is an affectation in it, 'tis natural to me. Do let the Printer's Devil cook it—and let me be 'as the casing air.'

You are too good in this Matter—were I in your state, I am certain I should have no thought but of discontent and illness—I might tho' be taught patience. I had an idea of giving no Preface however don't you think this had [bette]r go?—O let it, one should not be too afraid of committing faults.

The Climate here weighs us d[own] completely. Tom is quite low spirited. [It is] impossible to live in a country which is continually under hatches. Who would live in the Region of Mists, Game Laws, indemnity Bills &c when there is such a place as Italy? It is said this England from its Clime produces a Spleen able to engender the finest Sentiment—and covers the whole face of the Isle with Green*—so it ought, I'm sure. I should still like the Dedication simply as I said in my last.

I wanted to send you a few Songs written in your favorite Devon——it cannot be—Rain! Rain! Rain! I am going this Morning to take a fac simile of a Letter of Nelson's very much to his honor— you will be greatly pleased when you see it—in about a Week. What a spite it is one cannot get out the like way I went yesterday I found a lane bank'd on each side with store of Primroses—while the earlier bushes are beginning to leaf—

I shall hear a good Account of you soon.

Your Affectionate friend

John Keats

My Love to all and remember me to Taylor—

To John Taylor, 24 April 1818

Teignmouth Friday

My dear Taylor,

I think I Did very wrong to leave you to all the trouble of

Endymion—but I could not help it then—another time I shall be more bent to all sort of troubles and disagreeables—Young Men for some time have an idea that such a thing as happiness is to be had and therefore are extremely impatient under any unpleasant restraining—in time however, of such stuff is the world about them, they know better and instead of striving from Uneasiness greet it as an habitual sensation, a pannier which is to weigh upon them through life.

And in proportion to my disgust at the task is my sense of your kindness & anxiety—the book pleased me much—it is very free from faults; and although there are one or two words I should wish replaced, I see in many places an improvement greatly to the purpose—

I think those speeches which are related—those parts where the speaker repeats a speech—such as Glaucus' repetition of Circe's words, should have inverted commas to every line—In this there is a little confusion. If we divide the speeches into *identical* and *related*: and to the former put merely one inverted comma at the beginning and another at the end; and to the latter inverted commas before every line, the book will be better understood at the first glance. Look at pages 126 and 127 you will find in the 3 line the beginning of a *related* speech marked thus "Ah! art awake—while at the same time in the next page the continuation of the *identical speech* is mark'd in the same manner "Young Man of Latmos—You will find on the other side all the parts which should have inverted commas to every line—I was purposing to travel over the north this Summer—there is but one thing to prevent me—I know nothing I have read nothing and I mean to follow Solomon's directions of 'get Wisdom—get understanding'—I find cavalier days are gone by. I find that I can have no enjoyment in the World but continual drinking of Knowledge—I find there is no worthy pursuit but the idea of doing some good for the world—some do it with their society—some with their wit—some with their benevolence—some with a sort of power of conferring pleasure and good humour on all they meet and in a thousand ways all equally dutiful to the command of Great Nature—there is but one way for me—the road lies th[r]ough application study and thought. I will pursue it and to that end purpose retiring for some years. I have been hovering for some time between an exquisite sense of the luxurious and a love for Philosophy—were I calculated for the former I should be glad—but as I am not I shall turn all my soul to the latter. My Brother Tom is getting better and I hope I shall see both him and Reynolds well before I retire from the World. I shall see you soon and have some talk about what Books I shall take with me—

Your very sincere friend
John Keats

Remember me to Hessey—Woodhouse and Percy Street
I cannot discover any other error—the preface is well without those thing you have left out—Adieu—*

To J. H. Reynolds, 27 April 1818

Teignmouth Monday
My dear Reynolds.

It is an awful while since you have heard from me—I hope I may not be punished, when I see you well, and so anxious as you always are for me, with the remembrance of my so seldom writing when you were so horribly confined—the most unhappy hours in our lives are those in which we recollect times past to our own blushing—If we are immortal that must be the Hell—If I must be immortal, I hope it will be after having taken a little of "that watery labyrinth" in order to forget some of my schoolboy days & others since those.

I Have heard from George at different times how slowly you were recovering, it is a tedious thing—but all Medical Men will tell you how far a very gradual amendment is preferable; you will be strong after this, never fear.—We are here still enveloppd in clouds—I lay awake last night—listening to the Rain with a sense of being drown'd and rotted like a grain of wheat—There is a continual courtesy between the Heavens and the Earth.—the heavens rain down their unwelcomeness, and the Earth sends it up again to be returned to morrow. Tom has taken a fancy to a Physician here, Dr Turton, and I think is getting better—therefore I shall perhaps remain here some Months.—I have written to George for some Books—shall learn Greek, and very likely Italian—and in other ways prepare myself to ask Hazlitt in about a years time the best metaphysical road I can take.—For although I take poetry to be Chief, there is something else wanting to one who passes his life among Books and thoughts on Books—I long to feast upon old Homer as we have upon Shakespeare. and as I have lately upon Milton.—if you understand Greek, and would read me passages, now and then, explaining their meaning, 't would be, from its mistiness, perhaps a greater luxury than reading the thing one's self.—I shall be happy when I can do the same for you.—I have written for my folio Shakespeare, in which there is the first few stanzas of my "Pot of Basil": I have the rest here finish'd, and will copy the whole out fair shortly—and George will bring it to you—The Compliment is paid by us to Boccace, whether we publish or no:* so there is content in this world—mine is short— you must be deliberate about yours: you must not think of it till many months after you are quite well:—then put your passion to it,—and I shall be bound up with you in the shadows of mind, as we are in our matters of human life—Perhaps a Stanza or two* will not be too foreign to your Sickness.

> 'Were they unhappy then? It cannot be:
>   Too many tears &c &c——
>

> But for the general award of love &c
>
> She wept alone for Pleasures &c &c

I heard from Rice this morning—very witty—and have just written to Bailey—Don't you think I am brushing up in the letter way? and being in for it,—you shall hear again from me very shortly:—if you will promise not to put hand to paper for me until you can do it with a tolerable ease of health—except it be a line or two—Give my Love to your Mother and Sisters Remember me to the Butlers—not forgetting Sarah

Your affectionate friend
John Keats

To J. H. Reynolds, 3 May 1818

Teignmouth May 3ᵈ

My dear Reynolds.

What I complain of is that I have been in so an uneasy a state of Mind as not to be fit to write to an invalid. I cannot write to any length under a dis-guised feeling. I should have loaded you with an addition of gloom, which I am sure you do not want. I am now thank God in a humour to give you a good groats worth—for Tom, after a Night without a Wink of sleep, and overburdened with fever, has got up after a refreshing day sleep and is better than he has been for a long time; and you I trust have been again round the Common without any effect but refreshment.—As to the Matter I hope I can say with Sir Andrew "I have matter enough in my head"* in your favor And now, in the second place, for I reckon that I have finished my Imprimis, I am glad you blow up the weather—all through your letter there is a leaning towards a climate-curse. and you know what a delicate satisfaction there is in having a vexation anathematized: one would think there has been growing up for these last four thousand years, a grandchild Scion of the old forbidden tree, and that some modern Eve had just violated it; and that there was come with double charge, "Notus and After black with thunderous clouds from Sierra-leona"*—I shall breathe worsted stockings* sooner than I thought for. Tom wants to be in Town—we will have some such days upon the heath like that of last summer and why not with the same book: or what say you to a black Letter Chaucer printed in 1596: aye I've got one huzza! I shall have it bounden gothique a nice sombre binding—it will go a little way to unmodernize. And also I see no reason, because I have been away this last month, why I should not have a peep at your Spencerian*—notwithstanding you speak of your office,* in my thought a little too early, for I do not see why a Mind like yours is not capable of harbouring and digesting the whole Mystery of Law as easily as Parson Hugh does Pepins*—which did not hinder him from his poetic Canary—Were I to study physic or rather Medicine again,—I feel it would not make the least difference in my Poetry; when the Mind is in its infancy a Bias is in reality a Bias, but when we have acquired more strength, a Bias becomes no Bias. Every department of knowledge we see excellent and calculated

towards a great whole. I am so convinced of this, that I am glad at not
having given away my medical Books, which I shall again look over to
keep alive the little I know thitherwards; and moreover intend
through you and Rice to become a sort of Pip-civilian.* An extensive
knowledge is needful to thinking people*—it takes away the heat and
fever; and helps, by widening speculation, to ease the Burden of the
Mystery:* a thing I begin to understand a little, and which weighed
upon you in the most gloomy and true sentence in your Letter. The
difference of high Sensations with and without knowledge appears
to me this—in the latter case we are falling continually ten thousand
fathoms deep and being blown up again without wings and with all
[the] horror of a bare shouldered Creature—in the former case, our
shoulders are fledge, and we go thro' the same air and space without
fear. This is running one's rigs on the score of abstracted benefit—
when we come to human Life and the affections it is impossible how
a parallel of breast and head can be drawn—(you will forgive me for
thus privately treading out [of] my depth and take it for treading as
schoolboys tread the water)—it is impossible to know how far knowledge will console us for the death of a friend and the ill "that flesh is
heir to*—With respect to the affections and Poetry you must know
by a sympathy my thoughts that way; and I dare say these few lines
will be but a ratification: I wrote them on May-day—and intend to
finish the ode all in good time.—

> Mother of Hermes! and still youthful Maia!
>   May I sing to thee
> As thou wast hymned on the shores of Baiæ?
>   Or may I woo thee
> In earlier Sicilian? or thy smiles
> Seek as they once were sought, in Grecian isles,
> By Bards who died content in pleasant sward,
> Leaving great verse unto a little clan?
> O give me their old vigour, and unheard,
> Save of the quiet Primrose, and the span
> Of Heaven, and few ears
> Rounded by thee my song should die away
> Content as theirs
> Rich in the simple worship of a day.—

You may be anxious to know for fact to what sentence in your
Letter I allude. You say "I fear there is little chance of any thing else
in this life." You seem by that to have been going through with a
more painful and acute zest the same labyrinth that I have—I have
come to the same conclusion thus far. My Branchings out therefrom
have been numerous: one of them is the consideration of Wordsworth's genius and as a help, in the manner of gold being the meridian Line of worldly wealth,—how he differs from Milton.—And
here I have nothing but surmises, from an uncertainty whether Miltons apparently less anxiety for Humanity proceeds from his seeing
further or no than Wordsworth: And whether Wordsworth has in
truth epic passion, and martyrs himself to the human heart, the
main region of his song*—In regard to his genius alone—we find
what he says true as far as we have experienced and we can judge no
further but by larger experience—for axioms in philosophy are not
axioms until they are proved upon our pulses:* We read fine——
things but never feel them to thee full until we have gone the same
steps as the Author.—I know this is not plain; you will know exactly
my meaning when I say, that now I shall relish Hamlet more than I
ever have done—Or, better—You are sensible no man can set down
Venery as a bestial or joyless thing until he is sick of it and therefore
all philosophizing on it would be mere wording. Until we are sick, we
understand not;—in fine, as Byron says, "Knowledge is Sorrow";*
and I go on to say that "Sorrow is Wisdom"—and further for aught
we can know for certainty! "Wisdom is folly"—So you see how I
have run away from Wordsworth, and Milton; and shall still run
away from what was in my head, to observe, that some kind of letters
are good squares others handsome ovals, and others some orbicular,
others spheroid—and why should there not be another species with
two rough edges like a Rat-trap? I hope you will find all my long
letters of that species, and all will be well; for by merely touching the
spring delicately and etherially, the rough edged will fly immediately
into a proper compactness, and thus you may make a good wholesome loaf, with your own leven in it, of my fragments*—If you
cannot find this said Rat-trap sufficiently tractable—alas for me, it
being an impossibility in grain for my ink to stain otherwise: If I
scribble long letters I must play my vagaries. I must be too heavy, or
too light, for whole pages—I must be quaint and free of Tropes and

figures—I must play my draughts as I please, and for my advantage and your erudition, crown a white with a black, or a black with a white, and move into black or white, far and near as I please—I must go from Hazlitt to Patmore,* and make Wordsworth and Coleman* play at leap-frog—or keep one of them down a whole half holiday at fly the garter—"From Gray to Gay, from Little* to Shakespeare"— Also as a long cause requires two or more sittings of the Court, so a long letter will require two or more sittings of the Breech wherefore I shall resume after dinner.—

Have you not seen a Gull, an orc, a sea Mew, or any thing to bring this Line to a proper length, and also fill up this clear part; that like the Gull I may *dip**—I hope, not out of sight—and also, like a Gull, I hope to be lucky in a good sized fish—This crossing a letter is not without its association—for chequer work leads us naturally to a Milkmaid,* a Milkmaid to Hogarth Hogarth to Shakespeare Shakespear to Hazlitt—Hazlitt to Shakespeare and thus by merely pulling an apron string we set a pretty peal of Chimes at work—Let them chime on while, with your patience,—I will return to Wordsworth—whether or no he has an extended vision or a circum- scribed grandeur—whether he is an eagle in his nest, or on the wing—And to be more explicit and to show you how tall I stand by the giant, I will put down a simile of human life as far as I now perceive it; that is, to the point to which I say we both have arrived at—' Well—I compare human life to a large Mansion of Many Apartments, two of which I can only describe, the doors of the rest being as yet shut upon me—The first we step into we call the infant or thoughtless Chamber, in which we remain as long as we do not think—We remain there a long while, and notwithstanding the doors of the second Chamber remain wide open, showing a bright appear- ance, we care not to hasten to it; but are at length imperceptibly impelled by the awakening of the thinking principle—within us—we no sooner get into the second Chamber, which I shall call the Cham- ber of Maiden-Thought, than we become intoxicated with the light and the atmosphere, we see nothing but pleasant wonders, and think of delaying there for ever in delight: However among the effects this breathing is father of is that tremendous one of sharpening one's vision into the heart and nature of Man—of convincing ones nerves that the World is full of Misery and Heratbreak, Pain, Sickness and oppression—whereby This Chamber of Maiden Thought becomes gradually darken'd and at the same time on all sides of it many doors are set open—but all dark—all leading to dark passages—We see not the ballance of good and evil. We are in a Mist—*We* are now in that state—We feel the "burden of the Mystery," To this point was Wordsworth come, as far as I can conceive when he wrote 'Tintern Abbey' and it seems to me that his Genius is explorative of those dark Passages.* Now if we live, and go on thinking, we too shall explore them. he is a Genius and superior [to] us, in so far as he can, more than we, make discoveries, and shed a light in them—Here I must think Wordsworth is deeper than Milton—though I think it has depended more upon the general and gregarious advance of intellect,* than individual greatness of Mind—From the Paradise Lost and the other Works of Milton, I hope it is not too presuming, even between ourselves to say, his Philosophy, human and divine, may be tolerably understood by one not much advanced in years, In his time englishmen were just emancipated from a great superstition—and Men had got hold of certain points and resting places in reasoning which were too newly born to be doubted, and too much opposed by the Mass of Europe not to be thought etherial and authentically divine—who could gainsay his ideas on virtue, vice, and Chastity in Comus, just at the time of the dismissal of Cod-pieces and a hundred other disgraces? who would not rest satisfied with his hintings at good and evil in the Paradise Lost, when just free from the inquisition and burrning in Smithfield? The Reformation produced such immediate and great benefits, that Protestantism was considered under the immediate eye of heaven, and its own remaining Dogmas and superstitions, then, as it were, regenerated, constituted those resting places and seeming sure points of Reasoning—from that I have mentioned, Milton, whatever he may have thought in the sequel, appears to have been content with these by his writings—He did not think into the human heart, as Wordsworth has done—Yet Milton as a Philosopher, had sure as great powers as Wordsworth—What is then to be inferr'd? O many things—It proves there is really a grand march of intellect—, It proves that a mighty providence subdues the mightiest Minds to the service of the time being, whether it be in human Knowledge or Religion—I have often pitied a Tutor who has to hear "Nom^e:

Musa"—so often dinn'd into his ears—I hope you may not have the same pain in this scribbling—I may have read these things before, but I never had even a thus dim perception of them: and moreover I like to say my lesson to one who will endure my tediousness for my own sake—After all there is certainly something real in the World—Moore's present to Hazlitt is real—I like that Moore,* and am glad I saw him at the Theatre just before I left Town. Tom has spit a leetle blood this afternoon, and that is rather a damper—but I know—the truth is there is something real in the World Your third Chamber of Life shall be a lucky and a gentle one—stored with the wine of love—and the Bread of Friendship—When you see George if he should not have recēd a letter from me tell him he will find one at home most likely—tell Bailey I hope soon to see him—Remember me to all The leaves have been out here, for MONY a day—I have written to George for the first stanzas of my Isabel—I shall have them soon and will copy the whole out for you.

Your affectionate friend

John Keats.

To Benjamin Bailey, 21, 25 May 1818

My dear Bailey,   Hampstead Thursday—

I should have answered your letter on the moment—if I could have said yes to your invitation. What hinders me is insuperable; I will tell it at a little length. You know my Brother George has been out of employ for some time. it has weighed very much upon him, and driven him to scheme and turn over things in his Mind, the result has been his resolution to emigrate to the back settlements of America, become farmer and work with his own hands after purchacing 1400 hundred Acres of the American Government. This for many reasons has met with my entire consent—and the chief one is this—he is of too independent and liberal a Mind to get on in trade in this Country—in which a generous Ma⟨n⟩ with a scanty recourse must be ruined. I would sooner he should till the ground than bow to a Customer—there is no choice with him; he could not bring himself to the latter—I would not consent to his going alone—no: but that objection is done away with—he will marry before he sets sail a young Lady he has known some years—of a nature liberal and highspirited enough to follow him to the Banks of the Mississipi. He will set off in a month or six weeks, and you will see how I should wish to pass that time with him—and then I must set out on a journey of my own—Brown and I are going a pedestrian tour through the north of England and Scotland as far a[s] John o Grots. I have this morning such a Lethargy that I cannot write—the reason of my delaying is oftentimes from this feeling—I wait for a proper temper—Now you ask for an immediate answer I do not like to wait even till tomorrow—However I am now so depressed that I have not an Idea to put to paper—my hand feels like lead—and yet it is and unpleasant numbness it does not take away the pain of existence—I don't know what to write—Monday—You see how I have delayed—and even now I have but a confused idea of what I should be about my intellect must be in a degen[er]ating state—it must be for when I should be writing about god knows what I am troubling you with Moods of my own Mind or rather body—for Mind there is none.* I am in that temper that if I were under Water I would scarcely kick to come to the top—I know very well 't is all nonsense. In a short time I hope I shall be in a temper to fell [*for* feel] sensibly your mention of my Book—in vain have I waited till Monday to have any interest in that or in any thing else. I feel no spur at my Brothers going to America and am almost stony-hearted about his wedding. All this will blow over—all I am sorry for is having to write to you in such a time—but I cannot force my letters in a hot bed—I could not feel comfortable in making sentences for you—I am your debtor—I must ever remain so—nor do I wish to be clear of my *r*ational debt— There is a comfort in throwing oneself on the charity of ones friends—'t is like the albatros sleeping on its wings—I will be to you wine in the cellar and the more modestly or rather indolently I retire into the backward Bin, the more falerne will I be at the drinking. There is one thing I must mention. My Brother talks of sailing in a fortnight if so I will most probably be with you a week before I set out for Scotland. The middle of your first page should be suffic[i]ent to rouse me—what I said is true and I have dreamt of your mention of it and m⟨y⟩ not a[n]swering it has weighed on me since—If I com⟨e,⟩ I will bring your Letter and hear more fully your sentiments on one or two points. I will call about the Lectures at Taylors and at Little Britain tomorrow—Yesterday I dined with

Hazlitt; Barnes,* and Wilkie at Haydon's. The topic was the Duke of Wellington very amusingly pro and con'd. Reynolds has been getting much better; and Rice may begin to crow for he got a little so so at a Party of his and was none the worse for it the next morning. I hope I shall soon see you for we must have many new thoughts and feelings to analize, and to discover whether a little more knowledge has not made us more ignorant—

Your's affectionately John Keats—

To Benjamin Bailey, 10 June 1818

My dear Bailey,   London—
    I have been very much gratified and very much hurt by your Letters in the Oxford Paper:* because independent of that unlawful and mortal feeling of pleasure at praise, there is a glory in enthusia[s]m; and because the world is malignant enough to chuckle at the most honorable Simplicity. Yes on my Soul my dear Bailey you are too simple for the World—and that Idea makes me sick of it—How is it that by extreme opposites we have as it were got discont[ent]ed nerves—you have all your Life (I think so) believed every Body—I have suspected every Body—and although you have been so deceived you make a simple appeal—the world has something else to do, and I am glad of it—were it in my choice I would reject a petrarchal coronation—on accou[n]t of my dying day, and because women have Cancers. I should not by rights speak in this tone to you—for it is an incendiary spirit that would do so. Yet I am not old enough or magnanimous enough to anihilate self—and it would perhaps be paying you an ill compliment. I was in hopes some little time back to be able to releive your dullness by my spirits—to point out things in the world worth your enjoyment—and now I am never alone without rejoicing that there is such a thing as death—without placing my ultimate in the glory of dying for a great human purpose Perphaps if my affairs were in a different state I should not have written the above—you shall judge—I have two Brothers one is driven by the 'burden of Society' to America the other, with an exquisite love of Life, is in a lingering state—My Love for my Brothers from the early loss of our parents and even for earlier Misfortunes has grown into a affection 'passing the Love of Women'—I have been ill temper'd

93

with them. I have vex'd them—but the thought of them has always stifled the impression that any woman might otherwise have made upon me—I have a sister too and may not follow them, either to America or to the Grave—Life must be undergone, and I certainly derive a consolation from the thought of writing one or two more Poems before it ceases—I have heard some hints of your retireing to scotland—I should like to know your feeling on it—it seems rather remote—perhaps Gle[i]g will have a duty near you. I am not certain whether I shall be able to go my Journey on account of my Brother Tom and a little indisposition of my own—If I do not you shall see me soon—if no[t] on my return—or I'll quarter myself upon you in Scotland next Winter. I had know[n] my sister in Law some time before she was my Sister and was very fond of her. I like her better and better—she is the most disinterrested woman I ever knew—that is to say she goes beyond degree in it—To see an entirely disinter-rested Girl quite happy is the most pleasant and extraordinary thing in the world—it depends upon a thousand Circumstances—on my word 'tis extraordinary. Women must want Imagination and they may thank God for it—and so m[a]y we that a delicate being can feel happy without any sense of crime. It puzzles me and I have no sort of Logic to comfort me—I shall think it over. I am not at home and your letter being there I cannot look it over to answer any particular—only I must say I felt that passage of Dante—if I take any book with me it shall be those minute volumes of carey* for they will go into the aptest corner. Reynolds is getting I may say robust—his illness has been of service to him—like eny one just recoverd he is high-spirited. I hear also good accounts of Rice—With respects to domestic Literature—the Endinburgh Magasine in another blow up against Hunt calls me 'the amiable Mister Keats'* and I have more than a Laurel from the Quarterly Reviewers for they have *smothered* me in 'Foliage'* I want to read you my 'Pot of Basil' if you go to scotland I should much like to read it there to you among the Snows of next Winter. My Brothers' remembrances to you.

Your affectionate friend

John Keats—

To Tom Keats, 25–27 June 1818

Here beginneth my journal, this Thursday, the 25th day of June, Anno Domini 1818. This morning we arose at 4, and set off in a Scotch mist; put up once under a tree, and in fine, have walked wet and dry to this place, called in the vulgar tongue Endmoor, 17 miles; we have not been incommoded by our knapsacks; they serve capitally, and we shall go on very well.

June 26—I merely put *pro forma*, for there is no such thing as time and space, which by the way came forcibly upon me on seeing for the first hour the Lake and Mountains of Winander—I cannot describe them—they surpass my expectation—beautiful water—shores and islands green to the marge—mountains all round up to the clouds. We set out from Endmoor this morning, breakfasted at Kendal with a soldier who had been in all the wars for the last seventeen years—then we have walked to Bowne's* to dinner—said Bowne's situated on the Lake where we have just dined, and I am writing at this present. I took an oar to one of the islands to take up some trout for dinner, which they keep in porous boxes. I enquired of the waiter for Wordsworth—he said he knew him, and that he had been here a few days ago, canvassing for the Lowthers. What think you of that—Wordsworth versus Brougham!!* Sad—sad—sad—and yet the family has been his friend always. What can we say? We are now about seven miles from Rydale, and expect to see him to-morrow. You shall hear all about our visit.

There are many disfigurements to this Lake—not in the way of land or water. No; the two views we have had of it are of the most noble tenderness—they can never fade away—they make one forget the divisions of life; age, youth, poverty and riches; and refine one's sensual vision into a sort of north star which can never cease to be open lidded and stedfast over the wonders of the great Power. The disfigurement I mean is the miasma of London. I do suppose it contaminated with bucks and soldiers, and women of fashion—and hat-band ignorance. The border inhabitants are quite out of keeping with the romance about them, from a continual intercourse with London rank and fashion. But why should I grumble? They let me have a prime glass of soda water—O they are as good as their neighbors. But Lord Wordsworth, instead of being in retirement, has himself and his house full in the thick of fashionable visitors quite convenient to be pointed at all the summer long. When we had gone about half this morning, we began to get among the hills and to see the mountains grow up before us—the other half brought us to Wynandermere, 14 miles to dinner. The weather is capital for the views, but is now rather misty, and we are in doubt whether to walk to Ambleside to tea—it is five miles along the borders of the Lake. Loughrigg will swell up before us all the way—I have an amazing partiality for mountains in the clouds. There is nothing in Devon like this, and Brown says there is nothing in Wales to be compared to it. I must tell you, that in going through Cheshire and Lancashire, I saw the Welsh mountains at a distance. We have passed the two castles, Lancaster and Kendal. 27th—We walked here to Ambleside yesterday along the border of Winandermere all beautiful with wooded shores and Islands—our road was a winding lane, wooded on each side, and green overhead, full of Foxgloves—every now and then a glimpse of the Lake, and all the while Kirkstone and other large hills nestled together in a sort of grey black mist. Ambleside is at the northern extremity of the Lake. We arose this morning at six, because we call it a day of rest, having to call on Wordsworth who lives only two miles hence—before breakfast we went to see the Ambleside water fall. The morning beautiful—the walk easy among the hills. We, I may say, fortunately, missed the direct path, and after wandering a little, found it out by the noise—for, mark you, it is buried in trees, in the bottom of the valley—the stream itself is interesting throughout with "mazy error over pendant shades."* Milton meant a smooth river—this is buffeting all the way on a rocky bed ever various—but the waterfall itself, which I came suddenly upon, gave me a pleasant twinge. First we stood a little below the head about half way down the first fall, buried deep in trees, and saw it streaming down two more descents to the depth of near fifty feet—then we went on a jut of rock nearly level with the second fall-head, where the first fall was above us, and the third below our feet still—at the same time we saw that the water was divided by a sort of cataract island on whose other side burst out a glorious stream— then the thunder and the freshness. At the same time the different falls have as different characters; the first darting down the slate-rock like an arrow; the second spreading out like a fan—the third dashed into a mist—and the one on the other side of the rock a sort of mixture of all these. We afterwards moved away a space, and saw nearly the whole more mild, streaming silverly through the trees. What astonishes me more than any thing is the tone, the coloring, the slate, the stone, the moss, the rock-weed; or, if I may so say, the intellect, the countenance of such places. The space, the magnitude of mountains and waterfalls are well imagined before one sees them; but this countenance or intellectual tone must surpass every imagination and defy any remembrance. I shall learn poetry here and shall henceforth write more than ever, for the abstract endeavor of being able to add a mite to that mass of beauty which is harvested from these grand materials, by the finest spirits, and put into etherial existence for the relish of one's fellows. I cannot think with Hazlitt that these scenes make man appear little. I never forgot my stature so completely—I live in the eye; and my imagination, surpassed, is at rest—We shall see another waterfall near Rydal to which we shall proceed after having put these letters in the post office. I long to be at Carlisle, as I expect there a letter from George and one from you. Let any of my friends see my letters—they may not be interested in descriptions—descriptions are bad at all times—I did not intend to give you any; but how can I help it? I am anxious you should taste a little of our pleasure; it may not be an unpleasant thing, as you have not the fatigue. I am well in health. Direct henceforth to Port Patrick till the 12th July. Content that probably three or four pair of eyes whose owners I am rather partial to will run over these lines I remain; and moreover that I am your affectionate brother John.

To George and Georgiana Keats, 27, 28 June 1818

Foot of Helvellyn June 27

My dear George,

We have passed from Lancaster to Burton from Burton to En[d]moor, from En[d]moor to Kendal from Kendal to Bownes on turning down to which place there burst upon us the most beautiful and rich view of Winander mere and the surrounding Mountains— we dined at Bownes on Trout which I took an oar to fetch from some

Box preserves close on one of the little green Islands. After dinner we walked to Ambleside down a beautiful shady Lane along the Borders of the Lake with ample opportunity for Glimpses all the way—We slept at Ambleside not above two Miles from Rydal the Residence of Wordsworth We arose not very early on account of having marked this day for a day of rest—Before breakfast we visited the first waterfall I ever saw and certainly small as it is it surpassed my expectation, in what I have mentioned in my letter to Tom, in its tone and intellect its light shade slaty Rock, Moss and Rock weed— but you will see finer ones I will not describe by comparison a teapot spout—We ate a Monstrous Breakfast on our return (which by the way I do every morning) and after it proceeded to Wordsworths He was not at home nor was any Member of his family—I was much disappointed. I wrote a note for him and stuck it up over what I knew must be Miss Wordsworth's Portrait and set forth again & we visited two Waterfalls in the neighbourhood, and then went along by Rydal Water and Grasmere through its beautiful Vale—then through a defile in the Mountains into Cumberland and So to the foot of Helvellyn whose summit is out of sight four Miles off rise above rise—I have seen Kirkstone, Loughrigg and Silver How—and discovered without a hint "that ancient woman seated on Helm Craig."* This is the summary of what I have written to Tom and dispatched from Ambleside—I have had a great confidence in your being well able to support the fatigue of your Journey since I have felt how much new Objects contribute to keep off a sense of Ennui and fatigue 14 Miles here is not so much as the 4 from Hampstead to London. You will have an enexhaustible astonishment; with that and such a Companion you will be cheered on from day to day—I hope you will not have sail'd before this Letter reaches you—yet I do not know for I will have my Series to Tom coppied and sent to you by the first Packet you have from England. God send you both as good Health as I have now. Ha! my dear Sister George, I wish I knew what humour you were in that I might accomodate myself to any one of your Amiabilities—Shall it be a Sonnet or a Pun or an Acrostic, a Riddle or a Ballad—'perhaps it may turn out a Sang, and perhaps turn out a Sermon' I'll write you on my word the first and most likely the last I ever shall do, because it has strucke me—what shall it be about?

Give me your patience Sister while I frame
Enitials verse-wise of your golden name:
Or sue the fair Apollo and he will
Rouse from his Slumber heavy and instill
Great Love in me for thee and Poesy—
Imagine not that greatest Mastery
And kingdom over all the realms of verse
Nears more to heaven in aught than when we nurse
And surety give to
~~In its vast safety~~ Love and Brotherhood.—

Anthropopagi in Othello's Mood,
Ulysses stormed, and his enchanted Belt
~~by the sweet Muse are never never felt~~
Glow with the Muse but they are never felt
Unbosom'd so, and so eternal made,
Such selfsame insence in their Laurel shade
To all the regent sisters of the Nine
As this poor offering to thee Sister mine.

Kind Sister! aye this third name says you are
Enhanced has it been the Lord knows where.
Ah! may it taste to you like good old wine—
Take you ~~the~~ to real happiness and give
Sons daughters and a Home like honied hive.

June 28th I have slept and walked eight miles to Breakfast at Keswick
on derwent water—We could not mount Helvellyn for the mist so
gave it up with hopes of Skiddaw which we shall try tomorrow if it
be fine—to day we shall walk round Derwent water, and in our Way
see the Falls of Low-dore—The Approach to derwent water is rich
and magnificent beyond any means of conception—the Mountains
all round sublime and graceful and rich in colour—Woods and
wooded Islands here and there—at the same time in the distance
among Mountains of another aspect we see Bassenthwaite—I
⟨shall⟩ drop like a Hawk on the Post Office at Carlisle ⟨to ask for⟩
some Letters from you and Tom—

Sweet sweet is the greeting of eyes,
And sweet is the voice in its greeting,

When Adieux have grown old and goodbyes
Fade away where old time is retreating—

Warm the nerve of a welcoming hand
And earnest a kiss on the Brow,
When we meet over sea and o'er Land
Where furrows are new to the Plough.

This is all ⟨. . .⟩ in the m⟨. . .⟩ please a⟨. . .⟩ Letters as possi⟨bly . . .⟩* We will before many Years are over have written many folio volumes which as a Matter of self-defence to one whom you understand intends to be immortal in the best points and let all his Sins and peccadillos die away—I mean to say that the Book-sellers with [*for* will] rather decline printing ten folio volumes of Correspondence printed as close as the Apostles creed in a Watch paper—I have been looking out my dear Georgy for a joke or a Pun for you—there is none but the Names of romantic Misses on the Inn window Panes. You will of course have given me directions brother George where to direct on the other side of the Water. I have not had time to write to Henry*—for I have a journal to keep for Tom nearly enough to employ all my leisure—I am a day behind hand with him—I scarcely know how I shall manage Fanny and two or three others I have promised—We expect to be in Scotland in at most three days so you must if this should catch you before you set sail give me a line to Port-Patrick—

God bless you my dear Brother and Sister.

John—

To Tom Keats, *29 June, 1, 2 July 1818*

Keswick—June 29th 1818.

My dear Tom

I cannot make my Journal as distinct & actual as I could wish, from having been engaged in writing to George. & therefore I must tell you without circumstance that we proceeded from Ambleside to Rydal, saw the Waterfalls there, & called on Wordsworth, who was not at home, nor was any one of his family. I wrote a note & left it on the Mantlepiece. Thence on we came to the foot of Helvellyn, where we slept, but could not ascend it for the mist. I must mention that from Rydal we passed Thirlswater, & a fine pass in the Mountains from Helvellyn we came to Keswick on Derwent Water. The approach to Derwent Water surpassed Winandermere—it is richly wooded & shut in with rich-toned Mountains. From Helvellyn to Keswick was eight miles to Breakfast, After which we took a complete circuit of the Lake going about ten miles, & seeing on our way the Fall of Low-dore. I had an easy climb among the streams, about the fragments of Rocks & should have got I think to the summit, but unfortunately I was damped by slipping one leg into a squashy hole. There is no great body of water, but the accompaniment is delightful; for it ooses out from a cleft in perpendicular Rocks, all fledged with Ash & other beautiful trees. It is a strange thing how they got there. At the south end of the Lake, the Mountains of Bunowdale,* are perhaps as fine as any thing we have seen—On our return from this circuit, we ordered dinner, & set forth about a mile & a half on the Penrith road, to see the Druid temple. We had a fag up hill, rather too near dinner time, which was rendered void, by the gratification of seeing those aged stones, on a gentle rise in the midst of Mountains, which at that time darkened all round, except at the fresh opening of the vale of St. John. We went to bed rather fatigued, but not so much so as to hinder us getting up this morning, to mount Skiddaw It promised all along to be fair, & we had fagged & tugged nearly to the top, when at halfpast six there came a mist upon us & shut out the view; we did not however lose anything by it, we were high enough without mist, to see the coast of Scotland; the Irish sea; the hills beyond Lancaster; & nearly all the large ones of Cumberland & Westmoreland, particularly Helvellyn & Scawfell: It grew colder & colder as we ascended, & we were glad at about three parts of the way to taste a little rum which the Guide brought with him, mixed, mind ye with mountain water, I took two glasses going & one returning—It is about six miles from where I am writing to the top. so we have walked ten miles before Breakfast today. We went up with two others, very good sort of fellows, All felt on arising into the cold air, that same elevation, which a cold bath gives one—I felt as if I were going to a Tournament. Wordsworth's house is situated just on the rise of the foot of mount Rydall, his parlor window looks directly down Winandermere; I do not think I told you how fine the vale of Grassmere is, & how I discovered "the ancient woman seated on

Helm Crag."—We shall proceed immediately to Carlisle, intending
to enter Scotland on the 1st of July via——   July 1st—We are this
morning at Carlisle—After Skiddaw, we walked to Ireby the oldest
market town in Cumberland—where we were greatly amused by a
country dancing school, holden at the Tun,* it was indeed "no new
cotillon fresh from France."* No they kickit & jumpit with mettle
extraordinary, & whiskit, & fleckit, & toe'd it, & go'd it, & twirld it, &
wheel'd it, & stampt it, & sweated it, tattooing the floor like mad:
The differenc[e] between our country dances & these scotch figures,
is about the same as leisurely stirring a cup o' Tea & beating up a
batter pudding. I was extremely gratified to think, that if I had
pleasures they knew nothing of. they had also some into which I
could not possibly enter I hope I shall not return without having got
the Highland fling, there was as fine a row of boys & girls as you ever
saw, some beautiful faces, & one exquisite mouth. I never felt so near
the glory of Patriotism, the glory of making by any means a country
happier. This is what I like better than scenery. I fear our continued
moving from place to place, will prevent our becoming learned in
village affairs; we are mere creatures of Rivers, Lakes, & mountains.
Our yesterday's journey was from Ireby to Wigton, & from Wigton
to Carlisle—The Cathedral does not appear very fine; The Castle is
very Ancient, & of Brick The City is very various, old white washed
narrow streets; broad red brick ones more modern—I will tell you
anon, whether the inside of the Cathedral is worth looking at. It is
built of a sandy red stone or Brick. We have now walked 114 miles &
are merely a little tired in the thighs, & a little blistered; We shall ride
38 miles to Dumfries, where we shall linger a while, about Nithsdale
& Galloway, I have written two letters to Liverpool. I found a letter
from sister George. very delightful indeed. I shall preserve it in the
bottom of my knapsack for you.

—On visiting the Tomb of Burns—

The Town, the churchyard, & the setting sun,
The Clouds, the trees, the rounded hills all seem
Though beautiful, Cold—strange—as in a dream,
I dreamed long ago, now new begun
The shortlived, paly summer is but won
From winters argue, for one hours gleam;

Through saphire warm, their stars do never beam,
All is cold Beauty; pain is never done.
For who has mind to relish Minos-wise,
The real of Beauty, free from that dead hue
Fickly* imagination & sick pride
——* wan upon it! Burns! with honor due
I have oft honoured thee. Great shadow; hide
Thy face, I sin against thy native skies.

You will see by this sonnet that I am at Dumfries, we have dined in
Scotland. Burns' tomb is in the Churchyard corner, not very much
to my taste, though on a scale, large enough to show they wanted to
honour him—Mrs Burns lives in this place, most likely we shall see
her tomorrow—This Sonnet I have written in a strange mood, half
asleep. I know not how it is, the Clouds, the sky, the Houses, all seem
anti Grecian & anti Charlemagnish—I will endeavour to get rid of
my prejudices, & tell you fairly about the Scotch——   July 2nd In
Devonshire they say "Well where be yee going." Here it is, "How is
it all wi yoursel"—A man on the Coach said the horses took a Hellish heap o' drivin—the same fellow pointed out Burns' tomb with a
deal of life, "There de ye see it, amang the trees; white, wi a roond
tap." The first well dressed Scotchman we had any conversation
with, to our surprise confessed himself a Deist.* The careful manner
of his delivering his opinions, not before he had received several
encouraging hints from us, was very amusing—Yesterday was an
immense Horse fair at Dumfries, so that we met numbers of men &
women on the road, the women nearly all barefoot, with their shoes
& clean stockings in hand, ready to put on & look smart in the
Towns. There are plenty of wretched Cottages, where smoke has no
outlet but by the door—We have now begun upon whiskey, called
here *whuskey* very smart stuff it is—Mixed like our liquors with
sugar & water tis called toddy, very pretty drink, & much praised by
Burns.*

[R]   *To Fanny Keats, 2, 3, 5 July 1818*

My dear Fanny,   Dumfries July 2ⁿᵈ

I intended to have written to you from Kirkudbright the town I
shall be in tomorrow—but I will write now bec[a]use my knapsack
has worn my coat in the Seams, my coat has gone to the Taylors
and I have but one Coat to my back in these parts. I must tell you
how I went to Liverpool with George and our new Sister and the
Gentleman my fellow traveller through the Summer and
Autumn—We had a tolerable journey to Liverpool—which I left
the next morning before George was up for Lancaster—Then we
set off from Lancaster on foot with our knapsacks on, and have
walked a Little zig zag through the mountains and Lakes of
Cumberland and Westmoreland—We came from Carlisle yesterday
to this place—We are employed in going up Mountains, looking at
Strange towns prying into old ruins and eating very hearty break-
fasts. Here we are full in the Midst of broad Scotch 'How is it a'
wi yoursel'—the Girls are walking about bare footed and in the
worst cottages the Smoke finds its way out of the door—I shall
come home full of news for you and for fear I should choak
you by too great a dose at once I must make you used to it by a
letter or two—We have been taken for travelling Jewellers, Razor
sellers and Spectacle venders because friend Brown wears a pair—
The first place we stopped at with our knapsacks contained one
Richard Bradshaw a notorious tippler—He stood in the shape
of a ʒ* and ballanced himself as well as he could saying with his
nose right in Mʳ Browns face 'Do— yo u sell Spect—ta—cles?'
Mʳ Abbey says we are Don Quixotes—tell him we are more generally taken for Pedlars—All I hope is that we may not be taken
for excisemen in this whiskey country—We are generally up
about 5 walking before breakfast and we complete our 20 Miles
before dinner—Yesterday we visited Burns's Tomb and this
morning the fine Ruins of Lincluden—I had done thus far when
my coat came back fortified at all points—so as we lose no time
we set forth again through Galloway—all very pleasant and
pretty with no fatigue when one is used to it—We are in the
midst of Meg Merrilies' country of whom I suppose*—you have
heard—

Old Meg she was a Gipsey
   And liv'd upon the Moors
Her bed it was the brown heath turf
   And her house was out of doors

Her apples were swart blackberries
   Her currants pods o' broom
Her wine was dew o' the wild white rose
   Her book a churchyard tomb

Her Brothers were the craggy hills
   Her Sisters larchen trees—
Alone ~~wht~~ with her great family
   She liv'd as she did please—

                  morn
No breakfast has she many a ~~day~~
   No dinner many a noon
And 'stead of supper she would stare
   Full hard against the Moon—

But evey morn of woodbine fresh
   She made her garlanding
And every night the dark glen Yew
   She wove and she would sing—

And ~~sometimes~~ with her fingers old and brown
   She plaited Mats o' Rushes
And gave them to the Cottagers
   She met among the Bushes—

Old Meg was brave as Margaret Queen
   And tall as Amazon:
An old red blanket cloak she wore;
   A chip hat had she on—
God rest her aged bones somewhere
   She died full long agone!

If you like these sort of Ballads I will now and then scribble one for
you—if I send any to Tom I'll tell him to send them to you—I have
so many interruptions that I cannot manage to fill a Letter in one

day—since I scribbled the Song we have walked through a beautiful
Country to Kirkudbright—at which place I will write you a song
about myself—

There was a naughty Boy
    A naughty boy was he
He would not stop at home
    He could not quiet be—
        He took
        In his knapsack
        A Book
        Full of vowels
        And a shirt
        With some towels—
        A slight cap
        For night cap—
        A hair brush
        Comb ditto
        New Stockings
        For old ones
        Would split O!
        This knapsack
        Tight at 's back
        He revetted close
        And followe'd his Nose
        To the North
        To the North
And follow'd his nose
        To the North—

There was a naughty boy
    And a naughty boy was he
For nothing would he do
    But scribble poetry—
        He took
        An inkstand
        In his hand
        And a Pen
        Big as ten

In the other
And away
In a Pother
He ran
To the mountains
And fountains
And ghostes
And Postes
And witches
And ditches
And wrote
In his coat
When the weather
Was ~~warm~~ cool
Fear of gout
And without
When the w[e]ather
    warm
Was ~~cool~~—
Och the cha[r]m
When we choose
To follow ones nose
To the north
To the north
To follow one's nose to the north!

There was a naughty boy
  And a naughty boy we [*for* was] he
He kept little fishes
  In washing tubs three
    In spite
    Of the might
    Of the Maid
    Nor affraid
    Of his Granny-good—
    He often would
    Hurly burly
    Get up early

And go
By hook or crook
To the brook
And bring home
Miller's thumb
Tittle bat
Not over fat
Minnows small
As the stall
Of a glove
Not above
The size
Of a nice
Little Baby's
Little finger—
O he made
'T was his trade
Of Fish a pretty kettle
A kettle—A kettle
Of Fish a pretty kettle
A kettle!

There was a naughty Boy
And a naughty Boy was he
He ran away to Scotland
The people for to see—
There he found
That the ground
Was as hard
That a yard
Was a long,
That a song
Was as merry,
That a cherry
Was as red—
That lead
Was as weighty
That fourscore

Was as eighty
That a door
Was as wooden
As in england—
So he stood in
His shoes
And he wonderd
He wonderd
He stood in his
Shoes and he wonder'd—

My dear Fanny I am ashamed of writing you such stuff, nor would I if it were not for being tired after my days walking, and ready to tumble int⟨o bed⟩ so fatigued that when I am asleep you might sew my nose to my great toe and trundle me round the town like a Hoop without waking me—Then I get so hungry—a Ham goes but a very little way and fowls are like Larks to me—A Batch of Bread I make no more ado with than a sheet of parliament;* and I can eat a Bull's head as easily as I used to do Bull's eyes—I take a whole string of Pork Sausages down as easily as a Pen'orth of Lady's fingers*—Oh dear I must soon be contented with an acre or two of oaten cake a hogshead of Milk and a Cloaths basket of Eggs morning noon and night when I get among the Highlanders—Before we see them we shall pass into Ireland and have a chat with the Paddies, and look at the Giant's Cause-way which you must have heard of—I have not time to tell you particularly for I have to send a Journal to Tom of whom you shall hear all particulars or from me when I return—Since I began this we have walked sixty miles to newton stewart at which place I put in this Letter—tonight we sleep at Glenluce—tomorrow at Portpatrick and the next day we shall cross in the passage boat to Ireland—I hope Miss Abbey has quite recovered—Present my Respects to her and to Mr and Mrs Abbey—God bless you—

Your affectionate Brother John—
Do write me a Letter directed to *Inverness*. Scotland—

To Tom Keats, 3, 5, 7, 9 July 1818

My dear Tom,   Auchencairn July 3rd

I have not been able to keep up my journal completely on accou[n]t of other letters to George and one which I am writing to Fanny from which I have turned to loose no time whilst Brown is coppying a song about Meg Merrilies which I have just written for her—We are now in Meg Merrilies county and have this morning passed through some parts exactly suited to her—Kirkudbright County is very beautiful, very wild with craggy hills somewhat in the westmoreland fashion—we have come down from Dumfries to the sea coast part of it—The song I mention you would have from Dilke: but perhaps you would like it here—

[*A fair copy of the draft of 'Meg Merrilies' in the previous letter*]

Now I will return to Fanny—it rains. I may have time to go on here presently. July 5—You see I have missed a day from fanny's Letter. Yesterday was passed in Kircudbright—the Country is very rich—very fine—and with a little of Devon—I am now writing at Newton Stuart six Miles into Wigton—Our Landlady of yesterday said very few Southrens passed these ways—The children jabber away as in a foreign Language—The barefooted Girls look very much in keeping—I mean with the Scenery about them—Brown praises their cleanliness and appearance of comfort—the neatness of their cottages &c It may be—they are very squat among trees and fern and heaths and broom, on levels slopes and heights—They are very pleasant because they are very primitive—but I wish they were as snug as those up the Devonshire vallies—We are lodged and entertained in great varieties—we dined yesterday on dirty bacon dirtier eggs and dirtiest Potatoes with a slice of Salmon—we breakfast this morning in a nice carpeted Room with Sofa hair bottomed chairs and green-baized mehogany—A spring by the road side is always welcome—we drink water for dinner diluted with a Gill of whiskey. July 7th Yesterday Morning we set out from Glenluce going some distance round to see some Ruins—they were scarcely worth the while—we went on towards Stranrawier in a burning sun and had gone about six Miles when the Mail overtook us—we got up—were at Portpatrick in a jiffy, and I am writing now in little Ireland—The dialect on the neighbouring shores of Scotland and Ireland is much the same—yet I can perceive a great difference in the nations from the Chambermaid at this nate Inn kept by Mr Kelly—She is fair, kind and ready to laugh, because she is out of the horrible dominion of the Scotch kirk—A Scotch Girl stands in terrible awe of the Elders—poor little Susannas—They will scarcely laugh—they are greatly to be pitied and the kirk is greatly to be damn'd. These kirkmen have done scotland good (Query?) they have made Men, Women, Old Men Young Men old Women, young women boys, girls and infants all careful—so that they are formed into regular Phalanges of savers and gainers—such a thrifty army cannot fail to enrich their Country and give it a greater appearance of comfort than that of their poor irish neighbours—These kirkmen have done Scotland harm—they have banished puns and laughing and kissing (except in cases where the very danger and crime must make it very fine and gustful. I shall make a full stop at kissing for after that there should be a better paren*t*-thesis: and go on to remind you of the fate of Burns. Poor unfortunate fellow—his disposition was southern—how sad it is when a luxurious imagination is obliged in self defence to deaden its delicacy in vulgarity, and riot in thing[s] attainable that it may not have leisure to go mad after thing[s] which are not. No Man in such matters will be content with the experience of others—It is true that out of suffrance there is no greatness, no dignity; that in the most abstracted Pleasure there is no lasting happiness: yet who would not like to discover over again that Cleopatra was a Gipsey, Helen a Rogue and Ruth a deep one? I have not sufficient reasoning faculty to settle the doctrine of thrift—as it is consistent with the dignity of human Society—with the happiness of Cottagers—All I can do is by plump contrasts—Were the fingers made to squeeze a guinea or a white hand? Were the Lips made to hold a pen or a kiss? And yet in Cities Man is shut out from his fellows if he is poor, the Cottager must be dirty and very wretched if she be not thrifty—The present state of society demands this and this convinces me that the world is very young and in a very ignorant state—We live in a barbarous age. I would sooner be a wild deer than a Girl under the dominion of the kirk, and I would sooner be a wild hog than be the occasion of a Poor Creatures pennance before those execrable elders—It is not so far to the Giant's Cause way as we supposed—we thought it 70 and hear it is only 48 Miles—so we shall leave one of our knapsacks here at Donoghadee, take our immediate wants and be back in a week—when we shall proceed to the County of Ayr. In the Packet Yesterday we heard some Ballads from two old Men—one was a romance which seemed very poor—then there was the Battle of the Boyne—then Robin Huid as they call him—'Before the king you shall go, go, go, before the king you shall go.'* There were no Letters for me at Port Patrick so I am behind hand with you I dare say in news from George. Direct to Glasgow till the 17th of this month. 9th We stopped very little in Ireland and that you may not have leisere to marvel at our speedy return to Portpatrick I will tell you that is it as dear living in Ireland as at the Hummums*—thrice the expence of Scotland—it would have cost us £15 before our return—Moreover we found those 48 Miles to be irish ones which reach to 70 english—So having walked to Belfast one day and back to Donoghadee the next we left Ireland with a fair breeze—We slept last night at Port patrick where I was gratified by a letter from you. On our walk in Ireland we had too much opportunity to see the worse than nakedness, the rags, the dirt and misery of the poor common Irish—A Scotch cottage, though in that some times the Smoke has no exit but at the door, is a pallace to an irish one—We could observe that impetiosity in Man ⟨and b⟩oy and Woman—We had the pleasure of finding our way through a Peat-Bog—three miles long at least—dreary, black, dank, flat and spongy: here and there were poor dirty creatures and a few strong men cutting or carting peat. We heard on passing into Belfast through a most wretched suburb that most disgusting of all noises worse than the Bag pipe, the laugh of a Monkey, the chatter of women *solus* the scream of [a] Macaw—I mean the sound of the Shuttle—What a tremendous difficulty is the improvement of the condition of such people—I cannot conceive how a mind 'with child'* of Philantrophy could gra[s]p at possibility—with me it is absolute despair. At a miserable house of entertainment half way between Donaghadee and Bellfast were two Men Sitting at Whiskey one a Laborer and the other I took to be a drunken Weaver—The Laborer took me for a Frenchman and the other hinted at Bounty Money saying he was ready to take it—On calling for the Letters at Port patrick the man snapp'd out 'what

Regiment'? On our return from Bellfast we met a Sadan—the
Duchess of Dunghill—It is no laughing matter tho—Imagine the
worst dog kennel you ever saw placed upon two poles from a mouldy
fencing—In such a wretched thing sat a squalid old Woman squat
like an ape half starved from a scarcity of Buiscuit in its passage from
Madagascar to the cape,—with a pipe in her mouth and looking out
with a round-eyed skinny lidded, inanity—with a sort of horizontal
idiotic movement of her head—squab and lean she sat and puff'd out
the smoke while two ragged tattered Girls carried her along—What
a thing would be a history of her Life and sensations. I shall
endeavour when I know more and have though[t] a little more, to
give you my ideas of the difference between the scotch and irish—
The two Irishmen I mentioned were speaking of their treatment in
England when the Weaver said—'Ah you were a civil Man but I was
a drinker' Remember me to all—I intend writing to Haslam—but
dont tell him for fear I should delay—We left a notice at Portpatrick
that our Letters should be thence forwarded to Glasgow—Our quick
return from Ireland will occasion our passing Glasgow sooner than
we thought—so till further notice you must direct to Inverness
                         Your most affectionate Brother John—
Remember me to the Bentleys

To J. H. Reynolds, *11, 13 July 1818*

                                                        Maybole July 11.
My Dear Reynolds.
    I'll not run over the Ground we have passed, that would be merely
as bad as telling a dream—unless perhaps I do it in the manner of the
Laputan printing press*—that is I put down Mountains, Rivers
Lakes, dells, glens, Rocks, and Clouds, With beautiful enchanting,
gothic picturesque fine, delightful, enchancting, Grand, sublime—a
few Blisters &c—and now you have our journey thus far: where I
begin a letter to you because I am approaching Burns's Cottage very
fast—We have made continual enquiries from the time we saw his
Tomb at Dumfries—his name of course is known all about—his
great reputation among the plodding people is "that he wrote a good
MONY sensible things"—One of the pleasantest means of annulling

self is approaching such a shrine as the Cottage of Burns—we need not think of his misery—that is all gone—bad luck to it—I shall look upon it hereafter with unmixed pleasure as I do upon my Stratford on Avon day with Bailey—I shall fill this sheet for you in the Bardies Country, going no further than this till I get into the Town of Ayr which will be a 9 miles' walk to Tea—We were talking on different and indifferent things, when on a sudden we turned a corner upon the immediate County of Air—the Sight was as rich as possible—I had no Conception that the native place of Burns was so beautiful— the Idea I had was more desolate, his rigs of Barley seemed always to me but a few strips of Green on a cold hill—O prejudice! it was rich as Devon—I endeavour'd to drink in the Prospect, that I might spin it out to you as the silkworm makes silk from Mulbery leaves—I cannot recollect it—Besides all the Beauty, there were the Mountains of Annan [*for* Arran] Isle, black and huge over the Sea—We came down upon every thing suddenly—there were in our way, the 'bonny Doon,' with the Brig that Tam O' Shanter cross'ed—Kirk Alloway, Burns's Cottage and then the Brigs of Ayr—First we stood upon the Bridge across the Doon; surrounded by every Phantasy of Green in tree, Meadow, and Hill,—the Stream of the Doon, as a Farmer told us, is covered with trees from head to foot—you know those beautiful heaths so fresh against the weather of a summers evening—there was one stretching along behind the trees. I wish I knew always the humour my friends would be in at opening a letter of mine, to suit it to them nearly as possible I could always find an egg shell for Melancholy—and as for Merriment a Witty humour will turn any thing to Account—my head is sometimes in such a whirl in consider- ing the million likings and antipathies of our Moments—that I can get into no settled strain in my Letters—My Wig! Burns and sentimentality coming across you and frank Floodgate in the office— O scenery that thou shouldst be crush'd between two Puns—As for them I venture the rascalliest in the Scotch Region—I hope Brown does not put them punctually in his journal—If he does I must sit on the cutty-stool all next winter. We Went to Kirk allow'y "a Prophet is no Prophet in his own Country"—We went to the Cottage and took some Whiskey—I wrote a sonnet for the mere sake of writing some lines under the roof—they are so bad I cannot transcribe them—The Man at the Cottage was a great Bore with his Anecdotes—I hate the

rascal—his Life consists in fuz, fuzzy, fuzziest—He drinks glasses
five for the Quarter and twelve for the hour,*—he is a mahogany
faced old Jackass who knew Burns—He ought to be kicked for
having spoken to him. He calls himself "a curious old Bitch"—but
he is a flat old Dog—I sho^d like to employ Caliph Vatheck* to kick
him—O the flummery of a birth place! Cant! Cant! Cant! It is
enough to give a spirit the guts-ache—Many a true word they say is
spoken in jest—this may be because his gab hindered my
sublimity.—The flat dog made me write a flat sonnet—My dear
Reynolds—I cannot write about scenery and visitings—Fancy is
indeed less than a present palpable reality, but it is greater than
remembrance—you would lift your eyes from Homer only to see
close before you the real Isle of Tenedos.—you would rather read
Homer afterwards than remember yourself—One song of Burns's is
of more worth to you than all I could think for a whole year in his
native country—His Misery is a dead weight upon the nimbleness of
one's quill—I tried to forget it—to drink Toddy without any Care—
to write a merry Sonnet—it wont do—he talked with Bitches—he
drank with Blackguards, he was miserable—We can see horribly
clear in the works of such a man his whole life, as if we were God's
spies.—What were his addresses to Jean in the latter part of his
life—I should not speak so to you—yet why not—you are not in the
same case—you are in the right path, and you shall not be
deceived—I have spoken to you against Marriage, but it was
general—the Prospect in those matters has been to me so blank, that
I have not been unwilling to die—I would not now, for I have
inducements to Life—I must see my little Nephews* in America,
and I must see you marry your lovely Wife—My sensations are
sometimes deadened for weeks together—but believe me I have more
than once yearne'd for the time of your happiness to come, as much
as I could for myself after the lips of Juliet.—From the tenor of my
occasional rhodomontade in chitchat, you might have been deceived
concerning me in these points—upon my soul, I have been getting
more and more close to you every day, ever since I knew you, and
now one of the first pleasures I look to is your happy Marriage—the
more, since I have felt the pleasure of loving a sister in Law. I did not
think it possible to become so much attached in so short a time—
Things like these, and they are real, have made me resolve to have a

care of my health—you must be as careful—The rain has stopped us
to day at the end of a dozen Miles, yet we hope to see Loch-Lomond
the day after to Morrow;—I will piddle out my information, as Rice
says, next Winter at any time when a substitute is wanted for Vingt-
un. We bear the fatigue very well.—20 Miles a day in general—A
cloud came over us in getting up Skiddaw—I hope to be more lucky
in Ben Lomond—and more lucky still in Ben Nevis—what I think
you wo^d enjoy is poking about Ruins—sometimes Abbey, sometimes
Castle. The short stay we made in Ireland has left few
remembrances—but an old woman in a dog-kennel Sedan with a
pipe in her Mouth, is what I can never forget—I wish I may be able
to give you an idea of her—Remember me to your Mother and
Sisters, and tell your Mother how I hope she will pardon me for
having a scrap of paper pasted in the Book sent to her. I was driven
on all sides and had not time to call on Taylor—So Bailey is coming
to Cumberland*—well, if you'll let me know where at Inverness, I
[will] call on my return and pass a little time with him—I am glad
'tis not scotland—Tell my friends I do all I can for them, that is
drink their healths in Toddy—Perhaps I may have some lines by and
by to send you fresh on your own Letter—Tom has a few to shew
you.

your affectionate friend
John Keats

To Tom Keats, *10, 11, 13, 14 July 1818*

Ah! ken ye what I met the day
　Out oure the Mountains
A coming down by craggis grey
　An mossie fountains
A goud hair'd Marie yeve I pray
　Ane minute's guessing—
For that I met upon the way
　Is past expressing—
As I stood where a rocky brig
　A torrent crosses
I spied upon a misty rig
　A troup o Horses—

116

And as they trotted down the glen
　　I sped to meet them
To see if I might know the Men
　　To stop and greet them.
First Willie on his sleek mare came
　　At canting gallop
His long hair rustled like a flame
　　On board a shallop—
Then came his brother Rab and then
　　Young Peggy's Mither
And Peggy too—adown the glen
　　They went togither—
I saw her wrappit in her hood
　　Fra wind and raining—
~~There was a blush upon her~~
Her cheek was flush wi timid blood
　　Twixt growth and waning—
She turn'd her dazed head full oft
　　For thence her Brithers
Came riding with her Bridegroom soft
　　An mony ithers.
Young Tam came up an eyed me quick
　　With reddened cheek
Braw Tam was daffed like a chick
　　He coud na speak—
Ah Marie they are all 'gane hame
　　Through blustring weather
　　　　　full
An every heart is ~~light on~~ on flame
　　An light as feather
Ah! Marie they are all gone hame
　　Fra happy wedding,
Whilst I—Ah is it not a shame?
　　Sad tears am shedding—

————　　————　　————　　————

My dear Tom, Belantree July 10
The reason for my writing these lines was that Brown wanted to
impose a galloway song upon dilke—but it wont do—The subject I

got from meeting a wedding just as we came down into this place—
Where I am affraid we shall be emprisoned awhile by the weather—
Yesterday we came 27 Miles from Stranraer—enterd Ayrshire a little
beyond Cairn, and had our path th[r]ough a delightful Country. I
shall endeavour that you may follow our steps in this walk—it would
be uninteresting in a Book of Travels—it can not be interest⟨ing⟩
but by my having gone through it—When we left Cairn our Road lay
half way up the sides of a green mountainous shore, full of Clefts of
verdure and eternally varying—sometimes up sometimes down, and
over little Bridges going across green chasms of moss rock and
trees—winding about every where. After two or three Miles of this
we turned suddenly into a magnificent glen finely wooded in Parts—
seven Miles long—with a Mountain Stream winding down the
Midst—full of cottages in the most happy Situations—the sides of
the Hills coverd with sheep—the effect of cattle lowing I never had
so finely—At the end we had a gradual ascent and got among the
tops of the Mountains whence In a little time I descried in the Sea
Ailsa Rock 940 feet hight—it was 15 Miles distant and seemed close
upon us—The effect of ailsa with the peculiar perspective of the Sea
in connection with the ground we stood on, and the misty rain then
falling gave me a complete Idea of a deluge—Ailsa struck me very
suddenly—really I was a little alarmed—Thus far had I written
before we set out this morning—Now we are at Girvan 13 Miles
north of Belantree—Our Walk has been along a more grand shore to
day than yesterday—Ailsa beside us all the way—From the heights
we could see quite at home Cantire and the large Mountains of
~~Arran~~ Annan* one of the Hebrides—We are in comfortable Quarters. The Rain we feared held up bravely and it has been 'fu fine this
day"—⟨To⟩morrow we sh⟨all be⟩ at Ayr—

To Ailsa Rock—

    Hearken thou craggy ocean pyramid,
        Give answer by thy voice the Sea fowls screams!
        When were thy shoulders mantled in huge Streams?
    When from the Sun was thy broad forehead hid?
    How long ist since the mighty Power bid
        Thee heave to airy sleep from fathom dreams—
        Sleep in the Lap of Thunder or Sunbeams,

Or when grey clouds are thy cold Coverlid—
Thou answerst not for thou art dead asleep
         is but
Thy Life ~~has been will be~~ two dead eternities
The last in Air, the former in the deep—
  First with the Whales, last with the eglle skies—
Drown'd wast thou till an Earthquake made thee steep—
Another cannot wake thy giant Size!

This is the only Sonnet of any worth I have of late written—I hope
you will like it. 'T is now the 11th of July and we have come 8 Miles
to Breakfast to to Kirkoswald—I hope the next Kirk will be Kirk-
Alloway—I have nothing of consequence to say now concerning our
Journey—so I will speak as far as I can judge on the irish and
Scotch—I know nothing of the higher Classes. Yet I have a persuasion that there the Irish are victorious—As to the 'profanum vulgus'* I must incline to the scotch—They never laugh—but they are
always comparitively neat and clean—Their constitutions are not so
remote and puzzling as the irish—The Scotchman will never give a
decision on any point—he will never commit himself in a sentence
which may be refered to as a meridian in his notions of things—so
that you do not know him—and yet you may come in nigher neighbourhood to him than to the irishman who commits himself in so
many places that it dazes your head—A Scotchman's motive is more
easily discovered than an irishman's. A Scotchman will go wisely
about to deceive you, an irishman cunningly—An Irishman would
bluster out of any discovery to his disadvantage—A Scotchman
would retire perhaps without much desire of revenge—An Irishman
likes to be thought a gallous fellow—A scotchman is contented with
himself—It seems to me they are both sensible of the Character they
hold in England and act accordingly to Englishmen—Thus the
Scotchman will become over grave and over decent and the Irishman
over-impetuous. I like a Scotchman best because he is less of a
bore—I like the Irishman best because he ought to be more
comfortable—The Scotchman has made up his Mind within himself
in a sort of snail shell wisdom—The Irishman is full of strong
headed instinct—The Scotchman is farther in Humanity than the
Irishman—there his [*for* he] will stick perhaps when the Irishman

shall be refined beyond him—for the former thinks he cannot be improved the latter would grasp at it for ever, place but the good plain before him. Maybole—Since breakfast we have come only four Miles to dinner, not merely, for we have examined in the ⟨way⟩ t⟨wo⟩ Ruins, one of them very fine called Crossragual Abbey. there is a winding Staircase to the top of a little Watch Tower. July 13. *Kingswells*—I have been writing to Reynolds—therefore any particulars since Kirkoswald have escaped me—from said kirk we went to Maybole to dinner—then we set forward to Burnes's town Ayr—the Approach to it is extremely fine—quite outwent my expectations richly meadowed, wooded, heathed and rivuleted—with a grand Sea view terminated by the black Mountains of the isle of Annan. As soon as I saw them so nearly I said to myself 'How is it they did not beckon Burns to some grand attempt at Epic'—The bonny Doon is the sweetest river I ever saw overhung with fine trees as far as we could see—we stood some time on the Brig across it, over which Tam o' shanter fled—we took a pinch of snuff on the key stone— Then we proceeded to 'auld Kirk Alloway'—As we were looking at it a Farmer pointed out the spots where Mungo's Mither hang'd her-sel' and 'drunken Charlie brake's neck's bane'*—Then we pro-ceeded to the Cottage he was born in—there was a board to that effect by the door Side—it had the same effect as the same sort of memorial at Stradford on Avon—We drank some Toddy to Burns's Memory with an old Man who knew Burns—damn him—and damn his Anecdotes—he was a great bore—it was impossible for a South-ren to understand above 5 words in a hundred—There was some-thing good in his description of Burns's melancholy the last time he saw him. I was determined to write a sonnet in the Cottage—I did— but it is so bad I cannot venture it here—Next we walked into Ayr Town and before we went to Tea, saw the new Brig and the Auld Brig and wallace tower—Yesterday we dinned with a Traveller—We were talking about Kean—He said he had seen him at Glasgow 'in Othello in the Jew, I me an er, er, er, the Jew in Shylock' He got bother'd completely in vague ideas of the Jew in Othello, Shylock in the Jew, Shylock in Othello, Othello in Shylock, the Jew in Othello &c &c &c he left himself in a mess at last—Still satisfied with him-self he went to the Window and gave an abortive whistle of some tune or other—it might have been Handel. There is no end to these

Mistakes—he'll go and tell people how he has seen 'Malvolio in the Countess' 'Twehth [*for* Twelfth] night in 'Midsummer nights dream—Bottom in much ado about Nothing—Viola in Barrymore*—Antony in Cleopatra—Falstaff in the mouse Trap.— July 14 We enterd Glasgow last Evening under the most oppressive Stare a body could feel—When we had crossed the Bridge Brown look'd back and said its whole pop⟨ulation⟩ had turned to wonder at us—we came on till a drunken Man came up to me—I put him off with my Arm—he returned all up in Arms saying aloud that, 'he had seen all foreigners bu-u-u t he never saw the like o' me—I was obliged to mention the word Officer and Police before he would desist—The City of Glasgow I take to be a very fine one—I was astonished to hear it was twice the size of Edinburgh—It is built of Stone and has a much more solid appearance than London—We shall see the Cathedra⟨l⟩ this morning—they have devilled it into 'High Kirk—I want very much to know the name of the Ship George is g⟨one⟩ in—also what port he will land in—I know nothing about it—I hope you are leading a quiet Life and gradually improving—Make a long lounge of the whole Summer—by the time the Leaves fall I shall be near you with plenty of confab—there are a thousand things I cannot write—Take care of yourself—I mean in not being vexed or bothered at any thing—God bless you!   John—

To Tom Keats, 17, 18, 20, 21 July 1818

My dear Tom,   Cairn-something July 17th—

Here's Brown going on so that I cannot bring to Mind how the two last days have vanished—for example he says 'The Lady of the Lake went to Rock herself to sleep on Arthur's seat and the Lord of the Isles coming to Press a Piece and seeing her Assleep remembered their last meeting at Cony stone Water so touching her with one hand on the Vallis Lucis while he [*for* the] other un-Derwent her Whitehaven, Ireby stifled her clack man on, that he might her Anglesea and give her a Buchanan and said.'[1] I told you last how we were stared at in Glasgow—we are not out of the Crowd yet—Steam Boats on Loch Lomond and Barouches on its sides take a little from

---

[1] See Appendix, note 4.

the Pleasure of such romantic chaps as Brown and I—The Banks of
the Clyde are extremely beautiful—the north End of Loch Lomond
grand in excess—the entrance at the lower end to the narrow part
from a little distance is precious good—the Evening was beautiful
nothing could surpass our fortune in the weather—yet was I worldly
enough to wish for a fleet of chivalry Barges with Trumpets
and Banners just to die away before me into that blue place
among the mountains—I must give you an outline as well as I can*
Not B—the Water was a fine Blue silverd and the Mountains a dark
purple the Sun setting aslant behind them—meantime the head of
ben Lomond was covered with a rich Pink Cloud—We did not
ascend Ben Lomond—the price being very high and a half a day of
rest being quite acceptable—We were up at 4 this morning and have
walked to breakfast 15 Miles through two t[r]emendous Glens—at
the end of the first there is a place called rest and be thankful which
we took for an Inn—it was nothing but a Stone and so we were
cheated into 5 more Miles to Breakfast—I have just been bathing in
Loch fine a saltwater Lake opposite the Window—quite pat and
fresh but for the cursed Gad flies—damn 'em they have been at me
ever since I left the Swan and two necks*—

> All gentle folks who owe a grudge
>   To any living thing
> Open your ears and stay your t[r]udge
>   Whilst I in dudgeon sing—
>
> The gad fly he hath stung me sore
>   O may he ne'er sting you!
> But we have many a horrid bore
>   He may sting black and blue.
>
> Has any here an old grey Mare
>   With three Legs all her store
> O put it to her Buttocks bare
>   And Straight she'll run on four
>
> Has any here a Lawyer suit
>   Of 17, 43
> Take Lawyer's nose and put it to 't
>   And you the end will see

Is there a Man in Parliament
   Dum founder'd in his speech
O let his neighbour make a rent
   And put one in his breech

O Lowther how much better thou
   Hadst figur'd to'ther day
When to the folks thou madst a bow
   And hadst no more to say

If lucky gad fly had but ta'en
   His seat upon thine A — e
And put thee to a little pain
   To save thee from a worse.

Better than Southey it had been
   Better than Mr D——
Better than Wordsworth too I ween
   Better than Mr V——

Forgive me pray good people all
   For deviating so
In spirit sure I had a call—
   And now I on will go—

Has any here a daughter fair
   Too fond of reading novels
Too apt to fall in love with care
   And charming Mister Lovels*

O put a gadfly to that thing
   She keeps so white and pert
I mean the finger for the ring
   And it will breed a Wert—

Has any here a pious spouse
   Who seven times a day
Scolds as King David pray'd; to chouse
   And have her holy way—

O let a Gadfly's litt[l]e sting
   Persuade her sacred tongue

       That noises are a common thing
         But that her bell has rung

       And as this is the summum bo
         Num of all conquering
       I leave withouten wordes mo'
         The Gadfly's little sting

Last Evening we came round the End of Loch Fine to Inverary—the Duke of Argyle's Castle is very modern magnificent and more so from the place it is in—the woods seem old enough to remember to or three changes in the Crags about them—the Lake was beautiful and there was a Band at a distance by the Castle. I must say I enjoyed to or three common tunes—but nothing could stifle the horrors of a solo on the Bag-pipe—I thought the Beast would never have done— Yet was I doomed to hear another—On ente[r]ing Inverary we saw a Play Bill—Brown was knock'd up from new shoes—so I went to the Barn alone where I saw the Stranger* accompanied by a Bag pipe— There they went on about 'interesting creaters' and 'human nater'— till the Curtain fell and then Came the Bag pipe—When Mrs Haller fainted down went the Curtain and out came the Bagpipe—at the heartrending, shoemending reconciliation the Piper blew amain—I never read or saw this play before; not the Bag pipe, nor the wretched players themselves were little in comparison with it— thank heaven it has been scoffed at lately almost to a fashion—

       Of late two dainties were before me plac'd
         Sweet holy pure sacred and innocent
         From the ninth sphere to me benignly sent
       That Gods might know my own particlar taste—
       First the soft bag pipe mourn'd with zealous haste
         The Stranger next with head on bosom bent
         Sigh'd; rueful again the piteous bag-pipe went
                ings fresh did
     Again the Stranger sigh~~d in discontent~~ waste
     O Bag-pipe thou didst steal my heart away
         O Stranger thou my nerves from Pipe didst charm
     O Bag pipe—thou did'st reassert thy sway
         Again thou Stranger gave'st me fresh alarm—

> Alas! I could not choose. Ah! my poor heart
> Mum chance art thou with both obliged to part.

I think we are the luckiest fellows in Christendom—Brown could not proced this morning on account of his feet and lo there is thunder and rain—July 20th For these two days past we have been so badly accomodated more particularly in coarse food that I have not been at all in cue to write. Last night poor Brown with his feet blistered and scarcely able to walk, after a trudge of 20 Miles down the Side of Loch Awe had no supper but Eggs and Oat Cake—we have lost the sight of white bread entirely Now we had eaten nothing but Eggs all day—about 10 a piece and they had become sickening—. To day we have fared rather better—but no oat Cake wanting—we had a small Chicken and even a good bottle of Port—but all together the fare is too coarse—I feel it a little—another week will break us in—I forgot to tell you that when we came through Glencroe it was early in the morning and we were pleased with the noise of Shepherds Sheep and dogs in the misty heights close above us—we saw none of them for some time, till two came in sight creeping among the Craggs like Emmets, yet their voices came quite plainly to us—The Approach to Loch Awe was very solemn towards nightfall—the first glance was a streak of water deep in the Bases of large black Mountains—We had come along a complete mountain road, where if one listened there was not a sound but that of Mountain Streams We walked 20 Miles by the side of Loch Awe—evey ten steps creating a new and beautiful picture—sometimes through little wood—there are two islands on the Lake each with a beautiful ruin—one of them rich in ivy—We are detained this morning by the rain. I will tell you exactly where we are—We are between Loch Craignish and the Sea just opposite Long Island*—Yesterday our walk was of this description—the near Hills were not very lofty but many of their Steeps beautifully wooded—the distant Mountains in the Hebrides very grand the Saltwater Lakes coming up between Crags and Islands fulltided and scarcely ruffled—sometimes appearing as one large Lake, sometimes as th[r]ee distinct ones in different directions—At one point we saw afar off a rocky opening into the main Sea—We have also seen an Eagle or two. They move about without the least motion of Wings when in an indolent fit—I am for

the first time in a country where a foreign Language is spoken—they
gabble away Gælic at a vast rate—numbers of them speak English—
There are not many Kilts in Argylshire—At Fort William they say a
Man is not admitted into Society without one—the Ladies there
have a horror at the indecency of Breeches. I cannot give you a better
idea of Highland Life than by describing the place we are in—The
Inn or public is by far the best house in the immediate
neighbourhood—It has a white front with tolerable windows—the
table I am writing on suprises me as being a nice flapped Mehogany
one; at the same time the place has no watercloset nor anything like
it. You may if you peep see through the floor chinks into the ground
rooms. The old Grandmother of the house seems intelligent though
not over clean. N.B. No snuff being to be had in the village, she made
us some. The Guid Man is a rough looking hardy stout Man who I
think does not speak so much English as the Guid wife who is very
obliging and sensible and moreover though stockingless, has a pair of
old Shoes—Last night some Whisky Men sat up clattering Gælic till
I am sure one o'Clock to our great annoyance—There is a Gælic
testament on the Drawers in the next room—White and blue China
ware has crept all about here—Yesterday there passed a Donkey
laden with tin-pots—opposite the Window there are hills in a
Mist—a few Ash trees and a mountain stream at a little distance—
They possess a few head of Cattle—If you had gone round to the
back of the House just now—you would have seen more hills in a
Mist—some dozen wretched black Cottages scented of peat smoke
which finds is [*for* its] way by the door or a hole in the roof—a girl
here and there barefoot There was one little thing driving Cows
down a slope like a mad thing—there was another standing at the
cowhouse door rather pretty fac'd all up to the ankles in dirt—We
have walk'd 15 Miles in a soaking rain to Oban opposite the Isle of
Mull which is so near Staffa we had though[t] to pass to it—but the
expense is 7 Guineas and those rather extorted—Staffa you see is a
fashionable place and therefore every one concerned with it either
in this town or the Island are what you call up—'t is like paying
sixpence for an apple at the playhouse—this irritated me and
Brown was not best pleased—we have therefore resolved to set
northward for fort William tomorrow morning—I feel [*for* fell] upon
a bit of white Bread to day like a Sparrow—it was very fine—I

cannot manage the cursed Oatcake—Remember me to all and let me hear a good account of you at Inverness—I am sorry Georgy had not those Lines. Good bye.

Your affectionate Brother
John———

To Benjamin Bailey, 18, 22 July 1818

My dear Bailey,   Inverary July 18th

The only day I have had a chance of seeing you when you were last in London I took every advantage of—some devil led you out of the way—Now I have written to Reynolds to tell me where you will be in Cumberland—so that I cannot miss you—and when I see you the first thing I shall do will be to read that about Milton and Ceres and Proserpine—for though I am not going after you to John o' Grotts it will be but poetical to say so. And here Bailey I will say a few words written in a sane and sober Mind, a very scarce thing with me, for they may her⟨eaf⟩ter save you a great deal of trouble about me, which you do not deserve, and for which I ought to be ba[s]tinadoed. I carry all matters to an extreme—so that when I have any little vexation it grows in five Minutes into a theme for Sophocles—then and in that temper if I write to any friend I have so little selfpossession that I give him matter for grieving at the very time perhaps when I am laughing at a Pun. Your last Letter made me blush for the pain I had given you—I know my own disposition so well that I am certain of writing many times hereafter in the same strain to you— now you know how far to believe in them—you must allow for imagination—I know I shall not be able to help it. I am sorry you are grieved at my not continuing my visits to little Britain*—yet I think I have as far as a Man can do who has Books to read to [*for* and] subjects to think upon—for that reason I have been no where else except to Wentworth place so nigh at hand—moreover I have been too often in a state of health that made me think it prudent no[t] to hazard the night Air—Yet further I will confess to you that I cannot enjoy Society small or numerous—I am certain that our fair friends are glad I should come for the mere sake of my coming; but I am certain I bring with me a Vexation they are better without—If I can possibly at any time feel my temper coming upon me I refrain even from a promised visit. I am certain I have not a right feeling towards Women—at this moment I am striving to be just to them but I cannot—Is it because they fall so far beneath my Boyish imagination? When I was a Schoolboy I thought[t] a fair Woman a pure Goddess, my mind was a soft nest in which some one of them slept though she knew it not—I have no right to expect more than their reality. I thought them etherial above Men—I find then [*for* them] perhaps equal—great by comparison is very small—Insult may be inflicted in more ways than by Word or action—one who is tender of being insulted does not like to think an insult against another—I do not like to think insults in a Lady's Company—I commit a Crime with her which absence would have not known—Is it not extraordinary? When among Men I have no evil thoughts, no malice, no spleen—I feel free to speak or to be silent—I can listen and from every one I can learn—my hands are in my pockets I am free from all suspicion and comfortable. When I am among Women I have evil thoughts, malice spleen—I cannot speak or be silent—I am full of Suspicions and therefore listen to no thing—I am in a hurry to be gone—You must be charitable and put all this perversity to my being disappointed since Boyhood—Yet with such feelings I am happier alone among Crowds of men, by myself or with a friend or two— With all this trust me Bailey I have not the least idea that Men of different feelings and inclinations are more short sighted than myself—I never rejoiced more than at my Brother's Marriage and shall do so at that of any of my friends—. I must absolutely get over this—but how? The only way is to find the root of evil, and so cure it "with backward mutters of dissevering Power"* That is a difficult thing; for an obstinate Prejudice can seldom be produced but from a gordian complication of feelings, which must take time to unravell and care to keep unravelled—I could say a good deal about this but I will leave it in hopes of better and more worthy dispositions—and also content that I am wronging no one, for after all I do think better of Womankind than to suppose they care whether Mister John Keats five feet hight likes them or not. You appeared to wish to avoid any words on this subject—don't think it a bore my dear fellow—it shall be my Amen—I should not have consented to myself these four Months tramping in the highlands but that I thought it would give me more experience, rub off more Prejudice, use [me] to more hardship, identify finer scenes load me with grander Mountains, and strengthen more my reach in Poetry, than would stopping at home among Books even though I should reach Homer—By this time I am comparitively a a mountaineer—I have been among wilds and Mountains too much to break out much about the[i]r Grandeur. I have fed upon Oat cake—not long enough to be very much attached to it—The first Mountains I saw, though not so large as some I have since seen, weighed very solemnly upon me. The effect is wearing away—yet I like them mainely—We have come this evening with a Guide, for without was impossible, into the middle of the Isle of Mull, pursuing our cheap journey to Iona and perhaps staffa—We would not follow the common and fashionable mode from the great imposition of expense. We have come over heath and rock and river and bog to what in England would be called a horrid place—yet it belongs to a Shepherd pretty well off perhaps—The family speak not a word but gælic and we have not yet seen their faces for the smoke which after visiting every cr⟨a⟩nny, (not excepting my eyes very much incommoded for writing), finds it[s] way out at the ⟨door.⟩ I am more com⟨f⟩ortable than I could have imagined in such a place, and so is Brown—The People are all very kind. We lost our way a little yesterday and enquiring at a Cottage, a yound [*for* young] Woman without a word threw on her cloak and walked a Mile in a missling rain and splashy way to put us right again. I could not have had a greater pleasure in these parts than your mention of my Sister—She is very much prisoned from me—I am affraid it will be some time before I can take her to many places I wish—I trust we shall see you ere long in Cumberland—at least I hope I shall before my visit to America more than once I intend to pass a whole year with George if I live to the completion of the three next—My sisters well-fare and the hopes of such a stay in America will make me observe your advice—I shall be prudent and more careful of my health than I have been—I hope you will be about paying your first visit to Town after settling when we come into Cumberland—Cumberland however will be no distance to me after my present journey—I shall spin to you [in] a minute—I begin to get rather a contempt for distances. I hope you will have a nice convenient room for a Library. Now you are so well in health do keep it up by never missing your dinner, by not reading hard and by taking proper exercise. You'll have a horse I suppose so you must make a point of sweating him. You say I must study Dante—well the only Books I have with me are those three little Volumes. I read that fine passage you mention a few days ago. Your Letter followed me from Hampstead to Port Patrick and thence to Glasgow—you must think me by this time a very pretty fellow—One of the pleasantest bouts we have had was our walk to Burns's Cottage, over the Doon and past Kirk Alloway—I had determined to write a Sonnet in the Cottage. I did but lauk it was so wretched I destroyed it—howev^r in a few days afterwards I wrote some lines cousin-german to the Circumstance which I will transcribe or rather cross scribe in the front of this—Reynolds's illness has made him a new Man—he will be stronger than ever—before I left London he was really getting a fat face—Brown keeps on writing volumes of adventures to Dilke— when we get in of an evening and I have perhaps taken my rest on a couple of Chairs he affronts my indolence and Luxury by pulling out of his knapsack 1st his paper—2^{ndy} his pens and last his ink—Now I would not care if he would change about a little—I say now, why not Bailey take out his pens first sometimes—But I might as well tell a hen to hold up her head before she drinks instead of afterwards— Your affectionate friend

John Keats—

There is a joy in footing slow across a silent plain
Where Patriot Battle has been fought when Glory had the gain;
There is a pleasure on the heath where Druids old have been,
Where Mantles grey have rustled by and swept the nettles green:
There is a joy in every spot, made known by times of old,
New to the feet, although the tale a hundred times be told:
There is a deeper joy than all, more solemn in the heart,
More parching to the tongue than all, of more divine a smart,
When weary feet forget themselves upon a pleasant turf,
Upon hot sand, or flinty road, or Sea shore iron scurf,
Toward the Castle or the Cot where long ago was born
One who was great through mortal days and died of fame unshorn.
Light Hether bells may tremble then, but they are far away;
Woodlark may sing from sandy fern,—the Sun may hear his Lay;
Runnels may kiss the grass on shelves and shallows clear

But their low voices are not heard though come on travels drear;
Bloodred the sun may set b[e]hind black mountain peaks;
Blue tides may sluice and drench their time in Caves and weedy
    creeks;
Eagles may seem to sleep wing wide upon the Air;
Ring doves may fly convuls'd across to some high cedar'd lair;
But the forgotten eye is still fast wedded to the ground—
As Palmer's that with weariness mid desert shrine hath found.
At such a time the Soul's a Child, in Childhood is the brain
Forgotten is the worldly heart—alone, it beats in vain—
Aye if a Madman could have leave to pass a healthful day,
To tell his forehead's swoon and faint when first began decay,
He might make tremble many a Man whose Spirit had gone forth
To find a Bard's low Cradle place about the silent north.
Scanty the hour and few the steps beyond the Bourn of Care.
Beyond the sweet and bitter world—beyond it unaware;
Scanty the hour and few the steps because a longer stay
Would bar return and make a Man forget his mortal way.
O horrible! to lose the sight of well remember'd face,
Of Brother's eyes, Of Sister's Brow, constant to every place:
Filling the Air as on we move with Portraiture intense
More warm than those heroic tints that fill a Painter's sense—
When Shapes of old come striding by and visages of old.
Locks shining black, hair scanty grey and passions manifold.
No, No that horror cannot be—for at the Cable's length
Man feels the gentle Anchor pull and gladdens in its strength—
One hour half ideot he stands by mossy waterfall,
But in the very next he reads his Soul's memorial:
He reads it on the Mountain's height where chance he may sit down
Upon rough marble diadem, that Hills eternal crown.
Yet be the Anchor e'er so fast, room is there for a prayer
That Man may never loose his Mind ⟨on⟩ Mountains bleak and
    bare;
That he may stray league after League some great Berthplace to
    find,
And keep his vision clear from speck, his inward sight unblind—

To Tom Keats, 23, 26 July 1818

Dun an cullen

My dear Tom,

Just after my last had gone to the Post in came one of the Men with whom we endeavoured to agree about going to Staffa—he said what a pitty it was we should turn aside and not see the Curiosities. So we had a little talk and finally agreed that he should be our guide across the Isle of Mull—We set out, crossed two ferries, one to the isle of Kerrara of little distance, the other from Kerrara to Mull 9 Miles across—we did it in forty minutes with a fine Breeze—The road through the Island, or rather the track is the most dreary you can think of—betwe[e]n dreary Mountains—over bog and rock and river with our Breeches tucked up and our Stockings in hand— About eight o Clock we arrived at a shepherd's Hut into w⟨h⟩ich we could scarcely get for the Smoke through a door lower than my shoulders—We found our way into a little compartment with the rafters and turf thatch blackened with smoke—the earth floor full of Hills and Dales—We had some white Bread with us, made a good Supper and slept in our Clothes in some Blankets, our Guide snored on another little bed about an Arm's length off—This morning we came about sax Miles to Breakfast by rather a better path and we are now in by comparison a Mansion—Our Guide is I think a very obliging fellow—in the way this morning he sang us two Gælic songs—one made by a Mrs Brown on her husband's being drowned the other a jacobin one on Charles Stuart. For some days Brown has been enquiring out his Genealogy here—he thinks his Grandfather came from long Island—he got a parcel of people about him at a Cottage door last Evening—chatted with ane who had been a Miss Brown and who I think from a likeness must have been a Relation— he jawed with the old Woman—flattered a young one—kissed a child who was affraid of his Spectacles and finally drank a pint of Milk— They handle his Spectacles as we do a sensitive leaf—. July 26th Well—we had a most wretched walk of 37 Miles across the Island of Mull and then we crossed to Iona or Icolmkill from Icolmkill we took a boat at a bargain to take us to Staffa and land us at the head of Loch Nakgal whence we should only have to walk half the distance to Oban again and on a better road—All this is well pass'd and done with this singular piece of Luck that there was an intermission in the bad Weather just as we saw Staffa at which it is impossible to land but in a tolerable Calm Sea—But I will first mention Icolmkill—I know not whether you have heard much about this Island, I never did before I came nigh it. It is rich in the most interesting Antiqu[i]ties. Who would expect to find the ruins of a fine Cathedral Church, of Cloisters, Colleges, Mona[s]taries and Nunneries in so remote an Island? The Beginning of these things was in the sixth Century under the superstition of a would-be Bishop-saint who landed from Ireland and chose the spot from its Beauty—for at that time the now treeless place was covered with magnificent Woods. Columba in the Gaelic is Colm signifying Dove—Kill signifies church and I is as good as Island—so I-colm-kill means the Island of Saint Columba's Church—Now this Saint Columba became the Dominic of the barbarian Christians of the north and was famed also far south—but more especially was reverenced by the Scots the Picts the Norwegians the Irish. In a course of years perhaps the Iland was considered the most holy ground of the north, and the old kings of the afore mentioned nations chose it for their burial place—We were shown a spot in the Churchyard where they say 61 kings are buried 48 Scotch from Fergus 2nd to Macbeth 8 Irish 4 Norwegian and 1 french—they lie in rows compact—Then we were shown other matters of later date but still very ancient—many tombs of Highland Chieftains—their effigies in complete armour face upwards—black and moss covered—Abbots and Bishops of the island always of one of the chief Clans—There were plenty Macleans and Macdonnels, among these latter the famous Macdonel Lord of the Isles—There have been 300 Crosses in the Island but the Presbyterains destroyed all but two, one of which is a very fine one and completely covered with a shaggy coarse Moss—The old Schoolmaster an ignorant little man but reckoned very clever, showed us these things—He is a Macklean and as much above 4 foot as he is under 4 foot 3 inches—he stops at one glass of wiskey unless you press another and at the second unless you press a third. I am puzzled how to give you an Idea of Staffa. It can only be represented by a first rate drawing—One may compare the surface of the Island to a roof—this roof is supported by grand pillars of basalt standing together as thick as honey combs The finest thing is Fingal's Cave—it is entirely a hollowing

out of Basalt Pillars. Suppose now the Giants who rebelled against
Jove had taken a whole Mass of black Columns and bound them
together like bunches of matches—and then with immense Axes had
made a cavern in the body of these columns—of course the roof and
floor must be composed of the broken ends of the Columns—such is
fingal's Cave except that the Sea has done the work of excavations
and is continually dashing there—so that we walk along the sides of
the cave on the pillars which are left as if for convenient Stairs—the
roof is arched somewhat gothic wise and the length of some of the
entire side pillars is 50 feet—About the island you might seat an
army of Men each on a pillar—The length of the Cave is 120 feet
and from its extremity the view into the sea through the large Arch
at the entrance—the colour of the colums is a sort of black with a
lurking gloom of purple ther[e]in—For solemnity and grandeur it
far surpasses the finest Cathedrall—At the extremity of the Cave
there is a small perforation into another cave, at which the waters
meeting and buffetting each other there is sometimes produced a
report as of a cannon heard as far as Iona which must be 12 Miles—
As we approached in the boat there was such a fine swell of the sea
that the pillars appeared rising imm⟨ed⟩iately out of the crystal—
But it is impossible to describe it—

> Not Aladin magian
> Ever such a work began,
> Not the Wizard of the dee
> Ever such dream could see
> Not St John in Patmos isle
> In the passion of his toil
> When he saw the churches seven
> Golden aisled built up in heaven
> Gazed at such a rugged wonder.
> As I stood its roofing under
> Lo! I saw one sleeping there
> On the marble cold and bare
> While the surges washed his feet
> And his garments white did beat
> Drench'd about the sombre rocks,
> On his neck his well grown locks

Lifted dry above the Main
Were upon the curl again—
What is this and what art thou?
Whisper'd I and touch'd his brow.
What art thou and what is this?
Whisper'd I and strove to kiss
                          his eyes.
The Spirits hand to wake ~~him up~~
Up he started in a thrice.
I am Lycidas said he
Fam'd in funeral Minstrelsey—
This was architected thus
By the great Oceanus
Here his mighty waters play
Hollow Organs all the day
Here by turns his dolphins all
Finny palmer's great and small
Come to pay devotion due—
Each a mouth of pea[r]ls must strew
~~Many a Mortal comes to see~~
~~This Cathedrall of the S~~
Many a Mortal of these days
Dares to pass our sacred ways
Dares to touch audaciously
This Cathedral of the Sea—
I have been the Pontif priest
Where the Waters never rest
Where a fledgy sea bird choir
Soars for ever—holy fire
I have hid from Mortal Man.
~~Old~~ Proteus is my Sacristan.
But the stupid eye of Mortal
Hath pass'd beyond the Rocky portal
So for ever will I leave
Such a taint and soon unweave
All the magic of the place—
'T is now free to stupid face
To cutters and to fashion boats

To cravats and to Petticoats.
The great Sea shall war it down
For its fame shall not be blow⟨n⟩
At every farthing quadrille dance.
So saying with a Spirits glance
He dived—

I am sorry I am so indolent as to write such stuff as this—it cant be help'd—The western coast of Scotland is a most strange place—it is composed of rocks Mountains, mountainous and rocky Islands intersected by Lochs—you can go but a small distance any where from salt water in the highlands

I have a slight sore throat and think it best to stay a day or two at ⟨O⟩ban. Then we shall proceed to Fort William and Inverness—Where I am anxious to be on account if [*for of*] a Letter from you—Brown in his Letters puts down every little circumstance I should like to do the same but I ⟨c⟩onfess myself too indolent and besides next winter ⟨ever⟩y thing will come up in prime order as we verge on such and such things Have you heard in any way of George? I should think by this time he must have landed—I in my carelessness never thought of knowing where a letter would find him on the other side—I think Baltimore but I am affraid of directing to the wrong place—I shall begin some chequer work for him directly and it will be ripe for the post by the time I hear from you next after this—I assure you I often long for a seat and a Cup o' tea at well Walk—especially now that mountains, castles and Lakes are becoming common to me—yet I would rather summer it out for on the whole I am happier than when I have time to be glum—perhaps it may cure me—Immediately on my return I shall begin studying hard with a peep at the theatre now and then—and depend upon it I shall be very luxurious—With respect to Women I think I shall be able to conquer my passions hereafter better than I have yet done—You will help me to talk of george next winter and we will go now and then to see Fanny—Let me hear a good account of your health and comfort telling me truly how you do alone—

Remember me to all including M^r and Mrs Bentley—

Your most affectionate Brother

Joh⟨n⟩—

To Tom Keats, 3, 6 August 1818

My dear Tom,   Ah mio Ben.*   Letter Findlay August 3rd

We have made but poor progress Lately, chiefly from bad weather for my throat is in a fair way of getting quite well, so I have had nothing of consequence to tell you till yesterday when we went up Ben Nevis, the highest Mountain in Great Britain—On that account I will never ascend another in this empire—Skiddaw is no thing to it either in height or in difficulty. It is above 4300 feet from the Sea level and Fortwilliam stands at the head of a Salt water Lake, consequently we took it completely from that level. I am heartily glad it is done—it is almost like a fly crawling up a wainscoat—Imagine the task of mounting 10 Saint Pauls without the convenience of Stair cases. We set out about five in the morning with a Guide in the Tartan and Cap and soon arrived at the foot of the first ascent which we immediately began upon—after much fag and tug and a rest and a glass of whiskey apiece we gained the top of the first rise and saw then a tremendous chap above us which the guide said was still far from the top—After the first Rise our way lay along a heath valley in which there was a Loch—after about a Mile in this Valley we began upon the next ascent more fo[r]midable by far than the last and kept mounting with short intervals of rest untill we got above all vegetation, among nothing but loose Stones which lasted us to the very top—the Guide said we had three Miles of a stony ascent—we gained the first tolerable level after the valley to the height of what in the Valley we had thought the top and saw still above us another huge crag which still the Guide said was not the top—to that we made with an obstinate fag and having gained it there came on a Mist, so that from that part to the verry top we walked in a Mist. The whole immense head of the Mountain is composed of large loose stones—thousands of acres—Before we had got half way up we passed large patches of snow and near the top there is a chasm some hundred feet deep completely glutted with it—Talking of chasms they are the finest wonder of the whole—the[y] appear great rents in the very heart of the mountain though they are not, being at the side of it, but other huge crags arising round it give the appearance to Nevis of a shattered heart or Core in itself—These Chasms are 1500 feet in depth and are the most tremendous places I have ever seen—

they turn one giddy if you choose to give way to it—We tumbled in large stones and set the echoes at work in fine style. Sometimes these chasms are tolerably clear, sometimes there is a misty cloud which seems to steam up and sometimes they are entirely smothered with clouds—

After a little time the Mist cleared away but still there were large Clouds about attracted by old Ben to a certain distance so as to form as it appeared large dome curtains which kept sailing about, opening and shutting at intervals here and there and everywhere; so that although we did not see one vast wide extent of prospect all round we saw something perhaps finer—these cloud-veils opening with a dissolving motion and showing us the mountainous region beneath as through a loop hole—these Mouldy [*probably for* cloudy] loop holes ever varrying and discovering fresh prospect east, west north and South—Then it was misty again and again it was fair—then puff came a cold breeze of wind and bared a craggy chap we had not yet seen though in close neighbourhood—Every now and then we had over head blue Sky clear and the sun pretty wa[r]m. I do not know whether I can give you an Idea of the prospect from a large Mountain top—You are on a stony plain which of course makes you forget you are on any but low ground—the horison or rather edges of this plain being above 4000 feet above the Sea hide all the Country immediately beneath you, so that the next objects you see all round next to the edges of the flat top are the Summits of Mountains of some distance off—as you move about on all side[s] you see more or less of the near neighbour country according as the Mountain you stand upon is in different parts steep or rounded—but the most new thing of all is the sudden leap of the eye from the extremity of what appears a plain into so vast a distance On one part of the top there is a handsome pile of stones done pointedly by some soldiers of artillery, I climed onto them and so got a little higher than old Ben himself. It was not so cold as I expected—yet cold enough for a glass of Wiskey now and then—There is not a more fickle thing than the top of a Mountain—what would a Lady give to change her head-dress as often and with as little trouble!—There are a good many red deer upon Ben Nevis we did not see one—the dog we had with us keep [*for* kept] a very sharp look out and really languished for a bit of a worry—I have said nothing yet of out [*for* our] getting on among the loose stones large and small sometimes on two sometimes on three, sometimes four legs—sometimes two and stick, sometimes three and stick, then four again, then two⟨,⟩ then a jump, so that we kept on ringing changes on foot, hand, Stick, jump boggl⟨e,⟩ s[t]umble, foot, hand, foot, (very gingerly) stick again, and then again a game at all fours. . . .*

I felt it horribly—'T was the most vile descent—shook me all to pieces—Over leaf you will find a Sonnet I wrote on the top of Ben Nevis—We have just entered Inverness. I have three Letters from you and one [from] Fanny—and one from Dilke I would set about crossing this all over for you but I will first write to Fanny and Mrs Wilie then I will begin another to you and not before because I think it better you should have this as soon as possible—My Sore throat is not quite well and I intend stopping here a few days

> Read me a Lesson muse, and speak it loud
> Upon the top of Nevis blind in Mist!
> I look into the Chasms and a Shroud
> Vaprous doth hide them; just so much I wist
> Mankind do know of Hell: I look o'erhead
> And there is sullen Mist; even so much
> Mankind can tell of Heaven: Mist is spread
> Before the Earth beneath me—even such
> Even so vague is Man's sight of himself.
> Here are the craggy Stones beneath my feet;
> Thus much I know, that a poor witless elf
> I tread on them; that all my eye doth meet
>   Is mist and Crag—not only on this height
>   But in the World of thought and mental might—

Good bye till tomorrow

Your most affectionate Brother

John—

To Mrs James Wylie, 6 August 1818

My dear Madam—   Inverness 6th August 1818

 It was a great regret to me that I should leave all my friends, just at the moment when I might have helped to soften away the time for them. I wanted not to leave my Brother Tom, but more especially, believe me, I should like to have remained near you, were it but for an atom of consolation, after parting with so dear a daughter; My brother George has ever been more than a brother to me, he has been my greatest friend, & I can never forget the sacrifice you have made for his happiness. As I walk along the Mountains here, I am full of these things, & lay in wait, as it were, for the pleasure of seeing you, immediately on my return to town. I wish above all things, to say a word of Comfort to you, but I know not how. It is impossible to prove that black is white, It is impossible to make out, that sorrow is joy or joy is sorrow————Tom tells me that you called on Mr Haslam with a Newspaper giving an account of a Gentleman in a Fur cap, falling over a precipice in Kirkudbrightshire. If it was me, I did it in a dream, or in some magic interval between the first & second cup of tea; which is nothing extraordinary, when we hear that Mahomet, in getting out of Bed, upset a jug of water, & whilst it was falling, took a fortnight's trip as it seemed to Heaven: yet was back in time to save one drop of water being spilt. As for Fur caps I do not remember one beside my own, except at Carlisle—this was a very good Fur cap, I met in the High Street, & I daresay was the unfortunate one. I daresay that the fates seeing but two Fur caps in the North, thought it too extraordinary, & so threw the Dies which of them should be drowned. The lot fell upon Jonas—I daresay his name was Jonas. All I hope is, that the gaunt Ladies said not a word about hanging, if they did, I shall one day regret that I was not half drowned in Kirkudbright. Stop! let me see!—being half drowned by falling from a precipice is a very romantic affair—Why should I not take it to myself? Keep my secret & I will. How glorious to be introduced in a drawing room to a Lady who reads Novels, with— "M^r so & so—Miss so & so—Miss so & so. this is M^r so & so. who fell off a precipice, & was half drowned Now I refer it to you whether I should loose so fine an opportunity of making my fortune—No romance lady could resist me—None—Being run under a Waggon; side lamed at a playhouse; Apoplectic, through Brandy; & a thousand other tolerably decent things for badness would be nothing; but being tumbled over a precipice into the sea—Oh it would make my fortune—especially if you could continue to hint, from this bulletins authority, that I was not upset on my own account, but that I dashed into the waves after Jessy of Dumblane*—& pulled her out by the hair—But that, Alas! she was dead or she would have made me happy with her hand—however in this you may use your own discretion—But I must leave joking & seriously aver, that I have been *werry* romantic indeed, among these Mountains & Lakes. I have got wet through day after day, eaten oat cake, & drank whiskey, walked up to my knees in Bog, got a sore throat, gone to see Icolmkill & Staffa, met with wholesome food, just here & there as it happened; went up Ben Nevis, & N.B. came down again; Sometimes when I am rather tired, I lean rather languishingly on a Rock, & long for some famous Beauty to get down from her Palfrey in passing; approach me with—her saddle bags—& give me—a dozen or two capital roast beef sandwiches—When I come into a large town, you know there is no putting ones Knapsack into ones fob; so the people stare—We have been taken for Spectacle venders, Razor sellers, Jewellers, travelling linnen drapers, Spies, Excisemen, & many things else, I have no idea of—When I asked for letters at the Post Office, Port Patrick; the man asked what Regiment? I have had a peep also at little Ireland. Tell Henry I have not Camped quite on the bare Earth yet; but nearly as bad, in walking through Mull—for the Shepherds huts you can scarcely breathe in, for the smoke which they seem to endeavour to preserve for smoking on a large scale. Besides riding about 400, we have walked above 600 Miles, & may therefore reckon ourselves as set out.   I wish my dear Madam, that one of the greatest pleasures I shall have on my return, will be seeing you & that I shall ever be

> Yours with the greatest Respect & sincerity
>> John Keats—

To Fanny Keats, 19 August 1818

My dear Fanny,   Hampstead August 18th*

I am affraid you will [think] *me* very negligent in not having answered your Letter—I see it is dated June 12—I did not arrive at Inverness till the 8th* of this Month so I am very much concerned at your being disappointed so long a time. I did not intend to have returned to London so soon but have a bad sore throat from a cold I caught in the island of Mull: therefore I thought it best to get home as soon as possible and went on board the Smack from Cromarty—

We had a nine days passage and were landed at London Bridge yesterday—I shall have a good deal to tell you about Scotland—I would begin here but I have a confounded tooth ache—Tom has not been getting better since I left London and for the last fortnight has been worse than ever—he has been getting a little better for these two or three days—I shall ask Mr Abbey to let me bring you to Hampstead. If M^r A should see this Letter tell him that he still must if he pleases forward the Post Bill to Perth as I have empowered my fellow traveller to receive it—I have a few scotch pebbles for you from the Island of Icolmkill—I am affraid they are rather shabby—I did not go near the Mountain of Cairn Gorm—I do not know the Name of George's ship—the Name of the Port he has gone to is Philadelphia when[c]e he will travel to the Settlement* across the Country—I will tell you all about this when I see you—The Title of my last Book is 'Endymion' you shall have one soon—I would not advise you to play on the Flageolet however I will get you one if you please—I will speak to Mr Abbey on what you say concerning school—I am sorry for your poor Canary. You shall have another volume of my first Book. My tooth Ache keeps on so that I cannot writ[e] with any pleasure—all I can say now is that you Letter is a very nice one without fault and that you will hear from or see in a few days if his throat will let him,

　　　　　　　　　　　　　　　Your affectionate Brother
　　　　　　　　　　　　　　　　　　　John.

To C. W. Dilke, *20, 21 September 1818*

My dear Dilke,

According to the Wentworth place Bulletin you have left Brighton much improved: therefore now a few lines will be more of a pleasure than a bore. I have a few things to say to you and would fain begin upon them in this fo[u]rth line: but I have a Mind too well regulated to proceed upon any thing without due preliminary remarks—you may perhaps have observed that in the simple process of eating radishes I never begin at the root but constantly dip the little green head in the salt—that in the Game of Whist if I have an ace I constantly play it first—So how can I with any face begin without a dissertation on letter writing—Yet when I consider that a sheet of paper contains room only for three pages, and a half how can I do justice to such a pregnant subject? however as you have seen the history of the world stamped as it were by a diminishing glass in the form of a chronological Map, so will I 'with retractile claws'* draw this in to the form of a table—whereby it will occupy merely the remainder of this first page—

Folio——	Parsons, Lawyers, Statesmen, Phys[ic]ians out of place—Ut—Eustace—Thornton* out of practice or on their travels—
Fools cap—	1 superfine! rich or noble poets—ut Byron. 2 common ut egomet—
Quarto—	Projectors, Patentees, Presidents, Potatoe growers—
Bath	Boarding schools, and suburbans in general
Gilt edge	Dandies in general, male female and literary—
Octavo or tears	All who make use of a lascivious seal—
Duodec—	May be found for the most part on Milliners and Dressmakers Parlour tables—
Strip	At the Playhouse doors, or any where—
Slip	Being but a variation—
Snip	So called from its size being disguised by a twist—

I suppose you will have heard that Hazlitt has on foot a prosecution against Blackwood*—I dined with him a few days sinc[e] at Hessey's—there was not a word said about [it], though I understand he is excessively vexed—Reynolds by what I hear is almost over happy and Rice is in town. I have not seen him nor shall I for some time as my throat has become worse after getting well, and I am determined to stop at home till I am quite well—I was going to Town tomorrow with Mrs D. but I though[t] it best, to ask her excuse this morning—I wish I could say Tom was any better. His identity presses upon me so all day that I am obliged to go out—and although I intended to have given some time to study alone I am obliged to write, and plunge into abstract images to ease myself of his countenance his voice and feebleness—so that I live now in a continual fever—it must be poisonous to life although I feel well. Imagine 'the hateful siege of contraries'*—if I think of fame of poetry it seems a crime to me, and yet I must do so or suffer—I am sorry to give you pain—I am almost resolv'd to burn this—but I really have not self possession and magninimity enough to manage the thing othe[r]wise—after all it may be a nervousness proceeding from the Mercury—

Bailey I hear is gaining his Spirits and he will yet be what I once thought impossible a cheerful Man—I think he is not quite so much spoken of in Little Brittain. I forgot to ask Mʳˢ Dilke if she had any thing she wanted to say immediately to you—This morning look'd so unpromising that I did not think she would have gone—but I find she has on sending for some volumes of Gibbon—I was in a little funk yesterday, for I sent an unseal'd note of sham abuse, until I recollected from what I had heard Charles say,* that ⟨the ser⟩vant could neither read nor write—not even to her Mother as Charles observed. I have just had a Letter from Reynolds—he is going on gloriously. The following is a translation of a Line of Ronsard*—

'Love poured her Beauty into my warm veins'*—

You have passed your Romance and I never gave into it or else I think this line a feast for one of your Lovers—How goes it with Brown?

> Your sincere friend
> John Keats—

To J. H. Reynolds, 22 (?) September 1818

My dear Reynolds,

Believe me I have rather rejoiced in your happiness than fretted at your silence. Indeed I am grieved on your account that I am not at the same time happy—But I conjure you to think at Present of nothing but pleasure "Gather the rose &c"* Gorge the honey of life. I pity you as much that it cannot last for ever, as I do myself now drinking bitters.—Give yourself up to it—you cannot help it—and I have a Consolation in thinking so—I never was in love—Yet the voice and the shape of a woman has haunted me these two days—at such a time when the relief, the feverous relief of Poetry seems a much less crime—This morning Poetry has conquered—I have relapsed into those abstractions which are my only life—I feel escaped from a new strange and threatening sorrow.—And I am thankful for it—There is an awful warmth about my heart like a load of Immortality.

Poor Tom—that woman*—and Poetry were ringing changes in my senses—now I am in comparison happy—I am sensible this will distress you—you must forgive me. Had I known you would have set out so soon I could have sent you the 'Pot of Basil' for I had copied it out ready.—Here is a free translation of a Sonnet of Ronsard, which I think will please you—I have the loan of his works—they have great Beauties.

> Nature withheld Cassandra in the skies,
>   For more adornment, a full thousand years;
> She took their cream of Beauty's fairest dyes,
>   And shap'd and tinted her above all Peers:
> Meanwhile Love kept her dearly with his wings,
>   And underneath their shadow fill'd her eyes
> With such a richness that the cloudy Kings
>   Of high Olympus utter'd slavish sighs.
> When from the Heavens I saw her first descend,
>   My heart took fire, and only burning pains,
> They were my pleasures—they my Life's sad end;
>   Love pour'd her beauty into my warm veins.

I had not the original by me when I wrote it, and did not recollect the purport of the last lines—I should have seen Rice ere this—but I am confined by Sawrey's mandate in the house now, and have as yet only gone out in fear of the damp night—You know what an undangerous matter it is. I shall soon be quite recovered—Your offer I shall remember as though it had even now taken place in fact—I think it can not be—Tom is not up yet—I can not say he is better. I have not heard from George.

                    Yr affectte friend John Keats.

To J. A. Hessey, 8 October 1818

My dear Hessey,

You are very good in sending me the letter from the Chronicle—and I am very bad in not acknowledging such a kindness sooner.—pray forgive me—It has so chanced that I have had that paper every day—I have seen today's. I cannot but feel indebted to those Gentlemen who have taken my part*—As for the rest, I begin to get a little acquainted with my own strength and weakness.—Praise or blame has but a momentary effect on the man whose love of beauty in the abstract makes him a severe critic on his own Works. My own domestic criticism has given me pain without comparison beyond what Blackwood or the Quarterly could possibly inflict. and also when I feel I am right, no external praise can give me such a glow as my own solitary reperception & ratification of what is fine. J.S. is perfectly right in regard to the slipshod Endymion. That it is so is no fault of mine.—No!—though it may sound a little paradoxical. It is as good as I had power to make it—by myself—Had I been nervous about its being a perfect piece, & with that view asked advice, & trembled over every page, it would not have been written; for it is not in my nature to fumble—I will write independently.—I have written independently *without Judgment*—I may write independently *& with judgment* hereafter.—The Genius of Poetry must work out its own salvation in a man: It cannot be matured by law & precept, but by sensation & watchfulness in itself—That which is creative must create itself—In Endymion, I leaped headlong into the Sea, and thereby have become better acquainted with the Soundings, the quicksands, & the rocks, than if I had stayed upon the green shore, and piped a silly pipe, and took tea & comfortable advice.—I was never afraid of failure; for I would sooner fail than not be among the greatest—But I am nigh getting into a rant. So, with remembrances to Taylor & Woodhouse &c I am

Yrs very sincerely
John Keats.

To Fanny Keats, 26 October 1818

My dear Fanny,

I called on Mr Abbey in the beginning of last Week: when he seemed averse to letting you come again from having heard that you had been to other places besides Well Walk—I do not mean to say you did wrongly in speaking of it, for there should rightly be no objection to such things: but you know with what People we are obliged in the course of Childhood to associate; whose conduct forces us into duplicity and fa[l]shood to them. To the worst of People we should be openhearted: but it is as well as things are to be prudent in making any communication to any one, that may throw an impediment in the way of any of the little pleasures you may have. I do not recommend duplicity but prudence with such people. Perphaps I am talking too deeply for you: if you do not now, you will understand what I mean in the course of a few years. I think poor Tom is a little Better: he sends his love to you—I shall call on Mr Abbey tomorrow: when I hope to settle when to see you again. Mrs Dilke has been for some time at Brighton—she is expected home in a day or two. She will be pleased I am sure with your present. I will try for permission for you to remain here all Night should Mrs D. retu[r]n in time.

Your affectionate Brother
John—

To Richard Woodhouse, 27 October 1818

My dear Woodhouse,

Your Letter gave me a great satisfaction; more on account of its friendliness, than any relish of that matter in it which is accounted so acceptable in the 'genus irritabile' The best answer I can give you is in a clerklike manner to make some observations on two principle points, which seem to point like indices into the midst of the whole pro and con, about genius, and views and atchievements and ambition and cœtera. 1st As to the poetical Character itself, (I mean that sort of which, if I am any thing, I am a Member; that sort distinguished from the wordsworthian or egotistical sublime;* which is a thing per se and stands alone) it is not itself—it has no self—it is every thing and nothing—It has no character—it enjoys light and shade; it lives in gusto,* be it foul or fair, high or low, rich or poor, mean or elevated—It has as much delight in conceiving an Iago as an Imogen. What shocks the virtuous philosop[h]er, delights the camelion Poet. It does no harm from its relish of the dark side of things any more than from its taste for the bright one; because they both end in speculation. A Poet is the most unpoetical of any thing in existence; because he has no Identity—he is continually in for*—and filling some other Body—The Sun, the Moon, the Sea and Men and Women who are creatures of impulse are poetical and have about them an unchangeable attribute—the poet has none; no identity—he is certainly the most unpoetical of all God's Creatures. If then he has no self, and if I am a Poet, where is the Wonder that I should say I would ~~right~~ write no more? Might I not at that very instant [have] been cogitating on the Characters of saturn and Ops?* It is a wretched thing to confess: but is a very fact that not one word I ever utter can be taken for granted as an opinion growing out of my identical nature—how can it, when I have no nature? When I am in a room with People if I ever am free from speculating on creations of my own brain, then not myself goes home to myself: but the identity of every one in the room begins to [*for* so] to press upon me that, I am in a very little time an[ni]hilated—not only among Men; it would be the same in a Nursery of children: I know not whether I make myself wholly understood: I hope enough so to let you see that no dependence is to be placed on what I said that day.

In the second place I will speak of my views, and of the life I purpose to myself—I am ambitious of doing the world some good: if I should be spared that may be the work of maturer years—in the interval I will assay to reach to as high a summit in Poetry as the nerve bestowed upon me will suffer. The faint conceptions I have of Poems to come brings the blood frequently into my forehead—All I hope is that I may not lose all interest in human affairs—that the solitary indifference I feel for applause even from the finest Spirits, will not blunt any acuteness of vision I may have. I do not think it will—I feel assured I should write from the mere yearning and fondness I have for the Beautiful even if my night's labours should be burnt every morning and no eye ever shine upon them. But even now I am perhaps not speaking from myself; but from some character in whose soul I now live. I am sure however that this next sentence is from myself. I feel your anxiety, good opinion and friendliness in the highest degree, and am

> Your's most sincerely
> John Keats

To George and Georgiana Keats,
14, 16, 21, 24, 31 October 1818

My dear George; There was a part in your Letter which gave me a great deal of pain, that where you lament not receiving Letters from England—I intended to have written immediately on my return from Scotland (which was two Months earlier than I had intended on account of my own as well as Tom's health) but then I was told by ~~Haslam~~ M^rs W[ylie] that you had said you would not wish any one to write till we had heard from you. This I thought odd and now I see that it could not have been so; yet at the time I suffered my unreflecting head to be satisfied and went on in that sort of abstract careless and restless Life with which you are well acquainted. This sentence should it give you any uneasiness do not let it last for before I finish it will be explained away to your satisfaction—

I am g[r]ieved to say that I am not sorry you had not Letters at Philadelphia; you could have had no good news of Tom and I have been withheld on his account from beginning these many days; I could not bring myself to say the truth, that he is no better, but much worse—However it must be told, and you must my dear Brother and Sister take example frome me and bear up against any Calamity for my sake as I do for your's. Our's are ties which independent of their own Sentiment are sent us by providence to prevent the deleterious effects of one great, solitary grief. I have Fanny* and I have you— three people whose Happiness to me is sacred—and it does annul that selfish sorrow which I should otherwise fall into, living as I do with poor Tom who looks upon me as his only comfort—the tears will come into your Eyes—let them—and embrace each other— thank heaven for what happiness you have and after thinking a moment or two that you suffer in common with all Mankind hold it not a sin to regain your cheerfulness—I will relieve you of one uneasiness of overleaf: I retu[r]ned I said on account of my health—I am now well from a bad sore throat which came of bog trotting in the Island of Mull—of which you shall hear by the coppies I shall make from my Scotch Letters—Your content in each other is a delight to me which I cannot express—the Moon is now shining full and brilliant—she is the same to me in Matter, what you are to me in Spirit—If you were here my dear Sister I could not pronounce the words which I can write to you from a distance: I have a tenderness for you, and an admiration which I feel to be as great and more chaste than I can have for any woman in the world. You will mention Fanny—her character is not formed; her identity does not press upon me as yours does. I hope from the bottom of my heart that I may one day feel as much for her as I do for you—I know not how it is, but I have never made any acquaintance of my own—nearly all through your medium my dear Brother—through you I know not only a Sister but a glorious human being—And now I am talking of those to whom you have made me known I cannot forbear mention- ing Haslam as a most kind and obliging and constant friend—His behaviour to Tom during my absence and since my return has endeared him to me for ever—besides his anxiety about you. Tomor- row I shall call on your Mother and exchange information with her—On Tom's account I have not been able to pass so much time with her as I would otherwise have done—I have seen her but twice—on[c]e I dined with her and Charles—She was well, in good Spirits and I kept her laughing at my bad jokes—We went to tea at Mʳˢ Millar's and in going were particularly struck with the light and shade through the Gate way at the Horse Guards. I intend to write you such Volumes that it will be impossible for me to keep any order or method in what I write: that will come first which is uppermost in my Mind, not that which is uppermost in my heart—besides I should wish to give you a picture of our Lives here whenever by a touch I can do it; even as you must see by the last sentence our walk past Whitehall all in good health and spirits—this I am certain of, because I felt so much pleasure from the simple idea of your playing a game at Cricket—At Mʳˢ Millars I saw Henry quite well—there was Miss Keasle—and the goodnatured Miss Waldegrave*—Mʳˢ Millar began a long story and you know it is her Daughter's way to help her on as though her tongue were ill of the gout—Mʳˢ M. certainly tells a Story as though she had been taught her Alphabet in

Crutched Friars. Dilke has been very unwell; I found him very ailing on my return—he was under Medical care for some time, and then went to the Sea Side whence he has returned well—Poor little M^rs D—has had another gall-stone attack; she was well ere I returned—she is now at Brighton—Dilke was greatly pleased to hear from you and will write a Letter for me to enclose—He seems greatly desirous of hearing from you of the Settlement itself—I came by ship from Inverness and was nine days at Sea without being sick—a little Qualm now and then put me in mind of you—however as soon as you touch the thore [*for* shore] all the horrors of sick[n]ess are soon forgotten; as was the case with a Lady on board who could not hold her head up all the way. We had not been in the Thames an hour before her tongue began to some tune; paying off as it was fit she should all old scores. I was the only Englishman on board. There was a downright Scotchman who hearing that there had been a bad crop of Potatoes in England had brought some triumphant Specimens from Scotland—these he exhibited with national pride to all the Lightermen, and Watermen from the Nore to the Bridge. I fed upon beef all the way; not being able to eat the thick Porridge which the Ladies managed to manage with large awkward horn spoons into the bargain. Severn has had a narrow escape of his Life from a Typhous fever: he is now gaining strength—Reynolds has returned from a six weeks enjoyment in Devonshire, he is well and persuades me to publish my pot of Basil as an answer to the attacks made on me in Blackwood's Magazine and the Quarterly Review. There have been two Letters in my defence in the Chronicle and one in the Examiner, coppied from the Alfred Exeter paper, and written by Reynolds—I do not know who wrote those in the Chronicle—This is a mere matter of the moment—I think I shall be among the English Poets after my death. Even as a Matter of present interest the attempt to crush me in the Quarterly has only brought me more into notice and it is a common expression among book men "I wonder the Quarterly should cut its own throat.'*

It does me not the least harm in Society to make me appear little and rediculous: I know when a Man is superior to me and give him all due respect—he will be the last to laugh at me and as for the rest I feel that I make an impression upon them which insures me personal respect while I am in sight whatever they may say when my back is turned—Poor Haydon's eyes will not suffer him to proceed with his picture—he has been in the Country—I have seen him but once since my return—I hurry matters together here because I do not know when the Mail sails—I shall enqu[i]re tomorrow and then shall know whether to be particular or general in my letter—you shall have at least two sheets a day till it does sail whether it be three days or a fortnight—and then I will begin a fresh one for the next Month. The Miss Reynoldses are very kind to me—but they have lately displeased me much and in this way—Now I am coming the Richardson.* On my return, the first day I called they were in a sort of taking or bustle about a Cousin of theirs* who having fallen out with her Grandpapa in a serious manner, was invited by Mrs R—to take Asylum in her house—She is an east indian and ought to be her Grandfather's Heir. At the time I called Mrs R. was in conference with her up stairs and the young Ladies were warm in her praises down stairs calling her genteel, interesting and a thousand other pretty things to which I gave no heed, not being partial to 9 days wonders—Now all is completely changed—they hate her; and from what I hear she is not without faults—of a real kind: but she has othe[r]s which are more apt to make women of inferior charms hate her. She is not a Cleopatra; but she is at least a Charmian. She has a rich eastern look; she has fine eyes and fine manners. When she comes into a room she makes an impression the same as the Beauty of a Leopardess. She is too fine and too concious of her Self to repulse any Man who may address her—from habit she thinks that nothing *particular*.* I always find myself more at ease with such a woman; the picture before me always gives me a life and animation which I cannot possibly feel with any thing inferiour—I am at such times too much occupied in admiring to be awkward or on a tremble. I forget myself entirely because I live in her. You will by this time think I am in love with her; so before I go any further I will tell you I am not—she kept me awake one Night as a tune of Mozart's might do—I speak of the thing as a passtime and an amuzement than which I can feel none deeper than a conversation with an imperial woman the very 'yes' and 'no' of whose Lips is to me a Banquet. I dont cry to take the moon home with me in my Pocket not [*for* nor] do I fret to leave her behind me. I like her and her like because one has no *sensations*—what we both are is taken for granted—You will suppose

I have by this had much talk with her—no such thing—there are the Miss Reynoldses on the look out—They think I dont admire her because I did not stare at her—They call her a flirt to me—What a want of knowledge? she walks across a room in such a manner that a Man is drawn towards her with a magnetic Power. This they call flirting! they do not know things. They do not know what a Woman is. I believe tho' she has faults—the same as Charmian and Cleopatra might have had—Yet she is a fine thing speaking in a worldly way: for there are two distinct tempers of mind in which we judge of things—the worldly, theatrical and pantomimical; and the unearthly, spiritual and etherial—in the former Buonaparte, Lord Byron and this Charmian hold the first place in our Minds; in the latter John Howard, Bishop Hooker rocking his child's cradle* and you my dear Sister are the conquering feelings. As a Man in the world I love the rich talk of a Charmian; as an eternal Being I love the thought of you. I should like her to ruin me, and I should like you to save me. Do not think my dear Brother from this that my Passions are head long or likely to be ever of any pain to you—no

> "I am free from Men of Pleasure's cares
> By dint of feelings far more deep than theirs"

This is Lord Byron,* and is one of the finest things he has said—I have no town talk for you, as I have not been much among people—as for Politics they are in my opinion only sleepy because they will soon be too wide awake*—Perhaps not—for the long and continued Peace of England itself has given us notions of personal safety which are likely to prevent the reestablishment of our national Honesty—There is of a truth nothing manly or sterling in any part of the Government. There are many Madmen In the Country, I have no doubt, who would like to be beheaded on tower Hill merely for the sake of eclat, there are many Men like Hunt who from a principle of taste would like to see things go on better, there are many like Sir F. Burdett* who like to sit at the head of political dinners—but there are none prepared to suffer in obscurity for their Country—the motives of our wo[r]st Men are interest and of our best Vanity—We have no Milton, no Algernon Sidney*—Governers in these days loose the title of Man in exchange for that of Diplomat and Minister—We breathe in a sort of Official Atmosphere—All the departments of Government have strayed far from Spimpicity [*for* Simplicity] which is the greatest of Strength—there is as much difference in this respect between the present Government and oliver Cromwell's, as there is between the 12 Tables of Rome and the volumes of Civil Law which were digested by Justinian. A Man now entitlerd Chancellor has the same honour paid to him whether he be a Hog or a Lord Bacon. No sensation is created by Greatness but by the number of orders a Man has at his Button holes Notwithstand the part which the Liberals take in the Cause of Napoleon* I cannot but think he has done more harm to the life of Liberty than any one else could have done: not that the divine right Gentlemen have done or intend to do any good—no they have taken a Lesson of him and will do all the further harm he would have done without any of the good—The worst thing he has done is, that he has taught them how to organize their monstrous armies—The Emperor Alexander it is said intends to divide his Empire as did Diocletian—creating two Czars besides himself, and continuing the supreme Monarch of the whole—Should he do this and they for a series of Years keep peacable among themselves Russia may spread her conquest even to China—I think a very likely thing that China itself may fall Turkey certainly will—Meanwhile european north Russia will hold its horns against the rest of Europe, intrieguing constantly with France. Dilke, whom you know to be a Godwin perfectibil[it]y Man,* pleases himself with the idea that America will be the country to take up the human intellect where england leaves off—I differ there with him greatly—A country like the united states whose greatest Men are Franklins and Washingtons will never do that—They are great Men doubtless but how are they to be compared to those our countrey men Milton and the two Sidneys—The one is a philosophical Quaker full of mean and thrifty maxims the other sold the very Charger who had taken him through all his Battles—Those American's are great but they are not sublime Man—the humanity of the United States can never reach the sublime—Birkbeck's mind is too much in the American Stryle [*for* Style]—you must endeavour to infuse a little Spirit of another sort into the Settlement, always with great caution, for thereby you may do your descendents more good than you may imagine. If I had a prayer to make for any great good, next to Tom's recovery, it should be that one of your Children should be the first American Poet. I have a great mind to make a prophecy and they say prophecies work out their own fullfillment.

> 'Tis 'the witching time of night'
> Orbed is the Moon and bright
> And the Stars they glisten, glisten
> Seeming with bright eyes to listen
> For what listen they?
> For a song and for a cha[r]m
> See they glisten in alarm
> And the Moon is waxing warm
> To hear what I shall say.
> Moon keep wide thy golden ears
> Hearken Stars, and hearken Spheres
> Hearken thou eternal Sky
> I sing an infant's lullaby,
> A pretty Lullaby!
> Listen, Listen, listen, listen
> Glisten, glisten, glisten, glisten
> And hear my lullaby?
> Though the Rushes that will make
> Its cradle still are in the lake:
> Though the f linnen then that will be
> Its swathe is on the cotton tree;
> Though the wollen that will keep
> It wa[r]m, is on the silly sheep;
> Listen Stars light, listen, listen
> Glisten, Glisten, glisten, glisten
> And hear my lullaby!
> Child! I see thee! Child I've found thee
> Midst of the quiet all ~~the~~ around thee!
> Child I see thee! Ch[i]ld I spy thee
> And thy mother sweet is nigh thee!
> Child I know thee! Child no more
> But a Poet *ever*more
> See, See the Lyre, the Lyre
> In a flame of fire
> Upon the little cradle's top

Flaring, flaring, flaring.
Past the eyesight's bearing—
Awake it from its sleep
And see if it can keep
Its eyes upon the blaze.
Amaze, Amaze!
It stares, it stares, it stares
It dares what no one dares
It lifts its little hand into the flame
Unharm'd, and on the strings
                              sings
Paddles a little tune and ~~signs~~
With dumb endeavour sweetly!
Bard art thou completely!
Little Child
O' the western wild
Bard art thou completely!—
Sweetly, with dumb endeavour.—
A Poet now or never!
Litt[l]e Child
O' the western wild
A Poet now or never!

This is friday, I know not what day of the Month*—I will enquire
tomorrow for it is fit you should know the time I am writing. I went
to Town yesterday, and calling at Mʳˢ Millar's was told that your
Mother would not be found at home—I met Henry as I turned the
corner—I had no leisure to return, so I left the letters with him—He
was looking very well—Poor Tom is no better tonight—I am afraid
to ask him what Message I shall send from him—And here I could
go on complaining of my Misery, but I will keep myself cheerful for
your Sakes. With a great deal of trouble I have succeeded in getting
Fanny to Hampstead—she has been several times—Mʳ Lewis* has
been very kind to Tom all the Summer there has scar[c]e a day
passed but he has visited him, and not one day without bringing or
sending some fruit of the nicest kind. He has been very assiduous in
his enquiries after you—It would give the old Gentleman a great
pleasure if you would send him a Sheet enclosed in the next parcel to

me, after you receive this—how long it will be first—Why did I not write to Philadelphia? Really I am sorry for that neglect—I wish to go on writing ad infinitum, to you—I wish for interresting matter, and a pen as swift as the wind—But the fact is I go so little into the Crowd now that I have nothing fresh and fresh every day to speculate upon, except my own Whims and Theroies—I have been but once to Haydon's, onece to Hunt's, once to Rices, once to Hessey's I have not seen Taylor, I have not been to the Theatre—Now if I had been many times to all these and was still in the habit of going I could on my return at night have each day something new to tell you of without any stop—But now I have such a dearth that when I get to the end of this sentence and to the bottom of this page I much [*for* must] wait till I can find something interesting to you before I begin another.—After all it is not much matter what it may be about; for the very words from such a distance penned by this hand will be grateful to you—even though I were to coppy out the tale of Mother Hubbard or Little Red Riding Hood—I have been over to Dilke's this evening—there with Brown we have been talking of different and indifferent Matters—of Euclid, of Metaphisics of the Bible, of Shakspeare of the horrid System and conseque[nce]s of the fagging at great Schools—I know not yet how large a parcel I can send—I mean by way of Letters—I hope there can be no objection to my dowling up a qui[r]e made into a small compass—That is the manner in which I shall write. I shall send you more than Letters—I mean a tale—which I must begin on account of the activity of my Mind; of its inability to remain at rest—It must be prose and not very exciting. I must do this because in the way I am at present situated I have too many interruptions to a train of feeling to be able to w[r]ite Poetry—So I shall write this Tale, and if I think it worth while get a duplicate made before I send it off to you—This is a fresh beginning the 21ˢᵗ October—Charles and Henry were with us on Sunday and they brought me your Letter to your Mother—we agreed to get a Packet off to you as soon as possible. I shall dine with your Mother tomorrow, when they have promised to have their Letters ready. I shall send as soon as possible without thinking of the little you may have from me in the first parcel, as I intend as I said before to begin another Letter of more regular information. Here I want to communicate so largely in a little time that I am puzzled

where to direct my attention. Haslam has promised to let me know
from Capper and Hazlewood.* For want of something better I shall
proceed to give you some extracts from my Scotch Letters—Yet now
I think on it why not send you the letters themselves—I have three
of them at present—I beli[e]ve Haydon has two which I will get in
time. I dined with your Mother & Henry at Mrs Millar's on thursday
when they gave me their Letters Charles's I have not yet he has
promised to send it. The thought of sending my scotch Letters has
determined me to enclose a few more which I have received and
which will give you the best cue to how I am going on better than you
could otherwise know—Your Mother was well and was sorry I could
not stop later. I called on Hunt yesterday—it has been always my fate
to meet Ollier there—On thursday I walked with Hazlitt as far as
covent Garden: he was going to play Rackets—I think Tom has been
rather better these few last days—he has been less nervous. I expect
Reynolds tomorrow Since I wrote thus far I have met with that same
Lady again, whom I saw at Hastings and whom I met when we were
going to the English Opera. It was in a street which goes from
Bedford Row to Lamb's Conduit Street—I passed her and turrned
back—she seemed glad of it; glad to see me and not offended at my
passing her before We walked on towards Islington where we called
on a friend of her's who keeps a Boarding School. She has always
been an enigma to me*—she has ~~new~~ been in a Room with you and
with Reynolds and wishes we should be acquainted without any of
our common acquaintance knowing it. As we went along, some times
through shabby, sometimes through decent Street[s] I had my guessing at work, not knowing what it would be and prepared to meet any
surprise—First it ended at this Hou⟨s⟩e at Islington: on parting
from which I pressed to attend her home. She consented and then
again my thoughts were at work what it might lead to, tho' now they
had received a sort of genteel hint from the Boarding School. Our
Walk ended in 34 Gloucester Street Queen Square—not exactly so
for we went up stairs into her sitting room—a very tasty sort of place
with Books, Pictures a bronze statue of Buonaparte, Music, æolian
Harp; a Parrot a Linnet—A Case of choice Liquers &c &c &. she
behaved in the kindest manner—made me take home a Grouse for
Tom's dinner—Asked for my address for the purpose of sending
more game—As I had warmed with her before and kissed her—I

though[t] it would be living backwards not to do so again—she had a better taste: she perceived how much a thing of course it was and shrunk from it—not in a prudish way but in as I say a good taste— She cont[r]ived to disappoint me in a way which made me feel more pleasure than a simple kiss could do—she said I should please her much more if I would only press her hand and go away. Whether she was in a different disposition when I saw her before—or whether I have in fancy wrong'd her I cannot tell—I expect to pass some pleasant hours with her now and then: in which I feel I shall be of service to her in matters of knowledge and taste: if I can I will—I have no libidinous thought about her—she and your George are the only women à peu près de mon age whom I would be content to know for their mind and friendship alone—I shall in a short time write you as far as I know how I intend to pass my Life—I cannot think of those things now Tom is so unwell and weak. Notwithstand your Happiness and your recommendation I hope I shall never marry. Though the most beautiful Creature were waiting for me at the end of a Journey or a Walk; though the carpet were of Silk, the Curtains of the morning Clouds; the chairs and Sofa stuffed with Cygnet's down; the food Manna, the Wine beyond Claret, the Window opening on Winander mere, I should not feel—or rather my Happiness would not be so fine, as [*corrected from* and] my Soli- tude is sublime. Then instead of what I have described, there is a Sublimity to welcome me home—The roaring of the wind is my wife and the Stars through the window pane are my Children. The mighty abstract Idea I have of Beauty in all things stifles the more divided and minute domestic happiness—an amiable wife and sweet Children I contemplate as a part of that Bea⟨u⟩ty, but I must have a thousand of those beautiful particles to fill up my heart. I feel more and more every day, as my imagination strengthens, that I do not live in this world alone but in a thousand worlds—No sooner am I alone than shapes of epic greatness are stationed around me, and serve my Spirit the office o̶f̶ which is equivalent to a king's body guard—then 'Tragedy, with scepter'd pall, comes sweeping by" According to my state of mind I am with Achilles shouting in the Trenches or with Theocritus in the Vales of Sicily. Or I throw [*corrected from* through] my whole being into Triolus and repeating those lines, 'I wander, like a lost soul upon the stygian Banks staying for waftage,"* I melt into the air with a voluptuousness so delicate that I am content to be alone—These things combined with the opinion I have of the generallity of women—who appear to me as children to whom I would rather give a Sugar Plum than my time, form a barrier against Matrimony which I rejoice in. I have written this that you might see I have my share of the highest pleasures and that though I may choose to pass my days alone I shall be no Solitary. You see therre is nothing spleenical in all this. The only thing that can ever affect me personally for more than one short passing day, is any doubt about my powers for poetry—I seldom have any, and I look with hope to the nighing time when I shall have none. I am as happy as a Man can be—that is in myself I should be happy if Tom was well, and I knew you were passing pleasant days—Then I should be most enviable—with the yearning Passion I have for the beautiful, connected and made one with the ambition of my intellect. Th[i]nk of my Pleasure in Solitude, in comparison of my commerce with the world—there I am a child—there they do not know me not even my most intimate acquaintance—I give into their feelings as though I were refraining from irritating ⟨a⟩ little child—Some think me middling, others silly, others foolish—every one thinks he sees my weak side against my will; when in truth it is with my will—I am content to be thought all this because I have in my own breast so great a resource. This is one great reason why they like me so; because they can all show to advantage in a room, and eclipese from a certain tact one who is reckoned to be a good Poet—I hope I am not here playing tricks 'to make the angels weep': I think not: for I have not the least contempt for my species; and though it may sound paradoxical: my greatest elevations of soul leaves me every time more humbled—Enough of this—though in your Love for me you will not think it enough. Haslam has been here this morning, and has taken all the Letter's except this sheet, which I shall send him by the Twopenny, as he will put the Parcel in the Boston post Bag by the advice of Capper and Hazlewood, who assure him of the safety and expedition that way—the Parcel will be forwarded to Warder* and thence to you all the same. There will not be a Philadelphia Ship for these six weeks—by that time I shall have another Letter to you. Mind you I mark this Letter A. By the time you will receive this you will have I trust passed through the greatest of your fatigues. As it was with your Sea sickness I shall not hear of them till they are past. Do not set to your occupation with too great an a[n]xiety—take it calmly—and let your health be the prime consideration. I hope you will have a Son, and it is one of my first wishes to have him in my Arms—which I will do please God before he cuts one double tooth. Tom is rather more easy than he has been: but is still so nervous that I can not speak to him of these Matters—indeed it is the care I have had to keep his Mind aloof from feelings too acute that has made this Letter so short a one—I did not like to write before him a Letter he knew was to reach your hands—I cannot even now ask him for any Message—his heart speaks to you—Be as happy as you can. Think of me and for my sake be cheerful. Believe me my dear Brother and sister

Your anxious and affectionate Brother

John—

This day is my Birth day—
All our friends have been anxious in their enquiries and all send their rembrances

To James Rice, 24 November 1818

My dear Rice,   Well Walk—Novr 24—

Your amende honorable, I must call 'un surcroit d'amitié' for I am not at all sensible of any thing but that you were unfortunately engaged and I was unfortunately in a hurry. I completely understand your feeling in this mistake, and find in it that ballance of comfort which remains after regretting your uneasiness—I have long made up my Mind to take for granted the genuine heartedness of my friends notwithstanding any temporery ambiguousness in their behaviour or their tongues; nothing of which how[ev]er I had the least scent of this morning. I say completely understand; for I am everlastingly getting my mind into such like painful trammels—and am even at this moment suffering under them in the case of a friend of ours. I will tell you—Two most unfortunate and paralel slips—it seems downright preintention. A friend says to me 'Keats I shall go and see Severn this Week' 'Ah' says I 'You want him to take your Portrait' and again 'Keats' says a friend 'When will you come to town again' 'I will' says I 'let you have the Mss next week' In both these I appeared to attribute and [*for* an] interested motive to each of

my friends' questions—the first made him flush; the second made
him look angry—And yet I am innocent—in both cases my Mind
leapt over every interval to what I saw was per se a pleasant subject
with him—You see I have no allowances to make—you see how far I
am from supposing you could show me any neglect. I very much
regret the long time I have been obliged to exile from you—for I
have had one or two rather pleasant occasions to confer upon with
you—What I have heard from George is favorable—I expect soon a
Letter from the Settlement itself—

Your sincere friend
John Keats

I cannot give any good news of Tom—

To B. R. Haydon, 22 December 1818*

My dear Haydon,   Tuesday Wentworth Place—
    Upon my Soul I never felt your going out of the room at all—and
believe me I never rhodomontade any where but in your Company—
my general Life in Society is silence. I feel in myself all the vices of a
Poet, irritability, love of effect and admiration—and influenced by
such devils I may at times say more rediculous things than I am
aware of—but I will put a stop to that in a manner I have long
resolved upon—I will buy a gold ring and put it on my finger—and
from that time a Man of superior head shall never have occasion
to pity me, or one of inferior Nunskull to chuckle at me—I am
certainly more for greatness in a Shade than in the open day—I am
speaking as a mortal—I should say I value more the Priviledge of
seeing great things in loneliness—than the fame of a Prophet—Yet
here I am sinning—so I will turn to a thing I have thought on
more—I mean you[r] means till your Picture be finished: not only
now but for this year and half have I thought of it. Believe me
Haydon I have that sort of fire in my Heart that would sacrifice every
thing I have to your service—I speak without any reserve—I know
you would do so for me—I open my heart to you in a few words—I
will do this sooner than you shall be distressed: but let me be the last
stay—ask the rich lovers of art first—I'll tell you why—I have a little
money* which may enable me to study and to travel three or four
years—I never expect to get any thing by my Books: and moreover I

wish to avoid publishing—I admire Human Nature but I do not like *Men*—I should like to compose things honourable to Man—but not fingerable over by *Men*. So I am anxious to exist with[out] troubling the printer's devil or drawing upon Men's and Women's admiration—in which great solitude I hope God will give me strength to rejoice Try the long purses—but do not sell your drawing or I shall consider it a breach of friendship. I am sorry I was not at home when Salmon* called—Do write and let me know all you present whys and wherefores—

Your's most faithfully
John Keats

To George and Georgiana Keats,
16–18, 22, 29(?), 31 December 1818, 2–4 January 1819

B* My dear Brother and Sister,

You will have been prepared, before this reaches you for th⟨e⟩ worst news you could have, nay if Haslam's letter arrives in proper time, I have a consolation in thinking the first shock will be past before you receive this. The last days of poor Tom were of the most distressing nature; but his last moments were not so painful, and his very last was without a pang—I will not enter into any parsonic comments on death—yet the common observations of the common-est people on death are as true as their proverbs. I have scarce a doubt of immortality of some nature of [*for* or] other*—neither had Tom. My friends have been exceedingly kind to me every one of them—Brown detained me at his House. I suppose no one could have had their time made smoother than mine has been. During poor Tom's illness I was not able to write and since his death the task of beginning has been a hindrance to me. Within this last Week I have been every where—and I will tell you as nearly as possible how all go on—With Dilke and Brown I am quite thick—with Brown indeed I am going to domesticate—that is we shall keep house together—I Shall have the front parlour and he the back one—by which I shall avoid the noise of Bentley's Children—and be the better able to go on with my Studies—which [h]ave been greatly interrupted lately, so that I have not the Shadow of an idea of a book in my head, and my pen seems to have grown too goutty for verse. How are you going on now? The going[s] on of the world make me dizzy—there you are with Birkbeck—here I am with brown—sometimes I fancy an immense separation, and sometimes, as at present, a direct com-munication of spirit with you. That will be one of the grandeurs of immortality—there will be no space and consequently the only commerce between spirits will be by their intelligence of each other—when they will completely understand each other—while we in this world merely comp[r]ehend each other in different degrees— the highe⟨r⟩ the degree of good so higher is our Love and friendship—I have been so little used to writing lately that I am affraid you will not smoke my meaning so I will give an example— Suppose Brown or Haslam or any one whom I understand in the n⟨e⟩ther degree to what I do you, were in America, they would be so much the farth⟨er⟩ from me in proportion as their identity was less impressed upon me. Now the reason why I do not feel at the present moment so far from you is that I rememb⟨er⟩ your Ways and Man ners and actions; I known [*for* know] you manner of thinking, you manner of feeling: I know what shape your joy or your sorrow w⟨ou⟩ld take, I know the manner of you walking, standing, saunter- ing, sitting down, laugh⟨ing,⟩ punning, and every action so truly that you seem near to me. You will rem⟨em⟩ber me in the same manner— and the more when I tell you that I shall read a passage of Shakspeare every Sunday at ten o Clock—you read one ⟨a⟩t the same time and we shall be as near each other as blind bodies can be in the same room—I saw your Mother the day before yesterday, and intend now frequently to pass half a day with her—she sceem'd tolerably well. I called in Henrietta Street and so was speaking with you Mother about Miss Millar—we had a chat ab⟨out⟩ Heiresses—she told me I think of 7 or eight dying Swains. Charles was not at home. I think I have heard a little more talk about Miss Keasle—a⟨ll⟩ I know of her is, she had a new sort of shoe on of bright leather l⟨i⟩ke our Kna⟨p⟩sacks—Miss Millar gave me one of her confounded pinches. N.B. did not like it. Mrs Dilke went with me to see Fanny last week, and Haslam went with me last Sunday—she was well—she gets a little plumper and had a little Colour. On Sunday I brought from her a present of facescreens and a work bag for Mrs D. they were r⟨eall⟩y very pretty—From walthamstow we walked to Bethnal green*— were I fell [*for* felt] so tired from my long walk that I was obliged to go to Bed at ten—M^r and M^rs ⟨ . . . ⟩* were there—Haslam has been excess⟨iv⟩ely kind—and his anxiety about you is great⟨. I never⟩ meet him but we ⟨ha⟩ve some chat thereon⟨.⟩ He is always doing me some good turn—he gave me this thin paper for the purpose of writing to you. I have been passing an hour this morning with Mr Lewis—he wants news of you very much. Haydon was here yesterday—he amused us much by speaking of young Hopner who went with Captn Ross on a voyage of discovery to the Poles*—The Ship was sometimes entirely surrounded with vast mountains and crags of ice and in a few Minutes not a particle was to be seen all round the Horizon. Once they met with with so vast a Mass that th[e]y gave themselves over for lost; their last recourse was in meeting it with the Bowspit, which they did, and split it asunder and glided through it as it parted for a great distance—one Mile ane [*for* and] more Their eyes were so fatigued with the eternal dazzle and whiteness that they lay down on their backs upon deck to relieve their sight on the blue Sky. Hopner describes his dreadful weriness at the continual day—the sun ever moving in a circle round above their heads—so pressing upon him that he could not rid himself of the sensation even in the dark Hold of the Ship—The Esquimaux are de⟨s⟩cribed as the most wretched of Beings—they float from the Summer to their winter residences and back again like white Bears on the ice floats—They seem never to have washed, and so when their features move, the red skin shows beneath the cracking peal of dirt. They had no notion of any inhabitants in the World but themselves. The sailors who had not seen a Star for some time, when they came again southwards, on the hailing of the first revision, of one all ran upon deck with feelings of the most joyful nature. Haydon's eyes will not ⟨s⟩uffer him to proceed with his Picture—his Physician tells him he must remain two months more, inactive. Hunt keeps on in his old way—I am complete⟨ly⟩ tired of it all—He has lately publish'd a Pocket-Book call'd the litrerary Pocket-Book*—full of the most sickening stuff you can imagine. Reynolds is well—he has become an edinburgh Reviewer*—I have not heard from Bailey Rice I have seen very little of lately—and I am very sorry for it. The Miss R's are all as usual—Archer* above all people called on me one day—he wanted some information, by my means, from Hunt and Haydon, concerning some Man they knew. I got him what he wanted, but know none of the whys and wherefores. Poor Kirkman* left wentworth place one evening about ha⟨lf⟩ past eight and was stopped, beaten and robbed of his Watch in Pond Street. I saw him a few days since, he had not recovered from his bruize I called on Hazlitt the day I went to Romney Street—I gave John Hunt extracts from your Letters—he has taken no notice. I have seen Lamb lately—Brown and I were taken by Hunt to Novello's—there we were devastated and excruciated with bad and repeated puns—Brown dont want to go again. We went the other evening to see Brutus a new Trageday by Howard Payne, an American*—Kean was excellent—the play was very bad—It is the first time I have been since I went with you to the Lyceum—

Mʳˢ Brawne who took Brown's house for the Summer, still resides in Hampstead—she is a very nice woman—and her daughter senior* is ⟨I t⟩hink beautiful and elegant, graceful, silly, fashionable and strange we ⟨h⟩ave a li⟨ttle⟩ tiff now and then—and she behaves a little better, or I mus⟨t⟩ have sheered off—I find by a sidelong report from your Mother that I am to be invited to Miss Millar's birthday dance—Shall I dance with Miss Waldegrave? Eh! I shall be obliged to shirk a good many there—I s⟨hall⟩ be the only Dandy there—and indeed I merely comply with the invitation that the party may no[t] be entirely destitute of a specimen of that Race. I shall appear in a complete dress of purple Hat and all—with a list ⟨of⟩ the beauties I have conquered embroidered round my Calv⟨es.⟩

Thurs-
day This morning* is so very fine, I should have walked over to Walthamstow if I had thought of it yesterday—What are you doing this morning? Have you a clear hard frost as we have? How do you come on with the gun? Have you shot a Buffalo? Have you met with any Pheasants? My Thoughts are very frequently in a foreign Country—I live more out of England than in it—The Mountains of Tartary are a favourite lounge, if I happen to miss the Allegany ridge, or have no whim for Savoy. There must be great pleasure in pursuing game—pointing your gun—no, it wont do—now no—rabbit it—now bang—smoke and feathers—where is it? Shall you be able to get a good pointer or so? Have you seen Mʳ Trimmer—He is an acquaintance of Peachey's. Now I am not addressing miself to G. minor, and yet I am—for you are one—Have you some warm furs? By your next Letters I shall expect to hear exactly how you go on—smother nothing—let us have all—fair and foul all plain—Will the little bairn have made his entrance before you have this? Kiss it for me, and when it can first know a cheese from a Caterpillar show it my picture twice a Week—You will be glad to hear that Gifford's*

attack upon me has done me service—it has got my Book among several *Sets*—Nor must I forget to mention once more, what I suppose Haslam has told you, the present of a £25 note I had anonymously sent me—I have many things to tell you—the best way will be to make coppies of my correspondence; and I must not forget the Sonnet I received with the Note—Last Week I received the following from Woodhouse, whom you must recollect—"My dear Keats,— I send enclosed a Letter which, when read take the trouble to return to me. The History of its reaching me is this. My Cousin, Miss Frogley of Hounslow borrowed my copy of Endymion for a specified time—Before she had time to look into it; she and my friend Mr Hy Neville of Esher, who was house Surgeon to the late Princess Charlotte, insisted upon having it to read for a day or two, and undertook to make my Cousin's peace with me on account of the extra delay—Neville told me that one of the Misses Porter* (of romance Celebrity) had seen it on his table, dipped into it, and expressed a wish to read it—I desired he would keep it as long, and lend it to as many, as he pleased, provided it was not allowed to slumber on any one's shelf. I learned subsequently from Miss Frogley that these Ladies had requested of Mr Neville, if he was acquainted with the Author the Pleasure of an introduction—About a week back the enclosed was transmitted by Mr Neville to my Cousin, as a species of apology for keeping her so long without the Book—And she sent it to me, knowing it would give me Pleasure—I forward it to you for somewhat the same reason, but principally because it gives me the opportunity of naming to you (which It would have been fruitless to do before) the opening there is for an introduction to a class of society, from which you may possibly derive advantage as well as gratification, if you think proper to avail yourself of it. In such case I should be very happy to further your Wishes. But do just as you please. The whole is entirely entre nous— Your's &c—R.W." Well—now this is Miss Porter's Letter to Neville—"Dear Sir, As my Mother is sending a Messenger to Esher, I cannot but make the same the bearer of my regrets for not having had the pleasure of seeing you, the morning you called at the gate—I had given orders to be denied: I was so very unwell with my still adhæsive cold; but had I known it was you I should have taken off the interdict for a few minutes, to say, how very much I am delighted with Endymion—I had just finished the Poem, and have done as you permitted lent it to Miss Fitzgerald. I regret you are not personally acquainted with the Author: for I should have been happy to have acknowledged to him, through the advantage of your Communication the very rare delight my Sister and myself have enjoyed from this first fruits of Genius. I hope the ill-natured Review will not have damaged (or damped) such true Parnassian fire—it ought not for when Life is granted &c" and so she goes on—Now I feel more obliged than flattered by this—so obliged that I will not at present give you an extravaganza of a Lady Romancer. I will be introduced to them if it be merely for the pleasure of writing to you about it—I shall certainly see a new race of People—I shall more certainly have no time for them—Hunt has asked me to meet Tom Moore some day—so you shall hear of him. The night we went to Novello's there was a complete set to of Mozart and punning—I was so completely tired of it that if I were to follow my own inclinations I should never meet any one of that set again, not even Hunt—who is certainly a pleasant fellow in the main when you are with him—but in reallity he is vain, egotistical and disgusting in matters of taste and in morals—He understands many a beautiful thing; but then, instead of giving other minds credit for the same degree of perception as he himself possesses—he begins an explanation in such a curious manner that our taste and self-love is offended continually. Hunt does one harm by making fine things petty and beautiful things hateful— Through him I am indifferent to Mozart, I care not for white Busts—and many a glorious thing when associated with him becames [*for* becomes] a nothing—This distorts one's mind— make[s] one's thoughts bizarre—perplexes one in the standard of Beauty—Martin is very much irritated against Blackwood for printing some Letters in his Magazine which were Martin's property— he always found excuses for Blackwood till he himself was injured and now he is enraged—I have been several times thinking whether or not I should send you the examiners as Birkbeck no doubt has all the good periodical Publications—I will save them at all events.—I must not forget to mention how attentive and useful Mrs Bentley has been—I am sorry to leave her—but I must, and I hope she will not be much a looser by it—Bentley is very well—he has just brought me a cloathes' basket of Books. Brown has gone to town to day to take

his Nephews who are on a visit her[e] to see the Lions—I am passing
a Quiet day—which I have not done a long while—and if I do
continue so—I feel I must again begin with my poetry—for if I am
not in action mind or Body I am in pain—and from that I suffer
greatly by going into parties where from the rules of society and a
natural pride I am obliged to smother my Spirit and look like an
Idiot—because I feel my impulses given way to would too much
amaze them—I live under an everlasting restraint—Never relieved
except when I am composing—so I will write away. Friday. I think
you knew before you left England that my next subject would be 'the
fall of Hyperion" I went on a little with it last night—but it will take
some time to get into the vein again. I will not give you any extracts
because I wish the whole to make an impression—I have however a
few Poems which you will like and I will copy out on the next
sheet—I shall dine with Haydon on Sunday and go over to Walthamstow on Monday if the frost hold—I think also of going into Hampshire this Christmas to Mr Snooks*—they say I shall be very much
amused—But I dont know—I think I am in too huge a Mind for
study—I must do it—I must wait at home, and let those who wish
come to see me. I cannot always be (how do you spell it?) trapsing—
Here I must tell you that I have not been able to keep the journal or
write the Tale I promised—now I shall be able to do so—I will write
to Haslam this morning to know when the Packet sails and till it does
I will write someth[i]ng evey day—after that my journal shall go on
like clockwork—and you must not complain of its dullness—for
what I wish is to write a quantity to you—knowing well that dullness
itself will from me be interesting to you—You may conceive how this
not having been done has weighed upon me—I shall be able to judge
from your next what sort of information will be of most service or
amusement to you. Perhaps as you were fond of giving me sketches
of character you may like a little pic nic of scandal even across the
Atlantic—But now I must speak particularly to you my dear Sister—
for I know you love a little quizzing, better than a great bit of apple
dumpling—Do you know Uncle Red[d]all? He is a little Man with
an innocent, powdered, upright head; he lisps with a protruded
under lip—he has two Neices each one would weigh three of him—
one for height and the other for breadth—he knew Barttolozzi*—he
gave a supper and ranged his bottles of wine all up the kitchen and

cellar stairs—quite ignorant of what might be drank—it might have been a good joke to pour on the sly bottle after bottle into a washing tub and roar for more—If you were to trip him up it would discompose a Pigtail and bring his under lip nearer to his nose. He never had the good luck to loose a silk Handkerchef in a Crowd and therefore has only one topic of conversation—Bartolotzzi—Shall I give you Miss Brawn[e]? She is about my height—with a fine style of countenance of the lengthen'd sort—she wants sentiment in every feature—she manages to make her hair look well—her nostrills are fine—though a little painful—he[r] mouth is bad and good—he[r] Profil is better than her full-face which indeed is not full put [*for* but] pale and thin without showing any bone—Her shape is very graceful and so are her movements—her Arms are good her hands badish—her feet tolerable—she is not seventeen*—but she is ignorant—monstrous in her behaviour flying out in all directions, calling people such names—that I was forced lately to make use of the term *Minx*—this is I think no[t] from any innate vice but from a penchant she has for acting stylishly. I am however tired of such style and shall decline any more of it—She had a friend to visit her lately—you have known plenty such—Her face is raw as if she was standing out in a frost—her lips raw and seem always ready for a Pullet—she plays the Music without one sensation but the feel of the ivory at her fingers—she is a downright Miss without one set off—we hated her and smoked her and baited her, and I think drove her away—Miss B—thinks her a Paragon of fashion, and says she is the only woman she would change persons with—What a Stupe—She is superio[r] as a Rose to a Dandelion—When we went to bed Brown observed as he put out the Taper what an ugly old woman that Miss Robinson* would make—at which I must have groan'd aloud for I'm sure ten minutes. I have not seen the thing Kingston again—George will describe him to you—I shall insinuate some of these Creatures into a Comedy some day—and perhaps have Hunt among them—Scene, a little Parlour—Enter Hunt—Gattie*—Hazlitt—Mrs Novello—Ollier—Gattie) Ha! Hunt! got into you new house? Ha! Mrs Novello seen Altam and his Wife?* Mrs N. Yes (with a grin) *its* Mr Hunts is'nt it? Gattie. Hunts' no ha! Mr Olier I congratulate you upon the highest compliment I ever heard paid to the Book. Mr Haslit, I hope you are well (Hazlitt—yes Sir, no Sir—Mr Hunt (at the Music) La

Biondina &c M͏ʳ Hazlitt did you ever hear this—La Biondina &c—
Hazlitt—O no Sir—I never—Olier—Do Hunt give it us over
again—divino—Gattie / divino—Hunt when does your Pocket
Book come out—/ Hunt / What is this abso[r]bs me quite? O we are
sp[i]nning on a little, we shall floridize soon I hope—Such a thing
was very much wanting—people think of nothing but money-
getting—now for me I am rather inclined to the liberal side of
things—⟨but⟩ I am reckoned lax in my christian principles—& & &
&c——It is some days since I wrote the last page—and what have I
been about since I have no Idea—I dined at Haslam's on sunday—
with Haydon yesterday and saw Fanny in the morning—she was
well—just now I took out my poem to go on with it—but the
thought of my writing so little to you came upon me and I could not
get on—so I have began at random—and I have not a word to say—
and yet my thoughts are so full of you that I can do nothing else. I
shall be confined at Hampstead a few days on account of a sore
throat—the first thing I do will be to visit your Mother again—The
last time I saw Henry he show'd me his first engraving which I
thought capital—M͏ʳ Lewis called this morning and brought some
american Papers. I have not look'd into them—I think we ought to
have heard of you before this—I am in daily expectation of
Letters—Nil desperandum—M͏ʳˢ [*for* Mr.] Abbey wishes to take
Fanny from School—I shall strive all I can against that—There has
happened great Misfortune in the Drewe Family—old Drewe has
been dead some time; and lately George Drewe* expired in a fit—on
which account Reynolds has gone into Devonshire—He dined a few
days since at Horace Twisse's* with Liston and Charles Kemble*—I
see very little of him now, as I seldom go to little Britain because the
Ennui always seizes me there, and John Reynolds is very dull at
home—Nor have I seen Rice—How you are now going on is a Mystery to me—I hope a few days will clear it up. I never know the day of
the Month—It is very fine here to-day though I expect a Thunder-
cloud or rather a snow cloud in less than an hour—I am at present
alone at Wentworth place—Brown being at Chichester and M͏ʳ &
M͏ʳˢ Dilke making a little stay in Town. I know not what I should do
without a Sunshiny morning now and then—it clears up one's
spirits—Dilke and I frequently have some chat about you—I have
now and then some doubts but he seems to have a great confidence—

I think there will soon be perceptible a chance [*for* change] in the fashionable slang literature of the day—it seems to me that Reviews have had their day—that the public have been surfeited—there will soon be some new folly to keep the Parlours in talk—What it is I care not—We have seen three literary kings in our Time—Scott—Byron—and then the scotch nove⟨ls.⟩* All now appears to be dead—or I may mistake—literary Bodies may still keep up the Bustle which I do not hear—Haydon show'd me a letter he had received from Tripoli—Ritchey was well and in good Spirits, among Camels, Turbans, Palm Trees and sands—You may remember I promised to send him an Endymion which I did not—however he has one—you have one—One is in the Wilds of america—the other is on a Camel's back in the plains of Egypt. I am looking into a Book of Dubois's—he has written directions to the Players—one of them is very good. "In singing never mind the music—observe what time you please. It would be a pretty degradation indeed if you were obliged to confine your genius to the dull regularity of a fiddler—horse hair and cat's guts—no, let him keep *your* time and play *your* tune—*dodge him*"—I will now copy out the Letter and Sonnet I have spoken of—The outside cover was thus directed 'Messʳˢ Taylor and Hessey (Booksellers) No 93 Fleet Street London' and it contained this 'Messʳˢ Taylor and Hessey are requested to forward the enclosed letter by some *safe* mode of conveyance to the Author of Endymion, who is not known at Teignmouth: or if they have not his address, they will return the letter by post, directed as below, within *a fortnight* "Mʳ P. Fenbank* P.O. Teignmouth" 9ᵗʰ Novʳ 1818—In this sheet was enclosed the following—with a superscription 'Mʳ John Keats Teignmouth'—Then came Sonnet to John Keats—which I would not copy for any in the world but you—who know that I scout "mild light and loveliness" or any such nonsense in myself

> Star of high promise!—not to this dark age
>   Do thy mild light and loveliness belong;—
>   For it is blind intolerant and wrong;
> Dead to empyreal soarings, and the rage
> Of scoffing spirits bitter war doth wage
>   With all that hold integrity of song.
>   Yet thy clear beam shall shine through ages strong

To ripest times a light—and heritage.
And there breathe now who dote upon thy fame,
    Whom thy wild numbers wrap beyond their being,
Who love the freedom of thy Lays—their aim
    Above the scope of a dull tribe unseeing—
And there is one whose hand will never scant
From his poor store of fruits all *thou* can'st want.

November, 1818   turn over

I tu[r]n'd over and found a £25-note—Now this appears to me all
very proper—if I had refused it—I should have behaved in a very
bragadochio dunderheaded manner—and yet the present galls me a
little, and I do not know whether I shall not return it if I ever meet
with the donor—after whom to no purpose I have written—I have
your Minature on the Table George the great—its very like—
though not quite about the upper lip—I wish we had a better of
you little George—I must not forget to tell you that a few days
since I went with Dilke a shooting on the heath and stot [*for* shot] a
Tom-tit—There were as many guns abroad as Birds—I intended to
have been at Chichester this Wednesday—but on account of this
sore throat I wrote him (Brown) my excuse yesterday—
Thursday (I will date when I finish—I received a Note from Haslam
yesterday—asking if my letter is ready—now this is only the second
sheet—notwithstanding all my promises—But you must reflect
what hindrances I have had—However on sealing this I shall have
nothing to prevent my proceeding in a gradual journal—which will
increase in a Month to a considerable size. I will insert any little
pieces I may write—though I will not give any extracts from my
large poem* which is scarce began—I what [*for* want] to hear very
much whether Poetry and literature in general has gained or lost
interest with you—and what sort of writing is of the highest gust
with you now. With what sensation do you read Fielding?—and do
not Hogarth's pictures seem an old thing to you? Yet you are very
little more removed from general association than I am—recollect
that no Man can live but in one society at a time—his enjoyment in
the different states of human society must depend upon the Powers
of his Mind—that is you can imagine a roman triumph, or an
olympic game as well as I can. We with our bodily eyes see but the

fashion and Manners of one country for one age—and then we die—Now to me manners and customs long since passed whether among the Babylonians or the Bactrians are as real, or eveven more real than those among which I now live—My thoughts have turned lately this way—The more we know the more inadequacy we discover in the world to satisfy us—this is an old observation; but I have made up my Mind never to take any thing for granted—but even to examine the truth of the commonest proverbs—This however is true—Mrs Tighe and Beattie* once delighted me—now I see through them and can find nothing in them—or weakness—and yet how many they still delight! Perhaps a superior being may look upon Shakspeare in the same light—is it possible? No—This same inadequacy is discovered (forgive me little George you know I don't mean to put you in the mess) in Women with few exceptions—the Dress Maker, the blue Stocking and the most charming sentimentalist differ but in a Slight degree, and are equally smokeable—But I'll go no further—I may be speaking sacrilegiously—and on my word I have thought so little that I have not one opinion upon any thing except in matters of taste—I never can feel certain of any truth but from a clear perception of its Beauty—and I find myself very young minded even in that perceptive power—which I hope will encrease—A year ago I could not understand in the slightest degree Raphael's cartoons—now I begin to read them a little—and how did I lea[r]n to do so? By seeing something done in quite an opposite spirit—I mean a picture of Guido's in which all the Saints, instead of that heroic simplicity and unaffected grandeur which they inherit from Raphael, had each of them both in countenance and gesture all the canting, solemn melo dramatic mawkishness of Mackenzie's father Nicholas*—When I was last at Haydon's I look[ed] over a Book of Prints taken from the fresco of the Church at Milan the name of which I forget*—in it are comprised Specimens of the first and second age of art in Italy—I do not think I ever had a greater treat out of Shakspeare—Full of Romance and the most tender feeling—magnificence of draperies beyond any I ever saw not excepting Raphael's—But Grotesque to a curious pitch—yet still making up a fine whole—even finer to me than more accomplish'd works—as there was left so much room for Imagination. I have not heard one of this last course of Hazlitt's lecture's—They were upon

'Wit and Humour,' the english comic writers.' Saturday Jany 2nd Yesterday M^r [and] M^rs D and myself dined at Mrs Brawne's— nothing particular passed. I never intend here after to spend any time with Ladies unless they are handsome—you lose time to no purpose—For that reason I shall beg leave to decline going again to Redall's or Butlers or any Squad where a fine feature cannot be mustered among them all—and where all the evening's amusement consists in saying your good health' *your* good health, and YOUR good health—and (o I beg you pardon) your's Miss——.and such thing[s] not even dull enough to keep one awake—with respect to amiable speaking I can read—let my eyes be fed or I'll never go out to dinner any where—Perhaps you may have heard of the dinner given to Thos Moore in Dublin, because I have the account here by me in the Philadelphia democratic paper—The most pleasant thing that accured was the speech Mr Tom made on his Farthers health being drank—I am affraid a great part of my Letters are filled up with promises and what I will do rather than any great deal written—but here I say once for all—that circumstances prevented me from keeping my promise in my last, but now I affirm that as there will be nothing to hinder me I will keep a journal for you. That I have not yet done so you would forgive if you knew how many hours I have been repenting of my neglect—For I have no thought pervading me so constantly and frequently as that of you— my Poeem cannot frequently drive it away—you will retard it much more that [*for* than] You could by taking up my time if you were in England—I never forget you except after seeing now and then some beautiful woman—but that is a fever—the thought of you both is a passion with me but for the most part a calm one—I asked Dilke for a few lines for you—he has promised them—I shall send what I have written to Haslam on Monday Morning. what I can get into another sheet tomorrow I will—there are one or two little poems you might like—I have given up snuff very nearly quite—Dilke has promised to sit with me this evening, I wish he would come this minute for I want a pinch of snuff very much just now—I have none though in my own snuff box—My sore throat is much better to day—I think I might venture on a crust—Here are the Poems— they will explain themselves—as all poeems should do without any comment

Ever let the Fancy roam,
Pleasure never is at home.
At a touch sweet pleasure melteth
Like no bubbles when rain pelteth:
Then let winged fancy wander
To wards heaven still spread beyond her—
Open wide the mind's cage door
She'll dart forth and cloudward soar.
O sweet Fancy, let her loose!
Summer's joys are spoilt by use,
And the enjoying of the spring
Fades as doth its blossoming:
Autumn's red-lipp'd fruitage too
Blushing through the mist and dew
Cloys with kissing. What do then?
Sit thee in an ingle when
The sear faggot blazes bright,
Spirit of a winter night;
When the soundless earth is muffled,
And the caked snow is shuffled
From the Ploughboy's heavy shoon:
When the night doth meet the noon
In a dark conspiracy
To banish vesper from the sky.
Sit thee then and send abroad
With a Mind self overaw'd
Fancy high commission'd; send her,—
She'll have vassals to attend her—
She will bring thee, spite of frost,
Beauties that the Earth has lost;
She will bring thee all together
All delights of summer weather;
All the faery buds of May
On sp[r]ing turf or scented spray;
All the heaped Autumn's wealth
With a still, mysterious stealth;
She will mix these pleasures up,
Like three fit wines in a cup

And thou shalt quaff it—Thou shalt hear
Distant harvest carols clear,
Rustle of the reaped corn
Sweet Birds antheming the Morn;
And in the same moment hark
To the early April lark,
And the rooks with busy caw
Forraging for sticks and straw.
Thou shalt at one glance behold
The daisy and the marigold;
White plumed lillies and the first
Hegd⟨er⟩ow primrose that hath burst;
Shaded Hyacynth alway
Sapphire Queen of the Mid-may;—
And every leaf and every flower
Pearled with the same soft shower.
Thou shalt see the fieldmouse creep
Meagre from its celled sleep,
And the snake all winter shrank
Cast its skin on sunny bank;
Freckled nest eggs shalt thou see
Hatching in the hawthorn tree;
When the hen bird's wing doth rest
Quiet on its mossy nest—
Then the hurry and alarm
When the Beehive casts its swa[r]m—
Acorn's ripe down pattering
While the autumn breezes sing,
For the same sleek throated mouse
To store up in its winter house.
    O sweet Fancy, let her loose!
Evey joy is spoilt by use,
Every pleasure, every joy—
Not a Mistress but doth cloy.
Wheere's the cheek that doth not fade
Too much gaz'd at? Where's the Maid
Whose lip mature is ever new?
Where's the eye however blue

Doth not weary? Where's the face
One would meet in every place?
Where's the voice however soft
One would hear too oft and oft?
At a touch sweet pleasure melteth
Like to bubbles when rain pelteth.
Let then winged fancy find
Thee a Mistress to thy mind.
Dulcet-eyed as Cere's daughter
Ere the God of torment taught her
How to frown and how to chide:
With a waist, and with a side
White as Hebe's when her Zone
Slipp'd its golden clasp, and down
Fell her kirtle to her feet,
While she held the goblet sweet,
And Jove grew languid—Mistress fair,
Thou shalt have that tressed hair
Adonis tangled all for spite;
And the mouth he would not kiss,
And the treasure he would miss,
And the hand he would not press,
And the warmth he would distress,
    O the Ravishment—the Bliss!
Fancy has her there she is—
Never fulsome, ever new,
There she steps! and tell me who
Has a Mistress to [*for* so] divine?
Be the palate ne'er so fine
She cannot sicken.
                    Break the Mess [*for* Mesh]
Of the Fancy's silken leash
Where she's tether'd to the heart—
Quickly break her prison string
And such joys as these she'll bring
Let the winged fancy roam
Pleasure never is at home.

I did not think this had been so long a Poem—I have another not so long—but as it will more conveniently be coppied on the other side I will just put down here some observations on Caleb Williams by Hazlitt*—I meant to say St Leon for although he has mentioned all the Novels of Godwin very finely I do not quote them, but this only on account of its being a specimen of his usual abrupt manner, and fiery laconiscism—He says of St Leon 'He is a limb torn off from Society. In possession of eternal youth and beauty, he can feel no love; surrounded, tantalized and tormented with riches, he can do no good. The faces of Men pass before him as in a speculum; but he is attached to them by no common tie of sympathy or suffering. He is thrown back into himself and his own thoughts. He lives in the solitude of his own breast,—without wife or child or friend or Enemy in the world. *His is the solitude of the Soul, not of woods, or trees or mountains*—but the desert of society—the waste and oblivi[on] of the heart. He is himself alone. His existence is purely intellectual, and is therefore intolerable to one who has felt the rapture of affection, or the anguish of woe. .' As I am about it I might as well give you his caracter of Godwin as a Romancer "Whoever else is, it is pretty clear that the author of Caleb Williams is not the Author of waverly. Nothing can be more distinct or excellent in their several ways than these two writers. If the one owes almost every thing to external observation and traditional character, the other owes every thing to internal conception and contemplation of the possible workings of the human Mind. There is little knowledge of the world, little variety, neither an eye for the picturesque, nor a talent for the humourous in Caleb Williams, for instance, but you can not doubt for a moment of the originality of the work and the force of the conception. The impression made upon the reader is the exact measure of the strength of the authors genius. For the effect in Caleb Williams and St Leon, is entirely made out, not by facts nor dates, by blackletter or magazine learning, by transcript nor record, but by intense and patient study of the human heart, and by an imagination projecting itself into certain situations, and capable of working up its imaginary feelings to the height of reality." This appears to me quite correct—now I will copy the other Poem—it is on the double immortality of Poets—

Bards of Passion and of Mirth
Ye have left your souls on earth—
Have ye souls in heaven too
Double liv'd in regions new?
Yes—and those of heaven commune
With the s[p]heres of Sun & Moon;
With the noise of fountains wondrous,
And the parle of voices thundrous;
With the Whisper of heavens trees,
And one anothers, in soft ease
Seated on elysian Lawns,
Browsed by none but Dian's fawns;
Underneath large bluebells tented
Where the daisies are rose scented,
And the rose herself has got
Perfume that on Earth is not.
Where the nightingale doth sing
Not a senseless tranced thing;
But melodious truth divin
Philosophic numbers fine;
Tales and golden histories
Of Heaven and its Mysteries.

    Thus ye live on Earth and then
On the Earth ye live again;
And the souls ye left behind you
Teach us here the way to find you,
Where your other Souls are joying
Never slumber'd, never cloying.
Here your earth born souls still speak
To mortals of the little week
They must sojourn with their cares;
Of their sorrows and delights
Of their Passions and their spites;
Of their glory and their shame—
What doth strengthen and what maim.
Thus ye teach us every day
Wisdom though fled far away.
    Bards of Passion and of Mirth

> Ye have left your Souls on Earth
> Ye have souls in heaven too
> Double liv'd in Regions new!

These are specimens of a sort of rondeau which I think I shall become partial to—because you have one idea amplified with greater ease and more delight and freedom than in the sonnet—It is my intention to wait a few years before I publish any minor poems—and then I hope to have a volume of some worth—and which those people will realish who cannot bear the burthen of a long poem—In my journal I intend to copy the poems I write the days they are written—there is just room I see in this page to copy a little thing I wrote off to some Music as it was playing—

> I had a dove and the sweet dove died,
>   And I have thought it died of grieving:
> O what could it mourn for? it was tied
>   With a silken thread of my own hands weaving.
> Sweet little red-feet why did you die?
> Why would you leave me—sweet dove why?
> You live'd alone on the forest tree
> Why pretty thing could you not live with me?
> I kiss'd you oft, and I gave you white peas—
> Why not live sweet⟨ly as⟩ in the green trees—

Sunday.*
I have been dining with Dilke to day—He is up to his Ears in Walpole's letters Mr Manker* is there; I have come round to see if I can conjure up any thing for you—Kirkman came down to see me this morning—his family has been very badly off lately—He told me of a villainous trick of his Uncle William [Mathew] in Newgate Street who became sole Creditor to his father under pretence of serving him, and put an execution on his own Sister's goods—He went in to the family at Portsmouth; conversed with them, went out and sent in the Sherif's officer—He tells me too of abominable behaviour of Archer to Caroline Mathew—Archer has lived nearly at the Mathews these two years; he has been amusing Caroline all this time—and now he has written a Letter to Mrs M—declining on pretence of inability to support a wife as he would wish, all thoughts

of marriage. What is the worst is, Caroline is 27 years old*—It is an
abominable matter—He has called upon me twice lately—I was out
both times—What can it be for—There is a letter to day in the
Examiner to the Electors of westminster on Mr Hobhouse's
account—In it there is a good Character of Cobbet*—I have not the
paper by me or I would copy it—I do not think I have mentioned the
Discovery of an african kingdom—the account is much the same as
the first accounts of Mexico—all magnificence—there is a Book
being written about it*—I will read it and give you the cream in my
next. The ramance we have heard upon it runs thus: they have
window frames of gold—100,000 infantry—human sacrifices—The
Gentleman who is the adventurer has his wife with him—she I am
told is a beautiful little sylphid woman—her husband was to ha⟨ve⟩
been sacrificed to their Gods and was led through a Chamber filled
with different instruments of torture with priveledge to choose what
death he would die, without their having a thought of his aversion to
such a death they considering it a supreme distinction—However he
was let off and became a favorite with the King, who at last openly
patronised him; thoug⟨h⟩ at first on account of the Jealousy of his
Ministers he was wont to hold conversations with his Majesty in the
dark middle of the night—All this sounds a little Blue-beardish—
but I hope it is true—There is another thing I must mention of the
momentous kind;—but I must mind my periods in it—Mrs Dilke has
two Cats—a Mother and a Daughter—now the Mother is a tabby
and the daughter a black and white like the spotted child—Now it
appears ominous to me for the doors of both houses are opened
frequently—so that there is a complete thorough fare for both Cats
(there being no board up to the contrary) they may one and several
of them come into my room ad libitum. But no—the Tabby only
comes—whether from sympathy from ann the mai⟨d⟩ or me I can
not tell—or whether Brown has left behind him any atmospheric
sp[i]rit of Maidenhood I can not tell. The Cat is not an old Maid
herself—her daughter is a proof of it—I have questioned her—I
have look'd at the lines of her paw—I have felt her pulse—to no
purpose—Why should the *old* Cat come to me? I ask myself—and
myself has not a word to answer. It may come to light some day; if it
does you shall hear of it⟨.⟩ Kirkman this morning promised to write a
few lines for you and send them to Haslam. I do not think I have any

thing to say in the Business way—You will let me know what you would wish done with your property in England—What things you would wish sent out—but I am quite in the dark about what you are doing—if I do not hear soon I shall put on my Wings and be after you—I will in my next, and after I have seen your next letter—tell you my own particular idea of America. Your next letter will be the key by which I shall open your hearts and see what spaces want filling, with any particular information—Whether the affairs of Europe are more or less interesting to you—whether you would like to hear of the Theatre's—of the bear Garden—of the Boxers—the Painters—The Lecturers—the Dress—The Progress of Dandyism—The Progress of Courtship—or the fate of Mary Millar—being a full true and très particular account of Miss M's ten Suitors—How the first tried the effect of swearing; the second of stammering; the thi[r]d of whispering;—the fourth of sonnets—the fifth of spanish leather boots the sixth of flattering her body—the seventh of flattering her mind—the eighth of flattering himself—the ninth stuck to the Mother—the tenth kissed the Chambermaid and told her to tell her Mistress—But he was soon discharged his reading lead him into an error—he could not sport the Sir Lucius* to any advantage—And now for this time I bid you good by—I have been thing [for thinking] of these sheets so long that I appear in closing them to take my leave of you—but that is not it—I shall immediately as I send this off begin my journal—when some days ⟨I⟩ shall write no more than 10 lines and others 10 times as much⟨.⟩ Mrs Dilke is knocking at the wall for Tea is ready—I will tell you what sort of a tea it is and then bid you—Good bye—This is monday morning—no thing particular happened yesterday evening, except that ⟨just⟩ when the tray came up Mrs Dilke and I had a battle with celery stalks—she sends her love to you—I shall close this and send it immediately to Haslam—remaining ever

My dearest brother and sister
Your most affectionate Brother
John—

To B. R. Haydon, 10 (?) January 1819

My dear Haydon,   Wentworth place

We are very unlucky—I should have stopped to dine with you, but I knew I should not have been able to leave you in time for my plaguy sore throat; which is getting well—

I shall have a little trouble in procuring the Money* and a great ordeal to go through—No trouble indeed to any one else—or ordeal either—I mean I shall have to go to town some thrice, and stand in the Bank an hour or two—to me worse than any thing in Dante—I should have less chance with the people around me than Orpheus had with the Stones—I have been writing a little now and then lately: but nothing to speak off—being discontented and as it were moulting—yet I do not think I shall ever come to the rope or the Pistol: for after a day or two's melancholy, although I smoke* more and more my own insufficiency—I see by little and little more of what is to be done, and how it is to be done, should I ever be able to do it—On my Soul there should be some reward for that continual 'agonie ennuiyeuse." I was thinking of going into Hampshire for a few days: I have been delaying it longer than I intended—You shall see me soon; and do not be at all anxious, for *this* time I really will do, what I never did before in my life, business in good time, and properly—With respect to the Bond—it may be a satisfaction to you, to let me have it: but as you love me do not let there be any mention of interest, although we are mortal men—and bind ourselves for fear of death—

Your's for ever

John Keats—

To Fanny Keats, 11 February 1819

My dear Fanny,   Wentworth Place—

Feb^y—Thursday—

Your Letter to me at Bedhampton hurt me very much,—What objection can the[r]e be to your receiving a Letter from me? At Bedhampton I was unwell and did not go out of the Garden Gate but twice or thrice during the fortnight I was there—Since I came back I have been taking care of myself—I have been obliged to do so, and am now in hopes that by this care I shall get rid of a sore throat which has haunted me at intervals nearly a twelvemonth. I had always a presentiment of not being able to succeed in persuading Mr Abbey to let you remain longer at School—I am very sorry that he will not consent. I recommend you to keep up all that you know and to learn more by yourself however little. The time will come when you will be more pleased with Life—look forward to that time and, though it may appear a trifle, be careful not to let the idle and retired Life you lead fix any awkward habit or behaviour on you—whether you Sit or walk—endeavour to let it be in a seemly and if possible a graceful manner. We have been very little together: but you have not the less been with me in thought—You have no one in the world besides me who would sacrifice any thing for you—I feel myself the only Protector you have. In all your little troubles think of me with the thought that there is at least one person in England who if he could would help you out of them—I live in hopes of being able to make you happy—I should not perhaps write in this manner, if it were not for the fear of not being able to see you often, or long together—I am in hopes Mr Abbey will not object any more to your receiving a letter now and then from me—How unreasonable!—I want a few more lines from you for George—there are some young Men, acquaintances of a School-fellow of mine,* going out to Birkbeck's at the latter end of this Month—I am in expectation every day of hearing from George—I begin to fear his last letters Miscarried. I shall be in town tomorrow—if you should not be in town, I shall send this little parcel by the Walthamstow Coach. I think you will like Goldsmith. Write me soon—

Your affectionate Brother

John—

Wentworth Place—

My dear Haydon,

to day for exercise

To B. R. Haydon, 18 (?) February 1819

My dear Haydon,   Wentworth Place—

My throat has not suffered me yet to expose myself to the night air: however I have been to town in the day time—have had several interviews with my guardian—have written him a rather plain spoken Letter—which has had its effect; and he now seems inclined to put no stumbling block in my way: so that I see a good prospect of performing my promise What I should have lent you ere this if I could have got it, was belonging to poor Tom—and the difficulty is whether I am to inherit it before my Sister is of age; a period of six years—Should it be so I must incontinently take to Corderoy Trowsers. But I am nearly confident 't is all a Bam*—I shall see you soon—but do let me have a line to day or tomorrow concerning your health and spirits   Your sincere friend

John Keats

To Fanny Keats, 27 February 1819

My dear Fanny,   Wentworth Place Saturday Morn—

I intended to have not failed to do as you requested, and write you as you say once a fortnight. On looking to your letter I find there is no date; and not knowing how long it is since I received it I do not precisely know how great a sinner I am—I am getting quite well; and Mrs Dilke is getting on pretty well—You must pay no attention to Mrs Abbey's unfeeling and ignorant gabble—You can't stop an old woman's crying more than you can a Child's—The old woman is the greatest nuisance because she is too old for the rod. Many people live opposite a Blaksmith's till they cannot hear the hammer—I have been in Town for two or three days and came back last night. I have been a little concerned at not hearing from George—I continue in daily expectation. Keep on reading and play as much on the music and the grassplot as you can. I should like to take possession of those Grasplots for a Month or so; and send Mrs A—to Town to count coffee berries instead of currant Bunches, for I want you to teach me a few common dancing steps—and I would buy a Watch box to practise them in by myself—I think I had better always pay the postage of these Letters. I shall send you another book the first time I am in Town early enough to book it with one of the morning Walthamstow Coaches—You did not say a word about your Chilblains—Write me directly and let me know about them—Your Letter shall be answered like an echo—

Your affectionate Brother

John—

To B. R. Haydon, 8 March 1819

My dear Haydon,

You must be wondering where I am and what I am about! I am mostly at Hampstead, and about nothing; being in a sort of qui bono temper,* not exactly on the road to an epic poem. Nor must you think I have forgotten you. No, I have about every three days been to Abbey's and to the Law[y]ers. Do let me know how you have been getting on, and in what spirits you are.

You got out gloriously in yesterday's Examiner.* What a set of little people we live amongst. I went the other day into an iron-monger's shop, without any change in my sensations—men and tin kettles are much the same in these days. They do not study like children at five and thirty, but they talk like men at twenty. Conversation is not a search after knowledge, but an endeavour at effect. In this respect two most opposite men, Wordsworth and Hunt, are the same.* A friend of mine observed the other day that if Lord Bacon were to make any remark in a party of the present day, the conversation would stop on the sudden. I am convinced of this, and from this I have come to the resolution never to write for the sake of writing, or making a poem, but from running over with any little knowledge and experience which many years of reflection may perhaps give me—otherwise I will be dumb. What Imagination I have I shall enjoy, and greatly, for I have experienced the satisfaction of having great conceptions without the toil of sonnetteering. I will not spoil my love of gloom by writing an ode to darkness; and with respect to my liveli-hood I will not write for it, for I will not mix with that most vulgar of all crowds the literary. Such things I ratify by looking upon myself, and trying myself at lifting mental weights, as it were. I am three and twenty with little knowledge and middling intellect. It is true that in the height of enthusiasm I have been cheated into some fine passages, but that is nothing.

I have not been to see you because all my going out has been to town, and that has been a great deal. Write soon.

Yours constantly,
John Keats

To Fanny Keats, 13 March 1819

Wentworth Place

My dear Fanny,   March 13th

I have been employed lately in writing to George,—I do not send
him very short letters—but keep on day after day—There were some
young Men I think I told you of who were going to the Settlement:
they have changed their minds, and I am disappointed in my expectation of sending Letters by them—I went lately to the only dance I
have been to these twelve months or shall go to for twelve months
again—it was to our Brother in laws' cousin's—She gave a dance for
her Birthday and I went for the sake of Mrs Wylie—I am waiting every
day to hear from George. I trust there is no harm in the silence: other
people are in the same expectation as we are—On looking at your seal
I cannot tell whether it is done or not with a Tassi*—it seems to me to
be paste—As I went through Leicester Square lately I was going to
call and buy you some, but not knowing but you might have some I
would not run the chance of buying duplicates—Tell me if you have
any or if you would like any—and whether you would rather have
motto ones like that with which I seal this letter; or heads of great
Men such as Shakspeare, Milton &c—or fancy pieces of Art; such as
Fame, Adonis &c—those gentry you read of at the end of the English
Dictionary. Tell me also if you want any particular Book; or Pencils, or
drawing paper—any thing but live Stock—Though I will not now be
very severe on it, remembring how fond I used to be of Goldfinches,
Tomtits, Minnows, Mice, Ticklebacks, Dace, Cock salmons and all
the whole tribe of the Bushes and the Brooks: but verily they are
better in the Trees and the water—though I must confess even now a
partiality for a handsome Globe of goldfish—then I would have it
hold 10 pails of water and be fed continually fresh through a cool pipe
with another pipe to let through the floor—well ventilated they would
preserve all their beautiful silver and Crimson—Then I would put it
before a handsome painted window and shade it all round with
myrtles and Japonicas. I should like the window to open onto the
Lake of Geneva—and there I'd sit and read all day like the picture of
somebody reading—The weather now and then begins to feel like
spring; and therefore I have begun my walks on the heath again. M^{rs}
Dilke is getting better than she has been as she has at length taken a

Physician's advice—She ever and anon asks after you and always bids me remember her in my Letters to you—She is going to leave Hampstead for the sake of educating their Son Charles at the Westminster school.* We (Mr Brown and I) shall leave in the beginning of may; I do not know what I shall do or where be all the next Summer. Mrs Reynolds has had a sick house; but they are all well now—You see what news I can send you I do—we all live one day like the other as well as you do—the only difference is being sick and well—with the variations of single and double knocks; and the story of a dreadful fire in the Newspapers—I mentioned Mr Brown's name—yet I do not think I ever said a word about him to you—He is a friend of mine of two years standing—with whom I walked through Scotland; who has been very kind to me in many things when I most wanted his assistance and with whom I keep house till the first of M⟨ay—⟩ you will know him some day. The name of ⟨the⟩ young Man who came with me is—William Haslam—Ever, Your affectionate Brother
John.

To Joseph Severn, 29 March 1819

My dear Severn,   Wentworth Place—
Monday—af^t

Your note gave me some pain, not on my own account, but on yours—Of course I should mev [*for* never] suffer any petty vanity of mine to hinder you in any wise; and therefore I should say, 'put the miniature in the exhibition'* if only myself was to be hurt. But, will it not hurt you? What good can it do to any future picture—Even a large picture is lost in that canting place—what a drop of water in the ocean is a Miniature. Those who might chance to see it for the most part if they had ever heard of either of us—and know what we were and of what years would laugh at the puff of the one and the vanity of the other I am however in these matters a very bad judge—and would advise you to act in a way that appears to yourself the best for your interest. As your He[r]mia and Helena is finished send that without the prologue of a Miniature. I shall see you soon, if you do not pay me a visit sooner—there's a Bull for you.

Yours ever sincerely
John Keats—

To Fanny Keats, 31 March 1819

Wednesday—

My dear Fanny,

I shall be going to town tomorrow and will call at the Nursery on the road for those roots and seeds you want, which I will send by the Walthamstow stage. The best way, I thought, for you to lea[r]n to answer those questions,* is to read over the little book, which I sent from a Bookseller's in town, or you should have had a Letter with it—Tell me whether it will do: if not I will put down the answers for you—I have not yet heard from George—Perhaps if I just give you the heads of the answers it may be better—though I think you will find them all in that little book—

Ans^r 1—It was instituted by John the Baptist when he baptised those people in the river Jordan who beleved through him in the coming of Christ—and more particularly when he baptised christ himself.

2   It corresponds to the Jewish Circumscision

3   The meaning is that we are confirmed members of Christ It is not administered till 14 years of age because before that age the mind [is] not judged to be sufficiently mature and capable. The act of confirmation imposes on the Christian self circumspection; as by that ceremony the Christian duties of God fathers and god-mothers is annulled and put and end to—as you see in the catechisim—"they promise and vow three things in my name"—Confirmation absolves this obligation.

4   There are two Sacraments of our Church—Baptisim and the Lord's Supper. The Church of Rome has seven Sacraments. The church of Rome includes several ceremonies (I forget what they are) and the civil rite of marriage—I believe Confi[r]mation is a Sacrament with them—Extreme unction or the annointing the extremities of dying persons with holy water. The reason why we have but two Sacraments is—that it is proved from the Scriptures by the great protestant reformers—that only two are commanded by god—the rest adopted by the Church of Rome are human institutions.

5   You must here repeat your belief—and say the question is to hard for you.

6   Look in Isaia for "*A virgin shall conceive*" &c—Look in the Psalms for "*The Kings of the Earth set themselves and the Princes take*

counsel together" and "*they parted my Garments among them* &" and
"*My god, my god why has thou forsaken me* &c" In Jeremia "*Comfort
ye, comfort ye* &" In Daniel The stone cut out of the mountain
without hands that breaks the image in pieces is a type of the
Kingdom of Christ—Look at the 2ⁿᵈ Chat. Isaiah—Chap 7–9—'*For
unto us a Child is bo*[*r*]*n*" 11—Jeremiah Chap xxxi Micah Chap 5—
Zechariah Chap 6 and Chap 13 *verse* 6. Those I have marked will
be sufficient—You will remember their completion in the new
testament—

7ᵗʰ The communion of saints is the fruition they enjoy in heaven
among one another and in the Divinity of Christ—

8ᵗʰ It was instituded on the night of the feast of the Passover at the
Last supper with the Twelve; the night Judas betrayed Christ—and
you may see in the 26 Mathew—It corresponds to the "Feast of the
Passover in the Jewish Ritual—

9   They expected Christ to be a temporal Prince and being
disappointed, rejected him—

10   Look to the Catechisim—'What is your duty towards God?

11ᵗʰ The Prophecy to our first parents is this—Genesis 3 Chapter
—verse [15] "And I will put enmity between thee and the woman
and between thy seed and her seed; *it shall bruize thy head* and thou
shall bruize his heel—Christ the Son of David by dying on the Cross
triumphed over death and the grave from which he saved mankind;
and in that way did he 'bruize the Serpent's head"—

Your affectionate Parson

John—

To Fanny Keats, *12 April 1819*

My dear Fanny,   Wentworth Place
    I have been expecting a Letter from you about what the Parson
said to your answers—I have thought also of writing to you often, and
I am sorry to confess that my neglect of it has been but a small
instance of my idleness of late—which has been growing upon me, so
that it will require a great shake to get rid of it. I have written nothing,
and almost read nothing—but I must turn over a new leaf—One
most discouraging thing hinders me—we have no news yet from
George—so that I cannot with any confidence continue the Letter I

have been preparing for him. Many are in the same state with us and many have heard from the Settlement—They must be well however: and we must consider this silence as good news—I ordered some bulbous roots for you at the Gardeners, and they sent me some, but they were all in bud—and could not be sent, so I put them in our Garden There are some beautiful heaths now in bloom in Pots—either heaths or some seasonable plants I will send you instead—perhaps some that are not yet in bloom that you may see them come out—Tomorrow night I am going to a rout—a thing I am not at all in love with—Mr Dilke and his Family have left Hampstead—I shall dine with them to day in Westminster where I think I told you they were going to reside for the sake of sending their Son Charles to the ~~Blue~~ Westminster School. I think I mentioned the Death of Mr Haslam's Father—Yesterday week the two Mr Wylies dined with me. I hope you have good store of double violets—I think they are the Princesses of flowers and in a shower of rain, almost as fine as barley sugar drops are to a schoolboy's tongue. I suppose this fine weather the lambs tails give a frisk or two extraordinary—when a boy would cry huzza and a Girl O my! a little Lamb frisks its tail. I have not been lately through Leicester Square—the first time I do I will remember your Seals—I have thought it best to live in Town this Summer, chiefly for the sake of books, which cannot be had with any comfort in the Country—besides my Scotch jou[r]ney gave me a doze of the Picturesque with which I ought to be contented for some time. Westminster is the place I have pitched upon—the City or any place very confined would soon turn me pale and thin—which is to be avoided. You must make up your mind to get Stout this summer—indeed I have an idea we shall both be corpu⟨lent⟩ old folkes with tripple chins and stum⟨py⟩ thumbs—

> Your affectionate Brother
>
> John

To B. R. Haydon, *13 April 1819*

My dear Haydon,   Tuesday—

When I offered you assistance I thought I had it in my hand; I thought I had nothing to do, but to do. The difficulties I met with arose from the alertness and suspicion of Abbey; and especially

from the affairs being still in a Law[y]er's* hand—who has been
drain[i]ng our Property for the last 6 years of evey charge he could
make—I cannot do two things at once, and thus this affair has
stopped my pursuits in every way—from the first prospect I had of
difficulty. I assure you I have harrassed myself 10 times more than if
I alone had been concernned in so much gain or loss. I have also ever
told you the exact particulars as well as and as literally as my hopes
or fear could translate them—for it was only by parcels that I found
all those petty obstacles which for my own sake should not exist a
moment—and yet why not—for from my own imprudence and neglect all my accounts are entirely in my Guardians Power—This has
taught me a Lesson. hereafter I will be more correct. I find myself
possessed of much less than I thought for* and now if I had all on the
table all I could do would be to take from it a moderate two years
subsistence and lend you the rest; but I cannot say how soon I could
become possessed of it. This would be no sacrifice nor any matter
worth thinking of—much less than parting as I have more than once
done with little sums which might have gradually formed a library to
my taste—These sums amount to gether to nearly 200, which I have
but a chance of ever being repaid or paid at a very distant period. I
am humble enough to put this in writing from the sense I have of
your struggling situation and the great desire that you should [do]
me the justice to credit the unostentatious and willing state of my
nerves on all such occasions. It has not been my fault—I am doubly
hurt at the slight[l]y rep[r]oachful tone of your note ~~as well as~~ and at
the occasion of it,—for it must be some other disappointment; you
seem'd so sure of some important help when I last saw you—now
you have maimed me again; I was whole I had began reading again—
when your note came I was engaged in a Book—I dread as much as a
Plague the idle fever of two months more without any fruit. I will
walk over the first fine day: then see what aspect you affairs have
taken, and if they should continue gloomy walk into the City to
Abbey and get his consent for I am persuaded that to me alone he
will not concede a jot

To Fanny Keats, 1 May 1819

My dear Fanny,   Wentworth Place Saturday—

If it were but six o Clock in the morning I would set off to see you to day: if I should do so now I could not stop long enough for a how d'ye do—it is so long a walk through Hornsey and Tottenham—and as for Stage Coaching it besides that it is very expensive it is like going into the Boxes by way of the pit—I cannot go out on Sunday—but if on Monday it should promise as fair as to day I will put on a pair of loose easy palatable boots and me rendre chez vous—I continue increasing my letter to George to send it by one of Birkbeck's sons who is going out soon—so if you will let me have a few more lines, they will be in time—I am glad you got on so well with Monsr le Curè—is he a nice Clergyman—a great deal depends upon a cock'd hat and powder—not gun powder, lord love us, but lady-meal, violet-smooth, dainty-scented lilly-white, feather-soft, wigsby-dressing, coat-collar-spoiling whisker-reaching, pig-tail loving, swans down-puffing, parson-sweetening powder—I shall call in passing at the tottenham nursery and see if I can find some seasonable plants for you. That is the nearest place—or by our la' kin or lady kin, that is by the virgin Mary's kindred, is there not a twig-manufacturer in Walthamstow? M^r & Mrs Dilke are coming to dine with us to day—they will enjoy the country after Westminster—O there is nothing like fine weather, and health, and Books, and a fine country, and a contented Mind, and Diligent-habit of reading and thinking, and an amulet against the ennui—and, please heaven, a little claret-wine cool out of a cellar a mile deep—with a few or a good many ratafia cakes—a rocky basin to bathe in, a strawberry bed to say your prayers to Flora in, a pad nag to go you ten miles or so; two or three sensible people to chat with; two or th[r]ee spiteful folkes to spar with; two or three odd fishes to laugh at and two or three numskuls to argue with—instead of using dumb bells on a rainy day—

> Two or th[r]ee Posies
> With two or th[r]ee simples
> Two or three Noses
> With two or th[r]ee pimples—

> Two or th[r]ee wise men
> And two or three ninny's
> Two or th[r]ee purses
> And two or three guineas
> Two or three raps
> At two or three doors
> Two or three naps
> Of two or three hours—
> Two or th[r]ee Cats
> And two or three mice
> Two or th[r]ee sprats
> At a very great price—
> Two or three sandies
> And two or three tabbies
> Two or th[r]ee dandies—
> And two M^rs——mum!
> Two or three Smiles
> And two or three frowns
> Two or th[r]ee Miles
> To two or three towns
> Two or three pegs
> For two or three bonnets
> Two or three dove's eggs
> To hatch into sonnets—

Good bye I've an appoantment—can't stop pon word—good bye—
now dont get up—open the door myself—go-o-o d bye—see ye
Monday

                                                    J—K—

To George and Georgiana Keats, *14, 19 February, 3(?), 12, 13, 17, 19 March, 15, 16, 21, 30 April, 3 May 1819*

Letter C—   sunday Morn Feby 14—
My dear Brother & Sister—How is it we have not heard from you
from the Settlement yet? The Letters must surely have miscarried—
I am in expectation every day—Peachey wrote me a few days ago
saying some more acquaintances of his were preparing to set out for

Birkbeck—therefore I shall take the opportunity of sending you what I can muster in a sheet or two—I am still at Wentworth Place—indeed I have kept in doors lately. resolved if possible to rid myself of my sore throat—consequently i have not been to see your Mother since my return from Chichester—but my absence from her has been a great weight upon me—I say since my return from Chichester—I believe I told you I was going thither—I was nearly a fortnight at Mr John Snook's and a few days at old Mr Dilke's*—Nothing worth speaking of happened at either place—I took down some of the thin paper and wrote on it a little Poem call'd 'St Agnes Eve'—which you shall have as it is when I have finished the blank part of the rest for you—I went out twice at Chichester to old Dowager card parties—I see very little now, and very few Persons—being almost tired of Men and things—Brown and Dilke are very kind and considerate towards me—The Miss Reynoldses have been stoppi[n]g next door lately—but all very dull—Miss Brawne and I have every now and then a chat and a tiff—Brown and Dilke are walking round their Garden hands in Pockets making observations. The Literary world I know nothing about—There is a Poem from Rogers dead born—and another satire is expected from Byron call'd Don Giovanni—Yesterday I went to town for the first time for these three weeks—I met people from all parts and of all sets—Mr Towers*—one of the Holts—Mr Domine Williams—MrWoodhouse Mrs Hazlitt and Son—Mrs Webb—Mrs Septimus Brown—Mr Woodhouse was looking up at a Book-window in newgate street and being short-sighted twisted his Muscles into so queer a stupe* that I stood by in doubt whether it was him or his brother, if he has one and turning round saw Mr[s] Hazlitt with that little Nero her son—Woodhouse on his features subsiding proved to be Woodhouse and not his Brother—I have had a little business with Mr Abbey—From time to time he has behaved to me with a little Brusquerie—this hurt me a little especially wheen I knew him to be the only Man in England who dared to say a thing to me I did not approve of without its being resented or at least noticed—so I wrote him about it and have made an alteration in my favor—I expect from this to see more of Fanny—who has been quite shut out from me. I see Cobbet has been attacking the Settlement*—but I cannot tell what to believe—and shall be all out at elbous till I hear from you. I am invited to Miss

Millar's Birthday dance on the 19th I am nearly sure I shall no⟨t⟩ be able to go—a Dance would injure my throat very much. I see very little of Reynolds. Hunt I hear is going on very badly—I mean in money Matters I shall not be surprised to hear of the worst—Haydon too in consequence of his eyes is out at elbows. I live as prudently as it is possible for me to do. I have not seen Haslam lately—I have not seen Richards for this half year—Rice for three Months or C C. C.* for god knows when—When I last called in Hen[r]ietta Street—Mrs Millar was verry unwell—Miss Waldegrave as staid and self possessed as usual—Miss Millar was well—Henry was well—There are two new tragedies—one by the Apostate Man, and one by Miss Jane Porter*—Next week I am going to stop at Taylor's for a few days when I will see them bothe and tell you what they are—Mrs and Mr Bentley are well and all the young Carrots. I said nothing of consequence passed at Snook's—no more than this that I like the family very much Mr and Mrs Snook were very kind— we used to have over a little Religion and politicts together almost every evening—and sometimes about you—He proposed writing out for me all the best part of his experience in farming ~~for me to~~ to send to you if I should have an opportunity of talking to him about it I will get all I can at all events—but you may say in your answer to this what value you place upon such information. I have not seen Mr Lewis lately for I have shrunk from going up the hill—Mr Lewis went a few morning[s] ago to town with Mrs Brawne they talked about me—and I heard that Mr L Said a thing I am not at all contented with—Says he 'O, he is quite the little Poet' now this is abominable—you might as well say Buonaparte is quite the little Soldier—You see what it is to be under six foot and not a lord*— There is a long fuzz to day in the examiner about a young Man who delighted a young woman with a Valentine—I think it must be Ollier's.* Brown and I are thinking of passing the summer at Brussels if we do we shall go about the first of May—We i e Brown and I sit opposite one another all day authorizing (N.B. an s instead of a z would give a different meaning) He is at present writing a Story of an old Woman who lived in a forest and to whom the Devil or one [of] his Aid de feus came one night very late and in disguise—The old Dame sets before him pudding after pudding—mess after mess—which he devours and moreover casts his eyes up at a side of

Bacon hanging over his head and at the same times asks whither her Cat is a Rabbit—On going he leaves her three pips of eve's apple—and some how—she, having liv'd a virgin all her life, begins to repent of it and wishes herself beautiful enough to make all the world and even the other world fall in love with her—So it happens—she sets out from her smoaky Cottage in magnificent apparel; the first city She enters evey one falls in love with her—from the Prince to the Blacksmith. A young gentleman on his way to the church to be married leaves his unfortunate Bride and follows this nonsuch—A whole regiment of soldiers are smitten at once and follow her—A whole convent of Monks in corpus christi procession join the Soldiers—The Mayor and Corporation follow the same road—Old and young, deaf and dumb—all but the blind are smitten and form an immense concourse of people who—what Brown will do with them I know not—The devil himself falls in love with her flies away with her to a desert place—in consequence of which she lays an infinite number of Eggs—The Eggs being hatched from time to time fill the world with many nuisances such as John Knox—George Fox—Johanna Southcote—Gifford*—There have been within a fortnight eight failures of the highest consequence in London—Brown went a few evenings since to Davenport's* and on his coming in he talk'd about bad news in the City with such a face, I began to think of a national Bankruptcy—I did not feel much surprised—and was rather disappointed. Carlisle,* a Bookseller on the *Hone* principle has been issuing Pamphlets from his shop in fleet Street Called the Deist—he was conveyed to Newgate last Thursday—he intends making his own defence. I was surprised to hear from Taylor the amount of Murray the Booksellers last sale—what think you of £25,000? He sold 4000 coppies of Lord Byron. I am sitting opposite the Shakspeare I brought from the Isle of wight—and I never look at it but the silk tassels on it give me as much pleasure as the face of the Poet itself—except that I do not know how you are going on—In my next Packet as this is one by the way, I shall send you the Pot of Basil, St Agnes eve, and if I should have finished it a little thing call'd the 'eve of St Mark' you see what fine mother Radcliff names I have—It is not my fault—I did not search for them—I have not gone on with Hyperion—for to tell the truth I have not been in great cue for writing lately—I must wait for the sp[r]ing to rouse me up a

little—The only time I went out from Bedhampton was to see a
Chapel consecrated—Brown I and John Snook the boy, went in a
chaise behind a leaden horse Brown drove, but the horse did not
mind him—This Chapel is built by a Mr Way* a great Jew
converter—who in that line has spent one hundred thousand
Pounds—He maintains a great number of poor Jews—Of course his
communion plate was stolen—he spoke to the Clerk about it—The
Clerk said he was very sorry adding—'I dare shay your honour its
among ush' The Chapel is built in Mr Way's park—The Consecration was—not amusing—there were numbers of carriages, and his
house crammed with Clergy—they sanctified the Chapel—and it
being a wet day consecrated the burial ground through the vestry
window. I begin to hate Parsons—they did not make me love them
that day—when I saw them in their proper colours—A Parson is a
Lamb in a drawing room and a lion in a Vestry—The notions of
Society will not permit a Parson to give way to his temper in any
shape—so he festers in himself—his features get a peculiar diabolical self sufficient iron stupid exp[r]ession—He is continually
acting—His mind is against every Man and every Mans mind is
against him—He is an Hippocrite to the Believer and a Coward to
the unbeliever—He must be either a Knave or an Ideot—And there
is no Man so much to be pitied as an ideot parson. The soldier who is
cheated into an esprit du corps—by a red coat, a Band and Colours
for the purpose of nothing—is not half so pitiable as the Parson who
is led by the nose by the Bench of Bishops—and is smothered in
absurdities—a poor necessary subaltern of the Church—

Friday Feby 18 [*for* 19]—The day before yesterday I went to
Romney Street—your Mother was not at home—but I have just
written her that I shall see her on wednesday. I call'd on Mr Lewis
this morning—he is very well—and tells me not to be uneasy about
Letters the chances being so arbitrary—He is going on as usual
among his favorite democrat papers*—We had a chat as usual about
Cobbett: and the westminster electors. Dilke has lately been verry
much harrassed about the manner of educating his Son—he at
length decided for a public school—and then he did not know what
school—he at last has decided for Westminster; and as Charley is to
be a day boy, Dilke will remove to Westminster. We lead verry quiet
lives here—Dilke is at present in greek histories and antiquit[i]es—

and talks of nothing but the electors of Westminster and the retreat
of the ten-thousand—I never drink now above three glasses of
wine—and never any spirits and water. Though by the bye the other
day—Woodhouse took me to his coffee house—and ordered a Bottle
of Claret—now I like Claret whenever I can have Claret I must drink
it.—'t is the only palate affair that I am at all sensual in—Would it
not be a good Speck to send you some vine roots—could I [*for* it] be
done? I'll enquire—If you could make some wine like Claret to
d[r]ink on summer evenings in an arbour! For really 't is so fine—it
fills the mouth one's mouth with a gushing freshness—then goes
down cool and feverless—then you do not feel it quarelling with
your liver—no it is rather a Peace maker and lies as quiet as it did in
the grape—then it is as fragrant as the Queen Bee; and the more
ethereal Part of it mounts into the brain, not assaulting the cerebral
apartments like a bully in a bad house looking for his trul and hurrying from door to door bouncing against the waist-coat; but rather
walks like Aladin about his own enchanted palace so gently that you
do not feel his step—Other wines of a heavy and spirituous nature
transform a Man to a Silenus; this makes him a Hermes—and gives a
Woman the soul and imortality of Ariadne for whom Bacchus always
kept a good cellar of claret—and even of that he could never persuade her to take above two cups—I said this same Claret is the only
palate-passion I have I forgot game I must plead guilty to the breast
of a Partridge, the back of a hare, the backbone of a grouse, the wing
and side of a Pheasant and a Woodcock *passim* Talking of game (I
wish I could make it) the Lady whom I met at Hastings and of whom
I said something in my last I think,* has lately made me many presents of game, and enabled me to make as many—She made me take
home a Pheasant the other day which I gave to Mrs Dilke; on which,
tomorrow, Rice, Reynolds and the Wentworthians will dine next
door—The next I intend for your Mother. These moderate sheets of
paper are much more pleasant to write upon than those large thin
sheets which I hope you by this time have received—thought [*for*
though] that cant be now I think of it—I have not said in any Letter
yet a word about my affairs—in a word I am in no despair about
them—my poem has not at all succeeded—in the course of a year or
so I think I shall try the public again—in a selfish point of view I
should suffer my pride and my contempt of public opinion to hold

me silent—but for your's and fanny's sake I will pluck up a spirit, and try again—I have no doubt of success in a course of years if I persevere—but it must be patience—for the Reviews have enervated and made indolent mens minds—few think for themselves—These Reviews too are getting more and more powerful and especially the Quarterly—They are like a superstition which the more it prostrates the Crowd and the longer it continues the more powerful it becomes just in proportion to their increasing weakness—I was in hopes that when people saw, as they must do now, all the trickery and iniquity of these Plagues they would scout them, but no they are like the spectators at the Westminster cock-pit—they like the battle and do not care who wins or who looses—Brown is going on this morning with the story of his old woman and the Devil—He makes but slow progreess—the fact is it is a Libel on the Devil and as that person is ~~the~~ Brown's Muse, look ye, if he libels his own Muse how can he expect to write—Either Brown or his muse must turn tale— Yesterday was Charley Dilkes birth day—Brown and I were invited to tea—During the evening noth[i]ng passed worth notice but a little conversation between Mrs Dilke and Mrs Brawne—The subject was the watchman—It was ten o'Clock and Mrs Brawne, who lived during the summer in Brown's house and now lives in the Road, recognized her old Watchman's voice and said that he came as far as her now: 'indeed'; said 'Mrs D. 'does he turn the Corner?' There have been some Letters pass between me and Haslam: but I have not seen him lately—the day before yesterday—which I made a day of Business, I call'd upon him—he was out as usual—Brown has been walking up and down the room a breeding—now at this moment he is being delivered of a couplet—and I dare say will be as well as can be expected—Gracious—he has twins! I have a long Story to tell you about Bailey—I will say first the circumstances as plainly and as well as I can remember, and then I will make my comment. You know that Bailey was very much cut up about a little Jilt in the country somewhere; I thought he was in a dying state about it when at Oxford with him: little supposing as I have since heard, that he was at that very time making impatient Love to Marian Reynolds—and guess my astonishment at hearing after this that he had been trying at Miss Martin*—So matters have been. So Matters stood—when he got ordained and went to a Curacy near Carlisle where the family of the Gleigs reside—There his susceptible heart was conquered by Miss Gleig—and thereby all his connections in town have been annulled—both male and female—I do not now remember clearly the facts—These however I know—He showed his correspondence with Marian to Gleig—returnd all her Letters and asked for his own—he also wrote very abrubt Letters to Mrs Reynolds—I do not know any more of the Martin affair than I have written above—No doubt his conduct has been verry bad. The great thing to be considered is—whether it is want of delicacy and principle or want of Knowledge and polite experience—And again Weakness—yes that is it—and the want of a Wife—yes that is it—and then Marian made great Bones of him, although her Mother and sister have teased her very much about it. Her conduct has been very upright throughout the whole affair—She liked Bailey as a Brother—but not as a Husband—especially as he used to woo her with the Bible and Jeremy Taylor under his arm—they walked in no grove but Jeremy Taylors*—Marians obstinacy is some excuse—but his so quickly taking to miss Gleig can have no excuse—except that of a Ploughmans who wants a wife—The thing which sways me more against him than any thing else is Rice's conduct on the occasion; Rice would not make an immature resolve: he was ardent in his friendship for Bailey; he examined the whole for and against minutely; and he has abandoned Bailey entirely. All this I am not supposed by the Reynoldses to have any hint of—It will be a good Lesson to the Mother and Daughters—nothing would serve but Bailey—If you mentioned the word Tea pot—some one of them came out with an a propos about Bailey—noble fellow—fine fellow! was always in their mouths—this may teach them that the man who redicules romance is the most romantic of Men—that he who abuses women and slights them—loves them the most—that he who talks of roasting a Man alive would not do it when it came to the push—and above all that they are very shallow people who take every thing literal A Man's life of any worth is a continual allegory—and very few eyes can see the Mystery of his life—a life like the scriptures, figurative—which such people can no more make out than they can the hebrew Bible. Lord Byron cuts a figure—but he is not figurative—Shakspeare led a life of Allegory; his works are the comments on it—

On Monday* we had to dinner Severn & Cawthorn* the Bookseller & print virtuoso; in the evening Severn went home to paint & we other three went to the play to see Sheild's new tragedy* ycleped Evadné—In the morning Severn & I took a turn round the Museum, There is a Sphinx there of a ~~giant~~ size, & most voluptuous Egyptian expression, I had not seen it before—The play was bad even in comparison with *1818* the Augustan age of the Drama,* "Comme on sait" as Voltaire says.—the whole was made up of a virtuous young woman, an indignant brother, a suspecting lover, a libertine prince, a gratuitous villain, a street in Naples, a Cypress grove, lillies & roses, virtue & vice, a bloody sword, a spangled jacket, One Lady Olivia, One Miss ONeil alias Evadné, alias Bellamira, alias—Alias—Yea & I say unto you a greater than Elias—there was Abbot, & talking of Abbot his name puts me in mind of a Spelling book lesson, descriptive of the whole Dramatis personae—Abbot—Abbess—Actor—Actress—The play is a fine amusement as a friend of mine once said to me—"Do what you will" says he "A poor gentleman who wants a guinea, cannot spend his two shillings better than at the playhouse—   The pantomime was excellent, I had seen it before & enjoyed it again—   Your Mother & I had some talk about Miss H.—says I will Henry have that Miss H. a lath with a boddice, she who has been fine drawn—fit for nothing but to cut up into Cribbage pins, to the tune of 15.2;* One who is all muslin; all feathers & bone; Once in travelling she was made use of as a lynch pin; I hope he will not have her, though it is no uncommon thing to be *smitten with a staff*; though she might be very useful as his walking stick, his fishing rod, his toothpic—his hat stick (she runs so much in his head) let him turn farmer, she would cut into hurdles; let him write poetry she would be his turnstyle; Her gown is like a flag on a pole; she would do for him if he turn freemason; I hope she will prove a flag of truce;   When she sits languishing with her one foot, on a stool, & one elbow on the table, & her head inclined, she looks like the sign of the crooked billet—or the frontispeice to Cinderella or a teapaper wood cut of Mother Shipton at her studies; she is a make-believe—   She is bon a side a thin young—'Oman—But this is mere talk of a fellow creature; yet pardie I would not that Henry have her—Non volo ut eam possideat, nam, for it would be a bam, for it would be a sham—   Don't think I am writing a petition to the

Governors of St Lukes;* no, that would be in another style. May it please your worships; forasmuch as the undersigned has committed, transferred, given up, made over, consigned, and aberrated himself, to the art & mystery of poetry; for as much as he hath cut, rebuffed, affronted, huffed, & shirked, and taken stint, at all other employments, arts, mysteries, & occupations honest, middling & dishonest; for as much as he hath at sundry times, & in diverse places, told truth unto the men of this generation, & eke to the women, moreover; for as much as he hath kept a pair of boots that did not fit, & doth not admire Sheild's play, Leigh Hunt, Tom Moore, Bob Southey & Mr Rogers;* & does admire Wm Hazlitt: more over for as more, as he liketh half of Wordsworth, & none of Crabbe;* more over-est for for as most; as he hath written this page of penmanship—he prayeth your Worships to give him a lodging—witnessed by Rd Abbey & Co. cum familiaribus & Consanguiniis (signed) Count de Cockaigne— The nothing of the day is a machine called the Velocepede—It is a wheel-carriage to ride cock horse upon, sitting astride & pushing it along with the toes, a rudder wheel in hand. they will go seven miles an hour, A handsome gelding will come to eight guineas, however they will soon be cheaper, unless the army takes to them I look back upon the last month, & find nothing to write about, indeed I do not recollect one thing particular in it—It's all alike, we keep on breathing. The only amusement is a little scandal of however fine a shape, a laugh at a pun—& then after all we wonder how we could enjoy the scandal, or laugh at the pun,

I have been at different times turning it in my head whether I should go to Edinburgh & study for a physician; I am afraid I should not take kindly to it, I am sure I could not take fees—& yet I should like to do so; it is not worse than writing poems, & hanging them up to be flyblown on the Reviewshambles—Every body is in his own mess— Here is the parson at Hampstead quarreling with all the world, he is in the wrong by this same token; when the black Cloth was put up in the Church for the Queen's mourning, he asked the workmen to hang it the wrong side outwards, that it might be better when taken down, it being his perquisite—Parsons will always keep up their Character,* but as it is said there are some animals, the Ancients knew, which we do not; let us hope our posterity will miss the black badger with tri-cornered hat; Who knows but some Revisor of Buffon or Pliny,* may put an account of the parson in the Appendix; No one will then believe it any more than we believe in the Phoenix. I think we may class the lawyer in the same natural history of Monsters; a green bag will hold as much as a lawn sleeve— The only difference is that the one is fustian, & the other flimsy; I am not unwilling to read Church history at present & have Milnes* in my eye his is reckoned a very good one—March 12 Friday—I went to town yesterday chiefly for the purpose of seeing some young Men who were to take some Letters for us to you— through the medium of Peachey. I was surprised and disappointed at hearing they had changed their minds and did not purpose going so far as Birkbeck's—I was much disappointed; for I had counted upon seeing some persons who were to see you—and upon your seeing some who had seen me—I have not only lost this opportunity—but the sail of the Post-Packet to new york or Philadelphia—by which last, your Brothers have sent some Letters—The weather in town yesterday was so stifling that I could not remain there though I wanted much to see Kean in Hotspur—I have by me at present Hazlitt's Letter to Gifford*—perhaps you would like an extract or two from the high seasond parts—It begins thus. "Sir, You have an ugly trick of saying what is not true of any one you do not like; and it will be the object of this Letter to cure you of it. You say what you please of others; it is time you were told what you are. In doing this give me leave to borrow the familiarity of your style:—for the fidelity of the picture I shall be answerable. You are a little person, but a considerable cat's paw; and so far worthy of notice. Your clandestine connection with persons high in office constantly influences your opinions, and alone gives importence to them. You are the government critic, a character nicely differing from that of a government spy—the invisible link, that connects literature with the Police." Again—"Your employers Mr Gifford, do not pay their hirelings for nothing—for condescending to notice weak and wicked sophistry; for pointing out to contempt what excites no admiration; for cautiously selecting a few specimens of bad taste and bad grammar where nothing else is to be found "They want your invincible pertness, your mercenary malice, your impenetrable dullness, your barefaced impudence, your pragmatical self sufficiency, your hypocritical zeal, your pious frauds to stand in the gap of their Prejudices and pretensions, to fly blow and taint public opinion, to defeat independent efforts, to apply not the touch of the scorpion but the touch of the Torpedo to youthful hopes, to crawl and leave the slimy track of sophistry and lies over every work that does not 'dedicate its sweet leaves' to some Luminary of the tresury bench, or is not fostered in the hot bed of corruption—This is your office; "this is what is look'd for at your hands and this you do not baulk"—to sacrifice what little honesty and prostitute what little intellect you possess to any dirty job you are commission'd to execute. "They keep you as an ape does an apple in the corner of his jaw, first mouth'd to be at last swallow'd"—You are by appointment literary toad eater to greatness and taster to the court—You have a natural aversion to whatever differs from your own pretensions, and an acquired one for what gives offence to your superiors. Your vanity panders to your interest, and your malice truckles only to your love of Power. If your instinctive or premeditated abuse of your enviable trust were found wanting in a single instance; if you were to make a single slip in getting up your select committee of enquiry and greenbag report of the state of Letters, your occupation would be gone. You would never after obtain a squeeze of the hand from a great man, or a smile from a Punk of Quality. The great and powerful (whom you call wise and good) do not like to have the privacy of their self love startled by the obtrusive and unmanageable claims of Literature and Philosophy, except through the intervention of people like you, whom; if they have common penetration, they soon find out to be without any superiority of intellect; or if they do not whom they can despise for their meanness of soul. You "have the office opposite to saint Peter" You "keep a corner in the public mind, for foul prejudice and corrupt power to knot and gender in"; you volunteer your services to people of quality to ease scruples of mind and qualmes of conscience; you lay the flattering unction of venal prose and laurell'd verse to their souls—You persuade them that there is neither purity of morals, nor depth of understanding, except in themselves and their hangers on; and would prevent the unhallow'd names of Liberty and humanity from ever being whispered in years [*for* ears] polite! You, sir, do you not [do] all this? I cry you mercy then: I took you for the Editor of the Quarterly Review!" This is the sort of feu de joie he keeps up—there is another extract or two—one especially which I will copy tomorrow—for the candles are burnt down and I am using the wax taper—which has a long snuff on it—the fire is at its last click—I am sitting with my back to it with one foot rather askew upon the rug and the other with the heel a little elevated from the carpet—I am writing this on the Maid's tragedy which I have read since tea with Great pleasure—Besides this volume of Beaumont & Fletcher—there are on the tabl[e] two volumes of chaucer and a new work of Tom Moores call'd 'Tom Cribb's memorial to Congress—nothing in it—These are trifles—but I require nothing so much of you as that you will give me a like description of yourselves, however it may be when you are writing to me—Could I see the same thing done of any great Man long since dead it would be a great delight: as to know in what position Shakspeare sat when he began 'To be or not to be"—such thing[s] become interesting from distance of time or place. I hope you are both now in that sweet sleep which no two beings deserve more that [*for* than] you do—I must fancy you so—and please myself in the fancy of speaking a prayer and a blessing over you and your lives— God bless you—I whisper good night in your ears and you will dream of me—

Saturday 13 March. I have written to Fanny this morning; and received a note from Haslam—I was to have dined with him tomorrow: he give[s] me a bad account of his Father, who has not been in Town for 5 weeks—and is not well enough for company—Haslam is well—and from the prosperous state of some love affair he does not mind the double tides he has to work—I have been a Walk past westend—and was going to call at Mr Monkhouse's—but I did not, not being in the humour—I know not why Poetry and I have been so distant lately I must make some advances soon or she will cut me entirely. Hazlitt has this fine Passage in his Letter Gifford, in his Review of Hazlitt's characters of Shakspeare's plays, attacks the Coriolanus critique—He says that Hazlitt has slandered Shakspeare in saying that he had a leaning to the arbit[r]ary side of the question. Hazlitt thus defends himself "My words are "Coriolanus is a storehouse of political commonplaces. The Arguments for and against aristocracy and d[e]mocracy, on the Preveleges of the few and the claims of the many, on Liberty and slavery, power and the abuse of it, peace and war, are here very ably handled, with the spirit of a poet and the acuteness of a Philosopher. Shakspeare himself seems to have had a leaning to the arbit[r]ary side of the question, perhaps from some feeling of contempt for his own origin, and to have spared no occasion of ba[i]ting the rabble. *What he says of them is very true; what he says of their betters is also very true, though he dwells less upon it.*" I then proceed to account for this by shewing how it is that "the cause of the people is but little calculated for a subject for Poetry; or that the language of Poetry naturally falls in with the language of power." I affi[r]m, Sir, that Poetry, that the imagination, generally speaking, delights in power, in strong excitement, as well as in truth, in good, in right, whereas pure reason and the moral sense approve only of the true and good. I proceed to show that this general love or tendency to immediate excitement or theatrical effect, no matter how produced, gives a Bias to the imagination often [in]consistent with the greatest good, that in Poetry it triumphs over Principle, and bribes the passions to make a sacrifice of common humanity. You say that it does not, that there is no such original Sin in Poetry, that it makes no such sacrifice or unworthy compromise between poetical effect and the still small voice of reason—And how do you prove that there is no such principle giving a bias to the imagination, and a false colouring to poetry? Why by asking in reply to the instances where this principle operates, and where no other can with much modesty and simplicity—"But are these the only topics that afford delight in Poetry &c" No; but these objects do afford delight in poetry, and they afford it in proportion to their strong and often tragical effect, and not in proportion to their strong and often tragical effect,* and not in proportion to the good produced, or their desireableness in a moral point of view? "Do we read with more pleasure of the ravages of a beast of prey than of the Shepherds pipe upon the Mountain?" No but we do read with pleasure of the ravages of a beast of prey, and we do so on the principle I have stated, namely from the sense of power abstracted from the sense of good; and it is the same principle that makes us read with admiration and reconciles us in fact to the triumphant progress of the conquerers and mighty Hunters of mankind, who come to stope [*for* stop] the shepherd's Pipe upon the Mountains and sweep away his listening flock. Do you mean to deny that there is any thing imposing to the imagination in power, in grandeur, in outward shew, in the accumulation of individual wealth and luxury, at the expen[s]e of equal justice and the common weal? Do you deny that there is any thing in the "Pride, Pomp and Circumstance of glorious war, that makes ambition virtue'? in the eyes of admiring multitudes? Is this a new theory of the Pleasures of the imagination which says that the pleasures of the imagination do not take rise soly in the calculations of the understanding? Is it a paradox of my creating that "one murder makes a villain millions a Hero!" or is it not true that here, as in other cases, the enormity of the evil overpowers and makes a convert of the imagination by its very magnitude? You contradict my reasoning, because you know nothing of the question, and you think that no one has a right to understand what you do not. My offence against purity in the passage alluded to, "which contains the concentrated venom of my malignity," is, that I have admitted that there are tyrants and slaves abroad in the world; and you would hush the matter up, and pretend that there is no such thing in order that there may be nothing else. Farther I have explained the cause, the subtle sophistry of the human mind, that tolerates and pampers the evil in order to guard against its approaches; you would conceal the cause in order to prevent the cure, and to leave the proud flesh about the heart to harden and ossify into one impenetrabl[e] mass of selfishness and hypocrisy, that we may not "sympathise in the distresses of suffering virtue" in any case in which they come in competition with the fictitious [for factitious] wants and "imputed weaknesses of the great." You ask "are we gratified by the cruelties of Domitian or Nero?" No, not we—they were too petty and cowardly to strike the imagination at a distance; but the Roman senate tolerated them, addressed their perpetrators, exalted them into gods, the fathers of the[ir] people; they had pimps and scribblers of all sorts in their pay, their Senecas, &c till a turbulent rabble thinking that there were no injuries to Society greater than the endurance of unlimited and wanton oppression, put an end to the farce and abated the nuisance as well as they could. Had you and I lived in those times we should have been what we are now, I "a sour mal content," and you "a sweet courtier." The manner in which this is managed: the force and innate power with which it yeasts and works up itself—the feeling for the costume of society; is in a style of genius—He hath a demon as he himself says of Lord Byron—We are to have a party this evening—The Davenports from Church

row—I dont think you know any thing of them—they have paid me
a good deal of attention—I like Davenport himself—The names of
the rest are Miss Barnes Miss Winter with the Children—
⟨*Marc*⟩*h 17ᵗʰ*—Wednesday—On sunday I went to Davenports'
w[h]ere I dined—and had a nap. I cannot bare a day an[ni]hilated in
that manner—there is a great difference between an easy and an
uneasy indolence—An indolent day—fill'd with speculations even of
an unpleasant colour—is bearable and even pleasant alone—when
one's thoughts cannot find out any th[i]ng better in the world; and
experience has told us that locomotion is no change: but to have
nothing to do, and to be surrounded with unpleasant human identities; who press upon one just enough to prevent one getting into a
lazy position; and not enough to interest or rouse one; is a capital
punishment of a capital crime: for is not giving up, through goodna-
ture, one's time to people who have no light and shade a capital
crime? Yet what can I do?—they have been very kind and attentive to
me. I do not know what I did on monday—nothing—nothing—
nothing—I wish this was any thing extraordinary—Yesterday I went
to town: I called on Mʳ Abbey⟨;⟩ he began again (he has don[e] it
frequently lately) ⟨abou⟩t that ⟨hat-ma⟩king concern—saying he
wish you had hear⟨ken⟩ed to it: he wants to make me a H⟨at-
maker⟩—I really believe 't is all interested: for from the manner he
spoke withal and the card he gave me I think he is concerned in
⟨Hat-ma⟩king himself. He speaks well of Fanny⟨'s⟩ health—
Hodgkinson* is married—From this I think he takes a little
Latitude—Mʳ A was waiting very impatient[l]y for his return to the
counting house—and mean while observed how strange it was that
Hodgkinson should have been not able to walk two months ago and
that now he should be married.—"I do not,' says he 'think it will do
him any good: I should not be surprised if he should die of a consumption in a year or ⟨two.⟩ I called at Taylor's and found that he
and Hilto⟨n⟩ had set out to dine with me: so I followed them
immediately back—I walk'd with them townwards again as far as
Cambden Town and smoak'd home a Segar—This morning I have
been reading the '*False one*"* I have been up to Mʳˢ Bentley's—
shameful to say I was in bed at ten—I mean this morning—The
Blackwood's review has committed themselves in a scandalous
heresy—they have been putting up Hogg the ettrick shepherd

against Burns—The senseless villains. I have not seen Reynolds Rice or any of our set lately—. Reynolds is completely limed in the law: he is not only reconcil'd to it but hobbyhorses upon it—Blackwood wanted very much to see him—the scotch cannot manage by themselves at all—they want imagination—and that is why they are so fond of Hogg, who has a little of it—

Friday 19ᵗʰ Yesterday I got a black eye—the first time I took a Cr⟨icket⟩ bat—Brown who is always one's friend in a disaster ⟨app⟩lied a lee⟨ch to⟩ the eyelid, and there is no infla⟨mm⟩ation this morning though the ball hit me dir⟨ectl⟩y on the sight—'t was a white ball—I am glad it was not a clout—This is the second black eye I have had since leaving school—during all my ⟨scho⟩ol days I never had one at all—we must e⟨a⟩t a peck before we die—This morning I am in a sort of temper indolent and supremely careless: I long after a stanza or two of Thompson's Castle of indolence*—My passions are all alseep [*for* asleep] from my having slumbered till nearly eleven and weakened the animal fibre all over me to a delightful sensation about three degrees on this side of faintness—if I had teeth of pearl and the breath of lillies I should call it langour—but as I am + I must call it Laziness—In this state of effeminacy the fibres of the brain are relaxed in common with the rest of the body, and to such a happy degree that pleasure has no show of enticement and pain no unbearable frown. Neither Poetry, nor Ambition, nor Love have any alertness of countenance as they pass by me: they seem rather like three figures on a greek vase—a Man and two women— whom no one but myself could distinguish in their disguisement.* This is the only happiness; and is a rare instance of advantage in the body overpowering the Mind. I have this moment received a note from Haslam in which he expects the death of his Father who has been for some time in a state of insensibility—his mother bears up he says very well—I shall go to twon [*for* town] tommorrow to see him. This is the world—thus we cannot expect to give way many hours to pleasure—Circumstances are like Clouds continually gathering and bursting—While we are laughing the seed of some trouble is put into the wide arable land of events—while we are laughing it sprouts is [*for* it] grows and suddenly bears a poison fruit which we

+ especially as I have a black eye

must pluck*—Even so we have leisure to reason on the misfortunes of our friends; our own touch us too nearly for words. Very few men have ever arrived at a complete disinterestedness of Mind: very few have been influenced by a pure desire of the benefit of others—in the greater part of the Benefactors of & to Humanity some meretricious motive has sullied their greatness—some melodramatic scenery has facinated them—From the manner in which I feel Haslam's misfortune I perceive how far I am from any humble standard of disinterestedness—Yet this feeling ought to be carried to its highest pitch, as there is no fear of its ever injuring society—which it would do I fear pushed to an extremity—For in wild nature the Hawk would loose his Breakfast of Robins and the Robin his of Worms The Lion must starve as well as the swallow—The greater part of Men make their way with the same instinctiveness, the same unwandering eye from their purposes, the same animal eagerness as the Hawk—The Hawk wants a Mate, so does the Man—look at them both they set about it and procure on[e] in the same manner—They want both a nest and they both set about one in the same manner—they get their food in the same manner—The noble animal Man for his amusement smokes his pipe—the Hawk balances about the Clouds—that is the only difference of their leisures. This it is that makes the Amusement of Life—to a speculative Mind. I go among the Feilds and catch a glimpse of a stoat or a fieldmouse peeping out of the withered grass—the creature hath a purpose and its eyes are bright with it—I go amongst the buildings of a city and I see a Man hurrying along—to what? The Creature has a purpose and his eyes are bright with it. But then as Wordsworth says, "We have all one human heart"*—there is an ellectric fire in human nature tending to purify—so that among these human creature[s] there is continully some birth of new heroism—The pity is that we must wonder at it: as we should at finding a pearl in rubbish—I have no doubt that thousands of people never heard of have had hearts comp[l]etely disinterested: I can remember but two—Socrates and Jesus—their Histories evince it—What I heard a little time ago, Taylor observe with respect to Socrates, may be said of Jesus—That he was so great a man that though he transmitted no writing of his own to posterity, we have his Mind and his sayings and his greatness handed to us by others. It is to be lamented that the history of the latter was written and revised by Men interested in the pious frauds of Religion.* Yet through all this I see his splendour. Even here though I myself am pursueing the same instinctive course as the veriest human animal you can think of—I am however young writing at random—straining at particles of light in the midst of a great darkness—without knowing the bearing of any one assertion of any one opinion. Yet may I not in this be free from sin? May there not be superior beings amused with any graceful, though instinctive attitude my mind m[a]y fall into, as I am entertained with the alertness of a Stoat or the anxiety of a Deer? Though a quarrel in the streets is a thing to be hated, the energies displayed in it are fine; the commonest Man shows a grace in his quarrel—By a superior being our reasoning[s] may take the same tone—though erroneous they may be fine—This is the very thing in which consists poetry; and if so it is not so fine a thing as philosophy—For the same reason that an eagle is not so fine a thing as a truth—Give me this credit—Do you not think I strive—to know myself? Give me this credit—and you will not think that on my own accou[n]t I repeat Milton's lines

> "How charming is divine Philosophy
> Not harsh and crabbed as dull fools suppose
> But musical as is Apollo's lute"—*

No—no for myself—feeling grateful as I do to have got into a state of mind to relish them properly—Nothing ever becomes real till it is experienced*—Even a Proverb is no proverb to you till your Life has illustrated it—I am ever affraid that your anxiety for me will lead you to fear for the violence of my temperament continually smothered down: for that reason I did not intend to have sent you the following sonnet—but look over the two last pages and ask yourselves whether I have not that in me which will well bear the buffets of the world. It will be the best comment on my sonnet; it will show you that it was written with no Agony but that of ignorance; with no thirst of any thing but knowledge when pushed to the point though the first steps to it were throug[h] my human passions*—they went away, and I wrote with my Mind—and perhaps I must confess a little bit of my heart—

Why did I laugh tonight? No voice will tell:
　　No God, no Deamon of severe response
Deigns to reply from heaven or from Hell.—
　　Then to my human heart I turn at once—
Heart! thou and I are here sad and alone;
　　Say, wherefore did I laugh? O mortal pain!
O Darkness! Darkness! ever must I moan
　　To question Heaven and Hell and Heart in vain!
Why did I laugh? I know this being's lease
　　My fancy to its utmost blisses spreads:
Yet could I on this very midnight cease,*
　　And the world's gaudy ensigns see in shreds.
Verse, fame and Beauty are intense indeed
But Death intenser—Deaths is Life's high mead."

I went to ~~bead~~ bed, and enjoyed an uninterrupted sleep—Sane I
went to bed and sane I arose. || This is the 15th of April—you see
what a time it is since I wrote—all that time I have been day by day
expecting Letters from you—I write quite in the dark—In the hopes
of a Letter daily I have deferred that I might write in the light—I
was in town yesterday and at Taylors heard that young Brikbeck [*for*
Birkbeck] had been in Town and was set to forward in six or seven
days—so I shall dedicate that time to making up this parcel ready for
him—I wish I could hear from you to make me "whole and general
as the casing air" A few days after the 19th of april [*for* March] I
received a note from Haslam contain[i]ng the news of his father's
death—The Family has all been well—Haslam has his father's situation. The Framptons* have behaved well to him—The day before
yesterday I went to a rout at Sawrey's—it was made pleasant by
Reynolds being there, and our getting into conversation with one of
the most beautiful Girls I ever saw—She gave a remarkable pretti-
ness to all those commonplaces which most women who talk must
utter—I liked Mrs Sawrey very well. The Sunday before last your
Brothers were to come by a long invitation—so long that for the time
I forgot it when I promised Mrs Brawne to dine with her on the same
day—On recollecting my engagement with your Brothers I immediately excused myself with Mrs Brawn but she would not hear of it
and insisted on my bringing my friends with me. so we all dined at

Mrs Brawne's. I have been to Mrs Bentley's this morning and put all
the Letters two [*for* to] and from you and poor Tom and me—I have
found some of the correspondence between him and that degraded
Wells and Amena*—It is a wretched business. I do not know the
rights of it—but what I do know would I am sure affect you so much
that I am in two Minds whether I will tell you any thing about it—
And yet I do not see why—for any thing tho' it be unpleasant, that
calls to mind those we still love, has a compensation in itself for the
pain it occasions—so very likely tomorrow I may set about coppying
thee whole of what I have about it: with no sort of a Richardson self
satisfaction—I hate it to a sickness—and I am affraid more from
indolence of mind than any thing else I wonder how people exist
with all their worries. I have not been to Westminster but once lately
and that was to see Dilke in his new Lodgings—I think of living
somewhere in the neighbourhood myself—Your mothers was well by
your Brothers' account. I shall see her perhaps tomorrow—yes I
shall—We have had the Boys* here lately—they make a bit of a
racket—I shall not be sorry when they go. I found also this morning
in a note from George to you my dear sister a lock of your hair which
I shall this moment put in the miniature case. A few days ago Hunt
dined here and Brown invited Davenport to meet him. Davenport
from a sense of weakness thought it incumbent on him to show off—
and pursuant to that never ceased talking and boaring all day, till I
was completely fagged out—Brown grew melancholy—but Hunt
perceiving what a complimentary tendency all this had bore it
remarkably well—Brown grumbled about it for two or three days—
I went with Hunt to Sir John Leicester's gallery there I saw
Northcote—Hilton—Bewick and many more of great and Little
note. Haydons picture is of very little progress this last year—He
talk[s] about finishing it next year—Wordsworth is going to publish a
Poem called Peter Bell—what a perverse fellow it is! Why wilt he
talk about Peter Bells—I was told not to tell—but to you it will not
be tellings—Reynolds hearing that said Peter Bell was coming out,
took it into his head to write a skit upon it call'd Peter Bell.* He did
it as soon as thought on it is to be published this morning, and comes
out before the real Peter Bell, with this admirable motto from the
"Bold stroke for a Wife'* "'I am the real Simon Pure"' I[t] would be
just as well to trounce Lord Byron in the same manner. I am still at a

stand in versifying—I cannot do it yet with any pleasure—I mean
however to look round at my resources and means—and see what I
can do without poetry—To that end I shall live in Westminster—I
have no doubt of making by some means a little to help on or I shall
be left in the Lurch—with the burden of a little Pride—However I
look in time—The Dilkes like their lodging in Westminster tolerably
well. I cannot help thinking what a shame it is that poor Dilke should
give up his comfortable house & garden for his Son, whom he will
certainly ruin with too much care—The boy has nothing in his ears
all day but himself and the importance of his education—Dilke has
continually in his mouth "My Boy" This is what spoils princes: it
may have the same effect with Commoners. Mrs Dilke has been very
well lately—But what a shameful thing it is that for that obstinate
Boy Dilke should stifle himself in Town Lodgings and wear out his
Life by his continual apprehension of his Boys fate in Westminster-
school, with the rest of the Boys and the Masters—Every one has
some wear and tear—One would think Dilke ought to be quiet and
happy—but no—this one Boy—makes his face pale, his society
silent and his vigilanc⟨e⟩ jealous—He would I have no doubt quarrel with any one who snubb'd his Boy—With all this he has no
notion how to manage him O what a farce is our greatest cares! Yet
one must be in the pother for the sake of Clothes food and Lodging.
There has been a squabble between Kean and one Mr Bucke*—
There are faults on both sides—on Bucks the faults are positive to
the Question: Keans fault is a want of genteel knowledge and high
Policy—The formor writes knavishly foolish and the other silly
bombast. It was about a Tragedy written by said Mr Bucke; which it
appears Mr Kean kick'd at—is [*for* it] was so bad—. After a little
struggle of Mr Bucke's against Kean—drury Lane had the Policy to
bring it one [*for* on] and Kean the impolicy not to appear in it—It
was damn'd—The people in the Pit had a favou[r]ite call on the
night of "Buck Buck rise up" and "Buck Buck how many horns
do I hold up. Kotzebue the German Dramatist and traitor to his
country was murdered lately by a young student whose name I
forget—he stabbed himself immediately after crying out Germany!
Germany!* I was unfortunat⟨e⟩ to miss Richards the only time I
have been for many months to see him. Shall I treat you with a little
extempore.

When they were come unto the Faery's Court
They rang—no one at home—all gone to sport
And dance and kiss and love as faery's do
For Faries be as humans lovers true—
Amid the woods they were so lone and wild
Where even the Robin feels himself exild
And where the very brooks as if affraid
Hurry along to some less magic shade.
'No one at home'! the fretful princess cry'd
'And all for nothing such a drery ride
And all for nothing my new diamond cross
No one to see my persian feathers toss
No one to see my Ape, my Dwarf, my Fool
Or how I pace my otahaietan mule
Ape, Dwarf and Fool why stand you gaping there
Burst the door open, quick—or I declare
Ill switch you soundly and in pieces tear'.
The Dwarf began to tremble and the Ape
Star'd at the Fool, the Fool was all agape
The Princess grasp'd her switch but just in time
The dwarf with piteous face began to rhyme.
'O mighty Princess did you never hear tell
What your poor servants know but too too well
Know you the three 'great crimes' in faery land
The first alas! poor Dwarf I understand
I made a whipstock of a faery's wand
The next is snoring in their company
The next, the last the direst of the th[r]ee
Is making freee when they are not at home
I was a Prince—a baby p[r]ince—my doom
You see, I made a whipstock of a wand
My top has henceforth slept in faery land.
He was a P[r]ince, the Fool a grown up Prince
But he has never been a king's son since
He fell a snoring at a faery Ball—
Your poor Ape was a Prince, and he poor thing
Picklock'd a faerry's boudour—now no King
But ape—so pray your highness stay awhile

'T is sooth indeed We know it to our sorrow—
Persist and *you* may be an ape tomorrow—
While the Dwarf spake the Princess all for spite
Peal'd the brown hazel twig to lilly white
Clench'd her small teeth, and held her lips apart
Try'd to look unconcern'd with beating heart
They saw her highness had made up her mind
A quavering* like thee reeds before the wind—
And they had had it, but o happy chance
The Ape for very fear began to dance
And grin'd as all his ugliness did ache—
She staid her vixen fingers for his sake
He was so very ugly: then she took
Her pocket ~~glass~~ mirror and began to look
First at herself and at him and then
She smil'd at her own beauteous face again.
Yet for all this—for all her pretty face—
She took it in her head to see the place
Women gain little from experience
Either in Lovers husbands or expence
The more ~~their~~ beauty, the more fortune too
Beauty before the wide world never knew
So each Fair reasons—tho' it oft miscarries.
She thought *her* pretty face would please the faries
'My darling Ape I wont whip you to day
Give me the Picklock sirrah and go play—
They all three wept—but counsel was as vain
As crying cup biddy to drops of rain—
Yet lingeringly did the sad Ape forth draw
The Picklock from the Pocket in his Jaw.
The Princess took it and dismounting straigh⟨t⟩
Trip'd in blue silver'd slippers to the gate
And touch'd the wards, the Door ~~opes~~ full cou[r]teou[s]ly
Opened—she enter'd with her servants three
Again it clos'd and there was nothing seen
But the Mule grasing on the herbage green.

End of Canto xii

Canto the xiii

The Mule no sooner saw himself alone
Than he prick up his Ears—and 'said well done,
At least unhappy Prince I may be free—
No more a Princess shall side saddle me.
O king of Othaietè—tho a Mule
'Aye every inch a king'—tho—'Fortune's fool'
Well done—for by what Mr Dwarfy said
I would not give a sixpenc[e] for her head'
Even as he spake 'he trotted in high glee
To the knotty side of an old Pollard tree
And rub his sides against the mossed bark
Till his Girths burst and left him naked stark
Except his Bridle—how get rid of that
Buckled and tied with many a twist and plait
At last it struck him to pretend to sleep
And then the thievish Monkies down would creep
And filch the unpleasant trammels quite away
No sooner thought of than adown he lay
Sham'd a good snore—the Monkey-men descende[d]
And whom they thought to injure they brefriended.
They hung his Bridle on a topmost bough
And of he went run, trot, or any how—

———

Brown is gone to bed—and I am tired of rhyming—there is a north
wind blowing playing young gooseberry with the trees—I dont care
so it heps even with a side wind a Letter to me—for I cannot put
faith in any reports I hear of the Settlement some are good some
bad—Last Sunday I took a Walk towards highgate and in the lane
~~lead~~ that winds by the side of Lord Mansfield's park I met Mr Green
our Demonstrator at Guy's* in conversation with Coleridge—I
joined them, after enquiring by a look whether it would be
agreeable—I walked with him a[t] his alderman-after dinner pace for
near two miles I suppose In those two Miles he broached a thousand
things—let me see if I can give you a list—Nightingales, Poetry—on
Poetical sensation—Metaphysics—Different genera and species

of Dreams—Nightmare—a dream accompanied ~~with~~ by a sense
of touch—single and double touch—A dream related—First and
second consciousness—the difference explained between will
and Volition—so m[an]y metaphysicians from a want of smoking
the second consciousness—Monsters—the Kraken—Mermaids—
southey believes in them—southeys belief too much diluted—A
Ghost story—Good morning—I heard his voice as he came towards
me—I heard it as he moved away—I had heard it all the interval—if
it may be called so. He was civil enough to ask me to call on him at
Highgate Good Night! It looks so much like rain I shall not go to
town to day; but put it off till tomorrow—Brown this morning is
writing some spenserian stanzas against Mrs Miss Brawne and me; so
I shall amuse myself with him a little: in the manner of Spenser—

> He is to weet a melancholy Carle
> Thin in the waist, with bushy head of hair
> As hath the seeded thistle when in parle
> It holds the Zephyr ere it sendeth fair
> Its light balloons into the summer air
> Therto his beard had not began to bloom
> No brush had touch'd his chin or razor sheer
> No care had touch his cheek with mortal doom
> But new he was and bright as scarf from persian loom—

> Ne cared he for wine, or half and half
> Ne cared he for fish or flesh or fowl
> And sauces held he worthless as the chaff
>   'sdeign'd
> He ~~scorn'd~~ the swine heard at the wassail bowl
> Ne with lewd ribbalds sat he cheek by jowl
> Ne with sly Lemans in the scorner's chair
> But after water brooks this Pilgrim's soul
> Panted, and all his food was woodland air ·
> Though he would ofttimes feast on gilliflowers rare—

> The slang of cities in no wise he knew
> *Tipping the wink* to him was hethen greek
> He sipp'd no olden Tom or ruin blue*
> Or nantz,* or cheery brandy drank full meek

By many a Damsel hoarse and rouge of cheek
Nor did he know each aged Watchman's beat—
Nor in obscured perlieus would he seek
For curled Jewesses with ankles neat
Who as they walk abroad make tinkling with their feet—

This character would ensure him a situation in the establishment of patient Griselda—The servant has come for the little Browns this morning—they have been a toothache to me which I shall enjoy the riddance of—Their little voices are like wasps stings—'Some times am I all wound with Browns.' We had a claret feast some little while ago There were Dilke, Reynolds, Skinner,* Mancur, John Brown,* Martin, Brown and I—We all got a little tipsy—but pleasantly so—I enjoy Claret to a degree—I have been looking over the correspondence of the pretended Amena and Wells this evening—I now see the whole cruel deception—I think Wells must have had an accomplice in it—Amena's Letters are in a Man's language, and in a Man's hand imitating a woman's—The instigations to this diabolical scheme were vanity, and the love of intrigue. It was no thoughtless hoax—but a cruel deception on a sanguine Temperament, with every show of friendship. I do not think death too bad for the villain—The world will would look upon it in a different light should I expose it—they would call it a frolic—so I must be wary—but I consider it my duty to be prudently revengeful. I will hang over his head like a sword by a hair. I will be opium to his vanity—if I cannot injure his interests—He is a rat and he shall have ratsbane to his vanity—I will harm him all I possibly can—I have no doubt I shall be able to do so—Let us leave him to his misery alone except when we can throw in a little more—The fifth canto of Dante pleases me more and more—it is that one in which he meets with Paulo and Franchesca—I had passed many days in rather a low state of mind and in the midst of them I dreamt of being in that region of Hell. The dream was one of the most delightful enjoyments I ever had in my life—I floated about the whirling atmosphere as it is described with a beautiful figure to whose lips mine were joined at [*for* as] it seem'd for an age—and in the midst of all this cold and darkness I was warm—even flowery tree tops sprung up and we rested on them sometimes with the lightness of a cloud till the wind blew us away again—I tried a

Sonnet upon it—there are fourteen lines but nothing of what I felt in
it—o that I could dream it every night—

> As Hermes once took to his feathers light
> When lulled Argus, baffled, swoon'd and slept
> So on a delphic reed my idle spright
> So play'd, so charm'd so conquer'd, so bereft
> The dragon world of all its hundred eyes
> And seeing it asleep so fled away:—
> Not to pure Ida with its snow~~clad~~
> > cold skies
> Nor unto Tempe where Jove grieved that day,
> But to that second circle of sad hell,
> Where in the gust, the whirlwind and the flaw
> Of Rain and hailstones lovers need not tell
> Their sorrows—Pale were the sweet lips I saw
> Pale were the lips I kiss'd and fair the fo[r]m
> I floated with about that melancholy storm—

I want very very much a little of your wit my dear sister—a Letter or
two of yours just to bandy back a pun or two across the Atlantic and
send a quibble over the Floridas—Now you have by this time crum-
pled up your large Bonnet, what do you wear—a cap! do you put
your hair in papers of a night? do you pay the Miss Birkbeck's a
morning visit—have you any tea? or to [*for* do] you milk and water
with them—What place of Worship do you go to—the Quakers the
Moravians, the Unitarians or the Methodists—Are there any flowers
in bloom you like—any beautiful heaths—Any Streets full of Corset
Makers. What sort of shoes have you to fit those pretty feet of yours?
Do you desire Comp^ts to one another? Do you ride on Horseback?
What do you have for breakfast, dinner and supper? without mentioning lunch and bever and wet* and snack—and a bit to stay one's
stomach—Do you get any spirits—now you might easily distill some
whiskey—and going into the woods set up a whiskey spop [*for* shop]
for the Monkeys—Do you and the miss Birkbecks get groggy on any
thing—a little so so ish so as to be obliged to be seen home with a
Lantern—You may perhaps have a game at puss in the corner—
Ladies are warranted to play at this game though they have not
whiskers. Have you a fiddle in the Settlement—or at any rate a jew's

harp—which will play in spite of ones teeth—When you have noth-ing else to do for a whole day I tell you how you may employ it—First get up and when you are dress'd, as it would be pretty early, with a high wind in the woods give George a cold Pig* with my Comple-ments. Then you may saunter into the nearest coffee-house and after taking a dram and a look at the chronicle—go and frighten the wild boars upon the strength—you may as well bring one home for break-fast serving up the hoofs garnished with bristles and a grunt or two to accompany the singing of the kettle—then if George is not up give him a colder Pig always with my Compliments—When you are both set down to breakfast I advise you to eat your full share—but leave off immediately on feeling yourself inclined to any thing on the other side of the puffy—avoid that for it does not become young women—After you have eaten your breakfast—keep your eye upon dinner—it is the safest way—You should keep a Hawk's eye over your dinner and keep hovering over it till due time then pounce taking care not to break any plates—While you are hovering with your dinner in p[r]os-pect you may do a thousand things—put a hedgehog into Georges hat—pour a little water into his rifle—soak his boots in a pail of water—cut his jacket round into shreds like a roman kilt or the back of my grandmothers stays—sow *off* his buttons.

Yesterday I could not write a line I was so fat[i]gued for the day before, I went to town in the morning called on your Mother, and returned in time for a few friends we had to dinner. There were Taylor Woodhouse, Reynolds—we began cards at about 9 o'Clock, and the night coming on and continuing dark and rainy they could not think of returning to town—so we played at Cards till very daylight—and yesterday I was not worth a sixpence—Your mother was very well but anxious for a Letter. We had half an hours talk and no more for I was obliged to be home. Mrs and Miss Millar were well—and so was Miss Waldegrave—I have asked your Brothers here for next Sunday—When Reynolds was here ~~yeste~~ on Monday—he asked me to give Hunt a hint to take notice of his Peter Bell in the Examiner—the best thing I can do is to write a little notice of it myself which I will do here and copy it out if it should suit my Purpose—*Peter-Bell* There have been lately advertized two Books both Peter Bell by name; what stuff the one was made of might be seen by the motto, 'I am the real Simon Pure". This false florimel* has hurried from the press and obtruded herself into public notice while for ought we know the real one may be still wandering about the woods and mountains. Let us hope she may soon ~~make her appearance~~ and make good her right to the magic girdle—The Pamphleteering Archimage we can perceive has rather a splenetic love than a downright hatred to real florimels—if indeed they ~~sing~~ had been so christened—or had even a pretention to play at bob cherry* with Barbara Lewthwaite:* but he has a fixed aversion to those three rhyming Graces Alice Fell, Susan Gale and Betty Foy:* ~~and who can wonder at it?~~ and now at length especially to Peter Bell—fit Apollo. ~~The writer of this little skit from~~ understanding It may be seen from one or two passages ~~of~~ in this little skit, that the writer of it has felt the finer parts of Mr Wordsworth ~~Poetry~~, and perhaps expatiated with his more remote and sublimer muse; ~~who sits aloof in a cheerful sadness, and~~ This as far as it relates to Peter Bell is unlucky. The more he may love the sad embroidery of the Excursion; the more he will hate the coarse Samplers of Betty Foy and Alice Fell; and as they come from the same hand, the better will be able to imitate that which can be imitated. to wit Peter Bell—as far as can be imagined from the obstinate Name—We repeat, it is very unlucky—this real Simon Pure is in parts the very Man—There is a pernicious likeness in the scenery a 'pestilent humour' in the rhymes and an inveterate cadence in some of the Stanzas that must be lamented—If we are one part ~~pleased~~ amused at this we are th[r]ee parts sorry that an appreciator of Wordsworth should show so much temper at this really provoking name of Peter Bell—! This will do well enough—I have coppied it and enclosed it to Hunt—You will call it a little politic—seeing I keep clear of all parties. I say something for and against both parties—and suit it to the tune of the examiner—I mean to say I do not unsuit it—and I believe I think what I say nay I am sure I do—I and my conscience are in luck to day—which is an excellent thing—The other night I went to the Play with Rice, Reynolds and Martin—we saw a new dull and half damnd opera call'd 'the heart of Mid Lothian'* that was on Saturday—I stopt at Taylors on sunday with Woodhouse—and passed a quiet sort of pleasant day. I have been very much pleased with the Panorama* of the ships at the north Pole—with the icebergs, the Mountains, the Bears the Walrus—the seals the

225

Penguins—and a large whale floating back above water—it is impossible to describe the place—Wednesday Evening—*

La belle dame sans merci—

O what can ail thee knight at a[r]ms
    Alone and palely loitering?
The sedge has withered from the Lake
    And no birds sing!

O what can ail thee knight at a[r]ms
    So haggard and so woe begone?
The squirrel's granary is full
    And the harvest's done.

      a
I see ~~death's~~ lilly on thy brow
    With anguish moist and fever dew,
          a
And on thy cheeks ~~death's~~ fading rose
    Fast Withereth too—

I met a Lady in the ~~Wilds~~ Meads
    Full beautiful, a faery's child
Her hair was long, her foot was light
    And her eyes were wild—

I made a Garland for her head,
    And bracelets too, and fragrant Zones
She look'd at me as she'd did love
    And made sweet moan—

I set her on my pacing steed
    And nothing else saw all day long
For sidelong would she bend and sing
    A faerys song—

She found me roots of relish sweet
            manna
    And honey wild and ~~honey~~ dew
And sure in language strange she said
    I love thee true—

She took me to her elfin grot
                and sigh'd full sore
  And there she wept ~~and there she sighed full sore~~
And there I shut her wild wild eyes
  With kisses four.

And there she lulled me asleep
  And there I dream'd Ah Woe betide!
The latest dream I ever dreamt
  On the cold hill side

I saw pale kings and Princes too
  Pale warriors death pale were they all
They cried La belle dame sans merci
  Thee hath in thrall.

I saw their starv'd lips in the gloam
  ~~All tremble~~   gaped
  With horrid warning ∧ wide ~~agape~~
And I awoke and found me here
  On the cold hill's side

And this is way I ~~wither~~ sojourn here
  Alone and palely loitering:
Though the sedge is wither'd frome the Lak[e]
  And no birds sing—— . . . .

Why four kisses—you will say—why four because I wish to restrain the headlong impetuosity of my Muse—she would have fain said 'score' without hurting the rhyme—but we must temper the Imagination as the Critics say with Judgment. I was obliged to choose an even number that both eyes might have fair play: and to speak truly I think two a piece quite sufficient—Suppose I had said seven; there would have been three and a half a piece—a very awkward affair—and well got out of on my side—

Chorus of Faries ~~three~~ 4 Fire, air, earth and water—
    Salamander, Zephyr, Dusketha Breama—

Sal.   Happy happy glowing fire!
Zep.   Fragrant air, delicious light!

Dusk.   Let me to my glooms retire
Bream—I to ~~my~~ greenwood rivers bright.

Salam—

Happy, happy glowing fire
Dazzling bowers of soft retire!
Ever let my nourish'd wing
Like a bats s[t]ill wandering
Faintless fan
~~Ever beat~~ your fiery spaces
Spirit sole in deadly places
In unhaunted roar and blaze
Open eyes that never daze
Let me see the myriad shapes
Of Men and Beasts and Fish and apes
Portray'd in many a fiery den,
And wrough[t] by spumy bitumen
On the deep intenser roof
Arched every way aloof
Let me breathe upon my Skies
And anger their live tapestries
Free from cold and every care
Of chilly rain and shivring air.

Zephyr.

Spright of fire—away away!
Or your very roundelay
              newly
Will sear my plumeage ~~all~~ budded
                 all
From its quilled sheath ~~and~~ studded
with the selfsame dews that fell
On the May-grown Asphodel.
Spright of fire away away!

Breama

Spr[i]ght of fire, away away!
Zephyer blue eyed faery turn

228

And see my cool sedge shaded urn
Where its rests its mossy brim
Mid water mint and cresses dim
  And   in
~~Where~~ the flowers ~~amid~~ sweet troubles
Lift their eyes above the bubbles
Like our Queen when she would pleaise
To sleep and Oberon will tease—
Love me blue eyed Faery true
~~For in~~ soothly I am sick for you—

Zephyr—

Gentle Brema by the first
Violet young nature nurst
I will bathe myself with thee
So you sometime follow me
To my home far far in west
~~Far beyond the~~
Far beyond the search and quest
Of the golden browed sun—
Come with me oer tops of trees
To my fragrant Pallaces
Where they ever floating are
Beneath the cherish of a star
Call'd
~~Who with~~ Vesper—who with silver veil
Ever   Hides ~~his brightness~~ his brilliance pale
Ever gently drows'd doth keep
Twilight of the Fays to sleep
Fear not that your watry hair
Will thirst in drouthy ringlets there—
Clouds of stored summer rains
Thou shalt taste before the stains
Of the mountain soil they take
And too unlucent for thee make
      I love thee ch[r]ystal faery true
      Sooth I am as sick for you

Salam—

Out ye agueish Faeries out!
~~Chillier than the water~~
Chilly Lovers what a rout,
Keep ye with your frozen breath
Colder than the mortal death—
Adder-eyed Dusketha, speak
Shall we leave these ~~spr~~ and go seek
In the Earths wide Entrails old
Couches wa[r]m as theirs is cold
O for a fiery gloom and thee
Dusketha so enchantingly
Freck[l]e wing'd and lizard sided!

Dusketha

By thee spright will I be guided
I ~~lo~~ care not for cold or heat
Frost and and Flame or sparks or sleet
To my essence are the same
But I honor more the flame—
Spright of fire I follow thee
Wheresoever it m[a]y be,
To the ~~very fire~~ torrid spouts fountains
Underneath earth quaked mountains
Or at thy supreme desire
Touch the very pulse of fire
With my bare unlidded eyes

Salam—

Sweet Dusketha: Paradise!
Off ye icy spirits—fly
Frosty creatures of sky—

Dusketha

Breathe upon them fiery spright

Zephyr Brema to each other

~~let us fly~~
~~Ah, my love, my love~~
Away Away to our delight

Salam

while we
Go feed on icicles ~~will we~~
Bedded in tongued flames will be

Dusketha

Lead me to those fevrous glooms
Sp[r]ight of fire

Breana

Me to the blooms
~~Soft~~ Blue eyed Zephyr of those flowers
Far in the west w[h]ere the May cloud lours
And the beams of still vesper, where winds are all wist
Are shed through the rain and the milder mist
And twilight your floating bowers—

I have been reading lately two very different books Robertson's America* and Voltaire's Siecle De Louis xiv It is like walking arm and arm between Pizarro and the great-little Monarch. In How lementabl[e] a case do we see the great body of the people in both instances: in the first, where Men might seem to inherit quiet of Mind from unsophisticated senses; from uncontamination of civilisation; and especially from their being as it were estranged from the mutual helps of Society and its mutual injuries—and thereby more immediately under the Protection of Providence—even there they had mortal pains to bear as bad; or even worse than Baliffs, Debts and Poverties of civilised Life—The whole appears to resolve into this— that Man is originally 'a poor forked creature' subject to the same mischances as the beasts of the forest, destined to hardships and disquietude of some kind or other. If he improves by degrees his bodily accomodations and comforts—at each stage, at each accent there are waiting for him a fresh set of annoyances—he is mortal and there is still a heaven with its Stars abov[e] his head. The most interesting question that can come before us is, How far by the per-severing endeavours of a seldom appearing Socrates Mankind may be made happy—I can imagine such happiness carried to an extreme—but what must it end in?—Death—and who could in such a case bear with death—the whole troubles of life which are now frittered away in a series of years, would the[n] be accumulated for the last days of a being who instead of hailing its approach, would leave this world as Eve left Paradise—But in truth I do not at all believe in this sort of perfectibility*—the nature of the world will not admit of it—the inhabitants of the world will correspond to itself—Let the fish phil-osophise the ice away from the Rivers in winter time and they shall be at continual play in the tepid delight of summer. Look at the Poles and at the sands of Africa, Whirlpools and volcanoes—Let men exterminate them and I will say that they may arrive at earthly Happiness—The point at which Man may arrive is as far as the paralel state in inanimate nature and no further—For instance sup-pose a rose to have sensation, it blooms on a beautiful morning it enjoys itself—but there comes a cold wind, a hot sun—it cannot escape it, it cannot destroy its annoyances—they are as native to the world as itself: no more can man be happy in spite, the world[l]y elements will prey upon his nature—The common cognomen of this world among the misguided and superstitious is 'a vale of tears' from which we are to be redeemed by a certain arbitrary interposition of God and taken to Heaven—What a little circumscribe[d] straight-ened notion! Call the world if you Please "The vale of Soul-making"* Then you will find out the use of the world (I am speaking now in the highest terms for human nature admitting it to be immortal which I will here take for granted for the purpose of showing a thought which has struck me concerning it) I say '*Soul making*' Soul as distinguished from an Intelligence—There may be intelligences or sparks of the divinity in millions—but they are not Souls ~~the~~ till they acquire identities, till each one is personally itself. I[n]telligences are atoms of perception—they know and they see and they are pure, in short they are God—how then are Souls to be made? How then are these sparks which are God to have identity given them—so as ever to possess a bliss peculiar to each ones individual existence? How, but by the medium of a world like this? This point I sincerely wish to consider because I think it a grander system of salvation than the chrystain religion—or rather it is a system of Spirit-creation—This is effected by three grand materials acting the one upon the other for a series of years—These three Materials are the *Intelligence*—the *human heart* (as distinguished from intelligence or Mind) and the *World* or *Elemental space* suited for the proper action of *Mind and Heart* on each other for the purpose of forming the *Soul* or *Intelligence destined to possess the sense of Identity*. I can scarcely express what I but dimly perceive—and yet I think I perceive it—that you may judge the more clearly I will put it in the most homely form possible—I will call the *world* a School instituted for the purpose of teaching little children to read—I will call the *human heart* the *horn Book* used in that School— and I will call the *Child able to read, the Soul* made from that *school* and its *hornbook*. Do you not see how necessary a World of Pains and troubles is to school an Intelligence and make it a soul? A Place where the heart must feel and suffer in a thousand diverse ways! Not merely is the Heart a Hornbook, It is the Minds Bible, it is the Minds experience, it is the teat from which the Mind or intelligence sucks its identity—As various as the Lives of Men are—so various become their souls, and thus does God make individual beings, Souls, Identical Souls of the sparks of his own essence—This appears to me a faint sketch of a system of Salvation which does not affront our reason and humanity—I am convinced that many difficulties which christians labour under would vanish before it—There is one wh[i]ch even now Strikes me—the Salvation of Children—In them the Spark or intelligence returns to God without any identity—it having had no time to learn of, and be altered by, the heart—or seat of the human Passions—It is pretty generally suspected that the chr[i]stian scheme has been coppied from the ancient persian and greek Philosophers. Why may they not have made this simple thing even more simple for common apprehension by introducing Mediators and Personages in the same manner as in the hethen mythology abstractions are personified—Seriously I think it probable that this System of Soul-making—may have been the Parent of all the more palpable and personal Schemes of Redemption, among the Zoroastrians the Christians and the Hindoos. For as one part of the human species must have their carved Jupiter; so another part must have the palpable and named Mediator and saviour, their Christ their Oromanes and their Vishnu—If what I have said should not be plain enough, as I fear it

may not be, I will but [*for* put] you in the place where I began in this
series of thoughts—I mean, I began by seeing how man was formed
by circumstances—and what are circumstances?—but touchstones
of his heart—? and what are touch stones?—but proovings of his
hearrt?—and what are proovings of his heart but fortifiers or alterers
of his nature? and what is his altered nature but his soul?—and what
was his soul before it came into the world and had These provings
and alterations and perfectionings?—An intelligence—without
Identity—and how is this Identity to be made? Through the medium
of the Heart? And how is the heart to become this Medium but in a
world of Circumstances?—There now I think what with Poetry and
Theology you may thank your Stars that my pen is not very long
winded—Yesterday I received two Letters from your Mother and
Henry which I shall send by young Birkbeck with this—
Friday—April 30—Brown has been rummaging up some of my old
sins—that is to say sonnets I do not think you remember them, so I
will copy them out as well as two or three lately written—I have just
written one on Fame—which Brown is transcribing and he has his
book and mine I must employ myself perhaps in a sonnet on the
same subject—

On Fame

You cannot eat your cake and have it too

Proverb.

fever'd   Man

How ∧ is that ~~Man misled~~ who cannot look
    Upon his mortal days with temperate blood
    Who vexes all the leaves of his Life's book
      And robs his fair name of its maidenhood
It is as if the rose should pluck herself
    Or the ripe plumb finger its misty bloom
As if a clear Lake meddling with itself
          cloud
      Should ~~fill~~ its pureness with a muddy gloon [*for* gloom]
But the rose leaves herself upon the Briar
    For winds to kiss and grateful Bees to ~~taste~~ feed
        ~~will~~ still
And the ripe plumb ~~still~~ wears its dim attire

234

The undisturbed Lake has crystal space—
                    leasing the world for grace
Why then should Man ~~his own bright name deface~~
~~And spoil burn our pleasures in his selfish fire~~—
Spoil his salvation by a fierce miscreed

Another on Fame

Fame like a wayward girl will still be coy
    To those who woo her with too slavish knees
But makes surrender to some thoughtless boy
And dotes the more upon a heart at ease
She is a Gipsey will not speak to those
    Who have not learnt to be content without her
A Jilt whose ear was never whisper'd close
    Who think they scandal her who talk about her—
A very Gipsey is she Nilus born,
Sister in law to jealous Potiphar.—
Ye lovesick Bards, repay her scorn for scorn.
Ye lovelorn Artists madmen that ye are,
Make your best bow to her and bid adieu
Then if she likes it she will follow you—

To Sleep

O soft embalmer of the still midnight
    Shutting with careful fingers and benign
Our gloom-pleas'd eyes embowered from the light,
    Enshaded in forgetfulness divine—
O soothest sleep, if so it please the[e] close
    In midst of this thine hymn my willing eyes,
Or wait the amen, ere thy poppy throws
    Around my bed it[s] dewy Charities—
Then save me or the passed day will shine
Upon my pillow breeding many woes.
Save me from curious conscience that still lords
                                    a
Its strength for darkness, borrowing like ~~the~~ Mole—
Turn the key deftly in the oiled wards
And seal the hushed Casket of my soul.

The following Poem—the last I have written is the first and the only one with which I have taken even moderate pains—I have for the most part dash'd of[f] my lines in a hurry—This I have done leisurely—I think it reads the more richly for it and will I hope encourage me to write other thing[s] in even a more peacable and healthy spirit. You must recollect that Psyche was not embodied as a goddess before the time of Apulieus the Platonist who lived afteir the Agustan age, and consequently the Goddess was never worshipped or sacrificed to with any of the ancient fervour—and perhaps never thought of in the old religion*—I am more orthodox that [*for* than] to let a hethen Goddess be so neglected—

Ode to Psyche—

O Goddess hear these tuneless numbers, wrung
   By sweet enforcement, and remembrance dear,
And pardon that thy secrets should be sung
   Even into thine own soft-chonched ear!
Surely I dreamt to day; or did I see
The winged Psyche, with awaked eyes?
I wander'd in a forest thoughtlessly,
And on the sudden, fainting with surprise,
Saw two fair Creatures couched side by side
In deepest grass beneath the whisp'ring fan
Of leaves and trembled blossoms, where there ran
A Brooklet scarce espied
'Mid hush'd, cool-rooted flowers, fragrant eyed,
Blue, freckle-pink, and budded syrian
They lay, calm-breathing on the bedded grass.
Their arms embraced and their pinions too;
Their lips touch'd not, but had not bid adiew,
As if disjoined by soft-handed slumber,
And ready still past kisses to outnumber,
At tender eye dawn of aurorian love.
The winged boy I knew:
But who wast thou O þ happy dove?
His Psyche true?

O lastest born, and loveliest vision far
  Of all Olympus faded Hierarchy!
Fairer than Phœbe's sapphire-region'd star,
  Or Vesper amorous glow worm of the sky;
Fairer than these though Temple thou hadst none,
  Nor Altar heap'd with flowers;
Nor virgin choir to make delicious moan
  Upon the midnight hours;
No voice, no lute, no pipe no incense sweet
  From chain-swung Censer teeming
No shrine, no grove, no Oracle, no heat
  Of pale-mouth'd Prophet dreaming!

O Bloomiest! though too late for antique vows;
  Too, too late for the fond believing Lyre,
When holy were the haunted forest boughs,
  Holy the air, the water and the fire:
Yet even in these days so far retir'd
From happy Pieties, thy lucent fans,
Fluttering among the faint Olympians,
I see, and sing by my own eyes inspired.

O let me be thy Choir and make a moan
Upon the midnight hours;
Thy voice, thy lute, thy pipe, thy incense sweet
From swinged Censer teeming;
Thy shrine, thy Grove, thy Oracle, thy heat
Of pale-mouth'd Prophet dreaming!
Yes I will be thy Priest and build a fane
In some untrodden region of my Mind,
Where branched thoughts new grown with pleasant pain.
Instead of pines shall murmur in the wind.
Far, far around shall those dark cluster'd trees
Fledge the wild-ridged mountains steep by steep,
And there by Zephyrs, streams and birds and bees
                    lull'd
The moss-lain Dryads shall be ~~charmed~~ to sleep.
And in the midst of this wide-quietness
A rosy Sanctuary will I dress

With the wreath'd trellis of a working brain;
With buds and bells and stars without a mane [*for* name];
                         feign
With all the gardener, fancy e'er could ~~frame~~
Who breeding flowers will never breed the same—
And there shall be for thee all soft delight
  That shadowy thought can win;
A bright torch, and a casement ope at night,
  To let the warm Love in—

Here endethe ye Ode to Psyche

—————

Incipit altera Sonneta.

—————

I have been endeavouring to discover a better sonnet stanza than we have. The legitimate does not suit the language over-well from the pouncing rhymes—the other kind appears too elegiac—and the couplet at the end of it has seldom a pleasing effect—I do not pretend to have succeeded—It will explain itself—

    If by dull rhymes our english must be chaind
    And, like Andromeda, the Sonnet sweet,
    Fetterd in spite of pained Loveliness;
    Let us find out, if we must be constrain'd,
    Sandals more interwoven & complete
    To fit the naked foot of Poesy;
    Let us inspect the Lyre & weight the stress
    Of every chord & see what may be gained
    By ear industrious & attention meet,
    Misers of sound & syllable no less,
    Than Midas of his coinage, let us be
    Jealous of dead leaves in the bay wreath Crown;
    So if we may not let the Muse be free,
    She will be bound with Garlands of her own.

Here endeth the other Sonnet—this is the 3^d of May & every thing is in delightful forwardness; the violets are not withered, before the peeping of the first rose; You must let me know every thing, how parcels go & come, what papers you have, & what Newspapers you want, & other things—God bless you my dear Brother & Sister

Your ever Affectionate Brother

John Keats—

To Miss Jeffery,[1] 31 May 1819

C. Brown Esq^{re's}

My dear Lady,   Wentworth Place—Hampstead—

I was making a day or two ago a general conflagration of all old Letters and Memorandums, which had become of no interest to me—I made however, like the Barber-inquisitor in Don Quixote some reservations—among the rest your and your Sister's Letters. I assure you you had not entirely vanished from my Mind, or even become shadows in my remembrance: it only needed such a memento as your Letters to bring you back to me—Why have I not written before? Why did I not answer your Honiton Letter? I had no good news for you—every concern of ours, (ours I wish I could say) and still I must say *ours*—though George is in America and I have no Brother left—Though in the midst of my troubles I had no relation except my young sister I have had excellent friends. Mr B. at whose house I now am, invited me,—I have been with him ever since. I could not make up my mind to let you know these things. Nor should I now—but see what a little interest will do—I want you to do me a Favor; which I will first ask and then tell you the reasons. Enquire in the Villages round Teignmouth if there is any Lodging commodious for its cheapness; and let me know where it is and what price. I have the choice as it were of two Poisons (yet I ought not to call this a Poison) the one is voyaging to and from India* for a few years; the other is leading a fevrous life alone with Poetry—This latter will suit me best—for I cannot resolve to give up my Studies It strikes me it would not be quite so proper for you to make such inquiries—so give my love to your Mother and ask her to do it. Yes, I would rather conquer my indolence and strain my ne[r]ves at some grand Poem—than be in a dunder-headed indiaman—Pray let no

---

[1] See Appendix, note 5.

one in Teignmouth know any thing of this—Fanny must by this time have altered her name—perhaps you have also—are you all alive? Give my Comp^ts to M^rs—your Sister. I have had good news, (tho' 'tis a queerish world in which such things are call'd good) from George—he and his wife are well—I will tell you more soon— Especially dont let the Newfoundland fisherman know it—and especially no one else—I have been always till now almost as careless of the world as a fly—my troubles were all of the Imagination—My Brother George always stood between me and any dealings with the world—Now I find I must buffet it—I must take my stand upon some vantage ground and begin to fight—I must choose between despair & Energy—I choose the latter—though the world has taken on a quakerish look with me, which I once thought was impossible—

> 'Nothing can bring back the hour
> Of splendour in the grass and glory in the flower'*

I once thought this a Melancholist's dream—
  But why do I speak to you in this manner? No believe me I do not write for a mere selfish purpose—the manner in which I have written of myself will convince you. I do not do so to Strangers. I have not quite made up my mind—Write me on the receipt of this—and again at your Leisure; between whiles you shall hear from me again—

Your sincere friend
John Keats

To Miss Jeffery,[1] *9 June 1819*

Wentworth Place.

My Dear young Lady,—I am exceedingly obliged by your two letters—Why I did not answer your first immediately was that I have had a little aversion to the South of Devon from the continual remembrance of my Brother Tom. On that account I do not return to my old Lodgins in Hampstead though the people of the house have become friends of mine—This however I could think nothing of, it can do no more than keep one's thoughts employed for a day or two. I like your description of Bradley very much and I dare say shall

---

[1] See Appendix, note 5.

be there in the course of the summer; it would be immediately but that a friend with ill health and to whom I am greatly attached* call'd on me yesterday and proposed my spending a Month with him at the back of the Isle of Wight. This is just the thing at present—the morrow will take care of itself—I do not like the name of Bishop's Teigntown—I hope the road from Teignmouth to Bradley does not lie that way—Your advice about the Indiaman is a very wise advice, because it just suits me, though you are a little in the wrong concerning its destroying the energies of Mind: on the contrary it would be the finest thing in the world to strengthen them—To be thrown among people who care not for you, with whom you have no sympathies forces the Mind upon its own resources, and leaves it free to make its speculations of the differences of human character and to class them with the calmness of a Botanist. An Indiaman is a little world. One of the great reasons that the English have produced the finest writers in the world: is, that the English world has ill-treated them during their lives and foster'd them after their deaths. They have in general been trampled aside into the bye paths of life and seen the festerings of Society. They have not been treated like the Raphaels of Italy. And where is the Englishman and Poet who has given a magnifacent Entertainment at the christening of one of his Hero's Horses as Boyardo did?* He had a Castle in the Appenine. He was a noble Poet of Romance; not a miserable and mighty Poet of the human Heart. The middle age of Shakspeare was all c[l]ouded over; his days were not more happy than Hamlet's who is perhaps more like Shakspeare himself in his common every day Life than any other of his Characters—Ben Johnson was a common Soldier and in the Low countries, in the face of two armies, fought a single combat with a french Trooper and slew him—For all this I will not go on board an Indiaman, nor for examples sake run my head into dark alleys: I dare say my discipline is to come, and plenty of it too. I have been very idle lately, very averse to writing; both from the overpowering idea of our dead poets and from abatement of my love of fame. I hope I am a little more of a Philosopher than I was, consequently a little less of a versifying Pet-lamb.* I have put no more in Print or you should have had it. You will judge of my 1819 temper when I tell you that the thing I have most enjoyed this year has been writing an ode to Indolence. Why did you not make your long-haired sister put her great brown hard fist to paper and cross your Letter? Tell her when you write again that I expect chequer-work—My friend Mr. Brown is sitting opposite me employed in writing a Life of David. He reads me passages as he writes them stuffing my infidel mouth as though I were a young rook—Infidel Rooks do not provender with Elisha's Ravens. If he goes on as he has begun your new Church had better not proceed, for parsons will be superseeded—and of course the Clerks must follow. Give my love to your Mother with the assurance that I can never forget her anxiety for my Brother Tom. Believe also that I shall ever remember our leave-taking with *you*.

Ever sincerely yours'
John Keats.

To Fanny Keats, 9 June 1819

My dear Fanny,   Wentworth Place.

I shall be with you next monday at the farthest—I could not keep my promise of seeing you again in a week because I am in so unselted [*for* unsettled] a state of mind about what I am to do—I have given up the Idea of the Indiaman; I cannot resolve to give up my favorite studies: so I purpose to retire into the Country and set my Mind at work once more. A Friend of Mine who has an ill state of health called on me yesterday and proposed to spend a little time with him at the back of the Isle of Wight where he said we might live very cheaply—I agreed to his proposal. I have taken a great dislike to Town I never go there—some one is always calling one [*for* on] me and as we have spare beds they often stop a couple of days—I have written lately to some Acquaintances in Devonshire concer[n]ing a cheap Lodging and they have been very kind in letting me know all I wanted—They have described a pleasant place which I think I shall eventually retire to. How came you on With my young Master York-shire Man?* Did not Mrs A. sport her Carriage and one? They really surprised me with super civility—how did Mr A. manage it? How is the old tadpole gardener and little Master next door? it is to be hop'd they will both die some of these days. Not having been to Town I have not heard whether M^r A—purposes to retire from business. Do let me know if you have heard any thing more about it. I[f] he should not I shall be very disappointed—If any one deserves to be put to his shifts it is that Hodgkinson—As for the other he would live a long time upon his fat and be none the worse for a good long lent. How came milidi to give one Lisbon wine—had she drained the Gooseberry? Truly I cannot delay making another visit—asked to take Lunch, whether I will have ale, wine take sur g ar,—objection to green—like cream—thin bread and butter—another cup—agreeable—enough sugar—little more cream—too weak 12 shillin & &c &c lord I must come again

We are just going to Dinner I must must [*for* run] with this to the Post—Your affectionate Brother

John—

To B. R. Haydon, 17 June 1819

My dear Haydon,   Wentworth Place,
Thursday Morning

I know you will not be quite prepared for this, because your Pocket must needs be very low having been at ebb tide so long: but what can I do? mine is lower. I was the day before yesterday much in want of Money: but some news I had yesterday has driven me into necessity. I went to Abbey's for some Cash, and he put into my hand a Letter from my Aunt's Solicitor containing the pleasant information that she was about to file a Bill in Chancery against us*—Now in case of a defeat Abbey will be very undeservedly in the wrong box; so I could not ask him for any more money, nor can I till the affair is decided; and if it goes against him I must in conscience make over to him what little he may have remaining. My purpose is now to make one more attempt in the Press* if that fail, 'ye hear no more of me'* as Chaucer says—Brown has lent me some money for the present. Do borrow or beg some how what you can for me. Do not suppose I am at all uncomfortable about the matter in any other way than as it forces me to apply to the needy—I could not send you those lines, for I could not get the only copy of them before last ~~friday~~ Satu[r]-day evening. I sent them Mr Elmes on Monday*—I saw Monkhouse on sunday—he told me you were getting on with the Picture—I would have come over to you to day, but I am fully employed—

Your's ever sincerely
John Keats—

To Fanny Keats, 17 June 1819

My dear Fanny,   Wentworth Place

Still I cannot affo[r]d to spend money by Coachire and still my
throat is not well enough to warrant my walking—I went yesterday
to ask Mr Abbey for some money; but I could not on account of a
Letter he showed me from my Aunt's Solicitor—You do not understand the business—I trust it will not in the end be detrimental to
you. I am going to try the Press onece more and to that end shall
retire to live cheaply in the country and compose myself and verses
as well as I can—I have very good friends ready to help me—and I
am the more bound to be careful of the money they lend me—It will
all be well in the course of a year I hope—I am confident of it, so do
not let it trouble you at all—Mr Abbey showed me a Letter he had
received from George containing the news of the birth of a Niece for
us—and all doing well—he said he would take it to you—so I suppose to day you will see it. I was prepa[r]ing to enqu[i]re for a
Situation with an Apothecary, put [*for* but] Mr Brown persuads me
to try the press once more; so I will with all my industry and ability.
Mr Rice a friend of mine in ill health has proposed ret[i]ring to the
back of the isle of wight—which I hope will be cheap in the
summer—I am sure it will in the winter. Thence you shall frequently
hear from me and in the Letters I will coppy those lines I may write
which will be most pleasing to you in the confidence you will show
them to no one—I have not run quite aground yet I hope, having
written this morning to several people to whom I have lent money,
requesting repayment. I shall hencefore shake off my indolent fits,
and among other reformation be more diligent in writing to you and
mind you always answer me—I shall be obliged to go out of town on
Saturday and shall have no money till tomorrow, so I am very sorry
to think I shall not be able to come to Walthamstow—The Head M^r
Seve[r]n did of me is now too dear but here inclosed is a very capital
Profile done by Mr Brown. I will write again on Monday or
Tuesday—M^r and Mrs Dilke are well—

Your affectionate Brother

John—

To Fanny Brawne, 1 July 1819

Shanklin,
Isle of Wight, Thursday.

My dearest Lady,

I am glad I had not an opportunity of sending off a Letter which I wrote for you on Tuesday night—'twas too much like one out of Ro[u]sseau's Heloise.* I am more reasonable this morning. The morning is the only proper time for me to write to a beautiful Girl whom I love so much: for at night, when the lonely day has closed, and the lonely, silent, unmusical Chamber is waiting to receive me as into a Sepulchre, then believe me my passion gets entirely the sway, then I would not have you see those Rapsodies which I once thought it impossible I should ever give way to, and which I have often laughed at in another, for fear you should [think me] either too unhappy or perhaps a little mad. I am now at a very pleasant Cottage window, looking onto a beautiful hilly country, with a glimpse of the sea; the morning is very fine. I do not know how elastic my spirit might be, what pleasure I might have in living here and breathing and wandering as free as a stag about this beautiful Coast if the remembrance of you did not weigh so upon me. I have never known any unalloy'd Happiness for many days together: the death or sickness of some one has always spoilt my hours—and now when none such troubles oppress me, it is you must confess very hard that another sort of pain should haunt me. Ask yourself my love whether you are not very cruel to have so entrammelled me, so destroyed my freedom. Will you confess this in the Letter you must write immediately and do all you can to console me in it—make it rich as a draught of poppies to intoxicate me—write the softest words and kiss them that I may at least touch my lips where yours have been. For myself I know not how to express my devotion to so fair a form: I want a brighter word than bright, a fairer word than fair. I almost wish we were butterflies and liv'd but three summer days—three such days with you I could fill with more delight than fifty common years could ever contain. But however selfish I may feel, I am sure I could never act selfishly: as I told you a day or two before I left Hampstead, I will never return to London if my Fate does not turn up Pam* or at least a Court-card. Though I could centre my

Happiness in you, I cannot expect to engross your heart so entirely—indeed if I thought you felt as much for me as I do for you at this moment I do not think I could restrain myself from seeing you again tomorrow for the delight of one embrace. But no—I must live upon hope and Chance. In case of the worst that can happen, I shall still love you—but what hatred shall I have for another! Some lines I read the other day are continually ringing a peal in my ears:

> To see those eyes I prize above mine own
> Dart favors on another—
> And those sweet lips (yielding immortal nectar)
> Be gently press'd by any but myself—
> Think, think Francesca, what a cursed thing
> It were beyond expression!*

J.

Do write immediately. There is no Post from this Place, so you must address Post Office, Newport, Isle of Wight. I know before night I shall curse myself for having sent you so cold a Letter; yet it is better to do it as much as in my senses as possible. Be as kind as the distance will permit to your

J. Keats.

Present my Compliments to your mother, my love to Margaret* and best remembrances to your Brother—if you please so.

To Fanny Keats, 6 July 1819

Shanklin
Isle of Wight
Tuesday July 6th—

My dear Fanny,

I have just received another Letter from George—full of as good news as we can expect. I cannot inclose it to you as I could wish, because it contains matters of Business to which I must for a Week to come have an immediate reference. I think I told you the purpose for which I retired to this place—to try the fortune of my Pen once more, and indeed I have some confidence in my success: but in every event, believe me my dear sister, I shall be sufficiently comfortable,

as, if I cannot lead that life of competence and society I should wish,
I have enough knowledge of my gallipots* to ensure me an employment & maintainance. The Place I am in now I visited once before
and a very pretty place it is were it not for the bad Weather. Our
window looks over house tops and Cliffs onto the Sea, so that when
the Ships sail past the Cottage chimneys you may take them for
Weathercocks. We have Hill and Dale forest and Mead and plenty of
Lobsters. I was on the Portsmouth Coach the Sunday before last in
that heavy shower—and I may say I went to Portsmouth by water—I
got a little cold and as it always flies to my throat I am a little out of
sorts that way—There were on the Coach with me some common
french people, but very well behaved—there was a woman amongst
them to whom the poor Men in ragged coats were more gallant than
ever I saw gentleman to Lady at a Ball—When we got down to walk
up hill—one of them pick'd a rose, and on remounting gave it to the
woman with—'Ma'mselle—voila une bell rose!' I am so hard at work
that perhaps I should not have written to you for a day or two if
Georges Letter had not diverted my attention to the interests and
pleasure of those I love—and ever believe that when I do not behave
punctually it is from a very necessary occupation, and that my
silence is no proof of my not thinking of you, or that I want more
than a gentle philip to bring you image with every claim before me—
You have never seen mountains, or I might tell you that the hill at
Steephill is I think almost of as much consequence as Mount Rydal
on Lake Winander. Bonchurch too is a very delightful Place—as I
can see by the Cottages all romantic—covered with creepers and
honey-sickles with roses and eglantines peeping in at the windows.
Fit abodes, for the People I guess live in them, romantic old maids
fond of no⟨vels⟩ or soldiers widows with a pretty jointure—or a⟨ny⟩
body's widows or aunts or any things given to Poetry and a Piano
forte—as far as in 'em lies—as people say. If I could play upon the
Guitar I might make my fortune with an old song—and get t[w]o
blessings at once—a Lady's heart and the Rheumatism. But I am
almost affraid to peep at those little windows—for a pretty window
should show a pretty face, and as the world goes chances are against
me. I am living with a very good fellow indeed, a Mr Rice—He is
unfortunately labouring under a complaint which has for some years
been a burthen to him—This is a pain to me. He has a greater tact in

speaking to people of the village than I have, and in those matters is a great amusement as well [as] a good friend to me. He bought a ham the other day for say he 'Keats, I don't think a Ham is a wrong thing to have in a house.' Write to me, Shanklin Isle of Wight as soon as you can; for a Letter is a great treat to me here—believeing me ever your affectionate Brother, John—

[R]   *To Fanny Brawne, 8 July 1819*

July 8th

My sweet Girl,

Your Letter gave me more delight, than any thing in the world but yourself could do; indeed I am almost astonished that any absent one should have that luxurious power over my senses which I feel. Even when I am not thinking of you I receive your influence and a tenderer nature steeling upon me. All my thoughts, my unhappiest days and nights have I find not at all cured me of my love of Beauty, but made it so intense that I am miserable that you are not with me: or rather breathe in that dull sort of patience that cannot be called Life. I never knew before, what such a love as you have made me feel, was; I did not believe in it; my Fancy was affraid of it, lest it should burn me up. But if you will fully love me, though there may be some fire, 't will not be more than we can bear when moistened and bedewed with Pleasures. You mention 'horrid people' and ask me whether it depend upon them, whether I see you again—Do understand me, my love, in this—I have so much of you in my heart that I must turn Mentor when I see a chance of ha[r]m beffaling you. I would never see any thing but Pleasure in your eyes, love on your lips, and Happiness in your steps. I would wish to see you among those amusements suitable to your inclinations and spirits; so that our loves might be a delight in the midst of Pleasures agreeable enough, rather than a resource from vexations and cares—But I doubt much, in case of the worst, whether I shall be philosopher enough to follow my own Lessons: if I saw my resolution give you a pain I could not. Why may I not speak of your Beauty, since without that I could never have lov'd you—I cannot conceive any beginning of such love as I have for you but Beauty. There may be a sort of love for which, without the least sneer at it, I have the highest respect, and can admire it in others: but it has not the richness, the bloom, the full form, the enchantment of love after my own heart. So let me speak of you Beauty, though to my own endangering; if you could be so cruel to me as to try elsewhere its Power. You say you are affraid I shall think you do not love me—in saying this you make me ache the more to be near you. I am at the diligent use of my faculties here, I do not pass a day without sprawling some blank verse or tagging some rhymes; and here I must confess, that, (since I am on that subject,) I love you the more in that I believe you have liked me for my own sake and for nothing else—I have met with women whom I really think would like to be married to a Poem and to be given away by a Novel. I have seen your Comet, and only wish it was a sign that poor Rice would get well whose illness makes him rather a melancholy companion: and the more so as so to conquer his feelings and hide them from me, with a forc'd Pun. I kiss'd your writing over in the hope you had indulg'd me by leaving a trace of honey—What was your dream? Tell it me and I will tell you the interpretation thereof.

Ever yours my love!

John Keats—

Do not accuse me of delay—we have not here an opportunity of sending letters every day—Write speedily—

*To J. H. Reynolds, 11 July 1819**

My dear Reynolds,

*   *   *   *   *   *

You will be glad to hear under my own hand (tho' Rice says we are like sauntering Jack & Idle Joe)* how diligent I have been, & am being. I have finish'd the Act* and in the interval of beginning the 2^d have proceeded pretty well with Lamia, finishing the 1st part which consists of about 400 lines. I have great hopes of success, because I make use of my Judgment more deliberately than I yet have done; but in Case of failure with the world, I shall find my content. And here (as I know you have my good at heart as much as a Brother,) I can only repeat to you what I have said to George*—that however I sho^d like to enjoy what the competences of life procure, I am in no wise dashed at a different prospect. I have spent too many thoughtful days & moralized thro' too many nights for that, and fruitless wo^d they be indeed, if they did not by degrees make me look upon the affairs of the world with a healthy deliberation. I have of late been moulting: not for fresh feathers & wings: they are gone, and in their stead I hope to have a pair of patient sublunary legs. I have altered, not from a Chrysalis into a butterfly, but the Contrary. having two little loopholes, whence I may look out into the stage of the world: and that world on our coming here I almost forgot. The first time I sat down to write, I co^d scarcely believe in the necessity of so doing. It struck me as a great oddity—Yet the very corn which is now so beautiful, as if it had only took to ripening yesterday, is for the market: So, why sho^d I be delicate.—

To Fanny Brawne, 15 (?) July 1819

Shanklin
Thursday Evening

My love,

I have been in so irritable a state of health these two or three last days, that I did not think I should be able to write this week. Not that I was so ill, but so much so as only to be capable of an unhealthy teasing letter. To night I am greatly recovered only to feel the languor I have felt after you touched with ardency. You say you perhaps might have made me better: you would then have made me worse: now you could quite effect a cure: What fee my sweet Physician would I not give you to do so. Do not call it folly, when I tell you I took your letter last night to bed with me. In the morning I found your name on the sealing wax obliterated. I was startled at the bad omen till I recollected that it must have happened in my dreams, and they you know fall out by contraries. You must have found out by this time I am a little given to bode ill like the raven; it is my misfortune not my fault; it has proceeded from the general tenor of the circumstances of my life, and rendered every event suspicious. However I will no more trouble either you or myself with sad Prophecies; though so far I am pleased at it as it has given me opportunity to love your disinterestedness towards me. I can be a raven no more; you and pleasure take possession of me at the same moment. I am afraid you have been unwell. If through me illness have touched you (but it must be with a very gentle hand) I must be selfish enough to feel a little glad at it. Will you forgive me this? I have been reading lately an oriental tale of a very beautiful color—* It is of a city of melancholy men, all made so by this circumstance. Through a series of adventures each one of them by turns reach some gardens of Paradise where they meet with a most enchanting Lady; and just as they are going to embrace her, she bids them shut their eyes—they shut them—and on opening their eyes again find themselves descending to the earth in a magic basket. The remembrance of this Lady and their delights lost beyond all recovery render them melancholy ever after. How I applied this to you, my dear; how I palpitated at it; how the certainty that you were in the same world with myself, and though as beautiful, not so talismanic as that Lady; how I could not bear you should be so you must believe because I swear it by yourself. I cannot say when I shall get a volume ready. I have three or four stories half done, but as I cannot write for the mere sake of the press, I am obliged to let them progress or lie still as my fancy chooses. By Christmas perhaps they may appear, but I am not yet sure they ever will. 'Twill be no matter, for Poems are as common as newspapers and I do not see why it is a greater crime in me than in another to let the verses of an half-fledged brain tumble into the reading-rooms and drawing room windows. Rice has been better lately than usual: he is not suffering from any neglect of his parents who have for some years been able to appreciate him better than they did in his first youth, and are now devoted to his comfort. Tomorrow I shall, if my health continues to improve during the night, take a look fa[r]ther about the country, and spy at the parties about here who come hunting after the picturesque like beagles. It is astonishing how they raven down scenery like children do sweetmeats. The wondrous Chine here is a very great Lion: I wish I had as many guineas as there have been spy-glasses in it. I have been, I cannot tell why, in capital spirits this last hour. What reason? When I have to take my candle and retire to a lonely room, without the thought as I fall asleep, of seeing you tomorrow morning? or the next day, or the next—it takes on the appearance of impossibility and eternity—I will say a month—I will say I will see you in a month at most, though no one but yourself should see me; if it be but for an hour. I should not like to be so near you as London without being continually with you: after having once more kissed you Sweet I would rather be here alone at my task than in the bustle and hateful literary chit-chat. Meantime you must write to me—as I will every week—for your letters keep me alive. My sweet Girl I cannot speak my love for you. Good night! and

> Ever yours
> John Keats.

To Fanny Brawne, 25 July 1819

Sunday Night.

My sweet Girl,

I hope you did not blame me much for not obeying your request of a Letter on Saturday: we have had four in our small room playing at cards night and morning leaving me no undisturb'd opportunity to write. Now Rice and Martin are gone, I am at liberty. Brown to my sorrow confirms the account you give of your ill health. You cannot conceive how I ache to be with you: how I would die for one hour— —for what is in the world? I say you cannot conceive; it is impossible you should look with such eyes upon me as I have upon you: it cannot be. Forgive me if I wander a little this evening, for I have been all day employ'd in a very abstr[a]ct Poem and I am in deep love with you—two things which must excuse me. I have, believe me, not been an age in letting you take possession of me; the very first week I knew you I wrote myself your vassal; but burnt the Letter as the very next time I saw you I thought you manifested some dislike to me. If you should ever feel for Man at the first sight what I did for you, I am lost. Yet I should not quarrel with you, but hate myself if such a thing were to happen—only I should burst if the thing were not as fine as a Man as you are as a Woman. Perhaps I am too vehement, then fancy me on my knees, especially when I mention a part of you Letter which hurt me; you say speaking of Mr. Severn 'but you must be satisfied in knowing that I admired you much more than your friend.' My dear love, I cannot believe there ever was or ever could be any thing to admire in me especially as far as sight goes—I cannot be admired, I am not a thing to be admired. You are, I love you; all I

can bring you is a swooning admiration of your Beauty. I hold that
place among Men which snub-nos'd brunettes with meeting eye-
brows do among women—they are trash to me—unless I should find
one among them with a fire in her heart like the one that burns in
mine. You absorb me in spite of myself—you alone: for I look not
forward with any pleasure to what is call'd being settled in the world;
I tremble at domestic cares—yet for you I would meet them, though
if it would leave you the happier I would rather die than do so. I have
two luxuries to brood over in my walks, your Loveliness and the hour
of my death. O that I could have possession of them both in the same
minute. I hate the world: it batters too much the wings of my self-
will, and would I could take a sweet poison from your lips to send me
out of it. From no others would I take it. I am indeed astonish'd to
find myself so careless of all cha[r]ms but yours—remembring as I
do the time when even a bit of ribband was a matter of interest with
me. What softer words can I find for you after this—what it is I will
not read. Nor will I say more here, but in a Postscript answer any
thing else you may have mentioned in your Letter in so many
words—for I am distracted with a thousand thoughts. I will imagine
you Venus to night and pray, pray, pray to your star like a Hethen.

> Your's ever, fair Star,
>
> John Keats.

My seal is mark'd like a family table cloth with my mother's initial F
for Fanny: put between my Father's initials. You will soon hear from
me again. My respectful Compts to your Mother. Tell Margaret I'll
send her a reef of best rocks and tell Sam* I will give him my light
bay hunter if he will tie the Bishop hand and foot and pack him in a
hamper and send him down for me to bathe him for his health with a
Necklace of good snubby stones about his Neck.

To C. W. Dilke, 31 July 1819

> Shanklin Saturday Eveng

My dear Dilke,

I will not make my diligence an excuse for not writing to you
sooner—because I consider idleness a much better plea. A Man in
the hurry of business of any sort is expected and ought to be

expected to look to every thing—his mind is in a whirl, and what matters it—what whirl? But to require a Letter of a Man lost in idleness is the utmost cruelty, you cut the thread of his existence, you beat, you pummel him, You sell his goods and chattles, you put him in prison; you impale him; you c[r]ucify him—If I had not put pen to paper since I saw you this would be to me a vi et armis taking up before the Judge—but having got over my darling lounging habits a little; it is with scarcely any pain I come to this dating from Shankling and Dr Dilke, The Isle of Wight is but so so &c. Rice and I passed rather a dull time of it. I hope he will not repent coming with me. He was unwell and I was not in very good health: and I am affraid we made each other worse by acting upon each others spirits. We would grow as melancholy as need be. I confess I cannot bear a sick person in a House especially alone—it weighs upon me day and night—and more so when perhaps the Case is irretrievable—Indeed I think Rice is in a dangerous state. I have had a Letter from him which speaks favourably of his health at present—Brown and I are pretty well harnessed again to our dog-cart. I mean the Tragedy which goes on sinkingly—We are thinking of introducing an Elephant but have not historical referance within reach to determine us as to Otho's Menagerie. When Brown first mention'd this I took it for a Joke; however he brings such plausible reasons, and discourses so eloquently on the dramatic effect that I am giving it a serious consideration. The Art of Poetry is not sufficient for us, and if we get on in that as well as we do in painting we shall by next winter crush the Reviews and the royal Academy. Indeed if Brown would take a little of my advice he could not fail to be first pallet of his day. But odd as it may appear, he says plainly that he cannot see any force in my plea for putting Skies in the back ground—and leaving indian ink out of an ash tree—The other day he was sketching Shanklin Church and as I saw how the business was going on, I challenged him to a trial of Skill—he lent me Pencil and Paper—we keep the Sketches to contend for the Prize at the Gallerry—I will not say whose I think best—but really I do not think Brown's done to the top of the Art—A word or two on the Isle of Wight—I have been no further than Steephill. If I may guess I should [say] that there is no finer part in the Island than from this Place to Steephill—I do not hesitate to say it is fine. Bonchurch is the best. But I have been so many finer walks, with a back ground of lake and mountain instedd of the sea, that I am not much touch'd with it, though I credit it for all the Surprise I should have felt if it had taken my cockney maidenhead—But I may call myself an old Stager in the picturesque, and unless it be something very large and overpowering I cannot receive any extraordinary relish. I am sorry to hear that Charles is so much oppress'd at Westminster: though I am sure it will be the finest touch stone for his Metal in the world—His troubles will grow day by day less, as his age and strength increase. The very first Battle he wins will lift him from the Tribe of Manassah.* I do not know how I should feel were I a Father—but I hope I should strive with all my Power not to let the present trouble me—When your Boy shall be twenty, ask him about his childish troubles and he will have no more memory of them than you have of yours—Brown tells me Mrs Dilke sets off to day for Chichester—I am glad—I was going to say she had a fine day—but there has been a great Thunder cloud muttering over Hampshire all day—I hope she is now at supper with a good Appetite—So Reynolds's Piece succeeded*—that is all well. Papers have with thanks been duly received. We leave this Place on the 13th and will let you know where we may be a few days after—Brown says he will write when the fit comes on him. If you will stand law expences I'll beat him into one before his time—When I come to town I shall have a little talk with you about Brown and one Jenny Jacobs. Open daylight! he don't care. I am affraid the[r]e will be some more feet for little stockings*—of Keats' making. (I mean the feet.). Brown here tried at a piece of Wit but it failed him, as you see though long a brewing,—this is a 2^d lie*—Men should never despair—you see he has tried again and succeeded to a miracle—He wants to try again, but as I have a right to an inside place in my own Letter—I take possession. Your sincere friend. John Keats—

[R]   *To Fanny Brawne, 5, 6 August 1819*

My dear Girl,   Shanklin Thursday Night—
    You say you must not have any more such Letters as the last: I'll try that you shall not by running obstinate the other way—Indeed I have not fair play—I am not idle enough for proper downright love-letters—I leave this minute a scene in our Tragedy and see you

(think it not blasphemy) through the mist of Plots speeches, coun-
terplots and counter speeches—The Lover is madder than I am–I
am nothing to him—he has a figure like the Statue of Maleager* and
double distilled fire in his heart. Thank God for my diligence! were it
not for that I should be miserable. I encourage it, and strive not to
think of you—but when I have succeeded in doing so all day and as
far as midnight, you return as soon as this artificial excitement goes
off more severely from the fever I am left in—Upon my soul I
cannot say what you could like me for. I do not think myself a fright
any more than I do Mr A Mr B. and Mr C—yet if I were a woman I
should not like A— B. C. But enough of this—So you intend to hold
me to my promise of seeing you in a short time. I shall keep it with as
much sorrow as gladness: for I am not one of the Paladins of old who
livd upon water grass and smiles for years together—What though
would I not give to night for the gratification of my eyes alone? This
day week we shall move to Winchester; for I feel the want of a
Library. Brown will leave me there to pay a visit to Mr Snook at
Bedhampton: in his absence I will flit to you and back. I will stay
very little while; for as I am in a train of writing now I fear to disturb
it—let it have its course bad or good—in it I shall try my own
strength and the public pulse. At Winchester I shall get your Letters
more readily; and it being a cathedral City I shall have a pleasure
always a great one to me when near a Cathedral, of reading them
during the service up and down the Aisle—
Friday Morning Just as I had written thus far last night, Brown
came down in his morning coat and nightcap, saying he had been
refresh'd by a good sleep and was very hungry—I left him eating and
went to bed being too tired to enter into any discussions. You would
delight very greatly in the walks about here, the Cliffs, woods, hills,
sands, rocks &c about here. They are however not so fine but I shall
give them a hearty good bye to exchange them for my Cathedrall—
Yet again I am not so tired of Scenery as to hate Switzerland—We
might spend a pleasant Year at Berne or Zurich—if it should please
Venus to hear my 'Beseech thee to hear us O Goddess" And if she
should hear god forbid we should what people call, *settle*—turn into
a pond, a stagnant Lethe—a vile crescent, row or buildings. Better
be imprudent moveables than prudent fixtures—Open my Mouth at
the Street door like the Lion's head at Venice to receive hateful cards

Letters messages. Go out an⟨d⟩ wither at tea parties; freeze at dinners; bake at dance⟨s,⟩ simmer at routs. No my love, trust yourself to
me and I will find you nobler amusements; fortune favouring. I fear
you will not receive this till Sunday or Monday; as the irishman
would write do not in the mean while hate me—I long to be off for
Winchester for I begin to dislike the very door post⟨s⟩ here—the
names, the pebbles. You ask after my health, not telling me whether
you are better. I am quite well. You going out is no proof that you
are: how is it? Late hours will do you great harm—What fairing is it?
I was alone for a couple of days while Brown went gadding over the
country with his ancient knapsack. Now I like his society as wells
[*for* well] as any Man's, yet regretted his return—it broke in upon
me like a Thunderbolt—I had got in a dream among my Books—
really luxuriating in a solitude and silence you alone should have
disturb'd—

> Your ever affectionate
> John Keats—

To Benjamin Bailey [fragment], *14 August 1819*

*   *   *

We removed to Winchester for the convenience of a Library and find
it an exceeding pleasant Town, enriched with a beautiful Cathedrall
and surrounded by a fresh-looking country. We are in tolerably good
and cheap Lodgings. Within these two Months I have written 1500
Lines, most of which besides many more of prior composition you
will probably see by next Winter. I have written two Tales, one from
Boccacio call'd the Pot of Basil; and another call'd St Agnes' Eve on a
popular superstition; and a third call'd Lamia—(half finished—I
⟨hav⟩e a⟨I⟩so been writing parts of my Hyperion and ⟨c⟩ompleted
4 Acts of a Tragedy. It was the opinion of most of my friends that
I should never be able to ⟨write⟩ a ⟨s⟩cene—I will endeavour to wipe
awa⟨y the prejudice—⟩ I sincerely hope you will be pleased when my
Labours since we last saw each other shall reach you—One of my
Ambitions is to make as great a revolution in modern dramatic writing* as Kean has done in acting—another to upset the drawling of
the blue stocking literary world*—if in the course of a few years I do
these two things I ought to die content—and my friends should

drink a dozen of Claret on my Tomb—I am convinced more and
more every day that (excepting the human friend Philosopher) a fine
writer is the most genuine Being in the World—Shakspeare and the
paradise Lost every day become greater wonders to me—I look upon
fine Phrases like a Lover—I was glad to see, by a Passage in one of
Brown's Letters some time ago from the north that you were in such
good Spirits—Since that you have been married and in congra[tu]-
lating you I wish you every continuance of them—Present my
Respects to Mrs Bailey. This sounds oddly to me, and I dare say I do
it awkwardly enough: but I suppose by this time it is nothing new to
you—Brown's remembrances to you—As far as I know we shall
remain at Winchester for a goodish while—

Ever your sincere friend
John Keats.

To Fanny Brawne, 16 August 1819

Winchester August 17th*

My dear Girl—what shall I say for myself? I have been here four
days and not yet written you—'t is true I have had many teasing
letters of business to dismiss—and I have been in the Claws, like a
Serpent in an Eagle's, of the last act of our Tragedy—This is no
excuse; I know it; I do not presume to offer it—I have no right either
to ask a speedy answer to let me know how lenient you are—I must
remain some days in a Mist—I see you through a Mist: as I dare say
you do me by this time—Believe in the first Letters I wrote you: I
assure you I felt as I wrote—I could not write so now—The thousand images I have had pass through my brain—my uneasy spirits—
my unguess'd fate—all sp[r]ead as a veil between me and you—
Remember I have had no idle leisure to brood over you—'t is well
perhaps I have not—I could not have endured the throng of Jealousies that used to haunt me before I had plunged so deeply into
imaginary interests. I would feign, as my sails are set, sail on without
an interruption for a Brace of Months longer—I am in complete
cue—in the fever; and shall in these four Months do an immense
deal—This Page as my eye skims over it I see is excessively unlover-
like and ungallant—I cannot help it—I am no officer in yawning
quarters; no Parson-romeo—My Mind is heap'd to the full; stuff'd

like a cricket ball—if I strive to fill it more it would burst—I know
the generallity of women would hate me for this; that I should have
so unsoften'd so hard a Mind as to forget them; forget the brightest
realities for the dull imaginations of my own Brain—But I conjure
you to give it a fair thinking; and ask yourself whether 't is not better
to explain my feelings to you, than write artificial Passion—Besides
you would see through it—It would be vain to strive to deceive
you—'T is harsh, harsh, I know it—My heart seems now made of
iron—I could not write a proper answer to an invitation to Idalia—
You are my Judge: my forehead is on the ground—You seem
offended at a little simple innocent childish playfulness in my last—I
did not seriously mean to say that you were endeavouring to make
me keep my promise—I beg your pardon for it—'T is but *just* you
Pride should take the alarm—*seriously*—You say I may do as I
please—I do not think with any conscience I can; my cash-recourses
are for the present stopp'd; I fear for some time—I spend no money
but it increases my debts—I have all my life thought very little of
these matters—they seem not to belong to me—It may be a proud
sentence; but, by heaven, I am as entirely above all matters of interest
as the Sun is above the Earth—And though of my own money I
should be careless; of my Friends['] I must be spare. You see how I
go on—like so many strokes of a Hammer—I cannot help it—I am
impell'd, driven to it. I am not happy enough for silken Phrases, and
silver sentences—I can no more use soothing words to you than if I
were at this moment engaged in a charge of Cavalry—Then you will
say I should not write at all—Should I not? This Winchester is a fine
place; a beautiful Cathedral and many other ancient building[s] in
the Environs. The little coffin of a room at Shanklin, is changed for a
large room—where I can promenade at my pleasure—looks out onto
a beautiful—blank side of a house—It is strange I should like it
better than the view of the sea from our window at Shanklin—I
began to hate the very posts there—the voice of the old Lady over
the way was getting a great Plague—The Fisherman's face never
altered any more than our black tea-p⟨ot—⟩ the nob however was
knock'd off to my little relief⟨.⟩ I am g⟨ettin⟩g a great dislike of the
picturesque; and can only relish it over again by seeing you enjoy
it—One of the pleasantest things I have seen lately was at Cowes—
The Regent in his Yatch (I think they spell it) was anchored

oppoisite [*for* opposite]—a beautiful vessel—and all the Yatchs and boats on the coast, were passing and repassing it; and curcuiting and tacking about it in every direction—I never beheld any thing so, silent, light, and graceful—As we pass'd over to Southampton, there was nearly an accident—There came by a Boat well mann'd; with t[w]o naval officers at the stern—Our Bow-lines took the top of their little mast and snapped it off close by the bord—Had the mast been a little stouter they would have been upset—In so trifling an event I could not help admiring our seamen—Neither Officer nor man in the whole Boat moved a Muscle—they scar[c]ely notic'd it even with words—Forgive me for this flint-worded Letter—and believe and see that I cannot think of you without some sort of energy—though mal a propos—Even as I leave off—it seems to me that a few more moments thought of you would uncrystallize and dissolve me—I must not give way to it—but turn to my writing again—if I fail I shall die hard—O my love, your lips are growing sweet again to my fancy—I must forget them—Ever your affectionate

Keats—

To John Taylor, 23 August 1819

My dear Taylor— Winchester Monday morn.
24 Augst

You will perceive that I do not write you till I am forced by necessity: that I am sorry for. You must forgive me for entering abrubtly on the subject, merely p[r]efixing an intreaty that you will not consider my business manner of wording and proceeding any distrust of, or stirrup standing against you; but put it to the account of a desire of order and regularity—I have been rather unfortunate lately in money concerns—from a threatened chancery suit—I was deprived at once of all recourse to my Guardian I relied a little on some of my debts being paid—which are of a tolerable amount—but I have not had one pound refunded—For these three Months Brown has advanced me money: he is not at all flush and I am anxious to get some elsewhere—We have together been engaged (this I should wish to remain secret) in a Tragedy which I have just finish'd; and from which we hope to share moderate Profits—Being thus far connected, Brown proposed to me, to stand with me responsible for any money you may advance to me to drive through the summer—I must observe again that it is not from want of reliance on you readiness to assist me that I offer a ~~Bond~~ill; but as a relief to myself from a too lax sensation of Life—which ought to be responsible which requires chains for its own sake—duties to fulfil with the more earnestness the less strictly they are imposed Were I completely without hope— it might be different—but am I not right to rejoice in the idea of not being Burthensome to my friends? I feel every confidence that if I choose I may be a popular writer; that I will never be; but for all that I will get a livelihood—I equally dislike the favour of the public with the love of a woman—they are both a cloying treacle to the wings of independence.* I shall ever consider them (People) as debtors to me for verses, not myself to them for admiration—which I can do without. I have of late been indulging my spleen by composing a preface *at* them: after all resolving never to write a preface at all. 'There are so many verses,' would I have said to them', give me so much means to buy pleasure with as a relief to my hours of labour—You will observe at the end of this if you put down the Letter 'How a solitarry life engenders pride and egotism!' True: I know it does but this Pride and egotism will enable me to write finer things than any thing else could—so I will indulge it—Just so much as I am hu[m]bled by the genius above my grasp, am I exalted and look with hate and contempt upon the literary world—A Drummer boy who holds out his hand familiarly to a field marshall—that Drummer boy with me is the good word and favour of the public—Who would wish to be among the commonplace crowd of the little-famous—who are each individually lost in a throng made up of themselfes? is this worth louting or playing the hypocrite for? To beg suffrages* for a seat on the benches of a myriad aristocracy in Letters? This is not wise— I am not a wise man—T is Pride—I will give you a definition of a proud Man—He is a Man who has neither vanity nor wisdom— one fill'd with hatreds cannot be vain—neither can he be wise— Pardon me for hammering instead of writing—Remember me to Woodhouse, Hessey and all in Percey street—

Ever yours sincerly
John Keats

P.S. I have read what Brown has said on the other side—He agrees with me that this manner of proceeding might appear to harsh, distant and indelicate with you. This however will place all in a clear light. Had I to borrow money of Brown and were in your house, I should request the use of your name in the same manner—

[R]   *To J. H. Reynolds, 24 August 1819*

My dear Reynolds,   Winchest^r August 25th—

   By this Post I write to Rice who will tell you why we have left Shanklin; and how we like this Place—I have indeed scar[c]ely any thing else to say, leading so monotonous a life except I was to give you a history of sensations, and day-night mares. You would not find me at all unhappy in it; as all my thoughts and feelings which are of the selfish nature, home speculations every day continue to make me more Iron—I am convinced more and more day by day that fine writing is next to fine doing the top thing in the world; the Paradise Lost becomes a greater wonder—The more I know what my diligence may in time probably effect; the more does my heart distend with Pride and Obstinacy—I feel it in my power to become a popular writer—I feel it in my strength to refuse the poisonous suffrage of a public—My own being which I know to be becomes of more consequence to me than the crowds of Shadows in the Shape of Man and women that inhabit a kingdom. The Soul is a world of itself and has enough to do in its own home—Those whom I know already and who have grown as it were a part of myself I could not do without: but for the rest of Mankind they are as much a dream to me as Miltons Hierarchies. I think if I had a free and healthy and lasting organisation of heart and Lungs—as strong as an ox's—so as to be able [to bear] unhurt the shock of extreme thought and sensation without weariness, I could pass my Life very nearly alone though it should last eighty years. But I feel my Body too weak to support me to the height; I am obliged continually to check myself and strive to be nothing. It would be vain for me to endeavour after a more reasonable manner of writing to you: I have nothing to speak of but myself—and what can I say but what I feel? If you should have any reason to regret this state of excitement in me, I will turn the tide of your feelings in the right channel by mentioning that it is the only state for the best sort of Poetry—that is all I care for, all I live for. Forgive me for not filling up the whole sheet; Letters become so irksome to me that the next time I leave London I shall petition them all to be spar'd me. To give me credit for constancy and at the same time wa[i]ve letter writing will be the highest indulgence I can think of.

> Ever your affectionate friend
> John Keats

To Fanny Keats, 28 August 1819

My dear Fanny,   Winchester August 28th

You must forgive me for suffering so long a space to elapse between the dates of my letters. It is more than a fortnight since I left Shanklin, chiefly for the purpose of being near a tolerable Librarry, which after all is not to be found in this place—However we like it very much: it is the pleasantest Town I ever was in, and has the most reccommendations of any. There is a fine Cathedrall which to me is always a sourse of amusement; part of it built 1400 years ago; and the more modern by a magnificent Man, you may have read of in our History, called William of Wickham. The whole town is beautifully wooded—From the Hill at the eastern extremity you see a prospect of Streets, and old Buildings mixed up with Trees—Then There are the most beautiful streams about I ever saw—full of Trout—There is the Foundation of St Croix about half a mile in the fields—a charity greatly abused—We have a Collegiate School, a roman catholic School; a chapel ditto and a Nunnery! And what improves it all is, the fashionable inhabitants are all gone to Southampton. We are qui[e]t—except a fiddle that now and then goes like a gimlet through my Ears—Our Landlady's Son not being quite a Proficient—I have still been hard at work, having completed a Tragedy I think I spoke of to you—But there I fear all my labour will be thrown away for the present, as I hear Mr Kean is going to America—For all I can guess I shall remain here till the middle of October—when Mr Brown will return to his house at Hampstead: whither I shall return with him. I some time since sent the Letter I told you I had received from George to Haslam with a request to let you and Mrs Wylie see it: he sent it back to me for very insufficient reasons, without doing so; and I was so irritated by it that I would not send it travelling about by the post any more: besides the postage is very expensive. I know Mrs Wylie will think this a great neglect. I am sorry to say my temper gets the better of me—I will not send it again. Some correspondence I have had with Mr Abbey about George's affairs—and I must confess he has behaved very kindly to me as far as the wording of his Letter went—Have you heard any further mention of his retiring from Business? I am anxious to hear w[h]ether Hodgkinson, whose name I cannot bear to write,* will in any likelihood be thrown upon himself—The delightful Weather we have had for two Months is the highest gratification I could receive—no chill'd red noses—no shivering—but fair Atmosphere to think in—a clean towel mark'd with the mangle and a basin of clear Water to drench one's face with ten times a day: no need of much exercise—a Mile a day being quite sufficient—My greatest regret is that I have not been well enough to bathe though I have been two Months by the sea side and live now close to delicious bathing—Still I enjoy the Weather I adore fine Weather as the greatest blessing I can have. Give me Books, fruit, french wine and fine whether [*for* weather] and a little music out of doors, played by somebody I do not know—not pay the price of one's time for a gig—but a little chance music: and I can pass a summer very quietly without caring much about Fat Louis, fat Regent or the Duke of Wellington. Why have you not written to me? Because you were in expectation of George's Letter and so waited? Mr Brown is copying out our Tragedy of Otho the gre⟨at⟩ in a superb style—better than it deserves—there as I said is labour in vain for the present—I had hoped to give Kean another opportunity to shine. What can we do now? There is not another actor of Tragedy in all London or Europe—The Covent Garden Company is execrable—Young* is the best among them and he is a ranting, coxcombical tasteless Actor—A Disgust A Nausea—and yet the very best after Kean— What a set of barren asses are actors! I should like now to promenade round you Gardens—apple tasting—pear-tasting—plumb judging—apricot   nibbling—peach   sc[r]unching—Nectarine-sucking and Melon carving—I have also a great feeling for antiquated cherries full of sugar cracks—and a white currant tree kept for company—I admire lolling on a lawn by a water-lillied pond to eat white currants and see gold fish: and go to the Fair in the Evening if I'm good—There is not hope for that—one is sure to get

into some mess before evening—Have these hot days I brag of so
much been well or ill for your health? Let me hear soon—

Your affectionate Brother

John——

To John Taylor, 31 August 1819

Winchester Septr 1st

My dear Taylor,

Brown and I have been employed for these three weeks past from
time to time in writing to our different friends: a dead silence is our
ownly answer: we wait morning after morning and nothing: tuesday
is the day for the Examiner to arrive; this is the second tuesday
which has been barren even of a news paper—Men should be in
imitation of Spirits 'responsive to each others note'*—Instead of
that I pipe and no one hath danced—We have been cursing this
morning like Mandeville and Lisle*—With this I shall send by the
same Post a third Letter to a friend of mine—who though it is of
consequence has neither answered right or left—We have been much
in want of news from the Theatres having heard that Kean is going
to America—but no—not a word—Why I should come on you with
all these complaints, I cannot explain to myself: especially as I suspect you must be in the Country—Do answer me soon for I really
must know something. I must steer myself by the rudder of
information—And I am in want of a Month's cash—now believe me
I do not apply to you as if I thought you had a gold Mine. no. I
understand these matters well enough now having become well
acquainted with the disbu[r]sements every Man is tempted to make
beyond his means—From this time I have resolved myself to refuse
all such requests: tell me you are not flush and I shall thank you
heartily—That is a duty you owe to yourself as well as to *me*. I have
mulcted* Brown to much: let it be my last sin of the kind. I will try
what use it will be to insist on my debts being paid.

Ever yours sincerely

John Keats—

To J. A. Hessey, 5 September 1819

My dear Hessey,   Winchester, Sunday Sep^tr 5th

I received this morning yours of yesterday enclosing a 30£ bank post bill. I have been in fear of the Winchester Jail for some time: neither Brown nor myself could get an answer from any one—This morning I hear that some unknown part of a Sum due to me and for which I had been waiting three weeks has been sent to Chichester by mistake—Brown has borrow'd money of a freind of his in Hampshire—A few days ago we had but a few shillings left—and now between us we have 60£ besides what is waiting in the Chichester post office. To be a complete Midas I suppose some one will send me a pair of asses ears by the waggon—There has been such an embargo laid on our corresponde⟨nce⟩ that I can scar[c]ely believe your Letter was only dated yesterday—It seems miraculous—

Ever yours sincerely

John Keats.

I am sorry to hear such a bad account of himself from Taylor—

To John Taylor, 5 September 1819

Winchester Sep^tr 5th

My dear Taylor,

This morning I received yours of the 2nd and with it a Letter from Hessey enclosing a Bank post Bill of 30£—an ample sum I assure you: more I had no thought of. You should no[t] have delay'd so long in fleet Street; leading an inactive life as you did was breathing poison: you will find the country air do more for you than you expect. But it must be proper country air; you must choose a spot. What sort of a place is Retford? You should live in a dry, gravelly, barren, elevated country open to the currents of air, and such a place is generally furrnish'd with the finest springs—The neighbourhood of a rich inclosed fulsome manured arrable Land especially in a valley and almost as bad on a flat, would be almost as bad as the smoke of fleetstreet. Such a place as this was shanklin only open to the south east and surrounded by hills in every other direction— From this south east came the damps from the sea which having no

egress the air would for days together take on an unhealthy idio-
syncrasy altogether enervating and weakening as a city Smoke—I
felt it very much—Since I have been at Winchester I have been
improving in health—it is not so confined—and there is on one side
of the city a dry chalky down where the air is worth six pence a pint.
So if you do not get better at Retford do not impute it to your own
weakness before you have well considered the nature of the air and
soil—especially as Autumn is encroaching: for the autumn fogs over
a rich land is like the steam from cabbage water—What makes the
great difference between valemen flatland men, and Mountaineers?
The cultivation of the earth in a great measure—Our hea[l]th temperament and dispositions are taken more (notwithstanding the con-
tradiction of the history of cain and abel) from the air we breathe
than is generally imagined. See the difference between a Peasant and
a Butcher. I am convinced a great cause of it is the difference of the
air they breathe—The one takes his mingled with the fume of
slaughter the other with the damp exhalement from the glebe—The
teeming damp that comes from the plough furrow is of great effect
in taming the fierceness of a strong Man more than his labour—let
him be mowing furze upon a Mountain and at the days end his
thoughts will run upon a withe axe* if he ever had handled one, let
him leave the Plough and he will think qu[i]etly of his supper—
Agriculture is the tamer of men; the steam from the earth is like
drinking their mother's milk—It enervates their natures. This
appears a great cause of the imbecillity of the Chinese. And if this
sort of atmosphere is a mitigation to the energies of a strong man;
how much more must it injure a weak one—unoccupied—
unexerciced—For what is the cause of so many men maintaining a
good state in Cities but occupation—An idle man; a man who is not
sensitively alive to self interest in a city cannot continue long in good
Health—This is easily explained. If you were to walk liesurely
through an unwholesome path in the fens, with a little horror of
them you would be sure to have your ague. But let macbeth cross the
same path, with the dagger in the air leading him on, and he would
never have an ague or any thing like it. You should give these things a
serious consideration. Notts I believe is a flat County—You should
be on the slope of one of the dry barren hills in somersetshire. I am
convinced there is as harmful Air to be breath'd in the country as in

Town. I am greatly obliged to you for your Letter. Perhaps if you had had strength and spirits enough you would have felt offended by my offering a note of hand; or rather express'd it. However, I am sure you will give me credit for not in any wise mistrusting you; or imagining you would take advantage of any power I might give you over me. No, it proceeded from my serious resolve not to be a gratuitous borrower: from a great desire to be correct in money matters; to have in my desk the Chronicles of them to refer to, and know my worldly non-estate: besides in case of my death such documents would be but just: if merely as memorials of the friendly turns I had had done to me—Had I known of your illness I should not of written in such fierry phrase in my first Letter—I hope that shortly you will be able to bear six times as much. Brown likes the Tragedy very much: but he is not a fit judge, as I have only acted as Midwife to his plot, and of course he will be fond of his child. I do not think I can make you any extracts without spoiling the effect of the whole when you come to read it. I hope you will then not think my labour mispent. Since I finish'd it I have finish'd Lamia: and am now occupied in revising St Agnes' Eve and studying Italian. Ariosto I find as diffuse, in parts, as Spenser. I understand completely the difference between them—I will cross the letter with some lines from Lamia. Brown's kindest remembrances to you; and I am ever your most sincere friend

John Keats—

A haunting music, sole perhaps and lone
Supportress of the faery roof, made moan
Throughout, as fearful the whole charm might fade.
Fresh carved cedar, mimicking a glade
Of Palm and Plantain, met, from either side,
High in the midst in honour of the bride.
Two palms, and then two plantains, and so on,
From either side, their stems branch'd one to one
All down the aisled place; and beneath all
There ran a stream of lamps straight on from wall to wall.
So canopied lay an untasted feast
Teeming a perfume. Lamia regal drest
Silverly pac'd about, and as she went

In pale contented sort of discontent
Mission'd her viewless Servants to enrich
The splendid cornicing of nook and niche.
Between the Tree stems, wainscoted at first
Came jasper pannels; then, anon, there burst
Forth creeping imagery of slighter trees
And with the larger wove in small intricacies.
Approving all, she faded at self will,
And shut the chamber up close hush'd and still,
Complete, and ready for the revels rude,
When dreadful guests would come to spoil her solitude.

    The day came soon and all the gossip rout.
O senseless Lycius! Dolt! Fool! Madman! Lout!
Why would you murder happiness like yours,
And show to common eyes these secret bowers?

    The Herd came: and each guest, with buzzy brain,
Arriving at the Portal, gaz'd amain,
And enter'd won'dring; for they knew the Street,—
Remember'd it from childhood all complete,
Without a gap, but ne'er before had seen
That royal Porch, that high built fair demesne;
So in went one and all maz'd, curious and keen.
Save one; who look'd thereon with eye severe,
And, with calm-planted steps, walk'd in austere;
'T was Appolonius:—something to he laught;
As though some knotty problem, that had daft
His patient thought, and now begun to thaw,
And solve, and melt:—'t was just as he foresaw!

    Soft went the music, and the tables all
Sparkled beneath the viewless banneral
Of Magic; and dispos'd in double row
Seem'd edged Parterres of white bedded snow,
Adorne'd along the sides with living flowers
Conversing, laughing after sunny showers:
And, as the pleasant appetite entic'd,
Gush came the wine, and sheer the meats were slic'd.
Soft went the Music; the flat salver sang
Kiss'd by the emptied goblet,—and again it rang:

Swift bustled by the servants:—here's a health
Cries one—another—then, as if by stealth,
A Glutton drains a cup of Helicon,
Too fast down, down his throat the brief delight is gone.
"Where is that Music?" cries a Lady fair.
"Aye, where is it my dear? Up in the air"?
Another whispers 'Poo!' saith Glutton "Mum!"
Then makes his shiny mouth a knapkin for his thumb. & & &—

This is a good sample of the Story.*
Brown is going to Chi[che]ster and Bedhampton a visiting—I
shall be alone here for three weeks—expecting accounts of your
health

[R]   *To Fanny Brawne, 13 September 1819*

Fleet Street,* Monday Morn
My dear Girl,
   I have been hurried to Town by a Letter from my brother
George;* it is not of the brightest intelligenc[e] Am I mad or not? I
came by the Friday night coach—and have not yet been to Ham-
stead. Upon my soul it is not my fault, I cannot resolve to mix any
pleasure with my days: they go one like another undistinguishable. If
I were to see you to day it would destroy the half comfortable sullen-
ness I enjoy at present into dow[n]right perplexities. I love you too
much to venture to Hampstead, I feel it is not paying a visit, but
venturing into a fire. Que feraije? as the french novel writers say in
fun, and I in earnest: really what can I do? Knowing well that my life
must be passed in fatigue and trouble, I have been endeavouring to
wean myself from you: for to myself alone what can be much of a
misery? As far as they regard myself I can despise all events: but I
cannot cease to love you. This morn[i]ng I scarcely know what I am
doing. I am going to Walthamstow—I shall return to Winchester
tomorrow; whence you shall hear from me in a few days—I am a
Coward, I cannot bear the pain of being happy: t is out of the question: I must admit no thought of it.
                                        Yours ever affectionately
                                                    John Keats

To J. H. Reynolds, 21 September 1819

Winchester. Tuesday

My dear Reynolds,

I was very glad to hear from Woodhouse that you would meet in the Country. I hope you will pass some pleasant time together. Which I wish to make pleasanter by a brace of letters, very highly to be estimated, as really I have had very bad luck with this sort of game this season. I "kepen in solitarinesse,"* for Brown has gone a visiting. I am surprized myself at the pleasure I live alone in. I can give you no news of the place here, or any other idea of it but what I have to this effect written to George. Yesterday I say to him was a grand day for Winchester. They elected a Mayor—It was indeed high time the place should receive some sort of excitement. There was nothing going on: all asleep: not an old maid's sedan returning from a card party: and if any old woman got tipsy at Christenings they did not expose it in the streets. The first night tho' of our arrival here, there was a slight uproar took place at about 10 o' the Clock. We heard distinctly a noise patting down the high Street as of a walking cane of the good old Dowager breed; and a little minute after we heard a less voice observe "What a noise the ferril made—it must be loose"—Brown wanted to call the Constables, but I observed 'twas only a little breeze, and would soon pass over.—The side streets here are excessively maiden-lady like: the door steps always fresh from the flannel. The knockers have a staid serious, nay almost awful quietness about them.—I never saw so quiet a collection of Lions' & Rams' heads—The doors most part black. with a little brass handle just above the keyhole, so that in Winchester a man may very quietly shut himself out of his own house. How beautiful the season is now—How fine the air. A temperate sharpness about it. Really, without joking, chaste weather—Dian skies—I never lik'd stubble fields so much as now—Aye better than the chilly green of the spring. Somehow a stubble plain looks warm—in the same way that some pictures look warm—this struck me so much in my sunday's walk that I composed upon it.* I hope you are better employed than in gaping after weather. I have been at different times so happy as not to know what weather it was—No I will not copy a parcel of verses. I always somehow associate Chatterton with autumn. He is the purest writer in the English Language. He has no French idiom, or particles like Chaucer—'tis genuine English Idiom in English words. I have given up Hyperion—there were too many Miltonic inversions in it—Miltonic verse cannot be written but in an artful or rather artist's humour. I wish to give myself up to other sensations. English ought to be kept up. It may be interesting to you to pick out some lines from Hyperion and put a mark × to the false beauty proceeding from art, and one || to the true voice of feeling. Upon my soul 'twas imagination I cannot make the distinction—Every now & then there is a Miltonic intonation—But I cannot make the division properly. The fact is I must take a walk: for I am writing so long a letter to George; and have been employed at it all the morning. You will ask, have I heard from George. I am sorry to say not the best news—I hope for better—This is the reason among others that if I write to you it must be in such a scraplike way. I have no meridian to date Interests from, or measure circumstances—To night I am all in a mist; I scarcely know what's what—But you knowing my unsteady & vagarish disposition, will guess that all this turmoil will be settled by tomorrow morning. It strikes me to night that I have led a very odd sort of life for the two or three last years—Here & there—No anchor—I am glad of it.—If you can get a peep at Babbicomb before you leave the country, do.—I think it the finest place I have seen, or—is to be seen in the South. There is a Cottage there I took warm water at, that made up for the tea. I have lately skirk'd some friends of ours, and I advise you to do the same, I mean the blue-devils—I am never at home to them. You need not fear them while you remain in Devonshire. There will be some of the family waiting for you at the Coach office—but go by another Coach.—I shall beg leave to have a third opinion in the first discussion you have with Woodhouse—just half way—between both. You know I will not give up my argument—In my walk to day I stoop'd under a rail way that lay across my path, and ask'd myself "Why I did not get over" Because, answered I, "no one wanted to force you under"—I would give a guinea to be a reasonable man—good sound sense—a says what he thinks, and does what he says man—and did not take snuff—They say men near death however mad they may have been, come to their senses—I hope I shall here in this letter—there is a decent space to be very sensible in—many a good proverb has been in less—Nay I have heard of the statutes at large being chang'd into the Statutes at Small and printed for a watch paper. Your sisters by this time must have got the Devonshire ees—short ees—you know 'em—they are the prettiest ees in the Language. O how I admire the middle siz'd delicate Devonshire girls of about 15. There was one at an Inn door holding a quartern of brandy—the very thought of her kept me warm a whole stage—and a 16 miler too—"You'll pardon me for being jocular."*

Ever your affectionate friend.

John Keats—

To Richard Woodhouse, *21, 22 September 1819*

Dear Woodhouse,   Tuesday—

If you see what I have said to Reynolds before you come to your own dose you will put it between the bars unread; provided they have begun fires in Bath—I should like a bit of fire to night—one likes a bit of fire—How glorious the Blacksmiths' shops look now— I stood to night before one till I was verry near listing for one. Yes I should like a bit of fire—at a distance about 4 feet 'not quite hob nob'—as wordsworth says*—The fact was I left Town on Wednesday—determined to be in a hurry—You don't eat travelling—you're wrong—beef—beef—I like the look of a sign—The Coachman's face says eat eat, eat—I never feel more contemptible than when I am sitting by a good looking coachman—One is nothing—Perhaps I eat to persuade myself I am somebody. You must be when slice after slice—but it wont do—the Coachman nibbles a bit of bread—he's favour'd—he's had a Call—a Hercules Methodist—Does he live by bread alone? O that I were a Stage Manager—perhaps that's as old as 'doubling the Cape'—"How are ye old 'un? hey! why dont'e speak?' O that I had so sweet a Breast to sing as the Coachman hath! I'd give a penny for his Whistle—and bow to the Girls on the road—Bow—nonsense—'t is a nameless graceful slang action—Its effect on the women suited to it must be delightful. It touches 'em in the ribs—en passant—very off hand— very fine—Sed thongum formosa vale vale inquit Heigh ho la!* You like Poetry better—so you shall have some I was going to give Reynolds—

Season of Mists and mellow fruitfulness,
    Close bosom friend of the maturing sun;
Conspiring with him how to load and bless
    The vines with fruit that round the thatch eves run;
To bend with apples the moss'd cottage trees,
    And fill all fruit with ripeness to the core;
        To swell the gourd, and plump the hazle-shells
With a white kernel; to set budding more,
    And still more later flowers for the bees
    Untill they think wa[r]m days will never cease
        For summer has o'er brimm'd ther clammy Cells.

Who hath not seen thee oft, amid thy stores?
    Sometimes, whoever seeks abroad may find
Thee sitting careless on a granary floor,
    Thy hair soft-lifted by the winmowing wind;
Or on a half reap'd furrow sound asleep,
    Dased with the fume of poppies, while thy hook
        Spares the next swath and all its twined flowers;
And sometimes like a gleaner thou dost keep
    Stready thy laden head across a brook;
    Or by a Cyder press, with patient look.
        Thou watchest the last oozings hours by hours—

Where are the songs of spring? Aye, Where are they?
    Think not of them, thou hast thy music too.
While barred clouds bloom the soft-dying day
    And touch the stubble plains with rosy hue:
Then in a wailful quire the small gnats mourn
    Among the river sallows, borne aloft
        Or sinking as the light wind lives and dies;
And full grown Lambs loud bleat from hilly bourne:
    Hedge crickets sing, and now with treble soft
    The Red breast whistles from a garden Croft
        And gather'd Swallows twitter in the Skies—

I will give you a few lines from Hyperion on account of a word in the
last line of a fine sound—

> 'Mortal! that thou may'st understand aright
> I humanize my sayings to thine ear,
> Making comparisons of earthly things;
> Or thou might'st better listen to the wind
> Though it blows *legend-laden* th[r]ough the trees.

I think you will like the following description of the Temple of Saturn—

> I look'd around upon the carved sides
> Of an old sanctuary, with roof august
> Builded so high, it seem'd that filmed clouds
> Might sail beneath, as o'er the stars of heaven.
> So old the place was I remember none
> The like upon the earth; what I had seen
> Of grey Cathedrals, buttress'd walls, rent towers
> The superanuations of sunk realms,
> Or nature's rocks hard toil'd in winds and waves.
> Seem'd but the failing of decrepit things
> To that eternal-domed monument—
> Upon the marble, at my feet, there lay
> Store of strange vessels and large draperies
> Which needs had been of dyed asbestus wove,
> Or in that place the moth could not corrupt,
> So white the linen, so, in some, distinct
> Ran imageries from a sombre loom.
> All in a mingled heap confused there lay
> Robes, golden tongs, censer and chafing dish
> Girdles, and chains and holy jewelries.
> Turning from these, with awe once more I rais'd
> My eyes to fathom the space every way;
> The embossed roof, the silent massive range
> Of Columns north and south, ending in Mist
> Of nothing; then to the eastward where black gates
> Were shut against the Sunrise evermore—

I see I have completely lost my direction—So I e'n make you pay double postage. I had begun a sonnet in french of Ronsard—on my

word 't is verry capable of poetry—I was stop'd by a circumstance
not worth mentioning—I intended to call it La Platonique
Chevalresque—I like the second line—

> Non ne suis si audace a languire
>   De m'empresser au cœur vos tendres mains. &c

Here is what I had written for a sort of induction—*

> Fanatics have their dreams wherewith they weave
> A Paradise for a Sect; the savage too
> From forth the loftiest fashion of his sleep
> Guesses at Heaven: pity these have not
> Trac'd upon vellum, or wild indian leaf
> The shadows of melodious utterance:
> But bare of laurel they live, dream, and die,
> For Poesy alone can tell her dreams,
> With the fine spell of words alone can save
> Imagination from the sable charm
> And dumb enchantment—

My Poetry will never be fit for any thing it does n't cover its
ground well—You see he she is off her guard and does n't move a
peg though Prose is coming up in an awkward style enough—Now a
blow in the spondee will finish her—But let it get over this line of
circumvallation* if it can. These are unpleasant Phrase[s.]

Now for all this you two must write me a letter apiece—for as I know
you will interread one another—I am still writing to Reynolds as well
as yourself—As I say to George I am writing *to* you but *at* your
Wife—And dont forget to tell Reynold's of the fairy tale Undine*—
Ask him if he has read any of the American Brown's novels* that
Hazlitt speaks so much of—I have read one call'd Wieland—very
powerful—something like Godwin—Between Schiller and
Godwin—A Domestic prototype of S[c]hiller's Armenian*—More
clever in plot and incident than Godwin—A strange american scion
of the German trunk. Powerful genius—accomplish'd horrors—I
shall proceed tomorrow—Wednesday—I am all in a Mess here—
embowell'd in Winchester. I wrote two Letters to Brown one from

said Place, and one from London, and neither of them has reach'd him—I have written him a long one this morning and am so perplex'd as to be an object of Curiosity to you quiet People. I hire myself a show waggan and trumpetour. Here's the wonderful Man whose Letters wont go!—All the infernal imaginarry thunderstorms from the Post-office are beating upon me—so that 'unpoeted I write" Some curious body has detained my Letters—I am sure of it. They know not what to make of me—not an acquaintance in the Place—what can I be about? so they open my Letters—Being in a lodging house, and not so self will'd, but I am a little cowardly I dare not spout my rage against the Ceiling—Besides I should be run th[r]ough the Body by the major in the next room—I don't think his wife would attempt such a thing—Now I am going to be serious— After revolving certain circumstances in my Mind; chiefly connected with a late american letter—I have determined to take up my abode in a cheap Lodging in Town and get employment in some of our elegant Periodical Works—I will no longer live upon hopes—I shall carry my plan into execution speedily—I shall live in Westminster— from which a walk to the British Museum will be noisy and muddy—but otherwise pleasant enough—I shall enquire of Hazlitt how the figures of the market stand. O that I could [write] somthing agrestrural, pleasant, fountain-vo[i]c'd—not plague you will [*for* with] unconnected nonsense—But things won't leave me *alone*. I shall be in Town as soon as either of you—I only wait for an answer from Brown: if he receives mine which is now a very moot point—I will give you a few reasons why I shall persist in not publishing The Pot of Basil—It is too smokeable*—I can get it smoak'd at the Carpenters shaving chimney much more cheaply—There is too much inexperience of live [*for* life], and simplicity of knowledge in it— which might do very well after one's death—but not while one is alive. There are very few would look to the reality. I intend to use more finesse with the Public. It is possible to write fine things which cannot be laugh'd at in any way. Isabella is what I should call were I a reviewer 'A weak-sided Poem' with an amusing sober-sadness about it. Not that I do not think Reynolds and you are quite right about it—it is enough for me. But this will not do to be public—If I may so say, in my dramatic capacity I enter fully into the feeling: but in Propria Persona I should be apt to quiz it myself—There is no objection of this kind to Lamia—A good deal to St Agnes Eve—only not so glaring—Would a[s] I say I could write you something sylvestran. But I have no time to think: I am an otiosus-peroccupatus Man—I th[i]nk upon crutches, like the folks in your Pump room—Have you seen old Bramble yet*—they say he's on his last legs—The gout did not treat the old Man well so the Physician superseded it, and put the dropsy in office, who gets very fat upon his new employment, and behaves worse than the other to the old Man—But he'll have his house about his ears soon—We shall have another fall of Siege-arms—I suppose Mrs Humphrey persists in a big-belley—poor thing she little thinks how she is spo[i]ling the corners of her mouth—and making her nose quite a piminy. Mr Humphrey I hear was giving a Lecture in the gaming-room—When some one call'd out Spousey! I hear too he has received a challenge from a gentleman who lost that evening—The fact is Mr H. is a mere nothing out of his Bed-room.—Old Tabitha died in being bolstered up for a whist-party. They had to cut again—Chowder died long ago—Mrs H. laments that the last time they *put him* (i.e. to breed) he didn't take—They say he was a direct descendent of Cupid and Veney in the Spectator—This may be eisily known by the Parish Books—If you do not write in the course of a day or two: direct to me at Rice's—Let me know how you pass your times and how you are—

Your si⟨n⟩cere friend

John Keats—

Havn't heard from Taylor—

To Charles Brown [copy of part of letter], *22 September 1819*

*   *   *

Now I am going to enter on the subject of self. It is quite time I should set myself doing something, and live no longer upon hopes. I have never yet exerted myself. I am getting into an idle minded, vicious way of life, almost content to live upon others. In no period of my life have I acted with any self will, but in throwing up the apothecary-profession. That I do not repent of. Look at x x x x x x:* if he was not in the law he would be acquiring, by his abilities, something towards his support. My occupation is entirely literary; I will do so too. I will write, on the liberal side of the question,* for whoever will pay me. I have not known yet what it is to be diligent. I purpose living in town in a cheap lodging, and endeavouring, for a beginning, to get the theatricals of some paper. When I can afford to compose deliberate poems I will. I shall be in expectation of an answer to this. Look on my side of the question. I am convinced I am right. Suppose the Tragedy should succeed,—there will be no harm done. And here I will take an opportunity of making a remark or two on our friendship, and all your good offices to me. I have a natural timidity of mind in these matters: liking better to take the feeling between us for granted, than to speak of it. But, good God! what a short while you have known me! I feel it a sort of duty thus to recapitulate, however unpleasant it may be to you. You have been living for others more than any man I know. This is a vexation to me; because it has been depriving you, in the very prime of your life, of pleasures which it was your duty to procure. As I am speaking in general terms this may appear nonsense; you perhaps will not understand it: but if you can go over, day by day, any month of the last year,—you will know what I mean. On the whole, however, this is a subject that I cannot express myself upon. I speculate upon it frequently; and, believe me, the end of my speculations is always an anxiety for your happiness. This anxiety will not be one of the least incitements to the plan I purpose pursuing. I had got into a habit of mind of looking towards you as a help in all difficulties. This very habit would be the parent of idleness and difficulties. You will see it is a duty I owe myself to break the neck of it. I do nothing for my subsistence—make no exertion. At the end of another year, you shall applaud me,—not for verses, but for conduct. If you live at Hampstead next winter——I like x x x x x x x x x* and I cannot help it. On that account I had better not live there. While I have some immediate cash, I had better settle myself quietly, and fag on as others do. I shall apply to Hazlitt, who knows the market as well as any one, for something to bring me in a few pounds as soon as possible. I shall not suffer my pride to hinder me. The whisper may go round; I shall not hear it. If I can get an article in the "Edinburgh", I will. One must not be delicate. Nor let this disturb you longer than a moment. I look forward, with a good hope, that we shall one day be passing free, untrammelled, unanxious time together. That can never be if I continue a dead lump. x x x x x x x x x x x x x x* I shall be expecting anxiously an answer from you. If it does not arrive in a few days, this will have miscarried, and I shall come straight to x x x x* before I go to town, which you, I am sure, will agree had better be done while I still have some ready cash. By the middle of October I shall expect you in London. We will then set at the Theatres. If you have any thing to gainsay, I shall be even as the deaf adder which stoppeth her ears.

*   *   *

To C. W. Dilke, 22 September 1819

My dear Dilke,   Winchester Wednesday Eve—
    Whatever I take too for the time I cannot l[e]ave off in a hur[r]y; letter writing is the go now; I have consumed a Quire at least. You must give me credit, now, for a free Letter when it is in reality an interested one, on two points, the one requestive, the other verging to the pros and cons—As I expect they will lead me to seeing and conferring with you in a short time, I shall not enter at all upon a letter I have lately received from george of not the most comfortable intelligence: but proceed to these two points, which if you can theme out in sexions and subsexions for my edification, you will oblige me. The first I shall begin upon, the other will follow like a tail to a Comet. I have written to Brown on the subject, and can but go over the same Ground with you in a very short time, it not being more in length than the ordinary paces between the Wickets. It concerns a resolution I have taken to endeavour to acqu[i]re something by temporary writing in periodical works. You must agree with me how unwise it is to keep feeding upon hopes, which depending so much on the state of temper and imagination, appear gloomy or bright, near or afar off just as it happens—Now an act has three parts—to act, to do, and to perform—I mean I should *do* something for my immediate welfare—Even if I am swept away like a Spider from a drawing room I am determined to spin—home spun any thing for sale. Yea I will trafic. Any thing but Mortgage my Brain to Blackwood. I am determined not to layie like a dead lump. If Reynolds had not taken to the law, would he not be earning something? Why cannot I—You may say I want tact—that is easily

acqui[r]ed. You may be up to the slang of a cock pit in three battles.*
It is fortunate I have not before this been tempted to venture on the
common. I should a year or two ago have spoken my mind on every
subject with the utmost simplicity. I hope I have learnt a little better
and am confident I shall be able to cheat as well as any literary Jew of
the Market and shine up an article on any thing without much knowledge of the subject, aye like an orange. I would willingly have
recourse to other means. I cannot; I am fit for nothing but literature.
Wait for the issue of this Tragedy? No—there cannot be greater
uncertainties east west, north, and south than concerning dramatic
composition. How many months must I wait! Had I not better begin
to look about me now? If better events supersede this necessity what
harm will be done? I have no trust whatever on Poetry—I dont
wonder at it—the ma[r]vel it [*for* is] to me how people read so much
of it. I think you will see the reasonableness of my plan. To forward
it I purpose living in cheap Lodg[i]ng in Town, that I may be in the
reach of books and information, of which there is here a plentiful
lack. If I can [find] any place tolerably comfitable I will settle myself
and fag till I can afford to buy Pleasure—which if [I] never can
afford I must go Without—Talking of Pleasure, this moment I was
writing with one hand, and with the other holding to my Mouth a
Nectarine—good god how fine—It went down soft pulpy, slushy,
oozy—all its delicious embonpoint melted down my throat like a
large beatified Strawberry. I shall certainly breed. Now I come to my
request. Should you like me for a neighbour again? Come, plump it
out, I wont blush. I should also be in the neighbourhood of Mrs
Wylie, which I shoud be glad of, though that of course does not
influence me. Therefore will you look about Marsham, or rodney [*for*
Romney] street for a couple of rooms for me. Rooms like the gallants
legs in massingers time "as good as the times allow, Sir."* I have
written to day to Reynolds, and to Woodhouse. Do you know him?
He i⟨s⟩ a Friend of Taylors at whom Brown has taken one of his
funny odd dislikes. I'm sure he's wrong, because Woodhouse likes
my Poetry—conclusive. I ask your opinion and yet I must say to you
as to him, Brown that if you have any thing to say against it I shall be
as obstinate & heady as a Radical.* By the Examiner coming in your
hand writing you must be in Town. They have put [me] into spirits:
Notwithstand my aristocratic temper I cannot help being verry

much pleas'd with the present public proceedings.* I hope sincerely I shall be able to put a Mite of help to the Liberal side of the Question before I die. If you should have left Town again (for your Holidays cannot be up yet) let me know—when this is forwarded to you—A most extraordinary mischance has befallen two Letters I wrote Brown—one from London whither I was obliged to go on business for George; the other from this place since my return. I cant make it out. I am excessively sorry for it. I shall hear from Brown and from you almost together for I have sent him a Letter to day: you must positively agree with me or by the delicate toe nails of the virgin I will not open your Letters. If they are as David says 'suspicious looking letters"* I wont open them—If St John had been half as cunning he might have seen the revelations comfortably in his own room, without giving Angels the trouble of breaking open Seals. Remember me to Mrs D.—and the Westmonisteranian and believe me

Ever your sincere friend

John Keats—

To Charles Brown [copy of part of letter], 23 September 1819

*   *   *

Do not suffer me to disturb you unpleasantly: I do not mean that you should suffer me to occupy your thoughts, but to occupy them pleasantly: for, I assure you, I am as far from being unhappy as possible. Imaginary grievances have always been more my torment than real ones. You know this well. Real ones will never have any other effect upon me than to stimulate me to get out of or avoid them. This is easily accounted for. Our imaginary woes are conjured up by our passions, and are fostered by passionate feeling; our real ones come of themselves, and are opposed by an abstract exertion of mind. Real grievances are displacers of passion. The imaginary nail a man down for a sufferer, as on a cross; the real spur him up into an agent. I wish, at one view, you could see my heart towards you. 'Tis only from a high tone of feeling that I can put that word upon paper—out of poetry. I ought to have waited for your answer to my last before I wrote this. I felt, however, compelled to make a rejoinder to your's. I had written to x x x x* on the subject of my last,—I scarcely know whether I shall send my letter now. I think he would approve of my plan; it is so evident. Nay, I am convinced, out and out, that by prosing for awhile in periodical works I may maintain myself decently.

*   *   *

To George and Georgiana Keats,
17, 18, 20, 21, 24, 25, 27 September 1819

My dear George,   Winchester Septr Friday

I was closely employed in reading and composition, in this place, whither I had come from Shanklin, for the convenience of a library, when I received your last, dated July 24th You will have seen by the short Letter I wrote from Shanklin, how matters stand beetween us and Mrs Jennings. They had not at all mov'd and I knew no way of ove[r]coming the inveterate obstinacy of our affairs. On receiving your last I immediately took a place in the same night's coach for London—Mr Abbey behaved extremely well to me, appointed Monday evening at 7 to meet me and observed that he should drink tea at that hour. I gave him the inclosed note and showed him the last leaf of yours to me. He really appeared anxious about it; promised he would forward your money as quickly as possible—I think I mention'd that Walton was dead—He will apply to Mr Gliddon the partner; endeavour to get rid of Mrs Jennings's claim and be expeditious. He has received an answer from my Letter to Fry*—that is something. We are certainly in a very low estate: I say we, for I am in such a situation that were it not for the assistance of Brown & Taylor, I must be as badly off as a Man can be. I could not raise any sum by the promise of any Poem—no, not by the mortgage of my intellect. We must wait a little while. I really have hopes of success. I have finish'd a Tragedy which if it succeeds will enable me to sell what I may have in manuscript to a good avantage. I have pass'd my time in reading, writing and fretting—the last I intend to give up and stick to the other two. They are the only chances of benefit to us. Your wants will be a fresh spur to me. I assure you you shall more than share what I can get, whilst I am still young—the time may come when age will make me more selfish. I have not been well treated by the world—and yet I have capitally well—I do not know a Person to whom so many purse strings would fly open as to me—if I could possibly take advantage of them—which I cannot do for none of the owners of these purses are rich—Your present situation I will not suffer myself to dwell upon—when misfortunes are so real we are glad enough to escape them, and the thought of them. I cannot help thinking Mr Audubon a dishonest man—Why did he make you believe that he was a Man of Property?* How is it his circumstances have altered so suddenly? In truth I do not believe you fit to deal with the world; or at least the american worrld—But good God—who can avoid these chances—You have done your best—Take matters as coolly as you can and confidently expecting help from England, act as if no help was nigh. Mine I am sure is a tolerable tragedy—it would have been a bank to me, if just as I had finish'd it I had not heard of Kean's resolution to go to America. That was the worst news I could have had. There is no actor can do the principal character besides Kean. At Covent Garden there is a great chance of its being damn'd. Were it to succeed even there it would lift me out of the mire. I mean the mire of a bad reputation which is continually rising against me. My name with the literary fashionables is vulgar— I am a weaver boy* to them—a Tragedy would lift me out of this mess. And mess it is as far as it regards our Pockets—But be not cast down any more than I am. I feel I can bear real ills better than imaginary ones. Whenever I find myself growing vapourish, I rouse myself, wash and put on a clean shirt brush my hair and clothes, tie my shoestrings neatly and in fact adonize as I were going out—then all clean and comfortable I sit down to write. This I find the greatest relief—Besides I am becoming accustom'd to the privations of the pleasures of sense. In the midst of the world I live like a Hermit. I have forgot how to lay plans for enjoyment of any Pleasure. I feel I can bear any thing, any misery, even imp[r]isonment—so long as I have neither wife nor child. Perpaps you will say yours are your only comfort—they must be. I return'd to Winchester the day before yesterday and am now here alone, for Brown some days before I left, went to Bedhampton and there he will be for the next fortnight. The term of his house will be up in the middle of next month when we shall return to Hampstead. On Sunday I dined with your Mother and Henry and Charles in Henrietta Street—M^rs and Miss Millar were in the Country—Charles had been but a few days returned from Paris. I dare say you will have letters exp[r]essing the motives of his journey. Mrs Wylie and Miss Waldegrave seem as qu[i]et as two Mice there alone. I did not show your last—I thought it better not. For better times will certainly come and why should they be unhappy in the main time. On Monday Morning I went to Walthamstow—Fanny look'd better than I had seen her for some time. She complains of ~~my~~ not hearing from you appealing to me as if it was half my fault—I had been so long in retirement that London appeared a very odd place I could not make out I had so many acquaintance, and it was a whole day before I could feel among Men—I had another strange sensation there was not one house I felt any pleasure to call at. Reynolds was in the Country and saving himself I am p[r]ejudiced against all that family. Dilke and his wife and child were in the Country. Taylor was at Nottingham—I was out and every body was out. I walk'd about the Streets as in a strange land—Rice was the only one at home—I pass'd some time with him. I know him better since we have liv'd a month together in the isle of Wight. He is the most sensible, and even wise Man I know—he has a few John Bull prejudices: but they improve him. His illness is at times alarming. We are great friends, and there is no one I like to pass a day with better. Martin call'd in to bid him good bye before he set out for Dublin. If you would like to hear one of his jokes here is one which at the time we laugh'd at a good deal. A Miss — with three young Ladies, one of them Martin's sister had come a gadding in the Isle of wight and took for a few days a Cottage opposite ours— we dined with them one day, and as I was saying they had fish— Miss—said she thought *they tasted of the boat*—No says Martin very seriously they haven't been kept long enough. I saw Haslam he is very much occupied with love and business being one of Mr Saunders executors and Lover to a young woman He show'd me her Picture by Severn—I think she is, though not very cunning, too cunning for him. Nothing strikes me so forcibly with a sense of the rediculous as love—A Man in love I do think cuts the sorryest figure in the world—Even when I know a poor fool to be really in pain about it, I could burst out laughing in his face—His pathetic visage becomes irrisistable. Not that I take Haslam as a pattern for Lovers—he is a very worthy man and a good friend. His love is very amusing. Somewhere in the Spectator* is related an account of a Man inviting a party of stutter[e]rs and squinters to his table. 't would please me more to scrape together a party of Lovers, not to dinner—no to tea. The[re] would be no fighting as among Knights of old—

> Pensive they sit, and roll their languid eyes
> Nibble their to[a]sts, and cool their tea with sighs,
> Or else forget the purpose of the night
> Forget their tea—forget their appetite.
> See with cross'd arms they sit—ah hapless crew
> The fire is going out, and no one rings
> For coals, and therefore no coals betty brings.
> A Fly is in the milk pot—must he die
> Circled by a humane society?
> No no there m^r Wert[h]er takes his spoon
> Inverts it—dips the handle and lo, soon
> The little struggler sav'd from perils dark
> Across the teaboard draws a long wet mark.
> Romeo! Arise! take Snuffers by the handle
> There's a large Cauliflower in each candle.
> A winding-sheet—Ah me! I must away
> To no 7 just beyond the Circus gay.
> 'Alas' my friend! your Coat sits very well:
> Where may your Taylor live'?' 'I may not tell—
> 'O pardon me—I'm absent now and then"
> Where *might* my Taylor live?—I say again
> I cannot tell. let me no more be teas'd—
> He lives in wapping *might* live where he pleas'd

You see I cannot get on without writing as boys do at school a few nonsense verses—I begin them and before I have written six the whim has pass'd—if there is any th[i]ng deserving so respectable a name in them. I shall put in a bit of information any where just as it strikes me. Mr Abbey is to write to me as soon as he can bring matters to bear, and then I am to go to Town to tell him the means of forwarding to you through Capper and Hazlewood—I wonder I did not put this before—I shall go on tomorrow—it is so fine now I must take a bit of a walk—

Saturday—

With my inconstant disposition it is no wonder that this morning, amid all our bad times and misfortunes, I should feel so alert and well spirited. At this moment you are perhaps in a very different state of Mind. It is because my hopes are very paramount to my despair. I have been reading over a part of a short poem I have composed lately call'd 'Lamia'—and I am certain there is that sort of fire in it which must take hold of people in some way—give them either pleasant or unpleasant sensation. What they want is a sensation of some sort. I wish I could pitch the key of your spirits as high as mine is—but your organ loft is beyond the reach of my voice—I admire the exact admeasurement of my niece in your Mother's letter—O the little span long elf*—I am not in the least judge of the proper weight and size of an infant. Never trouble yourselves about that: she is sure to be a fine woman—Let her have only delicate nails both on hands and feet and teeth as small as a May-fly's. who will live you his life on a square inch of oak-leaf. And nails she must have quite different from the market women here who plough into the butter and make a quatter pound taste of it. I intend to w[r]ite a letter to you Wifie and there I may say more on this little plump subject—I hope she's plump—'Still harping on my daughter'— This Winchester is a place tolerably well suited to me; there is a fine Cathedral, a College, a Roman-Catholic Chapel, a Methodist do, an independent do,—and there is not one loom or any thing like manufacturing beyond bread & butter in the whole City. There are a number of rich Catholic[s] in the place. It is a respectable, ancient aristocratical place—and moreover it contains a nunnery—Our set are by no means so hail fellow, well met, on literary subjects as we were wont to be. Reynolds has turn'd to the law. Bye the bye, he brought out a little piece at the Lyceum call'd *one, two th[r]ee, four, by advertisement*. It met with complete success. The meaning of this odd title is explained when I tell you the principal actor is a mimic who takes off four of our best performers in the course of the farce— Our stage is loaded with mimics. I did not see the Piece being out of Town the whole time it was in progress. Dilke is entirely swallowed up in his boy: 't is really lamentable to what a pitch he carries a sort of parental mania—I had a Letter from him at Shanklin—He went on a word or two about the isle of Wight which is a bit of hobby horse of his; but he soon deviated to his boy. 'I am sitting' says he "at the window expecting my Boy from School." I suppose I told you some where that he lives in Westminster, and his boy goes to the School there. where he gets beaten, and every bruise he has and I dare say deserves is very bitter to Dilke. The Place I am speaking of, puts me in mind of a circumsta[n]ce occured lately at Dilkes—I think it very rich and dramatic and quite illustrative of the little quiet fun that he will enjoy sometimes. First I must tell you their house is at the corner of Great Smith Street, so that some of the windows look into one Street, and the back windows into another round the corner—Dilke had some old people to dinner, I know not who—but there were two old ladies among them—Brown was there—they had known him from a Child. Brown is very pleasant with old women, and on that day, it seems, behaved himself so winningly they [*for* that] they became hand and glove together and a little complimentary. Brown was obliged to depart early. He bid them good bye and pass'd into the passage—no sooner was his back turn'd than the old women began lauding him. When Brown had reach'd the Street door and was just going, Dilke threw up the Window and call'd 'Brown! Brown! They say you look younger than ever you did!' Brown went on and had just turn'd the corner into the other street when Dilke appeared at the back window crying "Brown! Brown! By God, they say you're handsome!" You see what a many words it requires to give any identity to a thing I could have told you in half a minute. I have been reading lately Burton's Anatomy of Melancholy; and I think you will be very much amused with a page I here coppy for you.* I call it a Feu de joie round the batteries of Fort St Hyphen-de-Phrase on the birthday of the Digamma. The whole alphabet was drawn up in a Phalanx on the cover of an old Dictionary. Band playing "Amo, Amas &c" "Every Lover admires his Mistress, though she be very deformed of herself, ill-favored, wrinkled, pimpled, pale, red, yellow, tann'd, tallow-fac'd, have a swoln juglers platter face, or a thin, lean, chitty face, have clouds in her face, be crooked, dry, bald, goggle-eyed, blear-eyed or with staring eyes, she looks like a squis'd cat, hold her head still awry, heavy, dull, hollow-eyed, black or yellow about the eyes, or squint-eyed, sparrow-mouth'd, Persean-hook-nosed, have a sharp fox nose, a red nose, China flat, great nose, nare simo patuloque, a nose like a promontory, gubber-tush'd, rotten teeth, black, uneven, brown teeth, beetle-brow'd, a witches beard, her breath stink all over the room, her nose drop winter and summer, with a Bavarian poke under her chin, a sharp chin, lave-eared, with a long crane's neck, which stands awry too, pendulis mammis her dugs like two double jugs, or else no dugs in the other extream, bloody-falln fingers, she have filthy, long, unpaired, nails, scabbed hands or wrists, a tan'd skin, a rotton carcass, crooked back, she stoops, is lame, splea footed, as slender in the middle as a cow in the wast, gowty legs, her ankles hang over her shooes, her feet stink, she breed lice, a meer changeling, a very monster, an aufe imperfect, her whole complexion savors, an harsh voice, incondite gesture, vile gate, a vast virago, or an ugly tit, a slug, a fat fustilugs, a trusse, a long lean rawbone, a Skeleton, a Sneaker, (si qua patent meliora puta) and to thy Judgement looks like a mard in a Lanthorn, whom thou couldst not fancy for a world, but hatest, loathest, and wouldst have spit in her face, or blow thy nose in her bosom, remedium amoris to another man, a dowdy, a Slut, a scold, a nasty rank, rammy, filthy, beastly quean, dishonest peradventure, obscene, base, beggarly, rude, foolish, untaught—peevish, Irus' daughter, Thersite's sister, Grobian's Scholler; if he love her once, he admires her for all this, he takes no notice of any such errors or imperfections of boddy or mind—" There's a dose for you—fine!! I would give my favou[r]ite leg to have written this as a speech in a Play: with what effect could Mathews* pop-gun it at the pit! This I th[i]nk will amuse you more than so much Poetry. Of that I do not like to copy any as I am affraid it is too mal apropo for you at present—and yet I will send you some—for by the time you receive it things in England may have taken a different turn. When I left Mr Abbey on monday evening I walk'd up Cheapside but returned to put some letters in the Post and met him again in Bucklersbury: we walk'd together th[r]ough the Poultry as far as the hatter's shop he has some concern in—He spoke of it in such a way to me, I though[t] he wanted me to make an offer to assist him in it. I do believe if I could be a hatter I might be one. He seems anxious about me. He began blowing up Lord Byron while I was sitting with him, however Says he the fellow says true things now & then; at which he took up a Magasine and read me some extracts from Don Juan, (Lord Byron's last flash poem) and particularly one against literary ambition.* I do think I must be well spoken of among sets, for Hodgkinson is more than polite, and the coffee-german* endeavour'd to be very close to me the other night at covent garden where I went at half-price before I tumbled into bed—Every one however distant an acquaintance behaves in the most conciliating manner to me—You will see I speak of this as a matter of interest. On the next Street [*for* sheet] I will give you a little politics. In every age there has been in England for some two or th[r]ee centuries subjects of great popular interest on the carpet: so that however great the uproar one can scarcely prophesy any material change in the government; for as loud disturbances have agitated this country many times. All civil[iz]ed countries become gradually more enlighten'd* and there should be a continual change for the better. Look at this Country at present and remember it when it was even though[t] impious to doubt the justice of a trial by Combat—From that time there has been a gradual change—Three great changes have been in progress—First for the better, next for the worse, and a third time for the better once more. The first was the gradual annihilation of the tyranny of the nobles when kings found it their interest to conciliate the common people, elevate them and be just to them. Just when baronial Power ceased and before standing armies were so dangerous, Taxes were few. kings were lifted by the people over the heads of their nobles, and those people held a rod over kings. The change for the worse in Europe was again this. The obligation of kings to the Multitude began to be forgotten—Custom had made noblemen the humble servants of kings—Then kings turned to the Nobles as the adorners of the[i]r power, the slaves of it, and from the people as creatures continually endeavouring to check them. Then in every kingdom there was a long struggle of kings to destroy all popular privileges. The english were the only people in europe who made a grand kick at this. They were slaves to Henry 8th but were freemen under william 3rd at the time the french were abject slaves under Lewis 14th The example of England, and the liberal writers of france and england sowed the seed of opposition to this Tyranny—and it was swelling in the ground till it burst out in the french revolution—That has had an unlucky termination. It put a stop to the rapid progress of free sentiments in England; and gave our Court hopes of turning back to the despotism of the 16 century. They have made a handle of this event in every way to undermine our freedom. They spread a horrid superstition against all inovation and improvement—The present struggle in England of the people is to destroy this superstition. What has rous'd them to do it is their distresses—Perpaps on this account the pres'ent distresses of this nation are a fortunate thing— tho so horrid in the[i]r experience. You will see I mean that the french Revolution but [*for* put] a tempor[a]ry stop to this third change, the change for the better—Now it is in progress again and I thing [*for* think] in an effectual one. This is no contest between whig and tory—but between right and wrong. There is scarcely a grain of party spirit now in England—Right and Wrong considered by each man abstractedly is the fashion. I know very little of these things. I am convinced however that apparently small causes make great alternations. There are little signs wherby we many [*for* may] know how matters are going on—This makes the business about Carlisle the Bookseller of great moment* in my mind. He has been selling deistical pamphlets, republished Tom Payne and many other works held in superstitious horror. He even has been selling for some time immense numbers of a work call 'The Deist' which comes out in weekly numbers—For this Conduct he I think has had above a dozen ~~Prosecutions~~ inditements issued against him; for which he has found Bail to the amount of many thousand Pounds—After all they are affraid to prosecute: they are affraid of his defence: it ~~will~~ would be published in all the papers all over the Empire: they shudder at this: the Trials would light a flame they could not extinguish. Do you not think this of great import? You will hear by the papers of the pro- ceedings at Manchester and Hunt's triumphal entry into London*— I[t] would take me a whole day and a quire of paper to give you any thing like detail—I will merely mention that it is calculated that 30,000 people were in the streets waiting for him—The whole dis- tance from the Angel Islington to the Crown and anchor* was lined with Multitudes. As I pass'd Colnaghi's window I saw a profil Por- traict of Sands* the destroyer of Kotzebue. His very look must inter- est every one in his favour—I suppose they have represented him in his college dress—He seems to me like a young Abelard—A fine Mouth, cheek bones (and this is no joke) full of sentiment; a fine unvulgar nose and plump temples. On looking over some Letters I found the one I wrote intended for you from the foot of Helvellyn to

Liverpool—but you had sail'd and therefore It was returned to me.
It contained among other nonsense an Acrostic of my Sister's
name—and a pretty long name it is. I wrote it in a great hurry which
you will see. Indeed I would not copy it if I thought it would ever be
seen by any but yourselves— . . .*

I ought to make a large Q* here: but I had better take the opportunity
of telling you I have got rid of my haunting sore throat—and conduct myself in a manner not to catch another You speak of Lord
Byron and me—There is this great difference between us. He
describes what he sees—I describe what I imagine—Mine is the
hardest task. You see the immense difference—The Edinburgh
review are affraid to touch upom [*for* upon] my Poem—They do not
know what to make of it—they do not like to condemn it and they
will not p[r]aise it for fear—They are as shy of it as I should be of
wearing a Quaker's hat—The fact is they have no real taste—they
dare not compromise their Judgements on so puzzling a Question—
If on my next Publication they should praise me and so lug in
Endymion—I will address [them] in a manner they will not at
all relish—The Cowardliness of the Edinburgh is worse than the
abuse of the Quarterly. Monday*—This day is a grand day for
winchester—they elect the Mayor. It was indeed high time the place
should have some sort of excitement. There was nothing going on—
all asleep—Not an old Maids Sedan returning from a card party—
and if any old women have got tipsy at christenings they have not
exposed themselves in the Street—The first night tho' of our arrival
here there was a slight uproar took place at about ten of the clock—
We heard distinctly a noise patting down the high street as of a
walking Cane of the good old dowager breed; and a little minute after
we heard a less voice obse[r]ve 'what a noise the ferr*i*l made.'—it
must be loose." Brown wanted to call the Constables, but I observed
't was only a little breeze and would soon pass over. The side-streets
here are excessively maiden lady like—The door steps always fresh
from the flannel. The knockers have a very staid ser[i]ous, nay almost
awful qu[i]etness about them—I never saw so quiet a collection
of Lions, and rams heads—The doors most part black with a little
brass handle just above the key hole—so that you may easily shut
yourself out of your own house—he! he! There is none of your
Lady Bellaston* rapping and ringing here—no thundering-Jupiter

footmen no opera-trebble-tattoos—but a modest lifting up of the knocker by a set of little wee old fingers that peep through the grey mittens, and a dying fall thereof—The great beauty of Poetry is, that it makes every thing every place interesting—The palatine venice and the abbotine Winchester are equally interesting—Some time since* I began a Poem call'd "the Eve of St Mark quite in the spirit of Town quietude. I th[i]nk it will give you the sensation of walking about an old county Town in a coolish evening. I know not yet whether I shall ever finish it—I will give it far as I have gone. *Ut tibi placent!**

> Upon a Sabbath day it fell;
> Thrice holy was the sabbath bell
> That call'd the folk to evening prayer.
> The City Streets were clean and fair
> Fron [*for* From] *w*holesome drench of April rains,
> And on the western window pains
> The chilly sunset faintly told
> Of immaturd, green vallies cold,
> Of the green, thorny, bloomless hedge,
> Of Rivers new with spring tide sedge,
> Of Primroses by shelter'd rills,
> And Dasies on the aguish hills.
> Thrice holy was the sabbath bell:
> The silent streets were crowded well
> With staid and pious companies
> Wa[r]m from their fireside oratries,
> And moving with demurest air
> To even song and vesper prayer.
> Each arched porch and entry low
> Was fill'd with patient crowd and slow,
> With whispers hush, and shuffling feet
> While play'd the organs loud and sweet.
>
> The Bells had ceas'd, the Prayers begun,
> And Bertha had not yet half done
> A curious volume, patch'd and torn,
> That all day long, from earliest morn,
> Had taken captive her fair eyes

Among its golden broideries:—
Perplex'd her with a thousand things—
The Stars of heaven, and Angels wings;
Martyrs in a fiery blaze;
Azure Saints 'mid silver rays;
Aron's breastplate, and the seven
Candlesticks John saw in heaven;
The winged Lion of St Mark,
And the Covenental Arck
With its many Misteries
Cherubim and golden Mice.

Bertha was a Maiden fair,
Dwelling in the old Minster square:
From her fireside she could see
Sidelong its rich antiquity,
Far as the Bishop's garden wall,
Where sycamores and elm trees tall
Full leav'd the forest had outstript,
By no sharp north wind ever nipt,
So sheltered by the mighty pile.

Bertha arose, and read awhile
With forehead 'gainst the window pane,—
Again she tried, and then again,
Until the dusk eve left her dark
Upon the Legend of St. Mark:
From pleated lawn-frill fine and thin
She lifted up her soft warm chin
With aching neck and swimming eyes
All daz'd with saintly imageries.

All was gloom, and silent all,
Save now and then the still foot fall
Of one returning homewards late
Past the echoing minster gate.
The clamourous daws that all the day
Above tree tops and towers play,
Pair by Pair had gone to rest,

Each in their ancient belfry nest
Where asleep they fall betimes
To music of the drowsy chimes.

   All was silent, all was gloom
Abroad and in the homely roon [*for* room];—
Down she sat, poor cheated soul,
And struck a swart Lamp from the coal,
Leaned forward with bright drooping hair
And slant book full against the glare.
Her shadow, in uneasy guise,
Hover'd about, a giant size,
On ceiling, beam, and old oak chair,
The Parrot's cage and pannel square,
And the warm-angled winter screne,
On which were many monsters seen,
Call'd, Doves of Siam, Lima Mice,
And legless birds of Paradise.
Macaw, and tender Av'davat.
And silken-furr'd Angora Cat.

   Untir'd she read—her shadow still
Glowerd about as it would fill
The room with gastly forms and shades—
As though some ghostly Queen of Spades
Had come to mock behind her back,
And dance, and ruffle her garments black.

   Untir'd she read the Legend page
Of holy Mark from youth to age,
On Land, on sea, in pagan-chains,
Rejoicing for his many pains.
Sometimes the learned Eremite
With golden star, or daggar bright,
Refer'd to pious poesies
Written in smallst crow quill size
Beneathe the text and thus the rhyme
Was parcell'd out from time to time:

What follows is an imitation of the Authors in Chaucer's time—'t is

more ancient than Chaucer himself and perhaps betwe[e]n him
and Gower

   ——Als writeth he of swevenis
Men han beforne they waken in blis,
When that hir friendes thinke hem bounde
In crimpide shroude farre under grounde:
And how a litling childe mote be
A scainte er its natavitie,
Gif that the modre (Gode her blesse)
Kepen in Solitarinesse,
And kissen devoute the holy croce.
Of Goddis love and Sathan's force
He writithe; and things many moe,
Of swiche thinges I may not show,
Bot I must tellen verilie
Somedele of Saintè Cicilie,
And chieflie what he auctoreth
Of Saintè Markis life and dethe.

I hope you will like this for all its Carelessness—I must take an
opportunity here to observe that though I am writing *to* you I am all
the while writing *at* your Wife—This explanation will account for
my speaking sometimes *hoity-toityishly*. Whereas if you were alone I
should sport a little more sober sadness. I am like a squinti[n]g
gentleman who saying soft things to one Lady ogles another—or
what is as bad in arguing with a person on his left hand appeals with
his eyes to one one [*for* on] the right. His Vision is elastic he bends it
to a certain object but having a patent sp[r]ing it flies off. Writing has
this disadvan[ta]ge of speaking. one cannot write a wink, or a nod, or
a grin, or a purse of the Lips, or a *smile*—*O law!* One can-[not] put
ones pinger [*for* finger] to one's nose, or yerk ye in the ribs, or lay
hold of your button in writing—but in all the most lively and titterly
parts of my Letter you must not fail to imagine me as the epic poets
say—now here, now there, now with one foot pointed at the ceiling,
now with another—now with my pen on my ear, now with my elbow
in my mouth—O my friends you loose the action—and attitude is
every thing as Fusili* said when he took up his leg like a Musket to

shoot a Swallow just darting behind his shoulder. And yet does not the word mum! go for ones finger beside the nose—I hope it does. I have to make use of the word Mum! before I tell you that Severn has got a little Baby—all his own let us hope—He told Brown he had given up painting and had tu[r]n'd modeller. I hope sincerely tis not a party concern; that no M^r — or **** is the real *Pinxit* and Severn the poor *Sculpsit*** to this work of art—You know he has long studied in the Life-Academy.* Haydon—yes your wife will say, 'here is a sum total account of Haydon again I wonder your Brother don't put a monthly bulleteen in the Philadelphia Papers about him—I wont hear—no—skip down to the bottom—aye and there are some more of his verses, skip (lullaby-by) them too" "No, lets go regularly through" "I wont hear a word about Haydon—bless the child, how rioty she is!—there go on there" Now pray go on here for I have a few words to say about Haydon—Before this Chancery threat had cut of every legitimate supp[l]y of Cash from me I had a little at my disposal: Haydon being very much in want I lent him 30£ of it. Now in this se-saw game of Life I got nearest to the ground and this chancery business rivetted me there so that I was sitting in that uneasy position where the seat slants so abominably. I applied to him for payment—he could not—that was no wonder. but goodman Delver, where was the wonder then, why marry, in this, he did not seem to care much about it—and let me go without my money with almost nonchalance when he aught to have sold his drawings to supply me. I shall perhaps still be acquainted with him, but for friendship that is at an end. Brown has been my friend in this he got him to sign a Bond payable at ~~two~~ three Months—Haslam has assisted me with the return of part of the money you lent him. Hunt—'there,' says your wife, 'there's another of those dull folkes—not a syllable about my friends—well—Hunt—what about Hunt pray—you little thing see how she bites my finger—my! is not this a tooth"—Well, when you have done with the tooth, read on—Not a syllable about your friends Here are some syllables. As far as I could smoke things on the Sunday before last, thus matters stood in Henrietta street—Henry was a greater blade than ever I remember to have seen him. He had on a very nice coat, a becoming waistcoat and buff trowsers—I think his face has lost a little of the spanish-brown, but no flesh. He carv'd some beef exactly to suit my appetite, as if I

had been measured for it. As I stood looking out of the window with
Charles after dinner, quizzing the Passengers, at which, I am sorry to
say he is too apt, I observed that his young, son of a gun's whiskers
had begun to curl and curl—little twists and twists; all down the
sides of his face getting properly thickish on the angles of the the
visage, He certainly will have a notable pair of Whiskers. "How shiny
your gown is in front" says Charles "Why, dont you see 't is an apron
says Henrry" Whereat I scrutiniz'd and behold your mother had a
purple stuff gown on, and over it an apron of the same colour, being
the same cloth that was used for the lining—and furthermore to
account for the shining it was the first day of wearing. I guess'd as
much of the Gown—but that is entre-nous. Charles likes england
better than france. They've got a fat, smiling, fair Cook as ever you
saw—she is a little lame, but that improves her. it makes her go more
swimmingly. When I ask'd 'Is Mrs Wylie within' she gave such a
large, five-and-thirty-year-old smile, it made me look round upon
the forth stair—it might have been the fifth—but that's a puzzle. I
shall never be able if I were to set myself a recollecting for a year, to
recollect that—I think I remember two or three specks in her teeth
but I really cant say exactly. Your mother said something about Miss
Keasle—what that was is quite a riddle to me now—Whether she
had got fatter or thinner, or broader or longer—straiter, or had taken
to the zig zags—Whether she had taken to, or left off, asses Milk—
that by the by she ought never to touch—how much better it would
be to put her out to nurse with the Wise woman of Brentford.* I can
say no more on so spare a subject. Miss Millar now is a different
morsell if one knew how to divide and subdivide, theme her out into
sections and subsections—Say a little on every part of her body as it
is divided in common with all her fellow creatures, in Moor's
Almanac. But Alas! I have not heard a word about her. no cue to
begin upon. There was indeed a buzz about her and her mother's
being at Old M^rs So and So's *who was like to die*—as the jews say—
but I dare say, keeping up their dialect, *she was not like to die*. I must
tell you a good thing Reynolds *did*: 't was the best thing he ever *said*.
You know at taking leave of a party at a door way, sometimes a Man
dallies and foolishes and gets awkward, and does not know how to
make off to advantage—Good bye—well—good-bye—and yet he
does not—go—good bye and so on—well—good bless you—You

know what I mean. Now Reynolds was in this predicament and got
out of it in a very witty way. He was leaving us at Hampstead. He
delay'd, and we were joking at him and even said, 'be off'—at which
he put the tails of his coat between his legs; and sneak'd off as nigh
like a spanial as could be. He went with flying colours: this is very
clever—I must, being upon the subject, tell you another good thing
of him; He began, for the service it might be of to him in the law, to
learn french. He had Lessons at the cheap rate of 2.6 per fag.* and
observed to Brown 'Gad says he, the man sells his Lessons so cheap
he must have stolen 'em.' You have heard of Hook the farce writer.
Horace Smith said to one who ask'd him if he knew Hook* "Oh yes'
Hook and I are very intimate." Theres a page of Wit for you—to put
John Bunyan's emblems* out of countenance.

Tuesday—You see I keep adding a sheet daily till I send the packet
off—which I shall not do for a few days as I am inclined to write a
good deal: for there can be nothing so remembrancing and enchain-
ing as a good long letter be it composed of what it may—From the
time you left me, our friends say I have altered completely—am not
the same person—perhaps in this letter I am for in a letter one takes
up one's existence from the time we last met—I dare say you have
altered also—evey man does—Our bodies every seven years are
completely fresh-materiald—seven years ago it was not this hand
that clench'd itself against Hammond*—We are like the relict garments of a Saint: the same and not the same: for the careful Monks
patch it and patch it for St Anthony's shirt. This is the reason why
men who had been bosom friends, on being separated for any number of years, afterwards meet coldly, neither of them knowing why—
The fact is they are both altered—Men who live together have a
silent moulding and influencing power over each other—They inter-
assimulate. 'T is an uneasy thought that in seven years the same
hands cannot greet each other again. All this may be obviated by a
willful and dramatic exercise of our Minds towards each other. Some
think I have lost that poetic ardour and fire 't is said I once had—the
fact is perhaps I have: but instead of that I hope I shall substitute a
more thoughtful and quiet power. I am more frequently, now, contented to read and think—but now & then, haunted with ambitious
thoughts. Qui[e]ter in my pulse, improved in my digestion; exerting
myself against vexing speculations—scarcely content to write the

best verses for the fever they leave behind. I want to compose without this fever. I hope I one day shall. You would scarcely imagine I could live alone so comfortably "Kepen in solitarinesse" I told Anne, the servent here, the other day, to say I was not at home if any one should call. I am not certain how I should endu[r]e loneliness and bad weather together. Now the time is beautiful. I take a walk every day for an hour before dinner and this is generally my walk—I go out at the back gate across one street, into the Cathedral yard, which is always interesting; then I pass under the trees along a paved path, pass the beautiful front of the Cathedral, turn to the left under a stone door way—then I am on the other side of the building—which leaving behind me I pass on through two college-like squares seemingly built for the dwelling place of Deans and Prebendaries— garnished with grass and shaded with trees. Then I pass through one of the old city gates and then you are in one College-Street through which I pass and at the end thereof crossing some meadows and at last a country alley of gardens I arrive, that is, my worship arrives at the foundation of Saint Cross, which is a very interesting old place, both for its gothic tower and alms-square and for the appropriation of its rich rents to ~~the~~ a relation of the Bishop of Winchester—Then I pass across St Cross meadows till you come to the most beautifully clear river—now this is only one mile of my walk I will spare you the other two till after supper when they would do you more good—You must avoid going the first mile just after dinner. I could almost advise you to put by all this nonsense until you are lifted out of your difficulties—but when you come to this part feel with confidence what I now feel that though there can be no stop put to troubles we are inheritors of there can be and must be and [*for* an] end to immediate difficulties. Rest in the confidence that I will not omit any exertion to benefit you by some means or other. If I cannot remit you hundreds, I will tens and if not that ones. Let the next year be managed by you as well as possible—the next month I mean for I trust you will soon receive Abbey's remittance. What he can send you will not be a sufficient capital to ensure you any command in America. What he has of mine I nearly have anticipated by debts. So I would advise you not to sink it, but to live upon it in hopes of my being able to encrease it—To this end I will devote whatever I may gain for a few years to come—at which period I must begin to think of a security of my own comforts when quiet will become more pleasant to me than the World—Still I would have you doubt my success—'T is at present the cast of a die with me. You say 'these things will be a great torment to me.' I shall not suffer them to be so. I shall only exert myself the more—while the seriousness of their nature will prevent me from missing up imaginary griefs. I have not had the blue devils once since I received your last—I am advised not to publish till it is seen whether the Tragedy will or not succeed— Should it, a few mo[n]ths may see me in the way of acquiring property; should it not it will be a drawback and I shall have to perform a longer literary Pilgrimage—You will perceive that it is quite out of my interest to come to America—What could I do there? How could I employ myself? Out of the reach of Libraries. You do not mention the name of the gentleman who assists you. 'T is an extraordinary thing. How could you do without that assistance? I will not trust myself with brooding over this. The following is an extract from a Letter of Reynolds to me. "I am glad to hear you are getting on so well with your writings. I hope you are not neglecting the revision of your Poems for the press: from which I expect more than you do"— the first thought that struck me on reading your last, was to mo[r]tgage a Poem to Murray:* but on more consideration I made up my mind not to do so: my reputation is very low: he would perhaps not have negociated my bill of intellect or given me a very small sum. I should have bound myself down for some time. 'T is best to meet present misfortunes; not for a momentary good to sacrifice great benefits which one's own untramell'd and free industry may bring one in the end. In all this do never think of me as in any way unhappy: I shall not be so. I have a great pleasure in thinking of my responsibility to you and shall do myself the greatest luxury if I can succeed in any way so as to be of assistance to you. We shall look back upon these times—even before our eyes are at all dim—I am convinced of it. But be careful of those Americans—I could almost advise you to come whenever you have the sum of 500£ to England—Those Americans will I am affraid still fleece you—If ever you should think of such a thing you must bear in mind the very different state of society here—The immense difficulties of the times—The great sum required per annum to maintain yourself in any decency. In fact the whole is with Providence. I know now [*for* not] how to advise you but by advising you to advise with yourself. In your next tell me at large your thoughts, about america; what chance there is of succeeding there: for it appears to me you have as yet been somehow deceived. I cannot help thinking Mr Audubon has deceived you. I shall not like the sight of him—I shall endeavour to avoid seeing him—You see how puzzled I am—I have no meridian to fix you to—being the Slave of what is to happen. I think I may bid you finally remain in good hopes: and not teise yourself with my changes and variations of Mind—If I say nothing decisive in any one particular part of my Letter, you may glean the truth from the whole pretty correctly—You may wonder why I had not put your affairs with Abbey in train on receiving your Letter before last, to which there will reach you a short answer dated from shanklin.* I did write and speak to Abbey but to no purpose. You last, with the enclosed note has appealed home to him—He will not see the necessity of a thing till he is hit in the mouth. 'T will be effectual—I am sorry to mix up foolish and serious things together—but in writing so much I am obliged to do so—and I hope sincerely the tenor of your mind will maintain itself better. In the course of a few months I shall be as good an Italian Scholar as I am a french one—I am reading Ariosto at present: not manageing more than six or eight stanzas at a time. When I have done this language so as to be able to read it tolerably well—I shall set myself to get complete in latin and there my learning must stop. I do not think of venturing upon Greek. I would not go even so far if I were not persuaded of the power the knowledge of any language gives one. the fact is I like to be acquainted with foreign languages. It is besides a nice way of filling up intervals &c Also the reading of Dante in [*for* is] well worth the while. And in latin there is a fund of curious literature of the middle ages—The Works of many great Men Aretine and Sanazarius and Machievel—I shall never become attach'd to a foreign idiom so as to put it into my writings. The Paradise lost though so fine in itself is a curruption of our Language—it should be kept as it is unique—a curiosity, a beautiful and grand Curiosity. The most remarkable Production of the world—A northern dialect accommodating itself to greek and latin inversions and intonations. The purest english I think—or what ought to be the purest—is Chatterton's—The Language had existed long enough to be entirely uncorrupted of Chaucer's gallicisms and still the old words are used—Chatterton's language is entirely northern—I prefer the native music of it to Milton's cut by feet I have but lately stood on my guard against Milton. Life to him would be death to me. Miltonic verse cannot be written but it [*for* in] the vein of art—I wish to devote myself to another sensation—

I have been obliged to intermiten your Letter for two days (this being Friday morn) from having had to attend to other correspondence. Brown who was at Bedhampton, went thence to Chichester, and I still directing my letters Bedhampton—there asore [*for* arose] a misunderstand about them—I began to suspect my Letters had been stopped from curiosity. However yesterday Brown had four Letters from me all in a Lump—and the matter is clear'd up—Brown complained very much in his Letter to me of yesterday of the great alteration the Disposition of Dilke has undergone—He thinks of nothing but 'Political Justice' and his Boy—Now the first political duty a Man ought to have a Mind to is the happiness of his friends. I wrote Brown a comment on the subject, wherein I explained what I thought of Dilke's Character. Which resolved itself into this conclusion. That Dilke was a Man who cannot feel he has a personal identity unless he has made up his Mind about every thing. The only means of strengthening one's intellect is to make up one's mind about nothing—to let the mind be a thoroughfare for all thoughts. Not a select party. The genus is not scarce in population. All the stubborn arguers you meet with are of the same brood—They never begin upon a subject they have not preresolved on. They want to hammer their nail into you and if you turn the point, still they think you wrong. Dilke will never come at a truth as long as he lives; because he is always trying at it. He is a Godwin-methodist.* I must not forget to mention that your mother show'd me the lock of hair—'t is of a very dark colour for so young a creature. When it is two feet in length I shall not stand a barley corn higher. That's not fair—one ought to go on growing as well as others—At the end of this sheet I shall stop for the present—and sent it off, you may expect another Letter immediately after it. As I never know the day of the mo[n]th but by chance I put here that this is *the 24th September*. I would wish you here to stop your ears, for I have a word or two to say to your Wife—My dear sister, In the first place I must quarrel with you for sending me such a shabby sheet of paper—though that is in some

degree made up for by the beautiful impress[i]on of the seal. You
should like to know what I was doing—The first of May—let me
see—I cannot recollect. I have all the Examiners ready to send—
They will be a great treat to you when they reach you—I shall pack
them up when my Business with Abbey has come to a good conclusion and the remittance is on the road to you—I have dealt round
your best wishes to our friends, like a pack of cards but being always
given to cheat, myself, I have turned up ace. You see I am making
game of you. I see you are not all all happy in that America. England
however would not be over happy for us if you were here. Perpaps
'twould be better to be teased herre than there. I must preach
patience to you both. No step hasty or injurious to you must be
taken. Your observation on the moschetos gives me great pleasure T
is excessively poetical and humane. You say let one large sheet be all
to me: You will find more than that in diffrent parts of this packet for
you. Certainly I have been caught in rains. A Catch in the rain
occasioned my last sore throat—but As for red-hair'd girls upon my
word I do not recollect ever having seen one—Are you quizzing me
or Miss Waldegrave when you talk of promenading. As for Pun-
making I wish it was as good a trade as pin-making—there is very
little business of that sort going on now. We struck for wages like the
manchester we[a]vers*—but to no purpose—so we are all out of
employ—I am more lucky than some you see by having an oportu-
nity of exporting a few—getting into a little foreign trade—which is
a comfortable thing. I wish one could get change for a pun in silver
currency. I would give three and a half any night to get into Drury-
pit—But they wont ring at all. No more will notes you will say—but
notes are differing things—though they make together a Pun
mote*—as the term goes. If I were your Son I shouldn't mind you,
though you rapt me with the Scissars—But lord! I should be out of
favor sin the little un be comm'd. You have made an Uncle of me,
you have, and I don't know what to make of myself. I suppose next
there'll be a Nevey.* You say—in may last, write directly. I have not
received your Letter above 10 days. The though[t] of you little girl
puts me in mind of a thing I heard a Mr Lamb say. A child in a[r]ms
was passing by his chair toward the mother, in the nurses a[r]ms—
Lamb took hold of the long clothes saying "Where, god bless me,
Where does it leave off?" *Saturday*. If you would prefer a joke or two

to any thing else I have too for you fresh hatchd. just ris as the Baker's wives say by the rolls. The first I play'd off at Brown—the second I play'd *on* on myself. Brown when he left me "Keats! says he "my good fellow (staggering upon his left heel, and fetching an irregular pirouette with his right) Keats says he (depressing his left eyebrow and elevating his right one ((tho by the way, at the moment, I did not know which was the right one)) Keats says he (still in the same posture but forthermore both his hands in his waistcoat pockets and jutting out his stomach) "Keats—my—go-o-ood fell o-o-o-ooh! says he (interlarding his exclamation with certain ventriloquial parentheses)—no this is all a lie—I Ic was as sober as a Judge when a judge happens to be sober; and said "Keats, if any Letters come for me—Do not forward them, but open them and give me the marrow of them in few words. At the time when I wrote my first to him no Letters had arrived—I thought I would invent one, and as I had not time to manufacture a long one I dabbed off as [*for* a] short one—and that was the reason of the joke succeeding beyond my expectations. Brown let his house to a Mr Benjamin a Jew. Now the water which furnishes the house is in a tank sided with a composition of lime and the lime imp[r]egnates the water unpleasantly—Taking advantage of this circumstance I pretended that Mr Benjamin had written the following short note—"Sir. By drinking your damn'd tank water I have got the gravel—what reparation can you make to me and my family? Nathan Benjamin" By a fortunate hit, I hit upon his right he[a]then name—his right Pronomen. Brown in consequence it appears wrote to the surprised Mr Benjamin the following "Sir, I cannot offer you any remuneration until your gravel shall have formed itself into a Stone when I will cut you with Pleasure. C. Brown" This of Browns Mr Benjamin has answered insisting on an explatinon [*for* explanation] of this singular circumstance. B. says "when I read your Letter and his following I roared, and in came Mr Snook who on reading them seem'd likely to burst the hoops of his fat sides—so the Joke has told well—Now for the one I played on myself—I must first give you the scene and the dramatis Personæ— There are an old M[a]jor and his youngish wife live in the next apartments to me—His bed room door opens at an angle with my sitting room door. Yesterday I was reading as demurely as a Parish Clerk when I heard a rap at the door—I got up and opened it—no one was to be seen—I listened and heard some one in the Major's room—Not content with this I went up stairs and down look'd in the cubboards—and watch'd—At last I set myself to read again not quite so demurely—when there came a louder rap—I arose determin'd to find out who it was—I look out the Stair cases were all silent—"This must be the Major's wife said I—at all events I will see the truth" so I rapt me at the Major's door and went in to the utter surprise and confusion of the Lady who was in reality there—after a little explanation, which I can no more describe than fly, I made my retreat from her convinced of my mistake. She is to all appearance a silly body and is really surprised about it—She must have been—for I have discoverd that a little girl in the house was the Rappee—I assure you she has nearly make me sneeze.* If the Lady tells tits I shall put a very grave and moral face on the matter with the old Gentleman, and make his little Boy a present of a humming top— My Dear George—This Monday morning the 27th I have received your last dated July 12th You say you have not heard from England these three months—Then my Letter from Shanklin wr[i]tten I think at the end of July cannot have reach'd you. You shall not have cause to think I neglect you. I have kept this back a little time in expectation of hearing from Mr Abbey—You will say I might have remained in Town to be Abbey's messenger in these affairs. That I offer'd him—but he in his answer convinced me he was anxious to bring the Business to an issue—He observed that by being himself the agent in the whole, people might be more expeditious. You say you have not heard for th[r]ee mo[n]ths and yet you letters have the tone of knowing how our affairs are situated by which I conjecture I acquainted you with them in a Letter previous to the Shanklin one. That I may not have done. To be certain I will here state that it is in consequence of Mrs Jennings threatning a Chancery suit that you have been kept from the receipt of monies and myself deprived of any help from Abbey—I am glad you say you keep up your Spirits— I hope you make a true statement on that score—Still keep them up—for we are all young—I can only repeat here that you shall hear from me again immediately—Notwithstanding their bad intelligence I have experienced some pleasure in receiving so correctly two Letters from you, as it give[s] me if I may so say a distant Idea of Proximity. This last improves upon my litle niece—Kiss her for me.

Do not fret yourself about the delay of money on account of any immediate opportunity being lost: for in a new country whoever has money must have opportunity of employing it in many ways. The report runs now more in favor of Kean stopping in England. If he should I have confident hopes of our Tragedy—If he smokes the hotblooded character of Ludolph—and he is the only actor that can do it—He will add to his own fame, and improve my fortune—I will give you a half dozen lines of it before I part as a specimen—

> "Not as a Swordsman would I pardon crave,
> But as a Son: the bronz'd Centurion
> Long-toil'd in foreign wars, *and whose high deeds*
> *Are shaded in a forest of tall spears*,
> *Known only to his troop*, hath greater plea
> Of favour with my Sire than I can have—"*

Believe me my dear brother and Sister—
Your affectionate and anxious Brother
John Keats

To C. W. Dilke, 1 October 1819

My dear Dilke,   Winchester Friday Octr 1st
   For sundry reasons, which I will explain to you when I come to Town, I have to request you will do me a great favor as I must call it knowing how great a Bore it is. That your imagination may not have time to take too great an alarm I state immediately that I want you to hire me a †couple of rooms in Westminster. Quietness and ch[e]apness are the essentials: but as I shall with Brown be returned by next Friday you cannot in that space have sufficient time to make any choice selection, and need not be very particular as I can when on the spot suit myself at leisure. Brown bids me remind you not to send the Examiners after the third. Tell Mrs D. I am obliged to her for the late ones which I see are directed in her hand—Excuse this mere business letter for I assure you I have not a syllable at hand on any subject in the world.

Your sincere friend
John Keats—

† A Sitting Room and bed room for myself alone.

To B. R. Haydon, 3 October 1819

My dear Haydon, Winchester Sunday Morn.

Certainly I might: but, a few Months pass away before we are aware; I have a great aversion, to letter writing which grows more and more upon me; and a greater to summon up circumstances before me of an unpleasant nature—I was not willing to trouble you with them. Could I have dated from my Palace in Milan you would have heard from me—Not even now will I mention a word of my affairs—only that "I Rab am here"* but shall not be here more than a Week more, as I purpose to settle in Town and work my way with the rest. I hope I shall never be so silly as to injure my health and industry for the future by speaking, writing or fretting about my non-estate. I have no quarrel, I assure you, of so weighty a nature, with the world, on my own account as I have on yours. I have done nothing—except for the amusement of a few people who refine upon their feelings till any thing in the ununderstandable way will go down with them—people predisposed for sentiment. I have no cause to complain because I am certain any thing really fine will in these days be felt. I have no doubt that if I had written Othello I should have been cheered by as good as Mob as Hunt.* So would you be now if the operation of painting was as universal as that of writing— It is not: and therefore it did behove men I could mention among whom I must place Sir G. Beaumont to have lifted you up above sordid cares—That this has not been done is a disgrace to the country. I know very little of Painting, yet your pictures follow me into the Country—when I am tired with reading I often think them over and as often condemn the spirit of modern Connoisseurs Upon the whole indeed you have no complaint to make being able to say what so few Men can "I have succeeded." On sitting down to write a few lines to you these are the uppermost in my mind, and however I may be beating about under the arctic while your spirit has passed the line, you may lay too a minute and consider I am earnest as far as I can see. Though at this present "I have great dispositions to *write*" I feel every day more and more content to read. Books are becoming more interesting and valuable to me—I may say I could not live without them. If in the course of a fortnight you can procure me a ticket to the british musœum I will make a better use of it than I did in the first instance. I shall go on with patience in the confidence that if I ever do any thing worth remembring the Reviewers will no more be able to stumble-block me than the Academy could you. They have the same quarrel with you that the scotch nobles had with Wallace— The fame they have lost through you is no joke to them. Had it not been for you Fuseli would have been not as he is major but maximus domo.* What the Reviewers can put a hindrance to must be—a nothing—or mediocre which is worse. I am sorry to say that since I saw you I have been guilty of—a practical Joke upon Brown which has had all the success of an innocent Wild fire among people— Some day in the next week you sh⟨a⟩ll hear it from me by word of Mouth—I hav⟨e not⟩ seen the portentous Book* which was scu⟨mm⟩er'd at you just as I left town. It may be light enough to serve you as a Cork Jacket and save you for a while the trouble of swimming. I heard the Man went raking and rummaging about like any Richardson. That and the Memoirs of Menage* are the first I shall be at. From Sʳ G— B's Lord Ms* and particularly Sʳ John Leicesters good lord deliver us—I shall expect to see your Picture plumped out like a ripe Peach—you would not be very willing to give me a slice of it—I came to this place in the hopes of meeting with a Library but was disappointed. The High Street is as quiet as a Lamb; the knockers are dieted To three raps per diem. The walks about are interesting—from the many old Buildings and arch ways—The view of the high street through the Gate of the City, in the beautiful September evening light has amused me frequently. The bad singing of the Cathedral I do not care to smoke.—being by myself I am not very coy in my taste. At Sᵗ Cross there is an interesting Picture of Albert Durers—who living in such warlike times perhaps was forced to paint in his Gauntlets—so we must make all allowances—

> I am my dear Haydon
> yours ever
> John Keats

Brown has a few words to say to you and will cross this

To Fanny Brawne, 11 October 1819

[25] College Street*

My sweet Girl,

I am living to day in yesterday: I was in a complete fa[s]cination all day. I feel myself at your mercy. Write me ever so few lines and tell you [*for* me] you will never for ever be less kind to me than yesterday—You dazzled me—There is nothing in the world so bright and delicate—When Brown came out with that seemingly true story again[s]t me last night, I felt it would be death to me if you had ever believed it—though against any one else I could muster up my obstinacy—Before I knew Brown could disprove it I was for the moment miserable. When shall we pass a day alone? I have had a thousand kisses, for which with my whole soul I thank love—but if you should deny me the thousand and first—'t would put me to the proof how great a misery I could live through. If you should ever carry your threat yesterday into execution—believe me 't is not my pride, my vanity or any petty passion would torment me—really 't would hurt my heart—I could not bear it—I have seen Mrs Dilke this morning—she says she will come with me any fine day—

Ever yours
John Keats

Ah hertè mine!*

[R]   *To Fanny Brawne, 13 October 1819*

25 College Street.

My dearest Girl,

This moment I have set myself to copy some verses out fair. I cannot proceed with any degree of content. I must write you a line or two and see if that will assist in dismissing you from my Mind for ever so short a time. Upon my Soul I can think of nothing else—The time is passed when I had power to advise and warn you again[s]t the unpromising morning of my Life—My love has made me selfish. I cannot exist without you—I am forgetful of every thing but seeing you again—my Life seems to stop there—I see no further. You have absorb'd me. I have a sensation at the present moment as though I was dissolving—I should be exquisitely miserable without the hope of soon seeing you. I should be affraid to separate myself far from you. My sweet Fanny, will your heart never change? My love, will it? I have no limit now to my love—You note came in just here—I cannot be happier away from you—'T is richer than an Argosy of Pearles. Do not threat me even in jest. I have been astonished that Men could die Martyrs for religion—I have shudder'd at it—I shudder no more—I could be martyr'd for my Religion—Love is my religion—I could die for that—I could die for you. My Creed is Love and you are its only tenet—You have ravish'd me away by a Power I cannot resist: and yet I could resist till I saw you; and even since I have seen you I have endeavoured often "to reason against the reasons of my Love."* I can do that no more—the pain would be too great—My Love is selfish—I cannot breathe without you.

Yours for ever

John Keats

To Fanny Brawne, 19 October 1819

Great Smith Street*

Tuesday Morn

My sweet Fanny,

On awakening from my three days dream ("I cry to dream again")* I find one and another astonish'd at my idleness and thoughtlessness—I was miserable last night—the morning is always restorative—I must be busy, or try to be so. I have several things to speak to you of tomorrow morning. Mrs Dilke I should think will tell you that I purpose living at Hampstead—I must impose chains upon myself—I shall be able to do nothing—I sho[u]ld like to cast the die for Love or death—I have no Patience with any thing else—if you ever intend to be cruel to me as you say in jest now but perhaps may sometimes be in earnest be so now—and I will—my mind is in a tremble, I cannot tell what I am writing.

Ever my love yours

John Keats

To Fanny Keats, 26 (?) October 1819

My dear Fanny,　　　　　　　　　　　　　　　　Wentworth Place

My Conscience is always reproaching me for neglecting you for so long a time. I have been returned from Winchester this fortnight and as yet I have not seen you. I have no excuse to offer—I should have no excuse. I shall expect to see you the next time I call on Mr A about Georges affairs which perplex me a great deal—I should have to day gone to see if you were in Town, but as I am in an i[n]dustrious humour (which is so necessary to my livelihood for the future) I am loath to break through it though it be merely for one day, for when I am inclined I can do a great deal in a day—I am more fond of pleasure than study (many men have prefer'd the latter) but I have become resolved to know something which you will credit when I tell you I have left off animal food that my brains may never henceforth be in a greater mist than is theirs by nature—I took Lodgings in Westminster for the purpose of being in the reach of Books, but am now returned to Hampstedd being induced to it by the habit I have acquired of this room I am now in and also from the pleasure of being free from paying any petty attentions to a diminutive house-keeping. Mr Brown has been my great friend for some time—without him I should have been in, perhaps, personal distress—as I know you love me though I do not deserve it, I am sure you will take pleasure in being a friend to Mr Brown even before you know him—My Lodgings for two or three days were close in the neighbourhood of Mrs Dilke who never sees me but she enquires after you—I have had letters from George lately which do not contain, as I think I told you in my last, the best news. I have hopes for the best—I trust in a good termination to his affairs which you please god will soon hear of—It is better you should not be teased with the particulars—The whole amount of the ill news is that his mercantile speculations have not had success in consequence of the general depression of trade in the whole province of Kentucky and indeed all america*—I have a couple of shells for you you will call pretty—

　　　　　　　　　　　　　　　　Your affectionate Brother

　　　　　　　　　　　　　　　　　　　　John—

To George and Georgiana Keats, 12 November 1819

My dear George,   Friday Evening
                                                         Nov^r

You must think my delay very great. I assure you it is no fault of mine. Not expecting you would want money so soon I did not send for the necessary power of attorney from Holland[1] before I received you Letter which reached me in the middle of the summer at Shanklin. I wrote for it then immediately and received it about ten days ago. You will also be much disappointed at the smallness of the Sum remitted to Warder's: there are two reasons for it, first that the Stocks are so very low, and secondly that Mr Abbey is unwilling to venture more till this business of Mrs Jennings's is completely at rest. Mr Abbey promised me to day that he would do all in his power to forward it expressing his wish that by the time it was settled she would make no claim the Stocks might recover themselves so that your property should not be sold out at so horrible a disadvantage. I know not what comfort to give you under these circumstances. Our affairs are in an awkward state. You have done as much as a man can do: I am not as yet fortunate. I should, in duty, endeavour to write you a Letter with a comfortable nonchalance, but how can I do so when you are in so perplexing a situation, and I not able to help you out of it. The distance between us is so great, the Posts so uncertain. We must hope. I am aff[r]aid you are no more than myself form'd for a gainer of money. I have been daily expecting to hear from you again. Does the steam boat make any return yet? Whether I shall at all be set affloat upon the world depends now upon the success of the Tragedy I spoke of. We have heard nothing from Elliston* who is now the Renter of Drury Lane since the piece was sent in which was three weeks and more ago. The reason may be that Kean has not return'd, whose opinion Elliston will partly rely on. Brown is still very sanguine. The moment I have any certain intelligence concerning it I will let you know. I have not been to see Fanny since my return from Winchester—I have written and received a Letter from her. Mr Abbey says she is getting stouter. I call'd in Rodney [*for* Romney] street about a fortnight since. Your Mother was quite well,

---

[1] See Appendix, note 6.

and Charles was to set out again for Paris on the day following. I do not call so often as I should do if I had any good news to tell—I am there in the character of a Prevaricator. I must not tell the truth. Mr Abbey shows at times a little anxiety about me he wanted me the other day to turn Bookseller. Why does he not make some such proposal to you? Yet he can not care much for I till yesterday had had no money of him for ten months and he never enquired how I liv'd: nor how I paid my last Christmas Bills (still unpaid) though I repeatedly mentioned them to him. We are not the only toilers and sufferers in the World. Hunt was arrested the other day.* He soon however dated from his own house again. Hazlitt has begun another course of Lectures, on the Writers of Elizabeth's reign*—I hear he quoted me in his last Lecture—Our Set still continue separate as we get older, each follows with more precision the bent of his own Mind. Brown and I by living together are an exception. Rice continues to every one his friendly behaviour his illness and his wit stick by him as usual. In a note to me the other day he sent the following Pun—*Tune—the Harlot's Lament*—

> Between the two P—x's I've lost every Lover,
>   But a difference I found 'twixt the great and the small:
> For by the Small Pox I gott ⎰pitted⎱ all over
>   By the other I did not get ⎱pitted⎰ at all.

Reynolds has settled in Lodgings very near to Rice's and seems set in for the Law. Dilke I call upon at his office the other day. We ta[l]ked about you; you being mostly my subject with him. He says you should have kept to your original design;* in which I differ with him entirely. I think you have done perfectly right. I have this moment received a Letter from Severn, whom I have not seen for some time, he tell me he has finish'd a picture of Spenser's Cave of despair which is designed to contend for the Prize at the Academy and is now hung up there for Judgement—He wishes me to see it. I have been endeavouring to write lately, but with little success as I require a little encouragement, as [*for* and a] little better fortun⟨e⟩ to befall you and happier news from you before I can wr⟨i⟩te with an untrammell'd mind. Nothing could have in all its circumstances fallen out worse for me than the last year has done, or could be more damping to my poetical talent—I comfort myself in the idea that you are a consolation to each other. Haslam told me the last time I saw him that he was about to write to you. He is entirely taken up with his Sweetheart—I feel very loath to write more than this Sheet—you must excuse the shortness of this Letter for the length of the last and the length of the next I hope, if any thing occurs to enspirit ⟨me a⟩ little. Fanny would like a Letter from you. I should ⟨think⟩ that Abbey from the delay of Waltons house has employed ⟨another⟩ Lawyer on our Business. Mrs Jennings has not instituted ⟨an⟩y action against us yet, nor has she withdrawn her claim I think I told you that even if she were to lose her cause we shold have to pay the expences of the Suit. You urg'd me to get Mr Abbey to advance you money—that he will by no means do—for besides the risk of the law (small enough indeed) he will never be persu[a]ded but you will loose it in America. For a bit of a treat in the heart of all this I had a most abusive Letter from Fry*—committing you and myself to destruction without reprieve—In your next Letter make some questions regularly upon which you wish to be in⟨form⟩ed concerning our's and any other subject and I will answer ⟨them as⟩ amply as I can—My dear Sister God bless you and your ⟨baby gir⟩l. The enquires about you are very frequent—My dear George I remain, in hopes,

Your most affectionate Brother
John Keats

To Joseph Severn, 15 November 1819

My dear Severn,   Wentworth Place
                                                   Monday Morn—

I am very sorry that on Tuesday I have an appointment in the City of an undeferable nature; and Brown on the same day has some business at Guildhall. I have not been able to figure your manner of executing the Cave of despair, therefore it will be at any rate a novelty and surprise to me—I trust on the right side. I shall call upon you some morning shortly early enought to catch you before you can get out—when we will proceed to the Academy. I think you must be suited with a good painting light in your Bay window. I wish you to return the Compliment by going with me to see a Poem I have hung up for the Prize in the Lecture Room of the surry Institution.* I have

many Rivals the most threatning are An Ode to Lord Castlereagh,*
and a news [*for* new] series of Hymns for the New, new Jerusalem*
Chapel—You had best put me into your Cave of despair*—

Ever yours sincerely

John Keats

To John Taylor, 17 November 1819

Wentworth Place

Wednesday,

My dear Taylor,

I have come to a determination not to publish any thing I have
now ready written; but for all that to publish a Poem before long and
that I hope to make a fine one. As the marvellous is the most enticing
and the surest guarantee of harmonious numbers I have been
endeavouring to persuade myself to untether Fancy and let her manage for herself—I and myself cannot agree about this at all. Wonders
are no wonders to me. I am more at Home amongst Men and
women. I would rather read Chaucer than Ariosto*—The little dramatic skill I may as yet have however badly it might show in a Drama
would I think be sufficient for a Poem—I wish to diffuse the colouring of St Agnes eve throughout a Poem in which Character and
Sentiment would be the figures to such drapery—Two or three such
Poems, if God should spare me, written in the course of the next six
years, would be a famous gradus ad Parnassum altissimum—I mean
they would nerve me up to the writing of a few fine Plays*—my
greatest ambition—when I do feel ambitious. I am sorry to say that is
very seldom. The subject we have once or twice talked of appears a
promising one, The Earl of Leicester's historry. I am this morning
reading Holingshed's Elisabeth,* You had some Books a while ago,
you promised to lend me, illustrative of my Subject. If you can lay
hold of them or any others which may be serviceable to me I know
you will encourage my low-spirited Muse by sending them—or
rather by letting me know when our Errand cart Man shall call with
my little Box. I will endeavour to set my self selfishly at work on this
Poem that is to be—

Your sincere friend

John Keats—

To James Rice, December 1819

Wentworth Place

My dear Rice,

As I want the coat on my back mended, I would be obliged if you will send me the one Brown left at your house, by the Bearer— During your late contest I hea[r]d regular reports of you; how that your time was entirely taken up, and you health improving—I shall call in the course of a few days and see wh[e]ther your promotion has made any difference in your Behaviour to us—I suppose Reynolds has given you an account of Brown and Elliston—As he has not rejected our Tragedy I shall not venture to call him directly a fool; but as he wishes to put it off till next season I cant help thinking him little better than a Knave—That it will not be acted this Season is yet uncertain—Perpaps we may give it another furbish and try it at covent Garden. 'T would do one's heart good to see Macready in Ludolph.* If you do not see me soon it will be from the humour of writing, which I have had for three days, continuing—I must say to the Muses what the maid says to the Man—"take me while the fit is on me"*—Would you like a true Story "There was a Man and his Wife who being to go a long journey on foot, in the course of their travels came to a River which rolled knee deep over the pebbles—In these cases the Man generally pulls off his shoes and stockings and carries the women over on his Back. This Man did so; and his Wife being pregnant and troubled, as in such cases is very common, with strange longings, took the strangest that ever was heard of—Seeing her Husband's foot, a hansome on [*for* one] enough, look very clean and tempting in the clear water, on their arrival at ⟨the⟩ other bank she earnestly demand⟨ed⟩ a bit of it; he being an affectionate fellow and fearing for the comeliness of his child gave her a bit which he cut off with his Clasp knife—Not satisfied she asked another morsel—supposing there might be twins he gave her a slice more. Not yet contented she craved another Piece. "You Wretch cries the Man, would you wish me to kill myself? take that!" Upon which he stabb'd her with the knife, cut her open and found three Children in her Belly two of them very comfortable with their mouth's shut, the third with its eyes and mouth stark staring open. "Who would have thought it"

cried the Wid[ow]er, and pursued his journey—, Brown has a little
rumbling in his Stomach this morning—

Ever yours sincerely
John Keats—

To Fanny Keats, 20 December 1819

My dear Fanny,   Wentworth Place
                                                 Monday Morn—
    When I saw you last, you ask'd me whether you should see me
again before Christmas—You would have seen me if I had been quite
well. I have not, though not unwell enough to have prevented me—
not indeed at all—but fearful le[s]t the weather should affect my
throat which on exertion or cold continually threatens me—By the
advice of my Doctor I have had a wa[r]m great Coat made and have
ordered some thick shoes—so furnish'd I shall be with you if it holds
a little fine before Christmas day—I have been very busy since I saw
you especially the last Week and shall be for some time, in preparing
some Poems to come out in the Sp[r]ing and also in h[e]ightening
the interest of our Tragedy—Of the Tragedy I can give you but news
semigood. It is accepted at Drury Lane with a promise of coming out
next season: as that will be too long a delay we have determined to
get Elliston to bring it out this Season or to transfer it to Covent
Garden.* This Elliston will not like, as we have every motive to
believe that Kean has perceived how suitable the principal Character
will be for him. My hopes of success in the literary world are now
better than ever—Mr Abbey, on my calling on him lately, appeared
anxious that I should apply myself to something else—He mentioned Tea Brokerage. I supposed he might perhaps mean to give me
the Brokerage of his concern, which might be executed with little
trouble and a good profit; and therefore said I should have no objection to it especially as at the same time it occured to me that I might
make over the business to George—I questioned him about it a few
days after. His mind takes odd turns. When I became a Suitor he
became coy. He did not seem so much inclined to serve me. He
described what I should have to do in the progress of business. It will
not suit me. I have given it up. I have not heard again from George
which rather disappoints me, as I wish to hear before I make any

fresh remittance of his property. I received a note from Mrs Dilke a few days ago inviting me to dine with her on Xmas day, which I shall do. Mr Brown and I go on in our old dog trot of Breakfast, dinner (not tea for we have left that off) supper Sleep, Confab, stirring the fire and reading. Whilst I was in the Country last summer Mrs Bentley tells me a woman in mour[n]ing call'd on me,—and talk'd something of an aunt of ours—I am so careless a fellow I did not enquire, but will particularly. On Tuesday I am going to hear some Schoolboys Speechify on breaking up day—I'll lay you a pocket pi[e]ce we shall have "My name is norval"* I have not yet look'd for the Letter you mention'd as it is mix'd up in a box full of papers—you must tell me, if you can recollect, the subject of it. This moment Bentley brought a Letter from George for me to deliver to Mrs Wylie—I shall see her and it before I see you. The direction was in his best hand, written with a good Pen and sealed with a Tassi[e]'s Shakspeare such as I gave you—We judge of peoples hearts by their Countenances; may we not judge of Letters in the same way? if so, the Letter does not contain unpleasant news—Good or bad spirits have an effect on the handwriting. This direction is at least unnervous and healthy. Our Sister is also well, or George would have made strange work with Ks and Ws. The little Baby is well o⟨r⟩ he would have formed precious vowels and Consonants—He sent off the Letter in a hurry, or the mail bag was rather a wa[r]m birth, or he has worn out his Seal, for the Shakespeare's head is flattened a little. This is close muggy weather as they say at the Ale houses—

> I am, ever, my dear Sister
> Yours affectionately
> John Keats—

1820

To Georgiana Wylie Keats,
                    13, 15, 17, 28 January 1820

My dear Sister,   Thursday Jany 13th 1820—
  By the time you receive this your troubles will be over—I wish
you knew they were half over; I mean that George is safe in England,
and in good health—To write to you by him is almost like following
ones own Letter in the Mail that it may not be quite so I will leave
common intelligence out of the question and write wide of him as I
can—I fear I must be dull having had no good-natured flip from
fortune's finger since I saw you, and so [*for* no] side way comfort in
the success of my friends—I could almost promise that if I had the
means I would accompany George back to america and pay you a
Visit of a few Months. I should not think much of the time or my
absence from my Books, or I have no right to think, for I am very
idle: but then I ought to be diligent and at least keep myself within
the reach of materials for diligence. Diligence! that I do not mean to
say, I should say dreaming over my Books, or rather other peoples
Books. George has promised to bring you to England when the five
years have elapsed, I regret very much that I shall not be able to see
you before that time; and even then then I must hope that your
affairs will be in so prosperous a way as to induce you to stop longer.
Yours is a hardish fate to be so divided from your friends and settled
among a people you hate—you will find it improve—you have a
heart that will take hold of your Children—Even Georges absence
will make things better—his return will ban[i]sh what must be your
greatest sorrow and at the same time minor ones with it. Robinson
Crusoe when he saw himself in danger of perishing on the Waters
look'd back to his island as to the haven of his Happiness and on
gaining it once more was more content with his Solitude. We smoke
George about his little Girl, he runs the common beaten road of

every father, as I dare say you do of every Mother—there is no Child like his Child—so original! original forsooth However I take you at your words; I have a lively faith that yours is the very gem of all Children—Aint I its Unkle? On Henry's Marriage there was a piece of Bride cake sent me—it miss'd its way—I suppose the Carrier or Coachman was a Conjurer and wanted it for his own private use— Last Sunday George and I dined at Millars—there were your Mother and Charles with Fool Lacon Esqre who sent the sly disinterested Shawl to Miss Millar with his own heathen name engraved in the Middle—Charles had a silk Handkerchief belonging to a Miss Grover with whom he pretended to be smitten and for her sake kept exhibiting and adoring the Handkerchief all the evening. Fool Lacon Esqre treated it with a little venturesome trembling Contumely, whereon Charles set him quietly down on the floor—from where he as quietly got up—This process was repeated at supper time, when your Mother said "If I were you Mr Lacon I would not let him do so." Fool Lacon Esqre did not offer any remark. He will undoubtedly die in his bed. Your Mother did not look quite so well on Sunday— Mrs Henry Wylie is excessively quiet before people, I hope she is always so. Yesterday we dined at Taylor's in Fleet—George left early after dinner to go to Deptford—He will make all square there for me—I could not go with him. I did not like the amusement— Haslam is a very good fellow indeed; he has been excessively anxious and kind to us. But is this fair? He has an innamorata at Deptford and he has been wanting me for some time past to see her. This is a thing which it is impossible not to shirk. A Man is like a Magnet, he must have a repelling end—so how am I to see Haslams lady and family if I even went; for by the time I got to greenwich I should have repell'd them to Blackheath and by the time I got to Deptford, they would be on Shooters hill, when I came to shooters Hill, they would alight at Chatham and so on till I drove them into the Sea, which I think might be inditeable—The Evening before yesterday we had a piano forte hop at Dilkes—There was very little amusement in the room but a Scotchman to hate—Some people you must have observed have a most unpleasant effect upon you when you see them speaking in profile—this Scotchman is the most accomplish'd fellow in this way I ever met with. The effect was complete—It went down like a dose of bitters and I hope will improve my digestion—At

Taylor's too there was a Scotchman—not quite so bad for he was as clean as he could get himself. Not having succeeded at Drury Lane with our Tragedy, we have been making some alterations and are about to try Covent Garden—Brown has just done patching up the Copy, as it is altered—The only reliance I had on it was in Kean's acting—I am *not* affraid it will be damn'd in the Garden—You said in one of your Letters that there was noth[i]ng but Haydon and Co in mine—There can be nothing of him in this for I never see him or Co—George has introduc'd to us an American of the Name of Hart—I like him in a Mod[e]rate way—He was at Mʳˢ Dilkes party; and sitting by me, we begun talking about english and American ladies—The Miss Reynolds' and some of their friends made not a very inticing row opposite us—I bade him mark them and form his Judgement of them—I told him I hated Englishmen because they were the only Men I knew. He does not understand this— Who would be Bragadocio to Johnny Bull? Johnny's house is his Castle, and a precious dull Castle it is. What a many Bull Castles there are in So and So Crescent—I never wish myself an unversd visitor an[d] news monger but when I write to you. I should like for a day or two to have somebody's knowledge, Mʳ Lacon's for instance of all the different folks of a wide acquaintance to tell you about—Only let me have his knowledge of family minutiæ and I would set them in a proper light but bless me I never go any where— my pen is no more garulous than my tongue—Any third person would think I was addressing myself to a Lover of Scandal. But we know we do not love scandal but fun, and if Scandal happens to be fun that is no fault of ours. There were very pretty pickings for me in Georges Letters about the Prairie Settlement, if I had had any taste to turn them to account in England. I knew a friend of Miss Andrews yet I never mention'd her to him: for after I had read the letter I really did not recollect her Story. Now I have been sitting here a half hour with my invention at work to say something about your Mother or Charles or Henry but it is in vain—I know not what to say—Three nights since George went with your Mother to the play—I hope she will soon see mine acted. I do not remember ever to have thank'd you for your tassels to my Shakspeare there he hangs so ably supported opposite me. I thank you now. It is a continual memento of you. If you should have a

Boy do not christen him John, and persuade George not to let his partiality for me come across—'T is a bad name, and goes against a Man—If my name had been Edmund I should have been more fortunate—I was surprised to hear of the State of Society at Louisville, is [*for* it] seems you are just as rediculous there as we are here—threepenny parties, half penny Dances—the best thing I have heard of is your Shooting, for it seems you follow the Gun. Give my Compliments to Mrs Audubon and tell her I cannot think her either good looking or honest—Tell Mr Audubon he's a fool—and Briggs that 't is well I was not M^r A—

Saturday Jany 15 It is strange that George having to stop so short ⟨a⟩ time in England I should not have seen him for nearly two days—He has been to ⟨H⟩aslam's and does not encourage me to follow his example—He had given promise to dine with the same party tomorrow, but has sent an excuse which I am glad of as we shall have a pleasant party with us tomorrow. We expect Charles here today—This is a beautiful day; I hope you will not quarrel with it if I call it an american one. The Sun comes upon the snow and makes a prettier candy than we have on twelvth cakes. George is busy this morning in making copies of my verses—He is making now one of an Ode to the nightingale, which is like reading an account of the b[l]ack hole at Calcutta on an ice bergh. You will say this is a matter of course, I am glad it is, I mean that I should like your Brothers more, the more I know them. I should spend much more time with them if our lives were more run in paralel, but we can talk but on one subject that is you—The more I know of Men the more I know how to value entire liberality in any of them. Thank God there are a great many who will sacrifice their worldly interest for a friend: I wish there were more who would sacrifice their passions. The worst of Men are those whose self interests are their passion—the next those whose passions are their self-interest. Upon the whole I dislike Mankind: whatever people on the other side of the question may advance they cannot deny that they are always surprised at hearing of a good action and never of a bad one. I am glad you have something [to] like in America, Doves—Gertrude of Wyoming* and Birkbeck's book should be bound up together like a Brace of Decoy Ducks— One is almost as poetical as the other. Precious miserable people at the Prarie. I have been sitting in the Sun whilest I wrote this till it became quite oppressive, this is very odd for January—The vulcan fire is the true natural heat for Winter: the Sun has nothing to do in winter but to give a 'little glooming light much like a Shade"*—Our irish servant has piqued me this morning by saying that her Father in Ireland was very much like my Shakspeare only he had more color than the Engraving. You will find on Georges return that I have not been neglecting your affairs. The delay was unfortunate, not faulty;—perhaps by this time you have received my three last letters not one of which had reach'd before George sail'd, I would give two ⟨pe⟩nce to have been over the world as much as he has—I wish I had money enough to do nothing but travel about for years—Were you now in England I dare say you would be able (setting aside the pleasure you would have in seeing your mother) to suck out more amusemement for Society than I am able to do. To me it is all as dull here as Louisville could be. I am tired of the Theatres. Almost all the parties I may chance to fall into I know by heart—I know the different Styles of talk in different places: what subjects will be started how it will proceed, like an acted play, from the first to the last Act— If I go to Hunt's I run my head into many-times heard puns and music. To Haydon's worn out discourses of poetry and painting: the Miss Reynolds I am affraid to speak to for fear of some sickly reiteration of Phrase or Sentiment. When they were at the dance the other night I tried manfully to sit near and talk to them, but to not [*for* no] purpose, and if I had 't would have been to no purpose still— My question or observation must have been an old one, and the rejoinder very antique indeed. At Dilkes I fall foul of Politics. 'T is best to remain aloof from people and like their good parts without being eternally troubled with the dull processes of their every day Lives. When once a person has smok'd the vapidness of the routine of Society he must have either self interest or the love of some sort of distinction to keep him in good humour with it. All I can say is that standing at Charing cross and looking east west north and south I can see nothing but dullness—I hope while I am young to live retired in the Country, when I grow in years and have a right to be idle I shall enjoy cities more. If the American Ladies are worse than the English they must be very bad—You say you should like your Emily brought up here. You had better bring her up yourself. You know a good number of english Ladies what encomium could you give of half a dozen of them—the greater part seem to me downright American. I have known more than one Mrs Audubon their affectation of fashion and politeness cannot transcend ours—Look at our Cheapside Trademans sons and daughters—only fit to be taken off by a plague—I hope now soon to come to the time when I shall never be forc'd to walk through the City and hate as I walk—

Monday Jany 17 George had a quick rejoinder to his Letter of excuse to Haslam so we had not his company yesterday which I was sorry for as there was our old set. I know three witty people all distinct in their excellence—Rice, Reynolds and Richards. Rice is the wisest, Reynolds the playfullest, Richards the out o' the wayest. The first makes you laugh and think, the second makes you laugh and not think, the third puzzles your head—I admire the first, I enjoy the second, I stare at the third—The first is Claret, the second Ginger beer, the third Crême de Bzrapqmdrag. The first is inspired by Minerva, the second by Mercury, the third by Harlequin Epigram Esqre—The first is neat in his dress, the second slovenly, the third uncomfortable—The first speaks adagio, the second alegretto, the third both together—The first is swiftean, the second Tom cribean,* the third Shandean—and yet these three Eans are not three Eans but one Ean. Charles came on Saturday, but went early: he seems to have schemes and plans and wants to get off—He is quite right, I am glad to see him employed at his years. You remember I wrote you a Story about a woman named Alice being made young again—or some such stuff—In your next Letter tell me whether I gave it as my own or whether I gave it as a matter Brown was employed upon at the time. He read it over to George the other day, and George said he had heard it all before—So Brown suspects I have been giving You his Story as my own—I should like to set him right in it by your Evidence. George has not return'd from Town when he does I shall tax his memory. We had a young, long, raw, lean Scotchman with us yesterday, calld Thornton—Rice for fun or for mistake would persist in calling him Stevenson—I know three people of no wit at all, each distinct in his excellence. A. B, and C, A is the soolishest [*for* foolishest], B the sulkiest, C is a negative—A makes you yawn, B makes you hate, as for C you never see him though he is six feet high. I bear the first, I forbear the second I am not certain that the third is. The first is gruel, the Second Ditch water, the third is spilt—he ought to be wip'd up A is inspired by Jack o' the Clock—B, has been dull'd by a russian Sargeant, C—they say is not his Mothers true Child but that she bought him of the Man who cries 'young Lambs to sell." T wang dillo dee. . This you must know is the Amen to nonsense. I know many places where Amen should be scratched out, rubb'd over with pou[n]ce made of Momus's* little finger bones, and in its place 'T wang-dillo-dee,' written. This is the word I shall henceforth be tempted to write at the end of most modern Poems—Every American Book ought to have it. It would be a good distinction in Saiety. My Lords Wellington, Castlereagh and Canning and many more would do well to wear T wang-dillo-dee written on their Backs instead of wearing ribbands in their Button holes—How many people would go sideways along walls and quickset hedges to keep their T wang dillo dee out of sight, or wear large pigtails to hide it. However there would be so many that the T wang dillo dees would keep one another in Countenance—which Brown cannot do for me. I have fallen away lately. Thieves and Murderers would gain rank in the world—for would any one of them have the poorness of Spirit to condescend to be a T wang dillo dee—"I have robb'd in many a dwelling house, I have kill'd many a fowl many a goose and many a Man," (would such a gentleman say) but thank heaven I was never yet a T wang dillo dee"—Some philosophers in the Moon who spy at our Globe as we do at theirs say that T wang dillo dee is written in large Letters on our Globe of Earth—They say the beginning of the T is just on the spot where London stands. London being built within the Flourish—*wan* reach downward and slant as far a [*for* as] Tumbutoo in africa, the tail of the G. goes slap across the Atlantic into the Rio della Plata—the remainder of the Letters wrap round new holland and the last exterminates on land we have not yet discovered. However I must be silent, these are dangerous times to libel a man in, much more a world.

Friday 27th [*for* 28th] I wish you would call me names. I deserve them so much. I have only written two sheets for you, to b[e] carry [*for* carried] by George and those I forgot to bring to town and have therefore to forward them to Liverpool ⟨George⟩ went this morning at 6 o Clock by the Liverpool Coach—His being on his journey to you, prevents me regreeting his short stay—I have no news of any sort to tell you. Henry is wife-bound in Cambden Town there is no getting him out. I am sorry he has not a prettier wife: indeed 't is a shame: she is not half a wife. I think I could find some of her relations in Buffon, or Captn Cook's voyages, or the ⟨hie⟩*rogue*glyphics in Moors almanack, or upon a chinese Clock door, the Shepherd-esses on her own mantle-piece, or in a *c*⟨*rue*⟩*l* sampler in which she may find herself worsted, or in a dutch toy shop windown [*for* window], or one of the Daughters in the Ark, or in any picture shop window. As I intend to retire into the Country where there will be no sort of news, I shall not be able to write you very long Letters—Besides I am affraid the Postage comes to too much; which till now I have not been aware of. We had a fine Packing up at ⟨*torn*⟩ other things I saw ⟨*torn*⟩ People in milata[r]y Bands are generally seriously occupied—none may or can laugh at their work but the Kettle Drums Long-drum D^o Triangle, and Cymbals—Thinking you might want a Ratcatcher I put your mother's old quaker-colour'd Cat into the top of your bonnet—she's wi' kitten, so you may expect to find a whole family—I hope the family will not grow too large for its Lodging. I shall send you a close written Sheet on the first of next Month but for fear of missing the Liverpool Post I must finish here. God bless you and your little Girl—

Your affectionate Brother
John Keats—

[R]   *To Fanny Brawne, 4 (?) February 1820*

Dearest Fanny, I shall send this the moment you return. They say I must remain confined to this room for some time. The consciousness that you love me will make a pleasant prison of the house next to yours. You must come and see me frequently: this evening, without fail—when you must not mind about my speaking in a low tone for I am ordered to do so though I *can* speak out.*

Yours ever
sweetest love.—

turn over   J Keats

Perhaps your Mother is not at home and so you must wait till she comes—You must see me to night and let me ~~have~~ hear you promise to come tomorrow—

Brown told me you were all out. I have been looking for the Stage the whole afternoon—Had I known this I could not have remained so silent all day—

To Fanny Keats, 6 February 1820

Wentworth Place
My dear Sister,   Sunday Morning.

I should not have sent those Letters* without some notice if Mr Brown had not persuaded me against it on account of an illness with which I was attackd on Thursday. After that I was resolved not to write till I should be on the mending hand: thank God, I am now so. From imprudently leaving off my great coat in the thaw I caught cold which flew to my Lungs. Every remedy that has been applied has taken the desired effect, and I have nothing now to do but stay within doors for some time. If I should be confined long I shall write to Mr Abbey to ask permission for you to visit me. George has been running great chance of a similar attack, but I hope the sea air will be his Physician in case of illness—the air out at sea is always more temperate than on land—George mentioned, in his Letters to us, something of Mr Abbey's regret concer[n]ing the silence kept up in his house. It is entirely the fault of his Manner—You must be careful always to wear warm cloathing not only in frost but in a Thaw—I have no news to tell you. The half built houses opposite us stand just as they were and seem dying of old age before they are brought up. The grass looks very dingy, the Celery is all gone, and there is nothing to enliven one but a few Cabbage Staks that seem fix'd on the superanuated List. Mrs Dilke has been ill but is better. Several of my friends have been to see me. Mrs Reynolds was here this morning and the two Mr Wylies. Brown has been very alert about me, though a little wheezy himself this weather. Evey body is ill. Yesterday evening Mr Davenport, a gentleman of hampstead sent me an invitation to supper, instead of his coming to see us, having so bad a cold he could not stir out—so you [see] tis the weather and I am among a thousand. Whenever you have an inflamatory fever never mind about eating. The day on which I was getting ill I felt this fever to a great height, and therefore almost entirely abstained from food the whole day. I have no doubt experienc'd a benefit from so doing—The Papers I see are full of anecdotes of the late king:* how he nodded to

a Coal heaver and laugh'd with a Quaker and lik'd boil'd Leg of
Mutton. Old Peter Pindar* is just dead: what will the old king and he
say to each other? Perhaps the king may confess that Peter was in the
right, and Peter maintain himse⟨lf⟩ to have been wrong. You shall
hear from me again on tuesday.

Your affectionate Brother
John.

To Fanny Keats, 8 February 1820

My dear Fanny—   Wentworth Place
Tuesday morn.

 I had a slight return of fever last night, which terminated favourably, and I am now tolerably well, though weak from small quantity
of food to which I am obliged to confine myself: I am sure a mouse
would starv[e] upon it. Mrs Wylie came yesterday. I have a very
pleasant room for a sick person. A Sopha bed is made up for me in
the front Parlour which looks on to the grass plot as you remember
Mrs Dilkes does. How much more comfortable than a dull room up
stairs, where one gets tired of the pattern of the bed curtains. Besides
I see all that passes—for instanc[e] now, this morning, if I had been
in my own room I should not have seen the coals brought in. On
sunday between the hours of twelve and one I descried a Pot boy. I
conjectured it might be the one o'Clock beer—Old women with
bobbins and red cloaks and unpresuming bonnets I see creeping
about the heath. Gipseys after hare skins and silver spoons. Then
goes by a fellow with a wooden clock under his arm that strikes a
hundred and more. Then comes the old french emigrant (who has
been very well to do in france) whith his hands joined behind on his
hips, and his face full of political schemes. Then passes Mr David
Lewis a very goodnatured, goodlooking old gentleman whas [*for*
who] has been very kind to Tom and George and me. As for those
fellows the Brickmakers they are always passing to and fro. I mus'n't
forget the two old maiden Ladies in well walk who have a Lap dog
between them, that they are very anxious about. It is a corpulent
Little Beast whom it is necessary to coax along with an ivory-tipp'd
cane. Carlo our Neighbour Mrs Brawne's dog and it meet sometimes.
Lappy thinks Carlo a devil of a fellow and so do his Mistresses. Well

they may—he would sweep 'em all down at a run; all for the Joke of it. I shall desire him to peruse the fable of the Boys and the frogs: though he prefers the tongues and the Bones.* You shall hear from me again the day after tomorrow—

> Your affectionate Brother
> John Keats

To Fanny Brawne, 10 (?) February 1820

My dearest Girl—

If illness makes such an agreeable variety in the manner of you eyes I should wish you sometimes to be ill. I wish I had read your note before you went last night that I might have assured you how far I was from suspecting any coldness: You had a just right to be a little silent to one who speaks so plainly to you. You must believe you shall, you will that I can do nothing say nothing think nothing of you but what has its spring in the Love which has so long been my pleasure and torment. On the night I was taken ill when so violent a rush of blood came to my Lungs that I felt nearly suffocated—I assure you I felt it possible I might not survive and at that moment though[t] of nothing but you—When I said to Brown 'this is unfortunate' I thought of you—'T is true that since the first two or three days other subjects have entered my head—I shall be looking forward to Health and the Spring and a regular routine of our old Walks. Your affectionate

> J.K—

To Fanny Brawne, February (?) 1820

My sweet love, I shall wait patiently till tomorrow before I see you, and in the mean time, if there is any need of such a thing, assure you by your Beauty, that whenever I have at any time written on a certain unpleasant subject, it has been with your welfare impress'd upon my mind. How hurt I should have been had you ever acceded to what is, notwithstanding, very reasonable! How much the more do I love you from the general result! In my present state of Health I feel too much separated from you and could almost speak to you in the words of Lorenzo's Ghost to Isabella

> Your Beauty grows upon me and I feel
> A greater love through all my essence steal.*

My greatest torment since I have known you has been the fear of you being a little inclined to the Cressid;* but that suspicion I dismiss utterly and remain happy in the surety of your Love, which I assure you is as much a wonder to me as a delight. Send me the words "Good night" to put under my pillow.

Dearest Fanny,
Your affectionate
J.K.

To Fanny Keats, *14 February 1820*

Wentworth Place

My dear Fanny,   Monday Morn—
I am improving but very gradually and suspect it will be a long while before I shall be able to walk six miles—The Sun appears half inclined to shine; if he obliges us I shall take a turn in the garden this morning. No one from Town has visited me since my last. I have had so many presents of jam and jellies that they would reach side by side the length of the sideboard. I hope I shall be well before it is all consumed. I am vex'd that Mr Abbey will not allow you pocket money sufficient. He has not behaved well—By detaining money from me and George when we most wanted it he has increased our expences. In consequence of such delay George was obliged to take his voyage to england which will be £150 out of his Pocket. I enclose you a Note—You shall hear from me again the day after tomorrow.

Your affectionate Brother
John

To Fanny Brawne, *February (?) 1820*

My dearest Girl,
According to all appearances I am to be separated from you as much as possible. How I shall be able to bear it, or whether it will not be worse than your presence now and then, I cannot tell. I must be patient, and in the meantime you must think of it as little as possible.

331

Let me not longer detain you from going to Town—there may be no end to this emprisoning of you. Perpaps you had better not come before tomorrow evening: send me however without fail a good night. You know our situation—what hope is there if I should be recoverd ever so soon—my very health with [*for* will] not suffer me to make any great exertion. I am reccommended not even to read poetry much less write it. I wish I had even a little hope. I cannot say forget me—but I would mention that there are impossibilities in the world. No more of this—I am not strong enough to be weaned—take no notice of it in your good night. Happen what may I shall ever be my dearest Love

> Your affectionate
>
> J—K—

To Fanny Brawne, February (?) 1820

My dearest Girl, how could it ever have been my wish to forget you? how could I have said such a thing? The utmost stretch my mind has been capable of was to endeavour to forget you for your own sake seeing what a change [*for* chance] there was of my remaining in a precarious state of health. I would have borne it as I would bear death if fate was in that humour: but I should as soon think of choosing to die as to part from you. Believe too my Love that our friends think and speak for the best, and if their best is not our best it is not their fault, When I am better I will speak with you at large on these subjects, if there is any occasion—I think there is none. I am rather nervous to day perhaps from being a little recovered and suffering my mind to take little excursions beyond the doors and windows. I take it for a good sign, but as it must not be encouraged you had better delay seeing me till tomorrow. Do not take the trouble of writing much: merely send me my goodnight. Remember me to your Mother and Margaret. Your affectionate

> J—K—

To James Rice, *14, 16 February 1820*

Wentworth Place

My dear Rice,   Monday Morn.

I have not been well enough to make any tolerable rejoinder to your kind Letter. I will as you advise be very chary of my health and spirits. I am sorry to hear of your relapse and hypochondriac symptoms attending it. Let us hope for the best as you say. I shall follow your example in looking to the future good rather than brooding upon present ill. I have not been so worn with lengthen'd illnesses as you have therefore cannot answer you on your own ground with respect to those haunting and deformed thoughts and feelings you speak of. When I have been or supposed myself in health I have had my share of them, especially within this last year. I may say that for 6 Months before I was taken ill I had not passed a tranquil day—Either that gloom overspred me or I was suffering under some passionate feeling, or if I turn'd to versify that acerbated the poison of either sensation. The Beauties of Nature had lost their power over me. How astonishingly (here I must premise that illness as far as I can judge in so short a time has relieved my Mind of a load of deceptive thoughts and images and makes me perceive things in a truer light)—How astonishingly does the chance of leaving the world impress a sense of its natural beauties on us. Like poor Falstaff, though I do not babble, I think of green fields. I muse with the greatest affection on every flower I have known from my infancy—their shapes and coulours as are [*for* are as] new to me as if I had just created them with a superhuman fancy—It is because they are connected with the most thoughtless and happiest moments of our Lives—I have seen foreign flowers in hothouses of the most beautiful nature, but I do not care a straw for them. The simple flowers of our sp[r]ing are what I want to see again.

Brown has left the inventive and taken to the imitative art—he is doing his forte which is copying Hogarth's heads.

He has just made a purchace of the methodist meeting Picture, which gave me a horrid dream a few nights ago. I hope I shall sit under the trees with you again in some such place as the isle of Wight—I do not mind a game at cards in a saw pit or waggon; but if

ever you catch me on a stage coach in the winter full against the wind
bring me down with a brace of bullets and I promise not to 'peach.
Rememberme [*for* Remember me] to Reynolds and say how much I
should like to hear from him: that Brown returned immediately after
he went on Sunday, and that I was vex'd at forgetting to ask him to
lunch for as he went towards the gate I saw he was fatigued and
hungr⟨y.⟩

> I am
>> my dear Rice
>>> ever most sincerly yours
>>>> John Keats

I have broken this open to let you know I was surprised at seeing it
on the table this morning; thinking it had gone long ago.

To Fanny Brawne, February (?) 1820

My dearest Fanny,

I read your note in bed last night, and that might be the reason of
my sleeping so much better. I th[i]nk Mr Brown is right in supposing
you may stop too long with me, so very nervous as I am. Send me
every evening a written Good night. If you come for a few minutes
about six it may be the best time. Should you ever fancy me too low-
spirited I must warn you to ascbribe [*for* ascribe] it to the medicine I
am at present taking which is of a nerve-shaking nature—I shall
impute any depression I may experience to this cause. I have been
writing with a vile old pen the whole week, which is excessively
ungallant. The fault is in the Quill: I have mended it and still it is
very much inclin'd to make blind es. However these last lines are in a
much better style of penmanship thof [*for* though] a little disfigured
by the smear of black currant jelly; which has made a little mark on
one of the Pages of Brown's Ben Jonson, the very best book he has. I
have lick'd it but it remains very purple*—I did not know whether to
say purple or blue, so in the mixture of the thought wrote purplue
which may be an excellent name for a colour made up of those two,
and would suit well to start next spring. Be very careful of open
doors and windows and going without your duffle grey—God bless
you Love!—

> J. Keats—

P.S. I am sitting in the back room—Remember me to your Mother—

To Fanny Brawne, February (?) 1820

My dear Fanny,

Do not let your mother suppose that you hurt me by writing at night. For some reason or other your last night's note was not so treasureable as former ones. I would fain that you call me *Love* still. To see you happy and in high spirits is a great consolation to me—still let me believe that you are not half so happy as my restoration would make you. I am nervous, I own, and may think myself worse than I really am; if so you must indulge me, and pamper with that sort of tenderness you have manifested towards me in different Letters. My sweet creature when I look back upon the pains and torments I have suffer'd for you from the day I left you to go to the Isle of Wight; the ecstasies in which I have pass'd some days and the miseries in their turn, I wonder the more at the Beauty which has kept up the spell so fervently. When I send this round I shall be in the front parlour watching to see you show yourself for a minute in the garden. How illness stands as a barrier betwixt me and you! Even if I was well——I must make myself as good a Philosopher as possible. Now I have had opportunities of passing nights anxious and awake I have found other thoughts intrude upon me. "If I should die," said I to myself, "I have left no immortal work behind me—nothing to make my friends proud of my memory—but I have lov'd the principle of beauty in all things, and if I had had time I would have made myself remember'd." Thoughts like these came very feebly whilst I was in health and every pulse beat for you—now you divide with this (may *I* say it?) "last infirmity of noble minds"* all my reflection.

God bless you, Love.

J. Keats.

[R]   *To Fanny Brawne, 24 (?) February 1820*

My dearest Girl,

Indeed I will not deceive you with respect to my Health. This is the fact as far as I know. I have been confined three weeks and am not yet well—this proves that there is something wrong about me which my constitution will either conquer or give way to—Let us hope for the best. Do you hear the Th[r]ush singing over the field? I think it is a sign of mild weather—so much the better for me. Like all Sinners now I am ill I philosophise aye out of my attachment to every thing, Trees, flowers, Thrushes Sp[r]ing, Summer, Claret &c &c aye [e]very thing but you——my Sister would be glad of my company a little longer. That Thrush is a fine fellow I hope he was fortunate in his choice this year—Do not send any more of my Books home. I have a great pleasure in the thought of you looking on them.

Ever yours

my sweet Fanny

J—K—

[R]   *To Fanny Brawne, 27 (?) February 1820*

My dearest Fanny,

I had a better night last night than I have had since my attack, and this morning I am the same as when you saw me. I have been turning over two volumes of Letters written between Ro[u]sseau and two Ladies in the perplexed strain of mingled finesse and sentiment in which the Ladies and gentlemen of those days were so clever, and which is still prevalent among Ladies of this Country who live in a state of resoning romance. The Likeness however only extends to the mannerism not to the dexterity. What would Rousseau have said at seeing our little correspondence! What would his Ladies have said! I don't care much—I would sooner have Shakspeare's opinion about the matter. The common gossiping of washerwomen must be less disgusting than the continual and eternal fence and attack of Rousseau and these sublime Petticoats. One calls herself Clara and her friend Julia two of Ro[u]sseau's Heroines—they all the same time christen poor Jean Jacques St Preux—who is the pure cavalier of his famous novel.* Thank God I am born in England with our own great

Men before my eyes—Thank god that you are fair and can love me without being Letter-written and sentimentaliz'd into it—Mr Barry Cornwall* has sent me another Book, his first, with a polite note—I must do what I can to make him sensible of the esteem I have for his kindness. If this north east would take a turn it would be so much the better for me. Good bye, my love, my dear love, my beauty—

love me for ever—

J—K—

[R]   *To J. H. Reynolds, 28 February 1820*

My dear Reynolds,

I have been improving since you saw me: my nights are better which I think is a very encouraging thing. You mention your cold in rather too slighting a manner—if you travel outside have some flannel aga[i]nst the wind—which I pope will not keep on at this rate when you are in the Packet boat. Should it rain do not stop upon deck though the Passengers should vomit themselves inside out. Keep under Hatches from all sort of wet. I am pretty well provided with Books at present, when you return I may give you a commission or two—Mr B. C. has sent me not only his Sicilian Story but yesterday his Dramatic Scenes—this is very polite and I shall do what I can to make him sensible I think so. I confess they tease me—they are composed of Amiability the Seasons, the Leaves, the Moon &c. upon which he rings (according to Hunt's expression) triple bob majors. However that is nothing—I think he likes poetry for its own sake, not his. I hope I shall soon bee well enough to proceed with my faries and set you about the notes on sundays and Stray-days*—If I had been well enough I should have liked to cross the water with you. Brown wishes you a pleasant voyage—Have fish for dinner at the sea ports, and dont forget a bottle of Claret. You will not meet with so much to hate at Brussels as at Paris.* Remember me to all my friends. If I were well enough I would paraphrase an ode of Horace's* for you, on your embarking in the seventy years ago style—the Packet will bear a comparison with a roman galley at any rate.

Ever yours affectionately

J. Keats

To Fanny Brawne, 29 (?) February 1820

My dear Fanny,

I think you had better not make any long stay with me when Mr Brown is at home—wh[en]ever he goes out you may bring your work. You will have a pleasant walk to day. I shall see you pass. I shall follow you with my eyes over the Heath. Will you come towards evening instead of before dinner—when you are gone, 't is past—if you do not come till the evening I have something to look forward to all day. Come round to my window for a moment when you have read this. Thank your Mother, for the preserves, for me. The raspberry will be too sweet not having any acid; therefore as you are so good a girl I shall make you a present of it. Good bye

My sweet Love!

J. Keats

[R]   To Fanny Brawne, 1 March (?) 1820

My dearest Fanny,

The power of your benediction is of not so weak a nature as to pass from the ring in four-and twenty hours—it is like a sacred Chalice once consecrated and ever consecrate. I shall kiss your name and mine where your Lips have been—Lips! why should a poor prisoner as I am talk about such things. Thank God, though I hold them the dearest pleasures in the universe, I have a consolation independent of them in the certainty of your affection. I could write a song in the style of Tom Moore's Pathetic about Memory* if that would be any relief to me—No. it would not. I will be as obstinate as a Robin, I will not sing in a cage—Health is my expected heaven and you are the Houri—this word I believe is both singular and plural—if only plural, never mind—you are a thousand of them.

Ever yours affectionately

my dearest—

J.K.

You had better not come to day—

To C. W. Dilke, 4 March 1820

My dear Dilke,

Since I saw you I have been gradually, too gradually perhaps, improving; and though under an interdict with respect to animal food living upon pseudo victuals, Brown says I have pick'd up a little flesh lately. If I can keep off inflammation for the next six weeks I trust I shall do very well. You certainly should have been at Martin's dinner for making an index is surely as dull work as engraving. Have you heard that the Bookseller is going to tie himself to the manger eat or not as he pleases? He says Rice shall have his foot on the fender notwithstanding. Reynolds is going to sail on the salt seas. Brown has been mightily progressing with his Hogarth. A damn'd melancholy picture it is, and during the first week of my illness it gave me a psalm singing nightmare, that made me almost faint away in my sleep. I know I am better, for I can bear the Picture. I have experienced a specimen of great politeness from Mr Barry Cornwall. He has sent me his books. Some time ago he had given his first publish'd book to Hunt for me; Hunt forgot to give it and Barry Cornwall thinking I had received it must have though[t] me [a] very neglectful fellow. Notwithstan[din]g he sent me his second book and on my explaining that I had not received his first he sent me that also. I am sorry to see by M^rs D's note that she has been so unwell with the spasms. Does she continue the Medicines that benefited her so much? I am affraid not. Remember me to her and say I shall not expect her at Hampstead next week unless the Weather changes for the warmer. It is better to run no chance of a supernumery cold in March. As for you you must come. You must improve in your penmanship; your writing is like the speaking of a child of three years old, very understandable to its father but to no one else. The worst is it looks well—no that is not the worst—the worst is, it is worse than Bailey's. Bailey's looks illegible and may perchance be read; your's looks very legible and may perchance not be read—I would endeavour to give you a facsimile of your word Thistlewood* if I were not minded on the instant that Lord chesterfield has done some such thing to his Son. Now I would not bathe in the same River with lord C. though I had the upper hand of the stream. I am grieved that in writing and speaking it is necessary to make use of the same particles as he did. Cobbet is expected to come in. O that I had two double plumpers* for him. The ministry are not so inimical to him but ~~they~~ it would like to put him out of Coventry. Casting my eye on the other side I see a long word written in a most vile manner, unbecoming a Critic. You must recollect I have served no apprenticeship to old plays. If the only copies of the greek and Latin Authors had been made by you, Bailey and Haydon they Were as good as lost. It has been said that the Character of a Man may be known by his hand writing—if the Character of the age may be known by the average goodness of said, what a slovenly age we live in. Look at Queen Elizabeth's Latin exercises and blush. Look at Milton's hand—I cant say a word for shakespeare—

Your sincere friend
John Keats

To Fanny Brawne, March (?) 1820

Sweetest Fanny,

You fear, sometimes, I do not love you so much as you wish? My dear Girl I love you ever and ever and without reserve. The more I have known you the more have I lov'd. In every way—even my jealousies have been agonies of Love, in the hottest fit I ever had I would have died for you. I have vex'd you too much. But for Love! Can I help it? You are always new. The last of your kisses was ever the sweetest; the last smile the brightest; the last movement the gracefullest. When you pass'd my window home yesterday, I was fill'd with as much admiration as if I had then seen you for the first time. You uttered a half complaint once that I only lov'd your Beauty. Have I nothing else then to love in you but that? Do not I see a heart naturally furnish'd with wings imprison itself with me? No ill prospect has been able to turn your thoughts a moment from me. This perhaps should be as much a subject of sorrow as joy—but I will not talk of that. Even if you did not love me I could not help an entire devotion to you: how much more deeply then must I feel for you knowing you love me. My Mind has been the most discontented and restless one that ever was put into a body too small for it. I never felt my Mind repose upon anything with complete and undistracted enjoyment—upon no person but you. When you are in the room my thoughts never fly out of window: you always concentrate my whole senses. The anxiety shown about our Loves in your last note is an immense pleasure to me: however you must not suffer such speculations to molest you any more: nor will I any more believe you can have the least pique against me. Brown is gone out—but here is Mrs. Wylie—when she is gone I shall be awake for you.—Remembrances to your Mother.

Your affectionate
J. Keats.

To Fanny Brawne, March (?) *1820*[1]

My dear Fanny,

I am much better this morning than I was a week ago: indeed I improve a little every day. I rely upon taking a walk with you upon the first of may: in the mean time undergoing a babylonish captivity I shall not be jew enough to hang up my harp upon a willow, but rather endeavour to clear up my arrears in versifying and with returning health begin upon something new: pursuant to which resolution it will be necessary to have my or rather Taylor's manuscript,* which you, if you please, will send by my Messenger either to day or tomorrow. Is M^r D with you today? You appear'd very much fatigued last night: you must look a little brighter this morning. I shall not suffer my little girl ever to be obscured like glass breath'd upon but always bright as it is her *nature to*. Feeding upon sham victuals and sitting by the fire will completely annul me. I have no need of an enchanted wax figure to duplicate me for I am melting in my proper person before the fire. If you meet with any thing better (worse) than common in your Magazines let me see it. Good bye my

sweetest Girl
J— K—

---

[1] See Appendix, note 7.

To Fanny Brawne, March (?) 1820

My dearest Fanny, I slept well last night and am no worse this morning for it. Day by day if I am not deceived I get a more unrestrain'd use of my Chest. The nearer a racer gets to the Goal the more his anxiety becomes so I lingering upon the borders of health feel my impatience increase. Perhaps on your account I have imagined my illness more serious than it is: how horrid was the chance of slipping into the ground instead of into your arms—the difference is amazing Love—Death must come at last; Man must die, as Shallow says; but before that is my fate I feign would try what more pleasures than you have given so sweet a creature as you can give. Let me have another op[p]ortunity of years before me and I will not die without being remember'd. Take care of yourself dear that we may both be well in the Summer. I do not at all fatigue myself with writing, having merely to put a line or two here and there, a Task which would worry a stout state of the body and mind, but which just suits me as I can do no more.

Your affectionate

J.K—

To Fanny Brawne, March (?) 1820

My dearest Fanny,

Though I shall see you in so short a time I cannot forbear sending you a few lines. You say I did not give you yesterday a minute account of my health. To-day I have left off the Medicine which I took to keep the pulse down and I find I can do very well without it, which is a very favourable sign, as it shows there is no inflammation remaining. You think I may be wearied at night you say: it is my best time; I am at my best about eight o'Clock. I received a Note from Mr. Proctor today. He says he cannot pay me a visit this weather as he is fearful of an inflammation in the Chest. What a horrid climate this is? or what careless inhabitants it has? You are one of them. My dear girl do not make a joke of it: do not expose yourself to the cold. There's the Thrush again—I can't afford it—he'll run me up a pretty Bill for Music—besides he ought to know I deal at Clementi's.* How can you bear so long an imprisonment at Hampstead? I shall always remember it with all the gusto that a monopolizing carle should. I could build an Altar to you for it.

> Your affectionate
>
> J.K.

To Fanny Keats, 20 March 1820

My dear Fanny,

According to your desire I write to day. It must be but a few lines for I have been attack'd several times with a palpitation at the heart and the Doctor says I must not make the slightest exertion. I am much the same to day as I have been for a week past. They say 't is nothing but debility and will entirely cease on my recovery of my strength, which is the object of my present diet.* As the Doctor will not suffer me to write I shall ask Mr Brown to let you hear news of me for the future if I should not get stronger soon. I hope I shall be well enough to co⟨me⟩ and see your flowers in bloom—

> Ever your most
>
> affectionate Brother
>
> John—

[R]　　　To Fanny Brawne, March (?) 1820

My dearest Girl,

In consequence of our company I suppose I shall not see you before tomorrow. I am much better to day—indeed all I have to complain of is want of strength and a little tightness in the Chest. I envied Sam's walk with you to day; which I will not do again as I may get very tired of envying. I imagine you now sitting in your new black dress which I like so much and if I were a little less selfish and more enthousiastic I should run round and surprise you with a knock at the door. I fear I am too prudent for a dying kind of Lover. Yet, there is a great difference between going off in warm blood like Romeo, and making one's exit like a frog in a frost—I had nothing particular to say to day, but not intending that there shall be any interruption to our correspondence (which at some future time I propose offering to Murray) I write something! God bless you my

343

sweet Love! Illness is a long lane, but I see you at the end of it, and shall mend my pace as well as possible

J—K

To Mrs James Wylie, 24 (?) March 1820

Wentworth Place
Friday. Morn.

My dear Mʳˢ Wylie,

I have been very negligent in not letting you hear from me for so long a time considering the anxiety I know you feel for me. Charles has been here this morning and will tell you that I am better. Just as he came in I was sitting down to write to you, and I shall not let his visit supersede these few lines. Charles enquired whether I had heard from George. It is impossible to guess whether he has landed yet, and if he has, it will take at least a month for any communication to reach us. I hope you keep your spirits a great height above the freezing point, and live in expectation of good news next summer. Louisville is not such a Monstrous distance: if Georgiana liv'd at york it would be just as far off. You see George will make nothing of the journey here and back. His absence will have been perhaps a fortunate event for Georgiana, for the pleasure of his return will be so great that it will wipe away the consciousness of many troubles felt before very deeply. She will see him return'd from us and be convinced that the separation is not so very formidable although the Atlantic is between. If George succeeds it will be better certainly that they should stop in America: if not why not return? It is better in ill luck to have at least the comfort of ones friends than to be shipwreck'd among American's. But I have good hopes as far as I can judge from what I have heard from George. He should by this time be taught Alertness and Carefulness—If they should stop in America for five or six years let us hope they may have about three Children: then the eldest will be getting old enough to be society. The very crying will keep their ears employed, and their spirits from being melancholy. Mʳˢ Millar I hear continues confined to her Chamber—if she would take my advice I should recommender [*for* recommend her] to keep it till the middle of april and then go to some Sea-town in Devonshire which is sheltered from the east wind—which blows down the channel very briskly even in april. Give my Compliments to Miss Millar and Miss Waldegra⟨ve.⟩*

To Fanny Keats, 1 April 1820

Wentworth Place
April 1ˢᵗ

My dear Fanny—

I am getting better every day and should think myself quite well were I not reminded every now and then by faintness and a tightness in the Chest. Send your Spaniel over to Hampsteead for I think I know where to find a Master or Mistress for him. You may depend upon it if you were even to turn it loose in the common road it would soon find an owner. If I keep improving as I have done I shall be able to come over to you in the course of a few weeks. I should take the advantage of your being in Town but I cannot bear the City though I have already ventured as far as the west end for the purpose of seeing Mʳ Haydon's Picture which is just finished and has m⟨ade its⟩ appearance.* I have not heard from George yet since he left liverpool. Mʳ Brown wrote to him as from me the other day—Mʳ B. wrote two Letters to Mʳ Abbey concerning me—Mʳ A. took no notice and of course Mʳ B. must give up such a correspondence when as the man said all the Letters are on one side—I write with greater ease than I had thought, threrfore [for therefore] you shall soon hear from me again. Your affectionate Brother—

John—

To Fanny Keats, 12 April 1820

Wentworth Place
12 April—

My dear Fanny—

Excuse these shabby scraps of paper I send you—and also from endeavouring to give you any consolation just at present for though my health is tolerably well I am too nervous to enter into any discussion in which my heart is concerned. Wait patiently and take care of your health being especially careful to keep yourself from low spirits which are great enemies to health. You are young and have only need of a little patience. I am not yet able to bear the fatigue of coming to Walthamstow though I have been to Town once or twice. I have thought of taking a change of air. You shall hear from me immediately on my moving any where. I will ask Mrs Dilke to pay you a visit if the weather holds fine, the first time I see her. The Dog is being attended to like a Prince.

Your affectionate Brother

John

To Fanny Keats, 21 April 1820

My dear Fanny,

I have been slowly improving since I wrote last. The Doctor assures me that there is nothing the matter with me except nervous irritability and a general weakness of the whole system which has proceeded from my anxiety of mind of late years and the too great excitement of poetry—Mr Brown is going to Scotland by the Smack, and I am advised for change of exercise and air to accompany him and give myself the chance of benefit from a Voyage. Mr H. Wylie call'd on me yesterday with a letter from George to his mother: George is safe on the other side of the water, perpaps by this time arrived at his home. I wish you were coming to town that I might see you; if you should be coming write to me, as it is quite a trouble to get by the coaches to Walthamstow. Should you not come to Town I must see you before I sail, at Walthamstow. They tell me I must study lines and tangents and squares and circles to put a little Ballast into my mind. We shall be going in a fortnight and therefore you will see me within that space. I expected sooner, but I have not been able to wenture to walk across the Country. Now the fine Weather is come you will not fine [*for* find] your time so irksome. You must be sensible how much I regret not being able to alleviate the unpleasantness of your situation, but trust my dear Fanny that better times are in wait for you.

Your affectionate Brother

John—

To Fanny Keats, 4 May 1820

Wentworth Place
My dear Fanny,   Thursday—
I went for the first time into the City the day before yesterday, for
before I was very disinclined to encounter the Scuffle, more from
nervousness than real illness; which notwithstanding I should not
have suffered to conquer me if I had not made up my mind not to go
to Scotland, but to remove to Kentish Town till Mr Brown returns.
Kentish Town is a Mile nearer to you than Hampstead—I have been
getting gradually better but am not so well as to trust myself to the
casualties of rain and sleeping out which I am liable to in visiting
you. Mr Brown goes on Saturday and by that time I shall have settled
in my new Lodging when I will certainly venture to you. You will
forgive me I hope when I confess that I endeavour to think of you as
little as possible and to let George dwell upon my mind but slightly.
The reason being that I am affraid to ruminate on any thing which
has the shade of difficulty or melancholy in it, as that sort of cogita-
tion is so pernicious to health, and it is only by health that I can be
enabled to alleviate your situation in future. For some time you must
do what you can of yourself for relief, and bear your mind up with
the consciousness that your situation cannot last for ever, and that
for the present you may console yourself against the reproaches of
Mrs Abbey. Whatever obligations you may have had to her ~~or her
Husband~~ you have none now as she has reproach'd you. I do not
know what property you have, but I will enquire into it: be sure
however that beyond the obligations that a Lodger may have to a
Landlord you have none to Mr Abbey—Let the surety of this make
you laugh at Mrs A's foolish tattle. Mrs Dilke's Brother has got your
Dog—She is now very well—still liable to Illness. I will get her to
come and see you if I can make up my mind on the propriety of
introducing a Strang[er] into Abbey's House. Be careful to let no
fretting injure you health as I have suffered it—health is the greatest
of blessings—with *heal⟨th⟩* and *hope* we should be content to live,
and so you will find as you grow older—I am
my dear Fanny
your affectionate Brother
John—

To Fanny Brawne, May (?) 1820*

Tuesday Morn—

My dearest Girl,

I wrote a Letter for you yesterday expecting to have seen your mother. I shall be selfish enough to send it though I know it may give you a little pain, because I wish you to see how unhappy I am for love of you, and endeavour as much as I can to entice you to give up your whole heart to me whose whole existence hangs upon you. You could not step or move an eyelid but it would shoot to my heart—I am greedy of you—Do not think of any thing but me. Do not live as if I was not existing—Do not forget me—But have I any right to say you forget me? Perhaps you think of me all day. Have I any right to wish you to be unhappy for me? You would forgive me for wishing it, if you knew the extreme passion I have that you should love me—and for you to love me as I do you, you must think of no one but me, much less write that sentence. Yesterday and this morning I have been haunted with a sweet vision—I have seen you the whole time in your shepherdess dress. How my senses have ached at it! How my heart has been devoted to it! How my eyes have been full of Tears at it! I[n]deed I think a real Love is enough to occupy the widest heart—Your going to town alone, when I heard of it was a shock to me—yet I expected it—*promise me you will not for some time, till I get better*. Promise me this and fill the paper full of the most endearing mames [*for* names]. If you cannot do so with good will, do my Love tell me—say what you think—confess if your heart is too much fasten'd on the world. Perhaps then I may see you at a greater distance, I may not be able to appropriate you so closely to myself. Were you to loose a favorite bird from the cage, how would your eyes ache after it as long as it was in sight; when out of sight you would recover a little. Perphaps if you would, if so it is, confess to me how many things are necessary to you besides me, I might be happier, by being less tantaliz'd. Well may you exclaim, how selfish, how cruel, not to let me enjoy my youth! to wish me to be unhappy! You must be so if you love me—upon my Soul I can be contented with nothing else. If you could really what is call'd enjoy yourself at a Party—if you can smile in peoples faces, and wish them to admire you *now*, you never have nor ever will love me—I see *life* in nothing but the cerrtainty of your Love—convince me of it my sweetest. If I am not somehow convinc'd I shall die of agony. If we love we must not live as other men and women do—I cannot brook the wolfsbane of fashion and foppery and tattle. You must be mine to die upon the rack if I want you. I do not pretend to say I have more feeling than my fellows— but I wish you seriously to look over my letters kind and unkind and consider whether the Person who wrote them can be able to endure much longer the agonies and uncertainties which you are so peculiarly made to create—My recovery of bodily hea[l]th will be of no benefit to me if you are not all mine when I am well. For god's sake save me—or tell me my passion is of too awful a nature for you. Again God bless you.

J.K.

No—my sweet Fanny—I am wrong. I do not want you to be unhappy—and yet I do, I must while there is so sweet a Beauty—my loveliest my darling! Good bye! I kiss you—O the torments!

To Fanny Brawne, May (?) 1820[1]

Wednesday Morng.

My dearest Girl,

I have been a walk this morning with a book in my hand, but as usual I have been occupied with nothing but you: I wish I could say in an agreeable manner. I am tormented day and night. They talk of my going to Italy. 'Tis certain I shall never recover if I am to be so long separate from you: yet with all this devotion to you I cannot persuade myself into any confidence of you. Past experience connected with the fact of my long separation from you gives me agonies which are scarcely to be talked of. When your mother comes I shall be very sudden and expert in asking her whether you have been to Mrs. Dilke's, for she might say no to make me easy. I am literally worn to death, which seems my only recourse. I cannot forget what has pass'd. What? nothing with a man of the world, but to me deathful. I will get rid of this as much as possible. When you were in the habit of flirting with Brown you would have left off, could your own

---

[1] See Appendix, note 8.

heart have felt one half of one pang mine did. Brown is a good sort of Man—he did not know he was doing me to death by inches. I feel the effect of every one of those hours in my side now; and for that cause, though he has done me many services, though I know his love and friendship for me, though at this moment I should be without pence were it not for his assistance, I will never see or speak to him until we are both old men, if we are to be. I *will* resent my heart having been made a football. You will call this madness. I have heard you say that it was not unpleasant to wait a few years—you have amusements—your mind is away—you have not brooded over one idea as I have, and how should you? You are to me an object intensely desireable—the air I breathe in a room empty of you is unhealthy. I am not the same to you—no—you can wait—you have a thousand activities—you can be happy without me. Any party, any thing to fill up the day has been enough. How have you pass'd this month? Who have you smil'd with? All this may seem savage in me. You do not feel as I do—you do not know what it is to love—one day you may— your time is not come. Ask yourself how many unhappy hours Keats has caused you in Loneliness. For myself I have been a Martyr the whole time, and for this reason I speak; the confession is forc'd from me by the torture. I appeal to you by the blood of that Christ you believe in: Do not write to me if you have done anything this month which it would have pained me to have seen. You may have altered— if you have not—if you still behave in dancing rooms and other societies as I have seen you—I do not want to live—if you have done so I wish this coming night may be my last. I cannot live without you, and not only you but *chaste you; virtuous you.* The Sun rises and sets, the day passes, and you follow the bent of your inclination to a certain extent—you have no conception of the quantity of miserable feeling that passes through me in a day.—Be serious! Love is not a plaything—and again do not write unless you can do it with a crystal conscience. I would sooner die for want of you than——

Yours for ever

J. Keats.

To Fanny Brawne, June (?) 1820

My dearest Fanny,

My head is puzzled this morning, and I scarce know what I shall say though I am full of a hundred things. 'T is certain I would rather be writing to you this morning, notwithstanding the alloy of grief in such an occupation, than enjoy any other pleasure, with health to boot, unconnected with you. Upon my soul I have loved you to the extreme. I wish you could know the Tenderness with which I continually brood over your different aspects of countenance, action and dress. I see you come down in the morning: I see you meet me at the Window—I see every thing over again eternally that I ever have seen. If I get on the pleasant clue I live in a sort of happy misery, if on the unpleasant 'tis miserable misery. You complain of my illtreating you in word thought and deed—I am sorry,—at times I feel bitterly sorry that I ever made you unhappy—my excuse is that those words have been wrung from me by the sha[r]pness of my feelings. At all events and in any case I have been wrong; could I believe that I did it without any cause, I should be the most sincere of Penitents. I could give way to my repentant feelings now, I could recant all my suspicions, I could mingle with you heart and Soul though absent, were it not for some parts of your Letters. Do you suppose it possible I could ever leave you? You know what I think of myself and what of you. You know that I should feel how much it was my loss and how little yours—My friends laugh at you! I know some of them—when I know them all I shall never think of them again as friends or even acquaintance. My friends have behaved well to me in every instance but one, and there they have b[e]come tatlers, and inquisitors into my conduct: spying upon a secret I would rather die than share it with any body's confidence. For this I cannot wish them well, I care not to see any of them again. If I am the Theme, I will not be the Friend of idle Gossips. Good gods what a shame it is our Loves should be so put into the microscope of a Coterie.* Their laughs should not affect you (I may perhaps give you reasons some day for these laughs, for I suspect a few people to hate me well enough, *for reasons I know of*, who have pretended a great friendship for me) when in competition with one, who if he never should see you again would make you the saint of his memory—

These Laughers, who do not like you, who envy you for your Beauty,
who would have God-bless'd-me from you for ever: who were ply-
ing me with disencouragements with respect to you eternally. People
are revengeful—do not mind them—do nothing but love me—if I
knew that for certain life and health will in such event be a heaven,
and death itself will be less painful. I long to believe in immortality I
shall never be ab⟨le⟩ to bid you an entire farewell. If I am destined
to be happy with you here—how short is the longest Life—I wish to
believe in immortality—I wish to live with you for ever. Do not let
my name ever pass between you and those laughers, if I have no
other merit than the great Love for you, that were sufficient to keep
me sacred and unmentioned in such society. If I have been cruel and
injust I swear my love has ever been greater than my cruelty which
last[s] but a minute whereas my Love come what will shall last for
ever If concessions to me has hurt your Pride, god knows I have had
little pride in my heart when thinking of you. Your name never
passes my Lips—do not let mine pass yours—Those People do not
like me. After ~~writing~~ reading my Letter you even then wish to see
me. I am strong enough to walk over—but I dare not. I shall feel so
much pain in parting with you again. My dearest love, I am affraid to
see you, I am strong but not strong enough to see you. Will my arm
be ever round you again. And if so shall I be obliged to leave you
again. My sweet Love! I am happy whilst I believe your first Letter.
Let me be but certain that you are mine heart and soul, and I could
die more happily than I could otherwise live. If you think me cruel—
if you think I have sleighted you—do muse it over again and see into
my heart—My Love to you is "true as truth's simplicity and simpler
than the infancy of truth"* as I think I once said before How could I
slight you? How threaten to leave you? not in the spirit of a Threat to
you—no—but in the spirit of Wretchedness in myself. My fairest,
my delicious, my angel Fanny! do not believe me such a vulgar
fellow. I will be as patient in illness and as believing in Love as I am
able—

> Yours for ever my dearest
> John Keats—

To John Taylor, *11 (?) June 1820*

My dear Taylor,

In reading over the proof of St Agnes' Eve since I left Fleet street I was struck with what appears to me an alteration in the 7th Stanza very much for the worse: the passage I mean stands thus

> "her maiden eyes incline
> Still on the floor, while many a sweeping train
> Pass by—"

Twas originally written

> "her maiden eyes divine
> Fix'd on the floor saw many a sweeping train
> Pass by—

My meaning is quite destroyed in the alteration. I do not use *train* for *concourse of passers by* but for ~~Skits~~ *Skirts* sweeping along the floor—In the first Stanza my copy reads—2nd line

> "bitter *chill* it was"

to avoid the echo cold in the next line.

ever yours sincerely
John Keats

To Charles Brown, *about 21 June 1820*

My dear Brown,

I have only been to x x x's once since you left, when x x x x* could not find your letters. Now this is bad of me. I should, in this instance, conquer the great aversion to breaking up my regular habits, which grows upon me more and more. True I have an excuse in the weather, which drives one from shelter to shelter in any little excursion. I have not heard from George. My book* is coming out with very low hopes, though not spirits on my part. This shall be my last trial; not succeeding, I shall try what I can do in the Apothecary line. When you hear from or see x x x x x x* it is probable you will hear some complaints against me, which this notice is not intended to forestall. The fact is I did behave badly; but it is to be attributed to my health, spirits, and the disadvantageous ground I stand on in society. I would go and accommodate matters, if I were not too weary of the world. I know that they are more happy and comfortable than I am; therefore why should I trouble myself about it? I foresee I shall know very few people in the course of a year or two. Men get such different habits, that they become as oil and vinegar to one another. Thus far I have a consciousness of having been pretty dull and heavy, both in subject and phrase; I might add, enigmatical. I am in the wrong, and the world is in the right, I have no doubt. Fact is, I have had so many kindnesses done me by so many people, that I am cheveaux-de-frised with benefits, which I must jump over or break down. I met x x x* in town a few days ago, who invited me to supper to meet Wordsworth, Southey, Lamb, Haydon, and some more; I was too careful of my health to risk being out at night. Talking of that, I continue to improve slowly, but, I think, surely. All the talk at present x x x x x x x x* There is a famous exhibition in Pall Mall of the old english portraits by Vandyck and Holbein, Sir Peter Lely and the great Sir Godfrey. Pleasant countenances predominate: so I will mention two or three unpleasant ones. There is James the first,—whose appearance would disgrace a "Society for the suppression of women;" so very squalid, and subdued to nothing he looks. Then, there is old Lord Burleigh, the high priest of economy, the political save-all, who has the appearance of a Pharisee just rebuffed by a gospel bon-mot. Then, there is George the second, very like an unintellectual Voltaire, troubled with the gout and a bad temper. Then, there is young Devereux, the favourite, with every appearance of as slang a boxer as any in the court; his face is cast in the mould of blackguardism with jockey-plaster. x x x x x I shall soon begin upon *Lucy Vaughan Lloyd.** I do not begin composition yet, being willing, in case of a relapse, to have nothing to reproach myself with. I hope the weather will give you the slip; let it show itself, and steal out of your company. x x x x x x When I have sent off this, I shall write another to some place about fifty miles in advance of you.

Good morning to you.

Your's ever sincerely,

John Keats.

To Fanny Keats, 23 June 1820

Friday Morn—*

My dear Fanny,

I had intended to delay seeing you till a Book which I am now publishing was out, expecting that to be the end of this Week when I would have brought it to Walthamstow: on receiving your Letter of course I set myself to come to town, but was not able for just as I was setting out yesterday morning a slight spitting of blood came on which returned rather more copiously at night. I have slept well and they tell me there is nothing material to fear. I will send my Book soon with a Letter which I have had

from George who   Your affectionate Brother
is with his family   John—
quite well.

To Fanny Brawne, 25 June (?) 1820

My dearest Girl,

I endeavour to make myself as patient as possible. Hunt amuses me very kindly—besides I have your ring on my finger and your flowers on the table. I shall not expect to see you yet because it would be so much pain to part with you again. When the Books you want came [*for* come] you shall have them. I am very well this afternoon. My dearest*

To Fanny Brawne, 4 July (?) 1820

Tuesday Af^tn

My dearest Fanny,

For this Week past I have been employed in marking the most beatutiful [*for* beautiful] passages in Spenser, intending it for you, and comforting myself in being somehow occupied to give you however small a pleasure. It has lightened my time very much. I am much better. God bless you.

Your affectionate
J. Keats

To Fanny Keats, 5 July 1820

Mortimer Terrace
Wednesday

My dear Fanny,

I have had no return of the spitting of blood, and for two or three days have been getting a little stronger. I have no hopes of an entire reestablishment of my health under some months of patience. My Physician tells me I must contrive to pass the Winter in Italy.* This is all very unfortunate for us—we have no recourse but patience, which I am now practicing better than ever I thought it possible for me. I have this moment received a Letter from Mr Brown, dated Dunvegan Castle, Island of Skye. He is very well in health and Spirits. My new publication has been out for some days and I have directed a Copy to be bound for you, which you will receive shortly. No one can regret Mr Hodgkinson's ill fortune: I must own illness has not made such a Saint of me as to prevent my rejoicing at his reverse. Keep yourself in as good hopes as possible; in case my illness should continue an unreasonable time many of my friends would I trust for my Sake do all in their power to console and amuse you, at the least word from me—You may depend upon it that in case my strength returns I will do all in my power to extricate you from the Abbies. Be above all things careful of your health which is the corner stone of all pleasure.

Your affectionate Brother
John—

To Fanny Keats, 22 July 1820

My dear Fanny,

I have been gaining Strength for some days: it would be well if I could at the same time say I [am] gaining hopes of a speedy recovery. My constitution has suffered very much for two or three years past, so as to be scar[c]ely able to make head against illness, which the natural activity and impatience of my Mind renders more dangerous—It will at all events be a very tedious affair, and you must expect to hear very little alteration of any sort in me for some time

You ought to have received a copy of my Book ten days ago I shall send another message to the Booksellers. One of the Mr Wylies will be here to day or to morrow when I will ask him to send you George's Letter. Writing the smallest note is so anoying to me that I have waited till I shall see him. Mr Hunt does every thing in his power to make the time pass as agreeably with me as possible. I read the greatest part of the day, and generally take two half hour walks a day up and down the terrace which is very much pester'd with cries, ballad singers, and street music. We have been so unfortunate for so long a time, every event has been of so depressing a nature that I must persuade myself to think some change will take place in the aspect of our affairs. I shall be upon the look out for a trump card—

> Your affectionate
> Brother, John—

[R]   *To Fanny Brawne, August (?) 1820*

> I do not write this till the last, that no eye
> may catch it.*

My dearest Girl,

I wish you could invent some means to make me at all happy without you. Every hour I am more and more concentrated in you; every thing else tastes like chaff in my Mouth. I feel it almost impossible to go to Italy—the fact is I cannot leave you, and shall never taste one minute's content until it pleases chance to let me live with you for good. But I will not go on at this rate. A person in health as you are can have no conception of the horrors that nerves and a temper like mine go through. What Island do your friends propose retiring to? I should be happy to go with you there alone, but in company I should object to it; the backbitings and jealousies of new colonists who have nothing else to amuse them selves, is unbearable. Mr Dilke came to see me yesterday, and gave me a very great deal more pain than pleasure. I shall never be able any more to endure to [*for* the] society of any of those who used to meet at Elm Cottage and Wentworth Place. The last two years taste like brass upon my Palate.* If I cannot live with you I will live alone. I do not think my health will improve much while I am separated from you. For all this I am averse to seeing you—I cannot bear flashes of light and return into my glooms again. I am not so unhappy now as I should be if I had seen you yesterday. To be happy with you seems such an impossibility! it requires a luckier Star than mine! it will never be. I enclose a passage from one of your Letters which I want you to alter a little—I want (if you will have it so) the matter express'd less coldly to me. If my health would bear it, I could write a Poem which I have in my head, which would be a consolation for people in such a situation as mine. I would show some one in Love as I am, with a person living in such Liberty as you do. Shakspeare always sums up matters in the most sovereign manner. Hamlet's heart was full of such Misery as mine is when he said to Ophelia "Go to a Nunnery, go, go!" Indeed I should like to give up the matter at once—I should like to die. I am sickened at the brute world which you are smiling with. I hate men and women more. I see nothing but thorns for the future—wherever I may be next winter in Italy or nowhere Brown will be living near you with his indecencies*—I see no prospect of any rest. Suppose me in Rome—well, I should there see you as in a magic glass going to and from town at all hours,——I wish you could infuse a little con-fidence in human nature into my heart. I cannot muster any—the world is too brutal for me—I am glad there is such a thing as the grave—I am sure I shall never have any rest till I get there At any rate I will indulge myself by never seeing any more Dilke or Brown or any of their Friends. I wish I was either in your a[r]ms full of faith or that a Thunder bolt would strike me.

God bless you—J.K—

To Fanny Keats, *13 August 1820*

Wentworth Place

My dear Fanny,

'T is a long time since I received your last. An accident of an unpleasant nature occured at Mʳ Hunt's and prevented me from answering you, that is to say made me nervous. That you may not suppose it worse I will mention that some one of Mʳ Hunt's house-hold opened a Letter of mine—upon which I immediately left Mortimer Terrace, with the intention of taking to Mʳˢ Bentley's again; fortunately I am not in so lone a situation, but am staying a short time with Mrs Brawne who lives in the House which was Mrs Dilke's. I am excessively nervous: a person I am not quite used to entering the room half choaks me—'T is not yet Consumption I believe, but it would be were I to remain in this climate all the Winter: so I am thinking of either voyageing or travelling to Italy. Yesterday I received an invitation from Mr Shelley, a Gentleman residing at Pisa, to spend the Winter with him: if I go I must be away in a Month or even less. I am glad you like the Poems, you must hope with me th⟨at⟩ time and health will pro⟨duce⟩ you some more. This is the first morning I have been able to sit to the paper and have many Letters to write if I can manage them. God bless you my dear Sister.

Your affectionate Brother
John—

To John Taylor, *13 August 1820*

Wentworth Place
Sat^y Morn.

My dear Taylor,

My Chest is in so nervous a State, that any thing extra such as speaking to an unaccostomed Person or writing a Note half suffocates me. This Journey to Italy wakes me at daylight every morning and haunts me horribly. I shall endeavour to go though it be with the sensation of marching up against a Battery. The first spep [*for* step] towards it is to know the expense of a Journey and a years residence: which if you will ascertain for me and let me know early you will greatly serve me. I have more to say but must desist for every line I write encreases the tightness of the Chest, and I have many more to do. I am convinced that this sort of thing does not continue for nothing—If you can come with any of our friends do.

Your sincere friend
John Keats—

[R]   *To Leigh Hunt, 13 (?) August 1820*

(An Amyntas)*

Wentworth Place

My dear Hunt,

You will be glad to hear I am going to delay a little time at M^rs
Brawnes. I hope to see you whenever you can get time for I feel really
attach'd to you for your many sympathies with me, and patience at
my lunes.* Will you send by the Bearess* Lucy Vaughn Lloyd: My
best rem^cs to Mrs Hunt—

Your affectionate frien⟨d⟩
John Keats

To Charles Brown, 14 August 1820

My dear Brown,

You may not have heard from x x x x or x x x x, or in any way,
that an attack of spitting of blood, and all its weakening con-
sequences, has prevented me from writing for so long a time. I have
matter now for a very long letter, but not news; so I must cut every
thing short. I shall make some confession, which you will be the
only person, for many reasons, I shall trust with. A winter in England would, I have not a doubt, kill me; so I have resolved to go to
Italy, either by sea or land. Not that I have any great hopes of
that,—for, I think, there is a core of disease in me not easy to pull
out. x x x x x x x x x x x x x x x x x* If I should die x x x x x I shall be
obliged to set off in less than a month. Do not, my dear Brown,
tease yourself about me. You must fill up your time as well as you
can, and as happily. You must think of my faults as lightly as you
can. When I have health I will bring up the long arrears of letters I
owe you. x x x x x x My book has had good success among literary
people,* and, I believe, has a moderate sale. I have seen very few
people we know. x x x has visited me more than any one. I would go
to x x x x x and make some inquiries after you, if I could with any
bearable sensation; but a person I am not quite used to causes an
oppression on my chest. Last week I received a letter from Shelley,
at Pisa, of a very kind nature, asking me to pass the winter with

him. Hunt has behaved very kindly to me. You shall hear from me again shortly.

> Your affectionate friend,
> John Keats.

To Percy Bysshe Shelley, 16 August 1820

Hampstead August 16th

My dear Shelley,

I am very much gratified that you, in a foreign country, and with a mind almost over occupied, should write to me in the strain of the Letter beside me. If I do not take advantage of your invitation it will be prevented by a circumstance I have very much at heart to prophesy—There is no doubt that an english winter would put an end to me, and do so in a lingering hateful manner, therefore I must either voyage or journey to Italy as a soldier marches up to a battery. My nerves at present are the worst part of me, yet they feel soothed when I think that come what extreme may, I shall not be destined to remain in one spot long enough to take a hatred of any four particular bed-posts. I am glad you take any pleasure in my poor Poem;—which I would willingly take the trouble to unwrite, if possible, did I care so much as I have done about Reputation. I received a copy of the Cenci, as from yourself from Hunt. There is only one part of it I am judge of; the Poetry, and dramatic effect, which by many spirits now a days is considered the mammon. A modern work it is said must have a purpose, which may be the God—*an artist* must serve Mammon—he must have "self concentration" selfishness perhaps. You I am sure will forgive me for sincerely remarking that you might curb your magnanimity and be more of an artist, and 'load every rift'* of your subject with ore The thought of such discipline must fall like cold chains upon you, who perhaps never sat with your wings furl'd for six Months together. And is not this extraordina[r]y talk for the writer of Endymion? whose mind was like a pack of scattered cards—I am pick'd up and sorted to a pip. My Imagination is a Monastry and I am its Monk—you must explain my metap^{cs} [*for* metaphysics] to yourself. I am in expectation of Prometheus every day. Could I have my own wish for its interest effected you would have it still in manuscript—

361

or be but now putting an end to the second act. I remember you advising me not to publish my first-blights, on Hampstead heath— I am returning advice upon your hands. Most of the Poems in the volume I send you have been written above two years, and would never have been publish'd but from a hope of gain; so you see I am inclined enough to take your advice now. I must exp[r]ess once more my deep sense of your kindness, adding my sincere thanks and respects for Mrs Shelley. In the hope of soon seeing you ⟨I⟩ remain

> most sincerely ⟨yours,⟩
> John Keats—

To Charles Brown, August (?) *1820*

My dear Brown,

x x x x x x* I ought to be off at the end of this week, as the cold winds begin to blow towards evening;—but I will wait till I have your answer to this. I am to be introduced, before I set out, to a Dr Clarke,* a physician settled at Rome, who promises to befriend me in every way at Rome. The sale of my book is very slow, though it has been very highly rated. One of the causes, I understand from different quarters, of the unpopularity of this new book, and the others also, is the offence the ladies take at me. On thinking that matter over, I am certain that I have said nothing in a spirit to displease any woman I would care to please: but still there is a tendency to class women in my books with roses and sweetmeats,—they never see themselves dominant. If ever I come to publish "Lucy Vaughan Lloyd", there will be some delicate picking for squeamish stomachs. I will say no more, but, waiting in anxiety for your answer, doff my hat, and make a purse as long as I can.

> Your affectionate friend,
> John Keats.

To Fanny Keats, 23 August 1820

Wentworth Place
Wednesday Morning

My dear Fanny,

It will give me great Pleasure to see you here, if you can contrive it; though I confess I should have written instead of calling upon you before I set out on my journey, from the wish of avoiding unpleasant partings. Meantime I will just notice some parts of your Letter. The Seal-breaking business is over blown—I think no more of it. A few days ago I wrote to Mr Brown, asking him to befriend me with his company to Rome. His answer is not yet come, and I do not know when it will, not being certain how far he may be from the Post Office to which my communication is addressed. Let us hope he will go with me. George certainly ought to have written to you: his troubles, anxieties and fatigues are not quite a sufficient excuse. In the course of time you will be sure to find that this neglect, is not forgetfulness. I am sorry to hear you have been so ill and in such low spirits. Now you are better, keep so. Do not suffer Your Mind to dwell on unpleasant reflections—that sort of thing has been the destruction of my health—Nothing is so bad as want of health—it makes one envy Scavengers and Cinder-sifters. There are enough real distresses and evils in wait for every one to try the most vigorous health. Not that I would say yours are not real—but they are such as to tempt you to employ your imagination on them, rather than endeavour to dismiss them entirely. Do not diet your mind with grief, it destroys the constitution; but let your chief care be of your health, and with that you will meet with your share of Pleasure in the world—do not doubt it. If I return well from Italy I will turn over a new leaf for you. I have been improving lately, and have very good hopes of 'turning a Neuk'* and cheating the Consumption. I am not well enough to write to George myself—Mr Haslam will do it for me, to whom I shall write to day, desiring him to mention as gently as possible your complaint—I am my dear Fanny

Your affectionate Brother
John.

[R]   *To Fanny Keats* [Dictated], *11 September 1820*

Monday Morn^g

My dear Fanny

In the hope of entirely re-establishing my health I shall leave England for Italy this week and, of course I shall not be able to see you before my departure. It is not illness that prevents me from writing but as I am recommended to avoid every sort of fatigue I have accepted the assistance of a friend,* who I have desired to write to you when I am gone and to communicate any intelligence she may hear of me. I am as well as I can expect and feel very impatient to get on board as the sea air is expected to be of great benefit to me. My present intention is to stay some time at Naples and then to proceed to Rome where I shall find several friends or at least several acquaintances. At any rate it will be a relief to quit this cold; wet, uncertain climate. I am not very fond of living in cities but there will be too much to amuse me, as soon as I am well enough to go out, to make me feel dull. I have received your parcel and intend to take it with me. You shall hear from me as often as possible, if I feel too tired to write myself I shall have some friend to do it for me; I have not yet heard from George nor can I expect to receive any letters from him before I leave

Your affectionate brot⟨her⟩

John—

To Charles Brown, 30 September 1820

Saturday Septr 28 [*for* 30]

Maria Crowther

off Yarmouth isle

of wight—

My dear Brown,

The time has not yet come for a pleasant Letter from me. I have delayed writing to you from time to time because I felt how impossible it was to enliven you with one heartening hope of my recovery; this morning in bed the matter struck me in a different manner; I thought I would write "while I was in some liking"* or I might become too ill to write at all and then if the desire to have written should become strong it would be a great affliction to me. I have many more Letters to write and I bless my stars that I have begun, for time seems to press,—this may be my best opportunity. We are in a calm and I am easy enough this morning. If my spirits seem too low you may in some degree impute it to our having been at sea a fort-might [*for* fortnight] without making any way. I was very disap-pointed at not meeting you at bedhampton [*for* Bedhampton], and am very provoked at the thought of you being at Chichester to day. I should have delighted in setting off for London for the sensation merely—for what should I do there? I could not leave my lungs or stomach or other worse things behind me. I wish to write on subjects that will not agitate me much—there is one I must mention and have done with it. Even if my body would recover of itself, this would prevent it—The very thing which I want to live most for will be a great occasion of my death. I cannot help it. Who can help it? Were I in health it would make me ill, and how can I bear it in my state? I dare say you will be able to guess on what subject I am harping—you know what was my greatest pain during the first part of my illness at your house. I wish for death every day and night to deliver me from these pains, and then I wish death away, for death would destroy even those pains which are better than nothing. Land and Sea, weak-ness and decline are great seperators, but death is the great divorcer for ever. When the pang of this thought has passed through my mind, I may say the bitterness of death is passed. I often wish for you that you might flatter me with the best. I think without my mention-ing it for my sake you would be a friend to Miss Brawne when I am dead. You think she has many faults—but, for my sake, think she has not one——if there is any thing you can do for her by word or deed I know you will do it. I am in a state at present in which woman merely as woman can have no more power over me than stocks and stones, and yet the difference of my sensations with respect to Miss Brawne and my Sister is amazing. The one seems to absorb the other to a degree incredible. I seldom think of my Brother and Sister in america. The thought of leaving Miss Brawne is beyond every thing horrible—the sense of darkness coming over me—I eternally see her figure eternally vanishing. Some of the phrases she was in the habit of using during my last nursing at Wen⟨t⟩worth place ring in my ears—Is there another Life? Shall I awake and find all this a dream? There must be we cannot be created for this sort of suffering. The receiving of this letter is to be one of yours—I will say nothing about our friendship or rather yours to me more than that as you deserve to escape you will never be so unhappy as I am. I should think of—you in my last moments. I shall endeavour to write to Miss Brawne if possible to day. A sudden stop to my life in the middle of one of these Letters would be no bad thing for it keeps one in a sort of fever awhile. Though fatigued with a Letter longer than any I have written for a long while it would be better to go on for ever than awake to a sense of contrary winds. We expect to put into Portland roads to night. The Captn the Crew and the Passengers are all illtemper'd and weary. I shall write to dilke. I feel as if I was closing my last letter to you—My dear Brown

Your affectionate friend
John Keats

To Frances Ricketts Brawne, 24 (?) October 1820

Octr 24 Naples Harbour
care Giovanni

My dear Mrs Brawne,

A few words will tell you what sort of a Passage we had, and what situation we are in, and few they must be on account of the Quarantine, our Letters being liable to be opened for the purpose of fumigation at the Health Office.* We have to remain in the vessel ten days and are, at present shut in a tier of ships. The sea air has been beneficial to me about to as great an extent as squally weather and bad accommodations and provisions has done harm—So I am about as I was—Give my Love to Fanny and tell her, if I were well there is enough in this Port of Naples to fill a quire of Paper—but it looks like a dream—every man who can row his boat and walk and talk seems a different being from myself—I do not feel in the world—It has been unfortunate for me that one of the Passengers is a young Lady in a Consumption—her imprudence has vexed me very much—the knowledge of her complaint—the flushings in her face, all her bad symptoms have preyed upon me—they would have done so had I been in good health. Severn now is a very good fellow but his nerves are too strong to be hurt by other peoples illnesses—I remember poor Rice wore me in the same way in the isle of wight—I shall feel a load off me when the Lady vanishes out of my sight. It is impossible to describe exactly in what state of health I am—at this moment I am suffering from indigestion very much, which makes such stuff of this Letter. I would always wish you to think me a little worse than I really am; not being of a sanguine disposition I am likely to succeed. If I do not recover your regret will be softened if I do your pleasure will be doubled—I dare not fix my Mind upon Fanny, I have not dared to think of her. The only comfort I have had that way has been in thinking for hours together of having the knife she gave me put in a silver-case—the hair in a Locket—and the Pocket Book in a gold net—Show her this. I dare say no more—Yet ⟨you⟩ must not believe I am so ill as this Letter may look for if ever there was a person born without the faculty of hoping I am he. Severn is writing to Haslam, and I have just asked him to request Haslam to send you his account of my health. O what an account I could give you of the Bay of Naples if I could once more feel myself a Citizen of this world—I feel a Spirit in my Brain would lay it forth pleasantly—O what a misery it is to have an intellect in splints! My Love again to Fanny—tell Tootts* I wish I could pitch her a basket of grapes—and tell Sam the fellows catch here with a line a little fish much like an anchovy, pull them up fast   Remember me to Mrs and Mr Dilke—mention to Brown that I wrote him a letter at Port-[s]mouth which I did not send and am in doubt if he ever will see it.

my dear Mrs Brawne

yours sincerely and affectionate

John Keats—

Good bye Fanny! god bless you

To Charles Brown, 1 November 1820

Naples. Wednesday first in November.

My dear Brown,

Yesterday we were let out of Quarantine, during which my health suffered more from bad air and a stifled cabin than it had done the whole voyage. The fresh air revived me a little, and I hope I am well enough this morning to write to you a short calm letter;—if that can be called one, in which I am afraid to speak of what I would the fainest dwell upon. As I have gone thus far into it, I must go on a little;—perhaps it may relieve the load of WRETCHEDNESS which presses upon me. The persuasion that I shall see her no more will kill me. I cannot q——* My dear Brown, I should have had her when I was in health, and I should have remained well. I can bear to die—I cannot bear to leave her. Oh, God! God! God! Every thing I have in my trunks that reminds me of her goes through me like a spear. The silk lining she put in my travelling cap scalds my head. My imagination is horribly vivid about her—I see her—I hear her. There is nothing in the world of sufficient interest to divert me from her a moment. This was the case when I was in England; I cannot recollect, without shuddering, the time that I was prisoner at Hunt's, and used to keep my eyes fixed on Hampstead all day. Then there was a good hope of seeing her again—Now!—O that I could be buried near where she lives! I am afraid to write to her—to receive a letter from her—to see her hand writing would break my heart— even to hear of her any how, to see her name written would be more than I can bear. My dear Brown, what am I to do? Where can I look for consolation or ease? If I had any chance of recovery, this passion would kill me. Indeed through the whole of my illness, both at your house and at Kentish Town, this fever has never ceased wearing me out. When you write to me, which you will do immediately, write to Rome (poste restante)—if she is well and happy, put a mark thus +, —if—Remember me to all. I will endeavour to bear my miseries patiently. A person in my state of health should not have such miseries to bear. Write a short note to my sister, saying you have heard from me. Severn is very well. If I were in better health I should urge your coming to Rome. I fear there is no one can give me any comfort. Is there any news of George? O, that something fortunate had ever happened to me or my brothers!—then I might hope,—but despair is forced upon me as a habit. My dear Brown, for my sake, be her advocate for ever. I cannot say a word about Naples; I do not feel at all concerned in the thousand novelties around me. I am afraid to write to her. I should like her to know that I do not forget her. Oh, Brown, I have coals of fire in my breast. It surprised me that the human heart is capable of containing and bearing so much misery.

Was I born for this end? God bless her, and her mother, and my sister, and George, and his wife, and you, and all!

Your ever affectionate friend,

John Keats.

Thursday. I was a day too early for the courier. He sets out now. I have been more calm to-day, though in a half dread of not continuing so. I said nothing of my health; I know nothing of it; you will hear Severn's account from x x x x x x.* I must leave off. You bring my thoughts too near to—

God bless you!

To Charles Brown, 30 November 1820

Rome. 30 November 1820.

My dear Brown,

'Tis the most difficult thing in the world to me to write a letter. My stomach continues so bad, that I feel it worse on opening any book,—yet I am much better than I was in Quarantine. Then I am afraid to encounter the proing and conning of any thing interesting to me in England. I have an habitual feeling of my real life having past, and that I am leading a posthumous existence. God knows how it would have been—but it appears to me—however, I will not speak of that subject. I must have been at Bedhampton nearly at the time you were writing to me from Chichester—how unfortunate—and to pass on the river too! There was my star predominant! I cannot answer any thing in your letter, which followed me from Naples to Rome, because I am afraid to look it over again. I am so weak (in mind) that I cannot bear the sight of any hand writing of a friend I love so much as I do you. Yet I ride the little horse,—and, at my worst, even in Quarantine, summoned up more puns, in a sort of desperation, in one week than in any year of my life. There is one thought enough to kill me—I have been well, healthy, alert &c, walking with her—and now—the knowledge of contrast, feeling for light and shade, all that information (primitive sense) necessary for a poem are great enemies to the recovery of the stomach. There, you rogue, I put you to the torture,—but you must bring your philosophy to bear—as I do mine, really—or how should I be able to live? Dr Clarke is very attentive to me; he says, there is very little the matter with my lungs, but my stomach, he says, is very bad. I am well disappointed in hearing good news from George,—for it runs in my head we shall all die young. I have not written to x x x x x yet, which he must think very neglectful; being anxious to send him a good account of my health, I have delayed it from week to week. If I recover, I will do all in my power to correct the mistakes made during sickness; and if I should not, all my faults will be forgiven. I shall write to x x x to-morrow, or next day. I will write to x x x x x in the middle of next week. Servern is very well, though he leads so dull a life with me. Remember me to all friends, and tell x x x x* I should not have left London without taking leave of him, but from being so low in body and mind. Write to George as soon as you receive this, and tell him how I am, as far as you can guess;—and also a note to my sister—who walks about my imagination like a ghost—she is so like Tom. I can scarcely bid you good bye even in a letter. I always made an awkward bow.

> God bless you!
> John Keats.

APPENDIX

Differences from Rollins, indicated in the texts of the letters by a footnote, are listed here, with detailed reasons for their adoption in this selection.

1. *To Benjamin Bailey, 28–30 October 1817* (page 30, line 13)

You must forgive although I have only written 300 Lines—they would have been five but I have been obliged to go to town. yesterday I called at Lambs— St Jane look'd very flush when I first went in but was much better before I left.

Rollins prints this at the end of the letter, calling it a 'second post-script', and saying that its position there is indicated by Keats. This seems a simple misunderstanding of two crosses put by Keats in his letter. Keats, finishing one page halfway through the letter with the words 'uncomfortable hours', then wrote the paragraph beginning 'You must forgive me' squeezed into another space he found on the paper. He put a cross before it and a cross after 'hours' to indicate the place where the paragraph should be inserted, and I have followed his directions, which make better sense of the whole sequence of the letter. Rollins rightly interpreted the 'yesterday' of the paragraph to mean 29 October; he did not perhaps consider the probability that Keats wrote it and the whole second half of the letter at night in the early hours of 30 October, when his visit to the Reynolds family of the previous evening would have become 'yesterday'.

2. *To Benjamin Bailey, 28–30 October 1817* (page 31, line 28)

—try whether I shall have grow[n] two lusty for my chair—by the fire side—and take a peep at my cordials Bower—

All editors, including Rollins, print the unknown word 'cardials'. Keats's *o*'s and *a*'s in this letter are very irregular, and 'cordials' makes sense in the context. It is the Regency slang word for semen. As 'chair' is slang for male sex and 'Bower' for female, the sentence is a sexual joke.

3. *To James Rice, 24 March 1818* (page 74, line 9)

—I have met with a Brace or twain of little Long heads—not a kit o' the german—

This is in the middle of an obscure passage, omitted by some editors, and uncommented upon by Rollins, who prints 'bit', though the word looks like 'kit', especially in the additional copy made by Woodhouse. 'Kit' again is slang for male sex, and the whole passage in which this occurs is clearly another piece of sexual joking, indicating that his correspondent, Rice, had left some bastards behind in that part of Devon.

4. *To Tom Keats, 17–21 July 1818* (page 121, line 27)

'The Lady of the Lake went to Rock herself to sleep on Arthur's seat and the Lord of the Isles coming to Press a Piece and seeing her Assleap remembered their last meeting at Cony stone Water so touching her with one hand on the Vallis Lucis while he [*for* the] other un-Derwent her Whitehaven, Ireby stifled her clack man on, that he might her Anglesea . . . '

Another piece of sexual joking, by Brown and reported verbatim by Keats. Rollins prints it without explanation and with 'Corry' when the manuscript clearly shows 'Cony', i.e. female sex. The pun on Coniston Water in the Lake District, since most of the other place-names are near by, is much more appropriate than Corrystone in Scotland, which all other editors have substituted, while showing obvious signs of embarrassment at the whole passage.

5. *To Miss Jeffery, 31 May and 9 June 1819* (pages 239 and 240)

Misled by the fact that none of the Keats boys could spell, and that Keats was particularly hazy about surnames, all Keats's editors, including Rollins, have invented a family in Teignmouth with a mother called Mrs. Margaret Jeff*rey*, and three daughters, Marian, Sarah, Fanny, and even possibly a fourth: this in spite of the fact that a descendant of this family was William Jeff*ery* Prowse (1836–1870), a humorous verse-writer.

Parish records show that the parents were William and Sarah Jeffery, who had two daughters, Mary-Ann, born 11 January 1798, and Sarah Frances, born 7 December 1799. The latter was known as both Sarah and Fanny; hence some of the confusion.

6. *To George and Georgiana Keats, 12 November 1819* (page 313, line 5)

Not expecting you would want money so soon I did not send for the necessary power of attorney from Holland before I received you Letter which reached me in the middle of the summer at Shanklin.

Rollins, not observing that the gaps which Keats habitually left in the middle of words are particularly wide throughout this letter, prints 'Holl and', though in a note he rejects the Buxton Formans' idea of 'Holt', and himself conjectures 'Holland', and then prints details of London solicitors called Holland. Aileen Ward, *John Keats: The Making of a Poet*, p. 294, first correctly identified this as a reference to the well-attested fact that one of the Keats trustees lived in Holland, though she then went on to name him as Keats's former guardian John Nowland Sandell who, in fact, had been dead for three years. He was almost certainly the man Fry, mentioned later in this letter.

7. *To Fanny Brawne, March (?) 1820* (page 341)

Rollins assigns this undated note to 'April (?) 1820'. He admits this is a guess. It must, however, with its reference to 'Feeding upon sham victuals', be before the second week in March, when Keats was put on normal diet by a new doctor, Robert Bree.

8. *To Fanny Brawne, May (?) 1820* (page 349)

The reasons for adopting this conjectural date instead of Rollins's '5 July (?) 1820' are cogently stated by J. R. Macgillivray, *Keats: A Bibliography and Reference Guide*, xxxv. Rollins argues that the sentence 'They talk of my going to Italy' indicates a time after 22 June, when Keats had his second haemorrhage; but there had been talk of his going to Italy much earlier in the year, and other parts of this letter seem to be connected with parts of other letters undoubtedly written well before this haemorrhage.

EXPLANATORY NOTES

KC *The Keats Circle*, ed. H. E. Rollins, 2 vols. (1948)
KSJ *Keats-Shelley Journal*

1816–1817

3 *the Sonnet to the Sun*: that is, Clarke himself.

and Darwin: Erasmus Darwin (1731–1802), author of many controversial works of poetry and science, including *The Botanic Garden* (1791). His attempt to preach enlightenment principles in heroic couplets had become deeply unfashionable, but Keats is reacting more against the poetry than the principles here.

G. Mathew: George Felton Mathew (1795–?), early friend whom Keats met in 1815. Mathew soon found Keats to be too much of 'the sceptical and republican school' (*KC* ii. 185), but for a time the two shared their intense poetic ambitions.

for an Action worthy of a God: Keats is thinking of Horace's *Ars Poetica*, l. 191. I am grateful to Christopher Pelling for this reference.

4 *daintie Davie*: see the chorus of Robert Burns's 'Now Rosy May'.

Haydon and all his Creation: a pun on B. R. Haydon the artist and the composer Haydn. Keats had only recently met Haydon, and was about to visit his studio. Punning is a marked feature of Keats's correspondence and was, as several letters show, a common entertainment among his friends.

Ollier's: Charles Ollier (1788–1859) and his brother James were the publishers of Keats's first volume *Poems* (1817) as well as Hunt's *Foliage* (1818) and the second edition of *The Story of Rimini* (1817). Keats and his brothers felt that the Olliers did too little to sell his volume.

the following: the letter is a response to Keats's visit to Haydon's studio. The sonnet records Keats's progressive notion of the spirit of the age in the 'mighty Workings in a distant Mart'. The great spirits are Haydon himself, Wordsworth, and Hunt.

5 *a fresh swarm of flies*: a reference to Aesop's fable of 'The Fox and the Hedgehog'.

must myself: the original letter is torn here. The preceding sentence adapts Falstaff's lines in *1 Henry IV*, II. iv. 468–74.

as small as a Wand": *The Two Gentlemen of Verona*, II. iii. 20.

broom furze": *The Tempest*, I. i. 70 misquoted.

5 *"There's my Comfort"*: *The Tempest*, II. ii. 56.

6 *Haydon's Picture*: *Christ's Entry into Jerusalem*, in which were painted the heads of Hazlitt, Wordsworth, and Keats. The painting was not finished until 1820. See below, p. 345.

Wilkinson's plan: an unsuccessful business scheme by George Keats.

7 *Birds eyes abate*: bird's eye, or germander speedwell, closes its petals in cloudy weather.

8 *"Do you not hear the Sea?"*: from *King Lear*, IV. vi. 4, where Edgar in disguise meets his blinded father.

9 *show the explanations to your sisters*: Keats was on good terms with the whole of the Reynolds family at this time, especially the mother and two of the daughters, Jane and Marian.

abysm of time—: *The Tempest*, I. ii. 328–30, and 50.

of Glory excellent: *The Faerie Queene*, I. v. i.

begin my Endymion: Keats wrote over 200 lines of the poem in the following week.

10 *coasted crab*: a pun (Keats is on the coast at Margate) on *A Midsummer Night's Dream*, II. i. 47–8. The 'little Gentleman' is Puck.

well acquainted with Bensley: Thomas Bensley printed the second edition of Hunt's *The Story of Rimini*. Clarke corrected the proofs.

Old Wood's: probably a bailiff; Hunt was often in debt.

Hazlitt's Southey: the leader in the *Examiner*, 4 May 1817, was an attack on religious intolerance and the law of blasphemy (currently being used by the government to silence radical opposition). The 'Foreign Intelligence' section of the paper contains an account of the Petzelians, an Austrian sect reported to practise human sacrifice as a form of atonement. Hazlitt's lengthy review of Southey's *A Letter to William Smith, Esq., M. P.* (1817) appeared in the same issue (and continued over the next two).

11 *to the Nymphs*: Hunt's poem 'The Nymphs' was eventually published in *Foliage* (1818). Keats goes on to suggest that Hunt cut or make 'a Horse shoe business' of a series of phrases. The cuts were not made.

12 *a bare Bodkin, in its modern sense)*: see *Hamlet*, II. i. 76, where 'bodkin' seems to refer to a stiletto pin. The 'modern sense' to which Keats refers may simply be a variant of 'bodikin' and hence a play on 'body'.

Shelley: with whom Hunt was staying in Marlow, Bucks. Shelley and Hunt had first met the previous December and had quickly become close, somewhat to Keats's discomfort.

out Master Vellum": Joseph Addison, *The Drummer*, IV. i.

Miss Kent: Hunt's sister-in-law, Elizabeth.

13 *heirs of all eternity*: *Love's Labour's Lost*, I. i. 1–7.

bill-pestilence: no less than Hunt, Keats was in financial difficulties for most of his short life. A substantial proportion of his inheritance had been spent on his medical training, but his guardian Richard Abbey was unhelpful and conceivably dishonest in his handling of Keats's financial affairs.

gathers Samphire dreadful trade": another reference to *King Lear*, IV. vi. 15. See above, p. 8.

they seem like Mice to mine: Keats expressed his sense of the failure of Pope and 'the French school' to live up to his idea of the poetic imagination in 'Sleep and Poetry', ll. 181–9. His views were typical of the Hunt circle. The Preface to Hunt's *Foliage* published in the following year provides a convenient summary of many of them.

15 *to have mine in*: another reference to Haydon's painting *Christ's Entry into Jerusalem*.

Shakspeare is enough: Keats did not meet Hazlitt until several months later, but he may have known his opinions on Shakespeare and other matters from his writing in the *Examiner*.

remarks of the Manuscript: Haydon reviewed 'Bonaparte. "Manuscrit venu de St. Hélène"' (1817) in the *Examiner*, 27 April and 4 May 1817. General Bertrand (1773–1844) was Napoleon's confidante.

reading Anthony and Cleopat[ra]: *Antony and Cleopatra*, III. v. 16–18, III. vi. 84–5, III. xii. 3–4, III. xiii. 31–4, 43–6.

16 *"deal in Lieutenantry"*: another reference to *Antony and Cleopatra*, III. xi. 38–9. Praise of Wellington was unusual in the liberal press.

the next as G.: George Keats.

the North: that is, to Wordsworth.

John Hunt: Leigh Hunt's brother; publisher and fellow founder of the *Examiner*.

Archimago or Urganda: an enchanter from Spenser's *The Faerie Queene* and enchantress from the medieval romance *Amadis of Gaul* respectively. Keats would have known the latter from Southey's *Amadis of Gaul* (1803). Only the allusion to Urganda really makes sense here, as she assists, whereas Archiago obstructs, the heroes in their respective quests. Urganda is also mentioned in the verse letter to J. H. Reynolds of 25 March 1818. See p. 76. I am grateful to Helen Moore for her help with this reference.

Sybils Leaves in Virgil: *Aeneid*, iii. 445–52. Keats had translated the poem for a competition at school as a boy.

the Ewe not bites": *The Tempest*, V. i. 37–8.

17 *Sir Novelty Fashion'(s)*: character in Colley Cibber's *Love's Last Shift*.

17 *twitter &c.*: Keats is slightly misquoting the opening lines of Wordsworth's 'Written in March, While Resting on the Bridge at the Foot of Brother's Water'.

19 *a visit to a young Man*: that is, Benjamin Bailey

20 *Original Poems*: Jane Taylor, *Essays in Rhyme* (1816) and with Ann Taylor, *Original Poems for Infant Minds* (1804). Both were Taylor and Hessey publications.

an overfeeding Schoolboy: the jingoism of this letter is inflected by the antipathy to 'the French school of poetry' associated with the Hunt circle. The fact that Hunt's ideas on taste were bound up with an attempt to present middle-class taste as more authentically British than élite culture should not be overlooked.

21 *and behind Mr Honeycomb"*: Oliver Goldsmith, *The Good Natur'd Man*, III. i. 252–4. The character's name is actually Honeywood.

personal talk": paraphrase of the opening of Wordsworth, 'Personal Talk'.

acherontic: infernal.

Montague: Elizabeth Montagu (1720–1800), well-known leader of the bluestockings.

22 *Orinda"*: Katherine Philips (1631–64). He goes on to quote from 'To Mrs. M. A. at Parting'. From her *Poems* (1710).

24 *of the Fletcher Kind*: Keats owned the 4-volume 1811 edition of Jonson, Beaumont, and Fletcher's *The Dramatic Works* (now at the Keats Museum, Hampstead).

Leech gatherer: Keats is referring to characters who appear in Wordsworth's 'Old Cumberland Beggar' and 'Resolution and Independence' respectively. John Martin (1791–1855) was a partner in the bookselling firm Rodwell and Martin of 46 New Bond Street.

reading his Table: Hazlitt collaborated with Leigh Hunt in a collection of essays, *The Round Table* (1817).

Hampton: Littlehampton, Sussex, where the Reynolds sisters were staying.

25 *is Crips*: Charles Cripps (b. 1796, Iffley, Oxford). Haydon was interested in taking Cripps, whose work he had seen in a previous visit to Oxford, as an apprentice. The attempt of Haydon's friends, including Keats, to raise a subscription on his behalf became a complicated matter, mentioned in several of the letters.

26 *There's Horace Smith*: Horace Smith (1779–1849), wealthy stockbroker, satirist, and novelist. He was a close friend of Hunt's, and, with his brother James (1775–1839), author of the successful *Rejected Addresses* (1812), a series of parodies on authors living and dead. Impressed by the early Keats poems that Charles Cowden Clarke showed Hunt, Smith seems to have met Keats at Hunt's Hampstead cottage in 1816.

web of our Life is of mingled Yarn": *All's Well that Ends Well*, IV. iii. 68.

Mrs Bentley's children: the Keats brothers were lodging with the Bentley family at 1 Well Walk, Hampstead.

27 *George in the spring*: this letter is now unknown.

through before Mrs Williams: probably a reference to Dr Johnson's friend and sometime hostess Anna Williams. Keats and his brother Tom had been facetiously annotating Johnson's critical notes to their set of Shakespeare. Hazlitt's *Characters of Shakespeare's Plays*, written in large part to refute Johnson's ideas, was published in July.

a Mockery at him at Hunts": some time in early spring 1817 the two poets exchanged crowns much to Keats's discomfort. See the sonnets 'On Receiving a Laurel Crown from Leigh Hunt' and 'To the Ladies who saw me Crown'd' and the apologetic ode to Apollo 'God of the golden bow'. See the account in W. J. Bate, *John Keats* (1984), 138–40. Such half-serious ceremonies, like sonnet-writing competitions, were not uncommon in the Hunt circle, to the derision of the Tory press.

for those Casts: that is, life masks of Keats.

you and Gleg: George Robert Gleig (1796–1888), student at Magdalen Hall, later an eminent clergyman and Bailey's brother-in-law.

28 *Ax Will*: probably a college servant.

improved my Health: mercury was often, although not exclusively, taken for venereal complaints.

the two R s: Rice and Reynolds. Bailey did not get this curacy. See p. 32.

an old Gent: an old poet, probably Chaucer.

30 *on Man's Mortality"*: Wordsworth, 'Ode: Intimations of Immortality', l. 202.

Hazlitt is right: Keats links two different essays by Hazlitt from *The Round Table* (1817): 'On Commonplace Critics' and 'On Manner'. The note on Wordsworth appears in the latter; the remarks on the reviews in the former. Later on in his career, Keats became more willing to criticize what Hazlitt called Wordsworth's 'Sunday-School philosophy'. Here Keats seems to feel that to dwell on the negative aspects of Wordsworth's poetry rather than to delight in the pleasures of the scenes he describes may be as 'commonplace' of Hazlitt as those who think like the reviewers. The sense of the grandeur of Wordsworth's poetry and its concern with 'the human heart' never entirely disappears from Keats's assessment. See the letter on the 'Mansion of Many Apartments' to Reynolds, pp. 89 ff.

31 *those Masks*: that is, Keats has not been able to get copies of the life mask mentioned in the previous letter.

Pæòna: Endymion's sister in the Keats poem.

31 *the Rock tarpeian*: *Coriolanus*, III. i. 211.

Coleridge's Lays: the first of Coleridge's 'Lay Sermons', *The Statesman's Manual*, was published in 1816. Bailey seems to have been preparing to read them. Much of Hazlitt's criticism of this period, obviously influencing Keats, was oriented against the conservative Christian thinking behind Coleridge's sermons.

Hopkinses and black beetles: H. J. Hopkins was a student at Magdalen Hall. 'Black beetles' probably refers to the University's beadles.

32 *your disappointment*: over the curacy mentioned in the previous letter.

the Proud Mans Contumely: *Hamlet*, III. i. 71.

33 *subscription*: that is, to pay for Cripps's tuition with Haydon.

the Endinburgh Magazine: see 'On the Cockney School of Poetry. No. I', *Blackwood's Edinburgh Magazine*, October 1817. The first of the famous attacks on the Cockney School which Byron, Shelley, and others erroneously blamed for the death of Keats. Two others were published in this series in November 1817 and July 1818 before a fourth directly attacked Keats in August 1818. Others followed in the series.

Webb Poetaster: Cornelius Webb or Webbe (*c.*1790–*c.*1848). The first two *Blackwood*'s articles were prefaced with these lines from Webb: 'Our talk shall be (a theme we never tire on) | Of Chaucer, Spenser, Shakespeare, Milton, Byron | (Our England's Dante)—Wordsworth—HUNT, and KEATS, The Muses' son of promise.' Hunt published some of Webb's poetry in his *Literary Pocket Book* (1822).

it is done: Rice played a part in Reynolds becoming articled to Francis Fladgate senior (1773–1821) to improve his prospects of marriage to Eliza Drewe. If there is an ominous tone to Keats's remarks, it originates in a sense of the parallels between Reynolds's case and his own. Reynolds had given up a clerkship to try his hand at living by his pen earlier in the year, a decision that seems to have influenced Keats to abandon his medical career. For Keats's hope that Reynolds would be able to keep up his literary aspirations despite his legal career, see pp. 86–7.

35 *and Whitehead*: J. F. C. Whitehead was another associate of Bailey's at Magdalen Hall.

capability of submission: a phrase that looks forward to the idea of 'Negative Capability', see p. 41 and note.

Men of Genius: the contrast between 'Men of Genius' and 'Men of Power' is picked up in the contrast Keats implies in the Negative Capability letter between himself and Coleridge. Later letters develop it in terms of the opposition between Shakespeare and Wordsworth (with Keats identified with the former). Hazlitt's influence is palpable in all these ideas. Bailey almost certainly encouraged Keats to read Hazlitt's *An Essay on the Principles of Human Action* (1805), as well as *The Round*

Table essays, while they were in Oxford together. Hazlitt believed, as the subtitle of his book indicated, in 'the natural disinterestedness of the human mind', that is, in its ability to abstract itself from its present being and by the same means of sympathetic identification enter into its own future being and the mind and feelings of others. Yet Hazlitt, unlike Keats, habitually describes this imaginative sympathy in terms of 'power', regardless of whether it develops a tendency towards self-love or benevolence, both of which are potential outcomes. For Keats the capabilities of his Men of Genius often seem more negative or submissive.

36 *the holiness of the Heart's affections and the truth of Imagination*: Hazlitt's influence is discernible again on this well-known sentiment. Hazlitt stressed the active role of imagination in our mental processes. The 'truths' that the imagination discovers are mediated for Hazlitt by their complex relationships with our 'affections'. They move us to action, he says in the *Essay* (1805), to the extent that they are 'sufficiently warm and vivid to excite in me an emotion of interest or passion'. This intensity or warmth seems to be what Keats means by 'Beauty'.

I sent in my last: that is, the passage of *Endymion* beginning at i. 177 and the poem 'O Sorrow' copied in the previous letter.

Adam's dream: Keats seems to refer to *Paradise Lost*, viii. 452–90. Hazlitt stressed the role of the imagination in bringing home to us ideas of our future selves or others that were not the result of either our present sensations or memories of our past ones.

O for a Life of Sensations rather than of Thoughts!: Hazlitt followed Hume in stressing the importance of the intensity of our impressions on our actions, that is, the power of imagination in mental processes. Although Keats acknowledges that disinterested philosophers, among whom he numbers Bailey, may sometimes need to put aside this influence in order to arrive at their truths, his sudden ejaculation seems to express a preference for the vivid 'impressions' of sensations over the dullness of 'thoughts' (to use Hume's vocabulary). Later discussions of the illusions of 'consequitive reasoning' are often made in relation to Dilke and his Godwinian belief that human benevolence was grounded not in the affections but in rational judgements. See p. 303 and note.

a finer tone and so repeated: an idea that seems to look forward to the 'vale of Soul-making' letter. See p. 232.

38 *your friend Christie*: Jonathan Henry Christie (?–1876). Christie fought a duel with John Scott (1788–1821), editor of the *London Magazine*, that resulted directly from J. G. Lockhart's *Blackwood's* reviews. Scott died of his wounds, but Christie was acquitted of murder. Ironically, Keats thought Scott was responsible for the essays in *Blackwood's* against the Cockney School. See p. 56.

38 *turn Rakehell*: 'a lewd or debauched fellow', which suggests 'go a *making*' means sowing his wild oats. Here Keats is proposing to indulge his literary rather than sexual appetites.

39 *Shakespear's Poems*: the passage which follows moves from Sonnet 12, to *Love's Labour's Lost*, v. iii. 538, to *Venus and Adonis*, to Sonnet 17, to Sonnet 19 ('thine antique pen'), to Sonnet 21, to Sonnet 13. See Andrew Bennett, *Keats, Narrative and Audience: The Posthumous Life of Writing* (Cambridge, 1994), 57. The reference to the snail's horns seems to be picked up in a letter to Haydon the following spring, see p. 79.

40 *to the rounce*: the word 'rounce', later pencilled in, seems to have been omitted by the copyist. The omission may be to do with the copyist's scruples over a bawdy pun, as a 'rounce' is part of a printing press that winds in and out. Here it is obviously a sexual image.

poems on the late Princess: Princess Charlotte Augusta died on 6 November 1817. The notice asking poets to stop sending in their verses appeared in the *Morning Chronicle*, 20 November.

a little pullet sperm, a few finch eggs: The Merry Wives of Windsor, III. v. 28, and *Troilus and Cressida*, v. i. 35.

Prince Arthur: King John, v. vii. 31. Note the unsympathetic view of monarchy expressed here.

hinc atque illinc: literally 'from one direction and from the other'.

& &: an omission by the copyist (who also misdated the letter).

Kean: Edmund Kean (1787/9–1833). Kean made his name with his performance as Shylock at Drury Lane in 1814. The review in the *Champion* makes it clear that Keats shared with Hazlitt—whose influence on the content and style of the review is palpable—a relish for the novel intensity or 'gusto' of Kean's acting style and his status as a social outsider. See the preference Keats expresses for the low company kept by Kean over the more fashionable circles inhabited by Horace Smith later in this letter.

his Luke in Riches: Luke Traffic in Sir J. B. Burges's *Riches: Or, The Wife and Brother* (1810).

41 *christmas Gambols & pastimes*: see Hunt's essays on 'Christmas and Other Old National Merry-Makings Considered', *Examiner*, 21 and 28 December 1817.

an essential service: T. J. Wooller (1786?–1853), author, printer, publisher, and editor of the *Black Dwarf* (1817–24) was tried for libelling the ministry and acquitted on 6 June. William Hone (1780–1842) radical journalist and publisher, was tried over 18–20 December on three charges of blasphemy for a series of political parodies on the church service. Both made skilful use of the courtroom situation to make a laughing stock of the proceedings brought against them. Keats seems to be responding to the detailed and entertaining accounts of Hone's trial that appeared in the *Examiner*,

21 December. Lord Ellenborough (1750–1818), who had sentenced John and Leigh Hunt to prison in 1813, presided over Hone's second and third trials. Popular opinion was that his death was hastened by the humiliation.

Wells: C. J. Wells (1800–79) was at school at Enfield with the Keats brothers, but the hoax he later perpetrated on Tom brought his friendship with John to an end. See p. 216 and note.

Christ rejected: both pictures by Benjamin West (1738–1820), American President of the Royal Academy. Reviewing West's *Picture of Christ Rejected* for the *Champion* on 26 June 1814, Hazlitt complained that it contained 'not one face or figure, hand or eye, which can be dwelt upon as an essence of its kind; as carrying truth, or beauty, or grandeur to that height of excellence to which they had been sometimes raised'. Keats like Hazlitt complains of the inability of West's picture to rouse the kind of 'greeting of the Spirit' he deemed necessary to the perception of any truth in Art.

Hill . . . one Du Bois: Thomas Hill, merchant and book collector; John Kingston, civil servant; Edward Dubois, editor of the *Monthly Mirror*. This group was memorably described by Coleridge as the 'Smith & Theodore Hook Squad' (to Charles Lamb, 30 June 1825). For Kingston's humiliation at the so-called 'Immortal Dinner', see p. 44.

Negative Capability: perhaps the best-known single phrase in Keats's letters, it obviously picks up and develops the idea of 'capability of submission' from the letter to Bailey (p. 35). Reading Hazlitt over the previous summer Keats would have known he stressed the ability of Shakespeare to throw himself into the life of his characters. See the discussion in my Introduction and the standard account in W. J. Bate's *Negative Capability* (1939).

42 *irritable reaching after fact & reason*: see his comments on 'consequitive reasoning' in the letter to Bailey, p. 36.

Penetralium: as several editors and critics have pointed out, there is no such word in Latin. Keats means something like 'penetrating insights'.

obliterates all consideration: Coleridge may appear here because of the two *Lay Sermons* (1816, 1817) and the *Biographia Literaria* (1817) which attempted to provide a foundation for knowledge and culture in a Christian metaphysics. Hazlitt described *The Statesman's Manual* (1816), the first of the sermons, as written to 'reprobate free inquiry'. Both Keats and Hazlitt stress the 'half knowledge' that made up the complex windings of human thought over Coleridge's desire to discover ultimate truths through reason. The role occupied by Coleridge in this comparison comes more often to be occupied by Dilke or Godwin and their ideas of 'perfectibility' in later letters. It may be significant, in this respect, that the dovetailing of ideas here had their origin in a discussion with Dilke.

42 *as Queen Mab was*: Shelley's *Queen Mab* (1813) was at the centre of a court case in 1817 over the custody of Shelley's children due to its 'immoral' content. Keats is also referring to *Laon and Cynthia*. Copies of the poem were published by the Olliers in December 1817, but recalled due to fears over its morality. The publishers forced changes on Shelley and reissued the poem as *The Revolt of Islam* in January 1818.

1818

43 *they have not put in*: in fact both were put in the 4 January issue of the *Champion*.

badly punc[t]uated: here he is referring to his review of Kean's acting in the *Champion* for 21 December 1817.

on Sawrey: Solomon Sawrey (1765–1835), the family doctor.

the Edge: a walk in Teignmouth.

we played a Concert: that is, by imitating musical instruments vocally.

and N. B. Severn Peter Pindars: Peter Pindar, or John Wolcot (1738–1819) was the greatest satirical poet of the period. He fixed the image of George III for satirists as a clottish 'Farmer George' over three decades from the 1780s. Although his political satires made him a sympathetic figure for Keats's circle anyway, Severn may have been particularly eager to drink his health because, originally a painter himself, Pindar had distinguished himself early on in his career with his unflattering *Odes to the Royal Academicians* (1782). Keats seems to look forward to meeting with Wolcot, p. 59, and reports his death to his sister Fanny, p. 329, in a reflection on the meeting of Peter Pindar with his old adversary George III in heaven.

Stephens: possibly Miss Stephens who had appeared in an adaptation of Sir Walter Scott's *Guy Mannering* at Covent Garden over 1817–18.

44 *pay through the Nose*: 'Pay through the nose', of course, means to pay an extravagant price for something. The pun revolves around the noisome conditions in the cheap gallery.

the Peachey family: James Peachey, attorney, had been at Enfield school with Keats.

and play it off: this sentence misquotes Prince Hal, *1 Henry IV*, II. iv. 16–18.

Sunday Evening at Haydon's: this episode has become known as the 'Immortal Dinner'. Keats's narration of events to his brothers rather confuses the chronology. The dinner took place on Sunday, 28 December, on the occasion of one of Wordsworth's rare visits to the capital. Wordsworth, Thomas Monkhouse, Charles Lamb, and Keats joined Haydon for dinner. Others dropped by, including John Kingston, who, unknown to Haydon, was Wordsworth's immediate superior in the civil service (Wordsworth had taken the post of Distributor of Stamps for Westmorland). There is a detailed description of events both in Haydon's *Autobiography* and the posthumously published *Diary* on which it was based. When Keats dropped in on Wordsworth the following Saturday he was disappointed to find him dressing formally out of deference to his superior (whose invitation Keats himself had declined). For Keats's distaste for Kingston, see pp. 80, 81, and 171.

Richer: that is, Joseph Ritchie (1788?–1819), explorer. John Scott had met George and Tom in Paris in September 1817.

Lamb: an early friend of Wordsworth and Coleridge, Charles Lamb managed to maintain good relations with them while also keeping in touch with liberal London circles that included Hazlitt and Hunt, to whom they were hostile. Hunt's Preface to *Foliage* (1818) described him as 'superior to both [Wordsworth and Coleridge] in what renders wisdom amiable and useful, which is social sentiment'. He wrote regularly for the London papers, including the *Examiner*.

Monkhouse: Thomas Monkhouse (1783–1825), a cousin of Mrs Wordsworth.

Landseer: John Landseer (1764–1852), painter and engraver.

Mrs Abbey: the wife of the trustee of Keats's estate, Richard Abbey, who reportedly had a low opinion of the entire Keats family.

on Haslam: William Haslam (1785?–1851) a solicitor and friend of the Keats brothers.

45 *Bob Harris in the Slips*: Harris may have been related to the family which managed Covent Garden. The slips were the sides of the gallery.

Miss Kents: in fact, one of Shelley's pseudonyms ('Elfin Knight') not Hunt's sister-in-law's. See the *Examiner*, 28 December 1817.

you're another": Keats is expressing a preference for Henry Fielding's *Tom Jones* over Sir Walter Scott's *The Antiquary* (1816). His love of the eighteenth-century English comic novelists Fielding, Sterne, and Smollett (and dislike of Richardson) is a little-noted but consistent feature of the letters.

Mr Redhall: G. S. Reddall, sword-cutler, 236 Piccadilly.

a very good thing: there follows the kind of exercise in bawdy punning typical of the Keats circle. *Mater Omnium* is 'Mother of All' and is clearly slang for the pudendum. Young Squibs seems to 'give' it as a toast on the women retiring, before being encouraged to blurt out the word 'cunt'. There follows an exchange of punning on 'Yard' (penis) and 'Pot' (vagina).

46 *as the casing Air*': *Macbeth*, III. iv. 22.

47 *depth of Taste*: note that Hazlitt has displaced Hunt from the triad of the sonnet of 16 November.

47 *disinterestedness*: an important concept for Keats, the use of this term to describe Bailey is almost certainly influenced by reading Hazlitt's *Essay* (1805). Many of Keats's best-known statements about poetry and identity, for instance those on 'Negative Capability' (p. 41 above) and 'the camelion poet' (p. 148), are clearly informed by his development of Hazlitt's ideas on disinterestedness.

48 *"the Devil rides upon a fiddle stick"*: *1 Henry IV*, II. iv. 481–2.

from the sunday: that is, at the 'Immortal Dinner' of 28 December.

last sunday's paper: the *Examiner*, of which Keats, for all the vicissitudes of his relationship with Hunt, was a devoted reader until his death.

49 *Hampstead*: probably a copying error for Hampshire.

& Bewick: William Bewick (1795–1866), artist. Pupil of Haydon from 1816.

of my first book: i.e. of *Endymion*, Book I.

in this business: that is, Keats agreed with Haydon that he should make a drawing of Keats as a frontispiece for the *Endymion* volume rather than illustrate the poem as Taylor had suggested. Neither idea was ever carried out.

written tale: that is, *Endymion*.

50 *than ever was written*: the stress here on the whirl of mental sensations and the buffetings of circumstance is picked up later in the letter in the idea of 'a kind of spiritual yeast in their frames which creates the ferment of existence'. The influence of Hazlitt's ideas on psychology is palpable once again. This brief comment anticipates the more famous 'vale of Soul-making' letter of 1819. See p. 232.

the twelve?: Bailey wrote on the address fold of the letter that this family 'was most kindly treated by poor Keats'.

51 *to Jane*: that is, Jane Reynolds.

binding: that is, an apprenticeship.

53 *Letter*: Keats never visited Bailey again. See p. 67 for the 'Letter'.

Surry institution: Hazlitt's second series of public lectures (the first in 1812 had been on philosophy) were given at the Surrey Institution, Blackfriars, 13 January to 3 March 1818. He attracted a largely middle-class, self-improving audience, many of whom—though by no means all—were Dissenters; broadly sympathetic to his political and religious views. The lectures were very popular, and the final one was delivered to an auditorium packed to the roof.

54 *far into the bowels of the Land"*: *Richard III*, v. ii. 3.

I may have made: writing to Shelley in 1820 (see p. 361) Keats mentions his rejection of advice from Shelley not to publish his first volume of poetry.

demme if I am: Keats is quoting from the manuscript of Horace Smith's 'Nehemiah Muggs' lent to him by the author (see pp. 60–2). The poem was never published in its entirety.

Rox: copyist's mistake for Cox, a medical bookseller. Hazlitt's 20 January lecture was on Chaucer and Spenser.

55 *a very gradual ripening of the intellectual powers*: from relatively early on in his career Keats narrates an idea of his own development as the product of an unconscious process, rather than the 'consequitive reasoning' that he associates at around this time with Bailey and Coleridge (see the Negative Capability letter, p. 41) and later with Dilke and Godwin (see his comments on Dilke as a Godwin-methodist, p. 303). This same idea of development operates in relation to his idea of the history of poetry (see his comments on Wordsworth and Milton, pp. 88, 90) and, indeed, his sense of political and cultural history more generally (see his comments on the grand march of the intellect, p. 90). In all these cases he tends to narrate his own position in terms of those, like Apollo in *Hyperion*, who are about to succeed to the next stage of development.

Queen! if: copying error for 'Queen of'.

Bombastes Furioso: three plays are being mentioned here: George Colman's *John Bull, Or, The Englishman's Fireside* (1803) and his *The Review, Or, Wags of Windsor* (1801), and W. B. Rhodes, *Bombastes Furioso* (1810).

56 *Tom's sake*: the actress has failed as Mary Thornberry in *John Bull*; she is dressed as Grace Gaylove the Quaker heroine of *The Review*. Phoebe Whitehorne is a woman who dresses as a soldier in *The Review*. Tom Shuffleton is a character in *John Bull*.

for his magazine: Archibald Constable (1774–1827) published the *Edinburgh* or *Scots Magazine*. Reynolds contributed several articles over 1818–19.

by Scott: the article discussed above, p. 33, was in fact written by J. G. Lockhart (1794–1854) and not John Scott, whom Tom had met in Paris.

57 *fold &c—*: *Endymion*, i. 777–81.

a kind of Pleasure Thermometer: another of the best-known phrases from the letters; it seems to look forward both to the 'Mansion of many Apartments' (p. 89) and 'vale of Soul-making' (p. 232) letters. Over the previous year with Bailey, he seems to have been weighing Hunt's doctrine of cheerfulness with the clergyman's Christian concern with the role of suffering in human life, but Keats's response again seems to resist a religious solution. Keats regularly places himself in the kind of developmental model suggested by 'a regular stepping of the Imagination towards a Truth'. See the idea of a 'gradual ripening' above, p. 55.

57 *of two pence*—: Reynolds had sent Keats two sonnets on Robin Hood by the twopenny post. Keats replied with 'Robin Hood' and 'Lines on the Mermaid Tavern'. Reynolds's sonnets were later published in the political journal *The Yellow Dwarf*, 21 February 1818, and reprinted in his *Garden of Florence* (1821). Note that Hazlitt quoted from one of them at the end of his 24 February lecture 'On Burns and the Old English Ballads'. For the political dimension of the Robin Hood motif, as well as other aspects of the context of the letter drawn on in the notes below, see John Barnard's excellent article 'Keats's "Robin Hood", John Hamilton Reynolds, and the "Old Poets"', *Proceedings of the British Academy*, 75, (1989), 181–200, and Nicholas Roe, *Keats and the Culture of Dissent* (1997), 141–55.

58 *Egotist*: the contrast between Wordsworth and Shakespeare on the basis of the former's egotism owes something to Hazlitt. Hazlitt's 'Observations on Mr Wordsworth's *Excursion*' declares of the poem: 'An intellectual egotism swallows up everything'. Yet it is only in this letter that Keats starts to express clear reservations about Wordsworth. Presumably this was the result of Keats thinking about the fact 'that Wordsworth has left a bad impression where–ever he visited in Town—by his egotism, Vanity and bigotry' (see p. 65) and partly the influence of Hazlitt's lectures on English poetry, which had begun in January. The lecture 'On Shakespeare and Milton', attended by Keats only a few days before he wrote this letter, described Shakespeare as 'the least of an egotist it was possible to be'. Keats developed his ideas on this contrast between Shakespeare and Wordsworth in the 'egotistical sublime' letter. See p. 58.

I will have no more of Wordsworth or Hunt in particular: one of the ironies of this letter is that many of the attitudes it expresses reflect the participation of both Keats and Reynolds in the Hunt circle. Keats and Reynolds had been introduced to each other by Hunt before October 1816 and the three of them were still meeting regularly when this letter was written. The Preface to Hunt's *Foliage* welcomed the 'revived love for our older and great school of poetry', and contrasted them with Wordsworth's gloominess. The attitudes Keats and Reynolds shared towards Hunt may reflect a need for them to clear a space for their own work, which they were only too aware was deeply influenced by Hunt. That is not to say that there were not real differences between Hunt and Keats (see my Introduction for a fuller discussion).

Manasseh: the reference to the tribe of Manasseh is to the elder but less important of the tribes of Israel descended from Joseph, but Keats may also have been thinking of the tyrannical king of that name.

"nice Eyed wagtails": the image appeared in Hunt's poem 'The Nymphs', eventually published in *Foliage* (1818), which Keats had seen—and tried to improve—in manuscript in May 1817. See the letter to Hunt, 10 May 1817, pp. 11.

"the Cherub Contemplation": a reference to Milton's *Il Penseroso*, l. 54.

a bough of wilding in his hand": see Wordsworth, 'The Two April Mornings', ll. 59–60.

Jacques "under an oak &c": *As You Like It*, II. i. 31.

the 4ᵗʰ Book of Childe Harold: the fourth Canto of Lord Byron's *Childe Harold* was published in April 1818.

59 *a few Catkins*: catkins presumably because of the way Keats's poems stretched down the page, and because hazel catkins fertilize filberts (hazel nuts).

&c: the copyist wrote down only the first line of each of the Keats sonnets.

the Land of Harpsicols: an archaic form of the word 'harpsichords', in line with the Elizabethan emphasis of the letter; the reference is probably to a musical evening at the Novellos' home. Vincent Novello (1781–1861) became a key figure in English musical life in the early nineteenth century. He edited collections of earlier music for professional organists and amateurs. His musical evenings provided a pattern of middle-class sociability of the sort mocked in the Cockney School reviews.

Hazlitts last Lecture . . . Thompson, Cowper & Crabbe: Hazlitt's lecture was given on 10 February. He disparaged Crabbe as a poet who 'collects all the petty vices of the human heart'.

the first night: *Fazio* by H. H. Milman (1791–1868) was presented at Covent Garden on 5 February 1818.

Mʳˢ Opie: Amelia Alderson Opie (1769–1853), poet and novelist.

60 *Mʳˢ Scott*: Caroline Colnaghi Scott was the wife of John Scott.

called on me: Henry Crabb Robinson (1775–1867), diarist, who does not mention the visit in any extant writings.

shall read them all: in fact only Hunt's 'The Nile' was published (in *Foliage*). Timed sonnet competitions on set subjects were a common pastime in the Hunt circle. Shelley's sonnet was 'Month after month the gather'd rains descend', not his better-known poem on an Egyptian theme 'Ozymandias'. Keats had contributed 'Sonnet to the Nile'.

on popular Preachers: 'Pulpit Oratory' appeared in the *Yellow Dwarf*, 7, 14, 28 February, and 4 April. The first three were signed 'Caius'. They reiterated the familiar Huntian doctrine of cheerfulness against the gloominess of Christianity.

Devon &c: Sir Richard Croft (1762–1818) had just shot himself after being accused of negligence over the death of Princess Charlotte (see above, p. 40). His suicide revived an old scandal that he had been involved in the exchange of infants in the Duke of Devonshire's family. Keats would have read about these things in the *Examiner*, 15 February 1818.

62 *thirty Pallaces"*: possibly a Buddhist reference, although there is no proof that Keats had any knowledge of Buddhism or of the other Indian sources of this image.

Indolence: the opening of Hazlitt's 10 February lecture 'On Thomson and Cowper' begins by laying stress on the former as the supreme poet of 'indolence'. Hazlitt tends to disparage this luxuriance rather more than Keats, who goes on to develop his idea of 'diligent Indolence', perhaps against Hazlitt's habitual stress on 'energy of mind', in the extended comparison of the bee and the flower later in this letter.

63 *a grand democracy of Forest Trees*: David Bromwich, *Hazlitt: The Mind of a Critic* (1983), 373–4, suggests a parallel in this passage with Hazlitt's answer to the question 'What is the people?' (*Examiner* for 7 March): 'Millions of men, like you, with hearts beating in their bosoms, blood circuating in their veins, with wants and appetites, and passions and anxious cares, and busy purposes and affections for others and a respect for themselves, and a desire for happiness, and a right to freedom, and a will to be free.'

64 *Miss Wylie*: Georgiana Augusta Wylie, who later married George.

essays on the elgin Marbles: Haydon had been a zealous advocate of the marbles as genuine examples of Greek art that ought to be acquired for the nation. He regarded his letter 'On the Judgment of Connoisseurs being Preferred to that of Professional Men', published simultaneously in the *Champion* and *Examiner*, as the decisive blow in the campaign. Both French and Italian translations were subsequently made. The marbles were installed in the British Museum by 17 January. Haydon took Keats to see them on 2 March. Keats's two sonnets commemorating the event appeared in the *Examiner* for 9 March.

Leslie's Uriel: the painting was not by Charles Robert Leslie (1794–1859) but his teacher Washington Allston (1779–1843). Keats had visited the British Institution in Pall Mall. James Stark (1794–1859) was awarded a prize by the directors of the Institution. Sir David Wilkie (1785–1841) was condemned in the 15 February issues of both the *Champion* and the *Examiner*.

65 *Butler's*: former neighbours of his family in Lambeth, Reynolds was lodging with them when he wrote to Keats in April.

to rights thereabouts: Le Mesurier was a close neighbour of Keats's grandmother in Church Street, Edmonton. The Haughtons have not been identified.

Voltaire and Gibbon: Keats may well have been reading Voltaire because of Hazlitt's lecture of 17 February on 'Swift, Young, Gray &c' (see below). Hazlitt specifically defended Voltaire against Wordsworth's strictures on him as a 'scoffer' in *The Excursion*. Attitudes to Voltaire had also been at the centre of squabbling between Haydon and Hunt. The former included Voltaire in the *Christ's Entry into Jerusalem* painting as a scoffer at religion. At the time of his death, Keats had three volumes by Voltaire in his library: *Siècle de Louis XIV* (see p. 231), *Essai sur les môeurs*, and *Dictionnaire Philosophique*.

many I know there: Hazlitt's lectures were a social event for Keats and his friends, and he in his turn seems to have responded to their interest. Hazlitt may have known of Keats's disappointment at the treatment of Chatterton at the close of the lecture on Swift *et al.* as he began his next lecture, 'On Burns'—with Keats in the audience—by apologizing for causing dissatisfaction 'to some persons, with whom I would willingly agree in all such matters'.

4th Canto: of *Childe Harold*, see above, p. 58.

Vanity and bigotry: by now a familiar aspect of Keats's comments on Wordsworth, but perhaps specifically picking up the mention of *The Excursion* in Hazlitt's lecture a few days before.

66 *follow quiet*: Keats refers to *Endymion*, i. 149 and 247.

a few Axioms: Hazlitt's emphasis on the power of intensity of expression in Art—and the example of Shakespeare—is clearly at work in the first two axioms. The idea of surprise combined with recognition suggests something of the way Hazlitt believed such intensity could make us see what we always seem to have known to be true. See *The Round Table* essay 'On Imitation': 'Art shows us nature, divested of the medium of our prejudices.' Compare with the letter on Adam's dream; see p. 36 above. The third of the axioms conforms with Hazlitt's view that it was a 'characteristic mark of the highest class of excellence to appear to come naturally from the mind of the author, without consciousness and effort'.

'O for a Muse of fire to ascend!': *Henry V*, Prologue, i.

a tall Ash top': *Endymion*, i. 334–5 and i. 495.

67 *to Percy Street*: the artists Peter De Wint (1784–1849) and William Hilton (1786–1839) lived in Percy Street. Hilton drew Keats, and after his death produced a portrait. Both contributed to the expenses of Keats's trip to Italy.

68 *Pulvis Ipecac. Simplex*: an emetic.

an Acrasian: Acrasia is a female enchantress in Spenser's *Faerie Queene*, who, like Homer's Circe, turns men into beasts and represents the destructive nature of sexual passion. Her Bower of Bliss is eventually destroyed by Sir Guyon (*FQ* II. v. 27; II. xii. 69–87).

69 *You know my ideas about Religion*: throughout their correspondence Keats admires Bailey's 'disinterested' commitment to serious study and thinking, but continually distances himself from his Christianity. Bailey's

'sermon' seems to be his pamphlet *Discourse inscribed to the memory of the Princess Charlotte* (1817).

69 *the ardour of the pursuer*: the stress on the role of the affections of the mind on truth is typical of Keats's letters and again owes a great deal to Hazlitt.

70 *as a Pecten*: a possible double meaning as pecten is both a comb/plectrum and a term for the pubis. I am grateful to Sara Lodge for pointing this out to me.

71 *Lydia Languish*: the heroine of R. B. Sheridan's *The Rivals*.

Damosel Radcliffe: Ann Radcliffe (1764–1823), Gothic novelist, whose writing is parodied in the passage that follows.

with bramble Bushes: a parody of Uncle Toby's language in Sterne's *Tristram Shandy*.

thou there, sweetheart!: 2 *Henry IV*, II. iv. 179.

72 *Answer to Salmasius*: Milton's *Pro Populo Anglicano Defensio* (1651) defended the Commonwealth's execution of Charles I against the attacks of Charles II's propagandist, Claude de Saumaise.

73 *all Bucks*: Charles Bucke (1781–1846), dramatist.

of Hengist: an anonymous play, published 1816.

Castlereaghs: Robert Stewart, Viscount Castlereagh (1739–1822). Foreign Secretary in Lord Liverpool's government, a hate-figure among liberals such as Keats, not least because of his role in the brutal suppression of the Irish rising of 1798.

74 *little Girls affairs*: a series of bawdy jokes on Rice's sexual activities in the West Country: 'secret' (here either the vagina or copulation), 'nail' (penis), 'kit' (male sexual organs), 'pepper' (the clap), 'drops' (the clap), and 'affair' (the vagina). See the description of the Devonian women as 'Acrasian,' above, p. 68.

75 *so, so,*: Junius Brutus Booth (1796–1852), actor. 'So-so' was cant for drunk.

77 *tease us out of thought*: see 'Ode on a Grecian Urn'.

78 *Moods of one's mind!*: Wordsworth used this phrase as a subtitle for a section of *Poems in Two Volumes* (1807). The banishment of these moods here would seem to be another expression of a preference for Shakespeare over Wordsworth. Hazlitt's 'Shakespeare and Milton' lecture had praised the former for not using poetry 'to fill up the dreary void with the Moods of their own Minds'.

Claude's Enchanted Castle: the title commonly used for Claude Lorraine's painting *Landscape with Psyche and the Palace of Amor* (the Psyche myth was a subject of continuing interest to Keats, see pp. 232 n. and 236). The painting was also a favourite of Hazlitt's (see his essay 'On the Ignorance of the Learned').

with my nonsense: Keats refers to a letter mainly of light verse not included in this selection.

79 *galligaskins*: breeches or leggings.

and snail-horn: see the reference to Shakespeare's *Venus and Adonis*, p. 39 above. The phrase 'composition and decomposition' and the ideas expressed here more generally seem to echo Hazlitt's *The Round Table* essay 'On Imitation', which discusses the way Art 'divides and decompounds objects into a thousand curious parts'. David Bromwich also draws attention to the way a similar vocabulary is used in Locke and—less positively—in Coleridge, both of which Keats may also have known. See Bromwich, *Hazlitt: The Mind of a Critic* (1983), 373–4.

with the Sea: see North's *Plutarch* (1676), 171.

the surly Warwick mans the Wall': *3 Henry VI*, v. i. 17.

bit of Italian: Haydon had mentioned Caroline Scott's black eyes ('occhi neri') in a letter of 25 March.

80 *Kingston's*: see *Merry Wives of Windsor*, i. iv. 24–5. Keats seems to be thinking of Wordsworth's deferential attitude to his superior John Kingston.

the thing: Keats's original preface to *Endymion*.

81 *Kingston Criticism*: Keats may be thinking specifically of Kingston's embarrassingly literal-minded questioning of Wordsworth at the 'Immortal Dinner'—ridiculed at the time by Lamb—about who was and was not a genius. The event was clearly in Keats's mind at this time. See p. 80.

82 *this Preface*: the new version that was actually published with the poem.

the Isle with Green: Matthew Green (1696–1737), who wrote *The Spleen* (1737).

84 *—Adieu—*: this postscript was added to a list of corrections not reprinted here.

85 *or no*: Keats and Reynolds planned a joint volume based on Boccaccio. Keats published only 'Isabella', but Reynolds included two poems based on Boccaccio in his *The Garden of Florence* (1821).

or two: the opening lines of 'Isabella', stanzas 12, 13, and 30 are indicated by the copyist.

86 *enough in my head"*: actually Abraham Slender in *The Merry Wives of Windsor*, i. i. 115. Keats was probably thinking of Sir Andrew Aguecheek in *Twelfth Night*.

from Sierra-leona": *Paradise Lost*, x. 702.

worsted stockings: that is, those of his landlady Mrs Bentley's children.

at your Spencerian: Reynolds's 'The Romance of Youth' printed in *The*

Garden of Florence (1821) or possibly his lodgings at Spencer Place or even punning on both.

86 *of your office*: i.e. in the law office of Francis Fladgate.

does Pepins: Sir Hugh Evans in *The Merry Wives of Windsor*, I. ii. 11–12.

87 *Pip-civilian*: an amateur lawyer.

needful to thinking people: Hazlitt's *Essay* (1805) took the view that 'our sympathy is always excited in proportion to our knowledge of the pain, and of the disposition and feelings of the sufferer'. Benevolent action depended on the extensive cultivation of our natural disposition to sympathy. Keats goes on to ask whether Wordsworth's imagination has really cultivated this extensive sympathy, martyred itself to the 'human heart', or fallen back on what Hazlitt took to be the easier route of referring everything to one's own past experience. Over the next few pages, Keats develops one of the best-known speculations on this matter. Although it has much to say about Milton, at its heart is really the comparison of Shakespeare and Wordsworth that had run through Hazlitt's lecture series that ended in March (see p. 89: 'Shakespear to Hazlitt to Shakespear . . . I will return to Wordsworth').

the Burden of the Mystery: Wordsworth's 'Tintern Abbey', l. 38.

is heir to: *Hamlet*, III. i. 63.

88 *the main region of his song*: see Wordsworth's unpublished *The Recluse*, I. i. 793, the passage containing this line had appeared in the Preface to *The Excursion*, l. 41.

proved upon our pulses: a staple idea of eighteenth-century sensationalist philosophy, and perhaps a specific echo of the interest of Hazlitt's *Essay* in what 'weighed upon the pulses of the blood'.

"Knowledge is Sorrow": Byron wrote 'Sorrow is Knowledge' in *Manfred* (1817), I. i. 10.

of my fragments: in a practical application of his ideas on imaginative sympathy, Keats hopes that Reynolds may be able to feel his way towards the meaning of his writing through familiarity with Keats's ways of thinking. The idea has specific echoes of Hazlitt's description of the effects of familiarity on the mind's operations in the 'Remarks' at the end of the 1805 *Essay*: 'By touching a spring, all obstacles are removed, the doors fly open, and the whole gallery is seen at a single glance—The mind has a capacity to perform any complex action the easier for having performed the same action before.'

89 *Hazlitt to Patmore*: Peter George Patmore (1765–1855), author and close friend of Hazlitt and Charles Lamb.

Coleman: George Colman, the younger (1762–1836), playwright

from Little: Thomas Moore had used the pseudonym Thomas Little.

I may dip: at this point Keats began to 'cross' his letter, that is, to write at right-angles across what he had already written. 'Dip' is the first word that dips into the other writing.

to a Milkmaid: possibly an allusion to Milton's *L'Allegro*, 65 and 96.

90 *his Genius is explorative of those dark Passages*: Keats may be suggesting that Wordsworth has explored the workings of the human heart to a certain point, but has not been able to develop it further. *The Excursion* offers a Christian consolation for suffering, but it may be significant that Keats places the emphasis on the much earlier 'Tintern Abbey'. Hazlitt took the view that he could find nothing 'in the larger poem equal to many of the detached pieces [such as 'Tintern Abbey'] in the Lyrical Ballads'. Keats later offers his ideas on the 'vale of Soul-making' as an advance on Christian ideas on suffering, see p. 232.

gregarious advance of intellect: see the comment on the 'grand march of intellect' later in the letter. Keats suggests that the developments he has been discussing are the products of a historical process of growth—a view perhaps more typical of Leigh Hunt than the sceptical Hazlitt—rather than the interventions of individual genius, and implicitly advances himself as its latest fruit (just as Wordsworth had succeeded Milton).

91 *I like that Moore*: probably Peter (not Thomas) Moore (1753–1828), MP and one of the managers of Drury Lane.

92 *for Mind there is none*: see the 'vale of Soul-making' idea, p. 232, which also rejects Christian notions of the soul for the more materialist idea of identity being formed by an intelligence responding to the buffetings of circumstance.

93 *Barnes*: Thomas Barnes (1786–1841), editor of *The Times*.

in the Oxford Paper: Bailey reviewed *Endymion* in the *Oxford University and City Herald*, 30 May and 6 June.

94 *volumes of carey*: Taylor and Hessey had just republished H. F. Cary's translation of *The Divine Comedy*.

Mister Keats': J. G. Lockhart, 'Letter from Z. to Leigh Hunt', *Blackwood's*, May 1818. The review quotes from the 'Great spirits now on earth are sojourning' and describes Keats as an 'amiable but infatuated bardling'.

in 'Foliage': Hunt's *Foliage* was reviewed in the *Quarterly*, January 1818, but Keats was not mentioned apart from a brief allusion to *Endymion*.

95 *to Bowne's*: Bowness on Lake Windermere.

Wordsworth versus Brougham!: William Lowther (later Earl Lonsdale) won the seat for the Tories against Henry Brougham, the Whig candidate. To Keats's disgust, Wordsworth was working as an agent for the Tory campaign. Henry Brougham (1778–1808) had been unofficial spokesman for the more radical wing of the Whig Party from 1810.

96 *over pendant shades"*: *Paradise Lost*, iv. 239.

98 *on Helm Craig"*: Wordsworth, 'Poems on the naming of Places. II. To Joanna', l. 56.

100 ⟨*bly . . .* ⟩: this part of the letter is torn.

to Henry: Georgiana's brother.

101 *Bunowdale*: copyist's error for Borrowdale.

102 *the Tun*: copyist's mistake for 'Sun'.

from France": Burns, 'Tam o'Shanter', l. 116.

103 *Fickly*: the word occurs in the folio *King Lear*, II. iv. 188.

——: word omitted by the copyist who queried 'Cast'.

confessed himself a Deist: the amusement stems presumably from the Scotsman not knowing the sympathies of Keats and Brown for Deism.

by Burns: the conclusion of the letter was omitted by the copyist.

104 *in the shape of a ℥*: sign for a fluid ounce.

I suppose: a draft of the poem eventually included in the 1820 volume followed. Meg Merrilies had appeared as a character in Sir Walter Scott's *Guy Mannering* (1815), but, according to Brown (*KC* ii. 61), Keats had not yet read the novel. Yet Keats may well have known of the character, who had quickly become popular, from reviews, stage versions (one of which was running while Keats was reviewing for the *Champion*), and paintings (one of which was hanging in the British Institution when he saw the Leslie and Wilkie paintings in February 1818). For details, see Claire Lamont, 'Meg the Gipsy in Scott and Keats', *English*, 36 (1987), 137–45.

109 *of parliament*: a thin flat cake.

Lady's fingers: peppermint.

112 *the king you shall go'*: a line from the popular ballad 'Robin Hood and the Bishop of Hereford'.

Hummums: a hotel near Covent Garden.

'with child': *The Faerie Queene*, I. v. i: 'The noble hart, that harbours vertuous thought, | And is with child of glorious great intent'. Keats's ideas on progress were clearly strained by the conditions he found on this walking tour, no less than by nursing his brother Tom and other personal circumstances.

113 *Laputan printing press*: see *Gulliver's Travels*, part III, ch. 5.

115 *for the hour*: Keats is parodying Coleridge's 'Christabel', l. 10.

Caliph Vatheck: see William Beckford's (1759–1844) *Vathek* (1786). Reynolds was a relative of Beckford.

little Nephews: George and Georgiana did not have their first son until 1827.

116 *to Cumberland*: Bailey was ordained in Carlisle a few days later.

118 *Annan*: Keats crossed out the wrong word, a mistake he continued to make.

119 *'profanum vulgus'*: that is, the common people, whose conditions he continuously monitors as he travels between the different countries and regions on his tour.

120 *neck's bane'*: all these quotations are from 'Tam o'Shanter'.

121 *Barrymore*: a well-known supporting actor of the time.

122 *as I can*: a rough sketch in ink is inserted here.

  and two necks: the London coaching inn from which Keats departed.

123 *Mister Lovels*: the name assumed by the hero of Scott's *The Antiquary*.

124 *the Stranger*: a play by Augustus von Kotzebue (1761–1819) first performed at Drury Lane in 1798. Reynolds described it as among 'the worst of German plays' in the *Champion* of 2 March 1817. For more on Kotzebue, see p. 217 and note.

125 *Long Island*: Luing Island.

127 *little Britain*: where George and Georgiana Keats lived.

128 *dissevering Power'*: Milton, *Comus*, l. 816.

137 *Ah mio Ben*: a pun on the popular song, 'Caro mio ben', by Giuseppe Giordani (1744–98).

139 *fours. . . .* : omitted is a comic account of a woman who climbed the mountain a few years earlier.

141 *Jessy of Dumblane*: heroine of popular Scottish song (various versions were available to Keats).

  August 18th: actually 19th.

  8th: actually 6th.

142 *to the Settlement*: George did not fulfill his intention of joining Morris Birkbeck's land settlement in Illinois.

143 *retractile claws'*: Cary's translation of Dante's *Inferno*, xvii. 101.

  Eustace—Thornton: J. C. Eustace, *A Tour of Italy* (1813), and Thomas Thornton, *The Present State of Turkey* (1807).

  a prosecution against Blackwood: the issue of *Blackwood*'s that viciously attacked Keats in its fourth Cockney School essay, August 1818, also used libellous language about Hazlitt in two articles. Hazlitt threatened to sue for libel, but the suit was dropped after the magazine made an out-of-court payment after its London agent, John Murray, withdrew his support.

  of contraries': *Paradise Lost*, ix. 121, 122.

144 *I had heard Charles say*: Dilke's only child, to whom he was devoted (to the irritation of Keats, as revealed in several of the letters that follow).

a Line of Ronsard: Woodhouse had loaned Keats a volume of Ronsard's works. The rest of the sonnet 'Nature ornant Cassandre' is freely translated in the next letter.

into my warm veins': a line from the sonnet translated in the next letter.

the rose &c': although the trope is a common one, Keats is probably referring to Fairfax's translation of Tasso's 'Gather the rose of love' from *Gerusalemme Liberata* (xvi. 15. 7) a copy of which Keats owned.

145 *that woman*: Jane Cox, whom Keats had met on a visit to the Reynolds family on 19 September. Her father seems to have died in the service of the East India Company. She was staying with the Reynolds family—Mrs Reynolds was her aunt—after becoming estranged from her grandfather. For a detailed account of Keats's feelings for her, see p. 152.

146 *who have taken my part*: letters to the *Morning Chronicle* defending him against J. W. Croker's ferocious attacks on *Endymion* in the *Quarterly*, September 1818. The letters appeared on 3 and 8 October and were signed J. S. [possibly for John Scott] and R. B. respectively.

147 *egotistical sublime*: much of the vocabulary and thinking behind this famous letter is derived from Hazlitt. Wordsworth's egotism was a recurrent theme of Hazlitt criticism; one routinely contrasted, as here, with Shakespeare's power of throwing himself into the lives of his fictional creations. The contrast to the detriment of Wordsworth seems to be more definitely affirmed here than in the 'Mansion of Many Apartments' letter, p. 89.

148 *it lives in gusto*: more of Hazlitt's habitual vocabulary. See Hazlitt's essay 'On Gusto' in *The Round Table* collection where it is defined as 'power or passion defining any object'. For Hazlitt, Shakespeare was the 'camelion Poet' above all others, because of his power to seize and communicate this defining intensity in his objects.

in for: possibly meaning 'informing'.

saturn and Ops: both of whom appear in *Hyperion*.

149 *I have Fanny*: from this time Keats started to write to his sister every fortnight.

150 *Miss Waldegrave*: who seems to have been a lodger of Henry Wylie's aunt, Mrs Millar.

151 *cut its own throat'*: Keats's own publisher, J. A. Hessey, seems to have taken this view. He wrote to his partner John Taylor on 23 October 1818 that 'Endymion begins to move at last—6 Copies have just been ordered by Simpkin & Marshall & one or two have been sold singly in the Shop —there is nothing like making a Stir for it—the papers have said so

much about it many persons will doubtless be curious to see what it does contain', *KC* i. 53.

152 *coming the Richardson*: like Samuel Richardson the novelist. Perhaps indicating the gossipy material Keats is passing on, but perhaps also indicating a Richardsonian style of 'writing to the moment'. Contrary to his generally positive treatment of the eighteenth-century novel tradition, Keats continually represents Richardson much as he represents blue-stocking opinion—with which Richardson was linked historically—in terms of an intrusive and gossipy censoriousness.

a Cousin of theirs: Jane Cox. See above, p. 145.

that nothing particular: i.e. she does not think Keats is making advances. Of course, this does not mean that he was not.

153 *his child's cradle*: Richard Hooker (1554?–1600) was not a bishop.

This is Lord Byron: in fact Leigh Hunt, *Story of Rimini*, iii. 121–2, misquoted.

soon be too wide awake: Keats is prophetic here. No less than for Keats's career as a poet, 1819 was in many ways to be an *annus mirabilis* for the radical movement.

Burdett: Sir Francis Burdett (1770–1844), aristocratic reformer. The decline in his reputation in reforming circles—reflected in Keats's comments here—coincided with the rise of the kind of mass platform politics that sat uneasily with his patrician attitudes. Many radicals felt that he had not done enough to press the case for political reform in Parliament. See the note to p. 183 below.

Milton, no Algernon Sidney: both appearing here as standard figures in the pantheon of liberty inherited from the seventeenth century and venerated by nearly all shades of reform-minded opinion. Note also the high opinion of Oliver Cromwell below.

154 *the Cause of Napoleon*: of whom the best known to Keats would have been Hazlitt.

a Godwin perfectibil[it]y Man: for Keats's reservations about the perfectibilarian philosophy of William Godwin's *Political Justice* (1793), see pp. 232, 303.

156 *day of the Month*: it was 16 October.

Mr Lewis: a neighbour who had strong democratic political sympathies. For his discussions with Keats on politics, see p. 200.

158 *Capper and Hazlewood*: stockbrokers who were also forwarding agents for mail to George.

an enigma to me: Mrs Isabella Jones, whom Keats had met at Hastings the previous summer. She seems to have been there with an elderly Whig gentlemen to whom she was close in some undefined way. Later and unbeknown to Keats, she also became intimate with his publisher John

Taylor. She seems to have had an inspiring effect on his poetry over the year that followed, and may have suggested the topic of 'The Eve of St Agnes' to Keats.

159 *staying for waftage"*: Theocritus was a Greek poet famed for his pastoral hymns to love. Keats is also thinking of Achilles fired with a desire to revenge his friend Patroclus in the *Iliad* and Troilus' anguish at the loss of Cressida (*Troilus and Cressida*, III. ii. 9–11).

160 *to Warder*: possibly the forwarding agents in the United States.

162 *December 1818*: this is the first letter in this selection written after the death of Keats's brother Tom.

a little money: Keats may be anticipating a settlement from the estate of Tom who had died a few weeks earlier.

163 *when Salmon*: Haydon's model and manservant was Corporal John Salmon.

1819

164 *B*: see p. 160; Keats had marked his previous letter to them 'A'.

of some nature of other: although Tom's death caused Keats to think seriously again about the matters of religion he had discussed with Bailey over much of 1817, especially in relation to the role of suffering in human experience, there is no reason to agree with Bailey (*KC* ii. 292) that this letter shows Keats to have been 'in no sense . . . an infidel'. For the commensurability of Deism with a belief in immortality, see Robert Ryan, *Keats: The Religious Sense*, (1976) 152–85.

165 *Bethnal green*: the area of London in which Haslam lived with his mother.

Mr and Mrs ⟨ . . . ⟩: torn paper makes the letter illegible here.

166 *to the Poles*: H. P. Hoppner (1795–1853) and Sir John Ross (1777–1856) were part of an expedition that rediscovered Baffin Bay. See the latter's *A Voyage of Discovery* (1819) for details similar to those provided by Keats.

litrerary Pocket-Book: despite the disparaging comments here, Hunt's *Literary Pocket-Book* (1819) contains the first printed versions of Keats's own 'Four Seasons Fill' and 'To Ailsa Rock'.

edinburgh Reviewer: that is, the *Scots* or *Edinburgh Magazine* not the *Edinburgh Review*. See note to p. 56.

Archer: probably the painter Archibald Archer.

Poor Kirkman: probably the stationer G. B. Kirkman, a relative of George Felton Mathew.

167 *Howard Payne, an American*: Payne's (1793–1852) *Brutus, Or, The Fall of Tarquin* opened on 3 December at Drury Lane. The *Examiner* gave it a more positive reception than Keats on 6 December 1818. Its subject—

the assassination of the Roman tyrant Tarquin—guaranteed it at least partial approval from those quarters.

daughter senior: the first mention of Fanny Brawne anywhere in the extant letters.

This morning: 17 December.

Gifford's: in fact Croker's attack. See p. 146 n.

168 *one of the Misses Porter*: Jane Porter (1776–1850). Porter was one of the earliest writers of historical romance, including, for instance *The Scottish Chiefs* (1804); her forays into drama were less successful with the public. She also collaborated on a series of popular romances with her sister Anna (1780–1832). Keats is typically condescending to a female admirer of his work, despite the fact that her writing was considerably better known than his at the time.

170 *Mr Snooks*: Dilke's brother-in-law, John Snook.

he knew Barttolozzi: Francesco Bartolozzi (1727–1815), celebrated painter and engraver.

171 *she is not seventeen*: in fact she was over 18.

that Miss Robinson: Caroline Robinson.

Gattie: John Byng Gattie, a relative of the Olliers.

Altam and his Wife: Ollier's *Altham and his Wife: A Domestic Tale* (1818).

172 *George Drewe*: Reynolds was engaged to his daughter Eliza Powell Drewe.

Horace Twisse's: Horace Twiss (1787–1849) wit, author, and politician; another member of Horace Smith's circle.

and Charles Kemble: John Liston (1776?–1846) and Kemble (1775–1854) were actors. Kemble was Kean's chief rival at the time. His more restrained style was often contrasted with Kean's 'gusto'.

173 *the scotch nove(ls)*: Keats is consciously praising Scott as poet and novelist. Scott's secret authorship of the 'scotch' or Waverley novels was 'no longer kept' according to the *Examiner*, 17 May 1818.

Fenbank: a pseudonym.

174 *my large poem*: 'Hyperion'.

175 *Mrs Tighe and Beattie*: the poets Mary Tighe (1772–1810) and James Beattie (1735–1803) whom Keats had been reading since his schooldays. These comments reflect Keats's continuing anxiety about his relationship with female readers and writers (note how quickly he turns to the topic of women in general and bluestockings in particular). Tighe's allegorical *Psyche* (1805/11) was extremely popular and a direct influence on the luxuriant style of his early poetry (see, for instance, 'Imitation of Spenser' and 'Calidore'). Yet despite his repudiation of Tighe for a more masculine poetics here, the influence continued, for instance, in the

Spenserianism of 'The Eve of St Agnes', written only a few weeks after this letter, and at the very least in the subject of 'Ode to Psyche'.

175 *Mackenzie's father Nicholas*: the sentimental Henry Mackenzie's (1745–1831) 'Story from Father Nicholas' appeared in *The Lounger*, 82–4 (1786). Despite the disparagement here, the relationship to Mackenzie's story may—as in the case of Tighe—be more complex than it seems. Mackenzie's preamble indicates that his purpose is a matter close to Keats's heart, that is, the idea that the deepest impressions are made 'when the understanding is addressed through the feelings'. The opposition Keats makes between 'grandeur' and 'mawkishness' suggests he is still trying to distance his interest in 'the human heart' from the effeminate associations of Mackenzie's brand of sensibility.

the name of which I forget: not frescoes from Milan, but Carlo Lasinio's *Pitture a fresco del Compo Santo di Pisa* (1812).

180 *on Caleb Williams by Hazlitt*: Keats is quoting from Hazlitt's lecture 'On the English Novelists'. The series, which Keats did not attend, 'On the English Comic Writers' ran from 3 November 1818 to 5 January 1819. The passage here seems to come from the lengthy notice in the *Examiner* for 27 December 1818, but Keats may have had access to the manuscript.

182 *Sunday*: 3 January 1819.

Manker: written Mancur elsewhere, a friend of Charles Brown.

183 *27 years old*: she was 26. Keats had written verses to Caroline and her sister Ann in 1815 ('To Some Ladies' and 'On Receiving a Curious Shell'), which he published in *Poems* (1817).

a good Character of Cobbet: William Cobbett (1763–1835) radical journalist, whose twopenny version of his *Political Register*—after originally appearing as a conservative paper—pioneered the spread of radical politics into a new mass readership at the beginning of the nineteenth century. Cobbett fled to America in 1817 when the government suspended habeas corpus (a measure he took to be primarily directed against himself). He returned to England in November 1819 in the wake of the Peterloo Massacre. The character sketch mentioned by Keats is a response to attacks on Burdett (see p. 153 n.) prior to the Westminster election of 1819. The sketch took the *Examiner*'s usual tack on Cobbett, that is, applauding his contribution to the revival of the cause of reform, but condemning his vanity and vulgarity. The election split reformist opinion between Burdett's man John Cam Hobhouse (1786–1869) and the more radical veteran reformer Major Cartwright (1740–1824). In the event, the Whig candidate George Lamb won the election in February. Keats was obviously keenly interested in the result. See p. 200 for his discussion of the issues with his democratic neighbour David Lewis.

written about it: T. E. Bowdich (1791–1824), *Mission from Cape Coast Castle to Ashantee* (1819).

184 *Sir Lucius*: the fiery Irishman Sir Lucius O' Trigger from Sheridan's *The Rivals*.

185 *procuring the Money*: see p. 162, where Keats seems to offer a loan.

I smoke: that is, 'discern' in cant. For a discussion of the whole range of meanings and anxieties Keats associated with this word, see James Chandler, *England in 1819* (1998), 398–402, who notes that its use roughly coincides with Keats's *annus mirabilis*.

186 *a School-fellow of mine*: James Peachey.

187 *a Bam*: a diversionary tactic.

188 *qui bono temper*: *Cui bono*, here, as often, used to express a sense of world weariness.

yesterday's Examiner: see the painter's own article 'Attacks on Mr Haydon', the *Examiner*, 7 March 1819.

Wordsworth and Hunt, are the same: Keats brings Hunt and Wordsworth together again in another attack on egotism and posturing. The Keatsian ideal of conversation as a means to truth is contrasted with the affectation he found in the public performances of these two very different literary figures.

189 *a Tassi*: these enamel gems had been made popular by James Tassie (1735–99) and his nephew William (1777–1860); the latter's shop was in Leicester Square. Keats took to using one in the shape of a lyre as a seal for his letters soon after Christmas 1818.

190 *at the Westminster school*: the Dilkes left Wentworth Place on 3 April, and the Brawne family moved in.

in the exhibition': Severn's miniature of Keats was shown in the Royal Academy Exhibition at Somerset House in May.

191 *those questions*: Fanny was undergoing instruction for her Confirmation from a clergyman. The help Keats provides here shows a good knowledge of the basic tenets of the Church of England. Ryan points out what would have been construed as a single error from the Anglican point of view, that is, his identification of John the Baptist rather than Christ as the founder of the rite of baptism. The way he signs off suggests his habitual anticlericalism in a letter otherwise uncharacteristically earnest about the 'parsonic' matters. See Ryan, *Keats: The Religious Sense*, 187–8.

194 *a Law[y]er's*: the solicitor was William Walton. There is no evidence that Keats was correct.

much less than I thought for: Keats's portion of Tom's estate was much less than he had expected.

197 *old Mr Dilke's*: actually he went to Snook's for the fortnight after Dilke's.

Mr Towers: Charles Cowden Clarke's brother-in-law.

a stupe: a medical term for a piece of flannel wrung out and used to foment a wound.

197 *attacking the Settlement*: see 'To Morris Birkbeck', *Cobbett's Weekly Political Register*, 6 and 13 February 1819.

198 *C C. C.*: Cowden Clarke.

and one by Miss Jane Porter: Richard Lalor Sheil (1791–1851) was the author of *The Apostate* presented at Covent Garden in 1817. His new play was *Evadne*. Jane Porter's tragedy *Switzerland* was a disaster and ran for one night only.

under six foot and not a lord: one of the best-known statements of Keats's sense of social discomfort. Although Lewis's point of view is rarely considered, it is possible his comment on Keats's pretensions is the perspective of a Cobbett-man (see p. 200 n.) on a reader of Hunt. The *Examiner* routinely disparaged Cobbett's lack of imagination and taste.

it must be Ollier's: actually the article was by Lamb, see the *Examiner*, 14 February.

199 *Knox ... Southcote—Gifford*: John Knox, Scottish religious reformer; George Fox, founder of the Quakers, and Joanna Southcott (1750–1814) popular prophet, all of whom the *Examiner* and its readers, like Keats, would probably have regarded as examples of the kind of deluded fanaticism that all too often appealed to the populace. Gifford was the editor of the *Quarterly* whom Keats suspected of writing its attack on *Endymion*. See his reference to Hazlitt's *Letter to William Gifford*, p. 206.

Davenport's: Burridge Davenport, a merchant who lived nearby in Hampstead.

Carlisle: Richard Carlile (1790–1843). Radical journalist, publisher, and freethinker. His blend of republicanism and Deism was responsible for reviving the reputation of Thomas Paine. He was arrested on 11 February for republishing Paine's *Age of Reason* and other freethinking works, but not tried (and found guilty) until October. The '*Hone* principle' marks Keats's recognition of the tactic of attacking the State through the Church. Keats gives a more accurate account of Carlile's case, p. 291.

200 *a Mr Way*: Stansted Park had recently been acquired by the wealthy evangelical philanthropist, Lewis Way (1772–1840). Way was devoted to the cause of converting the Jews. Keats was going to witness the consecration of the chapel Way had built in the cause. Obviously the tone of his account, not to mention the comments on Carlile's case earlier, indicates his religious scepticism, but the chapel does seem to have offered Keats another example of Gothic style to be later absorbed into 'The Eve of St Agnes'.

his favorite democrat papers: the phrase 'democrat paper', used, as it seems to me, here with a distancing effect, suggests the publications of Carlile, Cobbett, and Wooller, etc. rather than the *Examiner*. On the complications of the Westminster election, and Cobbett's opinions on it, see p. 183 and note.

201 *in my last I think*: Isabella Jones.

202 *Miss Martin*: Bailey's brother Edward was married to Elizabeth, sister of John Martin.

203 *but Jeremy Taylors*: Jeremy Taylor's *The Golden Grove* (1655) was a devotional manual.

204 *On Monday*: two paragraphs were left out of this letter, and sent on with the letter of 17–27 September, with this note (dated '1820' by mistake by the copyist):

> 18th September 1820—In looking over some of my papers, I found the above specimen of my carelessness—It is a sheet you ought to have had long ago my letter must have appeared very unconnected, but as I number the sheets you must have discovered how the mistake happened—how many things happened since I wrote it. How have I acted contrary to my resolves; The interval between writing this sheet, & the day I put this supplement to it, has been completely filled with generous & most friendly actions of Brown towards me. How frequently I forget to speak of things, which I think of & feel most. T"is very singular the idea about Buffon above, has been taken up by Hunt in the Examiner, in some papers which he calls 'A Preter-Natural History'

Hunt's essays appeared in the *Examiner*, 1, 8, and 15 August 1819.

Cawthorn: James Cawthorn of the British Library.

to see Sheild's new tragedy: copyist's mistake for 'Sheil'. See above, p. 198 n.

the Augustan age of the Drama: Stuart Sperry, 'Keats's Skepticism and Voltaire', *KSJ* 12 (1963), 75–93, points out that the allusion is sardonic. For Voltaire the Augustan age was one of artistic excellence, as made clear by his *Siècle de Louis XIV*, a text Keats was reading around this time (see p. 231).

to the tune of 15.2: a score in cribbage.

205 *St Lukes*: a lunatic asylum.

Mr Rogers: Samuel Rogers (1763–1855) wealthy and successful poet, admired by Byron. Hazlitt's lecture 'On the Living Poets' declared his work to be 'tantalizing, teasing, tripping, lisping *mimminee-pimminee*'. These 'lady-like' qualities were precisely what Keats feared that reviewers had 'smoked' in his own work. See my Introduction for a fuller discussion of this issue of Keats and femininity.

none of Crabbe: Keats's admiration for Hazlitt seems to have remained undiminished throughout his life. The half of Wordsworth he does not admire, one assumes, is a combination of what he came to see under Hazlitt's influence as the too palpable moral designs in *The Excursion* and elsewhere and what Hazlitt and others took to be his childish interest in country folk. For Keats on the former, see p. 58 and note above, and for his comments on Betty Foy *et al.*, below, p. 225. Hazlitt, of course, gave Crabbe 'an unmerciful licking' in his lectures on English poetry; see p. 59 above.

205 *Parsons will always keep up their Character*: a phrase that may echo Hazlitt's extended essay 'On the Clerical Character' in *The Yellow Dwarf*, 24, 31 January and 7 February 1818. Obviously these reflections are related to those on Way's chapel (p. 200) and Bailey's behaviour (pp. 202–3) towards Marian Reynolds.

206 *Buffon or Pliny*: Pliny was the Roman editor of a well-known encyclopaedia of natural history. George-Louis Buffon was a French naturalist and author of a multi-volume *Natural History* completed only after his death.

& have Milnes: copyist's error for Joseph Milner (1744–97), whose *History of the Church of Christ* (1794–1809) was completed by his brother Isaac.

Letter to Gifford: William Hazlitt, *A Letter to William Gifford* (1819). The brilliant invective of the pamphlet was a response to the hostile reviews in the *Quarterly* of Hazlitt's *The Round Table*, *Characters of Shakespeare's Plays*, and *Lectures on the English Poets*. In fact, Gifford himself only had a hand in the last. The delight in Hazlitt's coruscating attack is personal as well as ideological for Keats. Keats thought Gifford had written the attack on *Endymion* in the *Quarterly*. See pp. 167–8 and 199 above.

209 *and not in proportion to their strong and often tragical effect*: repetition due to Keats's hasty copying.

211 *Hodgkinson*: a junior partner in Abbey's firm with whom George Keats seems to have quarrelled when he worked in his guardian's office. Keats detested him, see pp. 243, 264.

the 'False one': Beaumont and Fletcher's *The False One*.

212 *Castle of indolence*: James Thomson's *The Castle of Indolence*.

disguisement: compare 'Ode on Indolence'.

213 *must pluck*: compare 'Ode on Melancholy'.

"We have all one human heart": Wordsworth's 'The old Cumberland Beggar', l. 153.

214 *pious frauds of Religion*: Ryan, *Keats: The Religious Sense*, 184, points out that this phrase was frequently used by Voltaire.

as is Apollo's lute": *Comus*, ll. 475–7.

Nothing ever becomes real till it is experienced: an idea fundamental to the sensationalist philosophy Keats imbibed from Hazlitt and elsewhere. See also pp. 36, 69, 88.

throug[h] my human passions: another step towards the 'vale of Soul-making' idea outlined on p. 232.

215 *could I on this very midnight cease*: compare 'Ode to a Nightingale', l. 56.

The Framptons: wholesale grocers, who employed Haslam's father.

216 *Wells and Amena*: C. J. Wells wrote letters signed 'Amena Bellefila' hoaxing Tom Keats into believing a girl was in love with him. Keats never forgave Wells.

the Boys: that is, Brown's nephews.

a skit upon it call'd Peter Bell: J. H. Reynolds's *Peter Bell A Lyrical ballad* was published anonymously by Taylor & Hessey on 15 April. Words-worth's poem, although written in 1798, did not appear until later that month. Reynolds's poem expresses the frustration with Wordsworth's egotism, moral didacticism, and ruralism of Keats and many others in his circle. Keats's opinion of the poem was published as a review in the *Examiner* for 25 April.

"Bold stroke for a Wife": in Susannah Centlivre's play of this title, Simon Pure is a 'quaking preacher'.

217 *and one Mr Bucke*: see p. 73 and note.

Germany! Germany!: Kotzebue was assassinated by the young student Karl Ludwig Sand on 23 March 1819. Widely regarded as a traitor to his native land, Kotzebue had been working in Germany as an agent of the Russian government. The *Examiner* covered the story closely throughout April, disapproving of assassination as a political method, but also taking the view that Sand's patriotism had been inflamed into fanaticism by the despots who had resumed control of Germany after the defeat of Napoleon. Sand did not succeed in killing himself, but lived to be executed soon afterwards. See p. 291, for Keats's idealized view of him.

219 *A quavering*: changed from 'they quaver'd' and 'And quaver'd'.

220 *at Guy's*: Joseph Henry Green (1791–1863) had been one of Keats's demonstrators at Guy's Hospital. Coleridge gave a brief account of this encounter in his *Table Talk* (1832).

221 *olden Tom or ruin blue*: both names for gin.

nantz: brandy.

222 *Skinner*: Robert Skynner, Brown's solicitor.

John Brown: Brown's brother, John Armitage Brown.

223 *bever and wet*: that is, a snack and a drink.

224 *a cold Pig*: that is, a splash of water to wake him up.

false florimel: a reference to *The Faerie Queene*, III. viii. 5–20.

225 *bob cherry*: a party game, but 'bob' was also slang for sexual intercourse.

with Barbara Lewthwaite: heroine of Wordsworth's 'The Pet Lamb'.

225 *those three rhyming Graces Alice Fell, Susan Gale and Betty Foy*: see Wordsworth's 'The Idiot Boy'. Keats expresses a preference for the grandeur of *The Excursion* over the poems of rustic life in the *Lyrical Ballads*. The latter were also routinely depreciated by Hazlitt, although he—and it seems Keats too eventually—preferred poems like 'Tintern Abbey' to the explicit morality of the longer poem.

'the heart of Mid Lothian': Daniel Terry's (1780?–1829) musical version of Scott's *The Heart of Midlothian* was presented at Covent Garden on 17 April.

with the Panorama: Sir John Franklin (1786–1847) set off in April on his first Arctic expedition. Henry Aston Barker's panorama in Leicester Square showed scenes of the coast of Spitzbergen. Panoramas were 360-degree paintings housed in a rotunda. Immensely popular, Barker's opened in 1793 and remained a landmark in the city until the 1860s.

226 *Wednesday Evening—*: 21 April.

231 *Robertson's America*: William Robertson's (1721–93), *The History of America* (1777) and Voltaire's *Le Siècle de Loius XIV*. Details from Robertson's book famously influenced the early sonnet 'On First Looking into Chapman's Homer'.

232 *this sort of perfectibility*: see the comments on Dilke's attachment to Godwin's ideas on perfectibility, p. 154, and, especially, p. 303.

vale of Soul-making': the discussion here seems to develop the idea of the Pleasure Thermometer from the letter to John Taylor of January 1818 (see p. 57) and build upon Hazlitt's ideas about the knowledge of the sufferings of others developing our moral character. Although it acknowledges the idea of an afterlife, it represents the soul as the product of the complex interplay of sensation and imagination outlined in Hazlitt's psychology contrary to the Christian doctrine against which it is explicitly developed. Once again Keats aligns himself with historical process on a personal and cultural level; he is implicitly presenting himself as a prophet of a new religion of the human heart that advances beyond Christianity, an idea relevant to the subject of 'Ode to Psyche' copied out later in the letter.

236 *in the old religion*: Keats is indebted to Lempriere's *Classical Dictionary*, which he owned, for the details, but he would also have known of the story from Mary Tighe's *Psyche; or, The Legend of Love*. See p. 175. It is also worth pointing out, given the importance of the name for Keats, Voltaire's *Dictionaire philosophique*, which Keats owned, identified Psyche with the sensations. This identification sits well with the riposte to Christian ideas of the soul in the 'vale of Soul-making' part of this letter. For a fuller discussion of this point, See James Chandler, *England in 1819* (1998), 413–14.

239 *to and from India*: faced with financial difficulties, including a potential

suit against Tom's estate (see p. 243), Keats was considering working as a ship's surgeon for the East India Company. Note that the idea crops up again in the next few letters.

240 *glory in the flower*: slightly misquoted lines from Wordsworth, 'Ode: Intimations of Immortality', ll. 181–2.

241 *to whom I am greatly attached*: James Rice.

as Boyardo did?: Matteo Maria Boiardo, author of *Orlando Innamorato*, ordered the church bells to be rung when he thought of a name for one of the characters in his poem.

a versifying Pet-lamb: see the 'Ode on Indolence'. A pointed comment to a female reader. One of several attempts by Keats around this time to distance himself from the influence of women as readers and writers and assert a masculine identity for his poetry. See pp. 175 and 257 and the discussion of Keats and women in the Introduction.

242 *Master Yorkshire Man*: probably a young relative of Abbey, who came from Yorkshire originally.

243 *Chancery against us*: the threatened suit against Tom's estate was never filed. The aunt is Mrs Margaret Jennings who had unsuccessfully filed a suit against Keats's mother in 1811. For details, see Andrew Motion, *Keats* (1997), 39 and 411–12. Motion suggests that Abbey misled Keats about the likelihood of the suit to quell his demands for money.

one more attempt in the Press: faced with the news of the threatened suit, Keats seems to have revised the dismissive attitude towards writing for money and the public often found in the letters (for an useful account of these changes in attitude, see Andrew Bennett's *Keats, Narrative and Audience: The Posthumous Life of Writing* (1994)). The next letter suggests Brown was also influential in this change of heart, which included co-writing *Otho the Great* for the stage.

'ye hear no more of me': Chaucer, *Legend of Good Women*, l. 1557.

sent them Mr Elmes on Monday: that is, 'Ode to a Nightingale'. The poem was published by James Elmes (1782–1862) in *Annals of the Fine Arts*, July 1819.

245 *Heloise*: in his essay on Rousseau in *The Round Table*, Hazlitt compared Rousseau to Wordsworth in so far as: 'His interest in his own thoughts and feelings was always wound up to the highest pitch.' Keats may be apologizing for becoming similarly obsessed with his own feelings in the letter he did not send.

turn up Pam: knave of clubs, the highest trump in five-card loo.

246 *were beyond expression!*: Philip Massinger's *Duke of Milan*, I. iii, misquoted.

love to Margaret: Fanny's sister.

247 *gallipots*: a nickname for an apothecary. The word was used in Lockhart's

review of *Poems* and *Endymion*, which may have been in Keats's mind here.

249   *To J. H. Reynolds, 11 July 1819*: an extract from a longer letter now lost.

  Jack & Idle Joe: see Matthew Prior 'An Epitaph' in *Poems on several Occasions*: 'Saunt'ring Jack and Idle Joan'.

  the Act: Keats was writing *Otho the Great* with Brown.

  what I have said to George: this letter has disappeared.

251   *an oriental tale of a very beautiful color*: Keats was reading Henry Weber's *Tales of the East* (1812), ii. 666–74.

253   *and tell Sam*: Fanny's brother.

255   *Manassah*: see p. 58 and note.

  Reynolds's Piece succeeded: a farce *One, Two, Three, Four, Five: By Advertisement*, first performed on 17 July 1819 and published soon afterwards. See the account of its success Keats gave to his brother and sister-in-law, p. 287.

  for little stockings: slang for illegitimate children.

  2ᵈ lie: the underlined phrases were written by Brown.

256   *the Statue of Maleager*: Meleager. The statue in the Vatican was widely regarded as one of the most beautiful statues ever made.

257   *revolution in modern dramatic writing*: an ambition which, given Keats's sustained interest in the theatre, perhaps ought to be taken more seriously than it usually is.

  another to upset the drawling of the blue stocking literary world: another assertion of freedom from female influence. See Introduction.

258   *August 17th*: during his stay at Winchester, Keats constantly made mistakes over the date, often postmarking his letters one day before the date he gives them, as here.

261   *the wings of independence*: note the tone of abrasive defensiveness in a letter asking his publisher for money. See the discussion of 'independence' in the Introduction.

  To beg suffrages: see Katherine Phillips, 'Upon a scandalous libel made by J. J.' which has the line 'To beg the Suffrage of a Vulgar Tongue'.

264   *Hodgkinson, whose name I cannot bear to write*: see p. 211 n.

  Young: Charles Mayne Young (1777–1856), actor. Kean did not, in fact, go to America that winter. Kean's availability was important not only because Keats greatly admired his acting, but also because he was essential to the play's commercial success.

265   *to each others note*': *Paradise Lost*, iv. 683.

  Mandeville and Lisle: characters from William Godwin's *Mandeville* (1817), who punctuate their hours of sitting silently together with bouts of violent cursing.

mulcted: literally 'to punish with a forfeit'; that is, Keats has borrowed too much from Brown already.

267 *a withe axe*: a primitive axe with a flexible handle.

270 *of the Story*: extensive changes were made to the published version.

Fleet Street: written from Taylor and Hessey's office.

my brother George: George's letter told Keats of his financial difficulties in America.

271 *in solitarinesse"*: from 'The Eve of St Mark', l. 106.

composed upon it: that is, 'To Autumn'.

273 *for being jocular*: the catchphrase of Master Vellum in Addison's play, *The Drummer*.

as wordsworth says: see 'The Idiot Boy', l. 289

Sed thongum formosa vale vale inquit Heigh ho la!: Virgil's *Eclogues*, iii. 79, has 'Et longum "formose, vale, vale," inquit, "Iolla"', that is, 'and he bade a long farewell, "fair Iollas, farewell, farewell"'. Keats uses 'thongum' to refer to the coachman's whip, raised to greet the young women he passes.

276 *a sort of induction*: that is, to 'The Fall of Hyperion'.

circumvallation: the lines of verse, across which he is now writing at right-angles.

the fairy tale Undine: George Soane, *Undine; or the Spirit of the Waters* (1818) translated from the German.

the American Brown's novels: that is, Charles Brockden Brown (1771–1810).

S[c]hiller's Armenian: William Render's 1800 translation of Schiller's *The Armenian; or, The Ghost Seer*.

277 *too smokeable*: here 'too easy to see through or mock'.

278 *old Bramble yet*: what follows is an imitation of Smollett's *Humphry Clinker* inspired by Woodhouse staying in Bath.

Look at x x x x x x: the omitted name is 'Reynolds'.

279 *the liberal side of the question*: like Hazlitt, whose advice Keats says on the next page he will seek, and Hunt. Keats is still thinking about a career in the press, but one which will not conflict with his ideological principles. See the discountenancing of writing for Tory papers such as *Blackwood's* in the letter to Dilke of the same day.

I like x x x x x x x x x: probably meaning Fanny Brawne.

280 *a dead lump. x x x x x x x x x x x x x x x*: omission by copyist.

straight to x x x x: either Chichester or Bedhampton.

281 *a cock pit in three battles*: a 'cock pit' was a slang term for the vagina.

'Battle' here, like 'throw', suggests sexual intercourse. The idea leads on to the phrase 'on the common', that is, Keats is presenting to Dilke the prospect of himself prostituting his talents.

281 *"as good as the times allow, Sir"*: Massinger, *A Very Woman*, III. i.

obstinate & heady as a Radical: although the distinction between 'radical' and 'liberal' was not rigorously applied in Keats's time, this phrase, with its implicit identification of radicalism with irresponsibility, does seem to contrast 'radical' politics with the 'liberal' side of the question he hopes to aid. For a fuller discussion of these terms, see my Introduction.

282 *present public proceedings*: these are detailed in the letter to George and Georgiana, see below, p. 291 and note.

looking letters": misquotation of Sheridan, *The Rivals*, IV. i. 77.

283 *to x x x x*: Dilke's name omitted by copyist.

my Letter to Fry: Fry seems to have been the other trustee of the Keats property appointed by Abbey after John Nowland Sandell died in 1816; see p. 315. He left for Holland some time after agreeing to act as trustee.

284 *a Man of Property*: John James Audubon (1785–1851), naturalist. Audubon had persuaded George to invest in a river trading-boat venture that failed.

I am a weaver boy: that is, an uneducated poet such as Samuel Bamford (1788–1872), who had recently published as the 'Weaver Boy'. Note Keats's sensitivity to being mistaken for a member of the working classes. See also p. 304.

286 *in the Spectator*: *The Spectator*, No. 371, 6 May 1712.

287 *span long elf*: Ben Jonson, *The Sad Shepherd*, II. viii. 53.

288 *I here coppy for you*: Robert Burton, *The Anatomy of Melancholy*, III. 2. iv. i.

289 *effect could Mathews*: Charles Mathews (1776–1835), popular comedian and another member of Horace Smith's circle of friends.

literary ambition: *Don Juan*, canto I, stanza 218.

290 *the coffee-german*: probably a relative or friend of Abbey in the coffee business.

gradually more enlighten'd: Keats's view of change is based on an idea of historical process rather than the kind of rational enlightenment associated, for instance, with Godwin's ideas of perfectibility. See his distaste for Dilke's Godwinian principles, p. 303.

291 *of great moment*: Keats updates and corrects the account of Carlile's arrest given earlier. See p. 199.

entry into London: Henry Hunt (1773–1835) had been on the platform at the Peterloo Masscre on St Peter's Field, Manchester, 16 August 1819. Ordered to arrest Hunt, the yeomanry charged an unarmed reform meeting killing ten people and injuring hundreds of others. Released on bail, Hunt led a procession into London from Manchester on 13 September where he was greeted by the enormous crowds described by Keats. For reformist opinion, Peterloo marked a defining moment in the struggle for political change that had been gathering pace from the end of the Napoleonic Wars. It became a symbol of the heartlessness and irresponsibility of the political élite, and encouraged many moderates to press for fundamental political change.

Crown and anchor: a tavern in the Strand long associated with political activities.

Sands: see above, p. 217.

292 *but yourselves— . . .* : Keats copies the acrostic along with a large section of the 23, 26 July letter to Tom (both with slight variations and additions) that have been omitted here.

a large Q: perhaps to indicate the end of the quotation from the letter to Tom.

Monday: this passage was repeated in the letter to Reynolds of 21 September.

Lady Bellaston: from Fielding's *Tom Jones*.

293 *Some time since*: on 13 February.

Ut tibi placent!: 'Take them as you please!'

296 *as Fusili*: Henri Fuseli (1741–1825), artist. Keats later puns on the words fusil = musket.

297 *the poor Sculpsit*: on engravings *Pinxit* referred to the original artist and *Sculpsit* to the engraver who made the copy. The point of the joke is that Severn may be the father only in name.

the Life-Academy: slang for brothel.

298 *woman of Brentford*: *The Merry Wives of Windsor*, IV. v. 24–5.

299 *2.6 per fag*: that is, per lesson.

he knew Hook: Theodore Hook (1788–1841), humourist and novelist. He was close to Smith.

John Bunyan's emblems: Bunyan's *Book for Boys and Girls* (1686) was called *Divine Emblems* in later editions.

against Hammond: Thomas Hammond, to whom Keats had been apprenticed in Edmonton from 1810 until he went to Guy's Hospital. Whatever their disagreement was about, Hammond must have supported Keats's application to Guy's (where Hammond himself had trained).

301 *a Poem to Murray*: John Murray (1778–1843), publisher. This would have felt like a particularly distasteful kind of prostitution to Keats, as Murray

was originally the London agent of *Blackwood's* and the publisher of the *Quarterly*. Presumably Keats was attracted by the commercial successes of Murray's authors, especially Byron.

302 *dated from shanklin*: this letter seems not to have survived.

303 *Godwin-methodist*: this judgement on Dilke here echoes Hazlitt's on Godwin himself. Hazlitt's discussion of Godwin in 'On the English Novelists' put forward the view that his utilitarian philosophy was guilty of abstracting 'the influence of reason or the understanding in moral questions and relations from that of habit, sense, association, local and personal attachment, natural affection, &c.'. When earlier in the letter Keats says he wishes to 'devote myself to another sensation', he is signalling a turn away from Milton's grandeur towards what Hazlitt's lecture called our 'imperfect, and mixed being'.

304 *the manchester we[a]vers*: the weavers of Manchester and the surrounding Lancashire went on strike during September and October 1818. They won short-lived concessions, but several of the leaders were prosecuted and imprisoned. In view of Keats's feelings about being thought of as a 'weaver-boy' (see p. 284), notice how Keats's joke subtly distances literary pun-makers from artisan pin-makers and weavers even as it seems to bring them together.

Pun mote: either a pun on *bon mot*, or if Keats meant to write 'note', on pound note.

Nevey: nephew.

306 *make me sneeze*: pun on 'rappee' (a kind of snuff).

307 *I can have—"*: *Otho the Great*, I. iii. 24–9.

308 *"I Rab am here"*: Burns, 'Second Epistle to J. Lapraik', l. 60.

as Hunt: Henry Hunt (see p. 291 and note).

309 *maximus domo*: Keats is suggesting that but for Haydon's achievement he would have been the greatest rather than merely one of the greater living artists.

the portentous Book: an attack by the art critic William Carey (1759–1839) in *A Desultory Exposition of an Anti-British System of Incendiary Publication* (1819).

Memoirs of Menage: Gilles Ménage's *Menagiana*.

Lord Ms: Sir George Beaumont (1753–1827) and the Earl of Mulgrave (1755–1831) were patrons with whom Haydon had fallen out.

310 *College Street*: in Westminster.

hertè mine!: a recurrent phrase in Chaucer's *Troilus and Criseyde*.

311 *against the reasons of my Love"*: John Ford, *'Tis Pity She's a Whore*, I. iii. 78.

Great Smith Street: that is, written from Dilke's house.

dream again"): *The Tempest*, III. ii. 141.

312 *indeed all america*: in 'the Panic of 1819', credit for pioneering ventures was difficult to obtain. There was also a shorter slump in England; see the next letter.

313 *nothing from Elliston*: Robert William Elliston (1774–1831), actor-manager, was considering the play for Drury Lane.

314 *Hunt was arrested the other day*: for debt. Leigh Hunt was about to move to Kentish Town in order to reduce his living expenses.

the Writers of Elizabeth's reign: Hazlitt's lectures were given at the Surrey Institution between 5 November and 24 December 1819. He quoted l. 237 of 'Sleep and Poetry' in his opening lecture. Keats was obviously thrilled to be mentioned in public by one of his heroes. He cannot help mentioning it again in the next letter.

your original design: that is, to have joined the Birkbeck settlement.

315 *from Fry*: see p. 283 and note.

the surry Institution: Keats is making a joking reference to Hazlitt's quotation from his works. See the previous letter for details.

316 *Ode to Lord Castlereagh*: I have not been able to trace any specific ode, but Keats may just mean Tory panegyric in general, or even the many attacks being written on the government in the wake of Peterloo.

new Jerusalem: here Keats is probably thinking of Joseph Proud's much reprinted *Hymns and Psalms for the Use of the Lord's New Church, signified by the New Jerusalem* (5th edition, 1818).

Cave of despair: Severn's painting (of a scene from *The Faerie Queene*) was hanging in the Royal Academy. He was awarded the gold medal in the following month.

Chaucer than Ariosto: signalling his interest in the human comedy of Chaucer's 'Men and women' over the wonders of Ariosto's romances.

a few fine Plays: a reiteration of his interest in a serious future in the theatre beyond *Otho the Great*.

Holingshed's Elisabeth: Raphael Holinshed, *Chronicles of England, Scotland, and Ireland*.

317 *to see Macready in Ludolph*: William Charles Macready (1793–1873), actor.

the fit is on me": Beaumont and Fletcher, *Wit without Money*, V. iv. 55.

318 *to Covent Garden*: this idea, which was Brown's, failed, and the play was not performed.

319 *"My name is norval"*: opening words of John Home's (1722–1808) *Douglas*, a popular recitation piece

323 *of Wyoming*: very popular poem of 1809 by Thomas Campbell (1777–1844) with an American setting.

324 *like a Shade"*: *The Faerie Queen*, I. i. 14.

325 *Tom cribean*: that is, his humour is like Thomas Moore's in *Tom Crib's Memorial to Congress* (1819). Keats may have read the extracts published in the *Examiner* in April 1819.

326 *Momus*: Greek god of satire and ridicule.

327 *I can speak out*: Keats had suffered a severe haemorrhage from the lungs on 3 February.

328 *those Letters*: letters from George written before he sailed from Liverpool.

the late king: George III died 29 January 1820.

329 *Old Peter Pindar*: See p. 43 and note.

330 *the tongues and the Bones*: *A Midsummer Night's Dream*, IV. i. 29 slightly altered.

331 *my essence steal*: 'Isabella', xl. 7–8.

to the Cressid: that is, to unfaithfulness.

334 *remains very purple*: first written 'purplue'.

335 *of noble minds"*: Milton's *Lycidas*, l. 71, misquoted.

336 *his famous novel*: the famous novel, of course, is *La Nouvelle Heloïse*, which Keats had in his library, but here he refers to *Correspondance originale et inédite de J. J. Rousseau avec Mme. Latour de Franqueville et M. du Peyrou* (1803).

337 *Mr Barry Cornwall*: pseudonym of Bryan Waller Procter (1787–1874). The books were his *Dramatic Scenes* (1819) and *A Sicilian Story* (1820). See the next letter.

and Stray-days: Keats is referring to his 'The Cap and Bells', which remained unfinished at his death, and for which Reynolds was to have written comic notes.

as at Paris: an opinion perhaps suggested by Tom's visit in 1817.

an Ode of Horace's: See *Odes*, i. 3.

338 *Pathetic about Memory*: Keats may be referring to any one of several melancholy lyrics by Moore.

339 *Thistlewood*: Dilke's letter had presumably been discussing the fate of Arthur Thistlewood (1770–1820), the ultra-radical arrested for his part in the conspiracy to assassinate the cabinet discovered on 23 February in a police raid on a stable in Cato Street. Within hours of their arrest, rumours were circulating that Thistlewood and his co-conspirators were the victims of *agents provocateurs*. Thistlewood was found guilty of high treason and hanged on 1 May.

340 *two double plumpers*: plumper: a vote given solely to one candidate when one has the right to vote for two or more. Cobbett stood at the Coventry election on 12 March 1820, but was defeated by a narrow margin. The *Examiner* of 12 March still shared Keats's expectation of a Cobbett victory and in a warming of its usual attitude towards him, also like Keats, welcomed the prospect of a representative in Parliament of 'the enlightened part of the poorer orders'.

341 *Taylor's manuscript*: that is, the *Lamia* volume.

342 *Clementi's*: Muzio Clementi (1752–1832) as well as being an important musician and composer ran a music publishing and instrument making firm in London.

343 *my present diet*: that is, his reversion to a non-vegetarian diet.

345 *and Miss Waldegra(ve.)*: ending cut away.

and has m(ade its) appearance: Haydon's *Christ's Entry into Jerusalem* was exhibited in the Egyptian Hall, Piccadilly, on 25 March.

348 *To Fanny Brawne, May (?) 1820*: written from Kentish Town, where Keats was now staying; see the previous letter.

351 *microscope of a Coterie*: many of Keats's friends did not approve of their relationship.

352 *infancy of truth"*: *Troilus and Cressida*, III. ii. 176–7.

353 *x x x's . . . when x x x x*: copyist's omissions, possibly referring to 'the Brawne's' and 'Abby' (Abigail O'Donoghue, Brown's housekeeper and mistress).

My book: the *Lamia* volume.

or see x x x x x x: probably 'the Dilkes'.

354 *I met x x x*: probably Monkhouse.

present x x x x x x x x: copyist's omissions.

Lucy Vaughan Lloyd: 'The Cap and Bells'.

355 *Friday Morn—*: written from Leigh Hunt's house in Kentish Town, where he had moved from his own lodgings because of blood spitting.

My dearest: signature cut away.

356 *Winter in Italy*: the recommendation was made by Dr George Darling, who attended many of the literary men in Keats's circle. Keats was also attended by Dr William Lambe.

357 *that no eye may catch it*: Keats was being careful that no one should see his affectionate opening in Hunt's crowded house.

brass upon my Palate: See *Hyperion*, i. 188–9.

358 *with his indecencies*: Brown had an illegitimate child by Abigail O'Donaghue, but Keats may also be referring—rather hypocritically—to the bawdy turn of mind both displayed in their letters.

360 *(An Amyntas)*: Keats dedicates this letter to Hunt, who had dedicated to him his poem *Amyntas, A Tale of the Woods* (1820).

patience at my lunes: presumably Keats is apologizing for his sensitivity over the opened letter among other things.

the Bearess: probably Fanny or Mrs Brawne.

to pull out. x x x x x x x x x x x x x x x: the copyist's omissions are impossible to supply.

good success among literary people: Keats is referring to the critical success of his *Lamia* volume.

361 *'load every rift'*: this famous piece of advice seems to draw on Matthew 6: 24 and *The Faerie Queene*, II. vii. 28, but its roots in Keats's thinking go back at least to his dislike of Wordsworth's moral designs on the reader and also connect with his more recent statements of his preference for a poetics of the affections over Godwinian principles.

362 *x x x x x x*: Brown said that this was a continuation of the secret in his former letter to Brown, and a request that Brown would go to Rome with him.

a Dʳ Clarke: Dr (later Sir) James Clarke (1788–1870).

363 *'turning a Neuk'*: Burns, 'To Miss Ferrier', l. 15.

364 *of a friend*: that is, Fanny Brawne, to whom Keats dictated this letter.

in some liking": *1 Henry IV*, III. iii. 5–6, slightly misquoted.

366 *at the Health Office*: the authorities kept the ship in quarantine because of an outbreak of typhus in London; the quarantine was extended further because a party of British sailors came on board who then had to stay in the ship a further seven days.

367 *tell Tootts*: nickname for Margaret Brawne.

368 *I cannot q——*: probably 'quiff' (that is, fuck).

369 *from x x x x x*: omission of 'Haslam' by copyist.

370 *tell x x x x*: names omitted by copyist here cannot be supplied.

SOURCES OF MANUSCRIPT LETTERS

Sources given below in abbreviated form are listed in full in the acknowledgements to the first edition on p. xi.

1816   9 October, Historical Society of Pennsylvania; 31 October, Berg Collection; 20 November, Harvard.

1817   10 May, 10 September, British Museum; 10, 11 May, 16 May, 28 September, 8 October, 28–30 October, 3 November, 22 November (to Bailey), Harvard.

1818   5 January, C. H. Pforzheimer, Jr.; 10 January, 23 January (to Bailey), 14 February, 21 February, 13 March, 24 March, 8 April, 17 April, 21, 25 May, 10 June, 27, 28 June, 3–9 July, 18, 22 July, 23, 26 July, 3, 6 August, 27 October, 14–31 October, 24 November, 22 December, Harvard; 23 January (to Taylor), 10–14 July, 19 August, 26 October, British Museum; 30 January, 27 February, 24 April, 2–5 July, Morgan Library; 19 February, Robert H. Taylor; 17–21 July, 20, 21 September, Keats Museum.

1819   16 December (1818)–4 January, 10 (?) January, 18 (?) February, 29 March, 13 April, 1 May, 14 February–3 May, 31 May, 17 June (to Haydon), 25 July, 14 August, 16 August, 23 August, 31 August, 5 September (to Hessey), 5 September (to Taylor), 21, 22 September, 3 October, 11 October, 19 October, 15 November, December (to Rice), Harvard; 11 February, 27 February, 13 March, 12 April, 9 June (to Fanny Keats), 17 June (to Fanny Keats), 6 July, 28 August, 26 (?) October, 20 December, British Museum; 31 March, 31 July, 22 September (to Dilke), 1 October, Keats Museum; 8 July, 12 November, Historical Society of Pennsylvania; 5, 6 August, Maine Historical Society; 24 August, Berg Collection; 13 September, Archibald S. Alexander; 17–27 September, 17 November, Morgan Library; 13 October, Haverford College.

1820   13–28 January (first 8 pages), 28 February, University of Texas; 13–28 January (last 2 pages beginning 'Friday 27th'), Yale University: 6 February, 8 February, 14 February, 20 March, 1 April, 12 April, 21 April, 4 May, 23 June, 5 July, 22 July, 13 August (to Fanny Keats), 16 August, 23 August, British Museum; 10 (?) February, 2 letters of February (?) to Fanny Brawne (pp. 331,

332), 14, 16 February, February (?) to Fanny Brawne (p. 334), 29 (?) February, March (?) to Fanny Brawne (p. 342), 24 (?) March, June (?) to Fanny Brawne (p. 351), 11 (?) June, 25 June (?), 4 July (?), 30 September, Harvard; 24 (?) February, Indiana University; 27 (?) February, Princeton University; 1 March (?), Roger Barrett; 4 March, May (?) to Fanny Brawne (p. 348), 24 (?) October, Keats Museum; March (?) to Fanny Brawne (p. 341), Archibald S. Alexander; March (?) to Fanny Brawne (p. 343), Robert H. Taylor; August (?) to Fanny Brawne (p. 357), 13 (?) August, Berg Collection; 13 August (to John Taylor), Morgan Library; 11 September, Keats–Shelley Memorial House, Rome.

KEATS'S CORRESPONDENTS

BAILEY, BENJAMIN (1791–1853). Keats met Bailey, an undergraduate at Oxford at the time, through Reynolds and Rice in the spring of 1817. He stayed with Bailey that autumn in Oxford, where he learnt from Bailey's interest in Dante, Hazlitt, Milton, and Wordsworth. Keats credited Bailey with a 'philosophic' or 'disinterested' concern for human suffering. Bailey defended *Endymion* in two *Oxford Herald* articles in early summer 1818. Soon afterwards he was ordained and became curate in Carlisle. He had seemed to be courting Mariane Reynolds, but married his Bishop's daughter in 1819. Keats was disillusioned at what he saw as Bailey's duplicity in the matter.

BRAWNE, FRANCES (Fanny) (1800–65). Probably met Keats some time in the summer of 1818 when she and her mother and siblings (Samuel and Margaret 'Toots') rented Brown's half of Wentworth Place. Her paternal grandfather, like Keats's, had been an innkeeper. The Brawne family rented Dilke's half of Wentworth Place from April 1819; Keats moved in with Brown in October. Keats seems to have proposed in December 1818. They were engaged with her mother's approval the following year. She corresponded with Fanny Keats after his death. Several of Keats's friends —some of whom strongly disapproved of the relationship—comment on her vivacity and independence.

BRAWNE, FRANCES RICKETTS (Mrs Samuel) (1778?–1829). Widowed mother of Fanny. She seems to have welcomed Keats's engagement with her daughter despite the fragility of both his health and financial situation. She nursed Keats with her daughter prior to his departure for Italy.

BROWN, CHARLES ARMITAGE (1787–1842). One of Keats's closest and most supportive friends. Brown had returned to Britain from Russia in 1810 after a failed business venture. His comic opera *Narensky* was successfully performed at Drury Lane in 1814. He met Keats some time in 1817, and the following year they toured together in the north. After Tom Keats died, Keats became Brown's tenant at Wentworth Place (the house he jointly owned with Charles Dilke). In September 1819, Brown was informally married to his housekeeper Abigail O'Donoghue with whom he had a son.

CLARKE, CHARLES COWDEN (1787–1877). Author and lecturer, son of Keats's schoolteacher at Enfield. He taught at the school himself, and had a great influence on Keats in the early years. It was Cowden Clarke who encouraged him to read the *Examiner* and fed his liberal politics and developing literary tastes. He also introduced Keats to Leigh Hunt. Cowden Clarke moved to Ramsgate in 1817, and was less often in contact with Keats thereafter. He married Mary, the daughter of Vincent Novello.

DILKE, CHARLES WENTWORTH (1789–1864). Civil servant and author, joint owner of Wentworth Place with his old school friend Brown. The interest he shared with many of Keats's friends in Elizabethan and Jacobean drama is reflected in his continuation of Dodsley's *Old Plays* (1814–16). He seems to have met Keats at some time in 1817, after which time the poet frequently visited Dilke and his wife Maria. In April 1819 Dilke moved to Westminster to be near his son who was at school there. Although Keats was sometimes irritated by his obsessive concern for his son and unsympathetic to his brand of Godwinian radicalism, he was a close and trusted friend. After Keats's death he supervised Fanny's financial affairs, initiating an action against Richard Abbey, and later became editor of the *Athenaeum*.

HAYDON, BENJAMIN ROBERT (1786–1846). History painter who came to London to study at the Royal Academy in 1804. His paintings tended to be on a grand scale dealing with epic subjects, but he struggled with failing eyesight and financial difficulties. Haydon was a fervent admirer of the Elgin marbles, to which he introduced Keats, and regarded himself as the decisive factor in the government's decision to buy them. He met Keats at Hunt's during October 1816. Hunt and Haydon often argued, especially over religious matters, and over 1816–17 they fought for influence over Keats. The 'Immortal Dinner' attended by Wordsworth, Lamb, and Keats took place in Haydon's studio in December 1817. Haydon included Keats in his painting *Christ's Entry into Jerusalem* (not exhibited in public until 1820), but their friendship cooled later when Haydon refused to repay a loan.

HESSEY, JAMES AUGUSTUS (1785–1870). Partner with John Taylor of Taylor and Hessey publishers. The firm took over *Poems* (1817) from the Olliers and published Keats's other two volumes of verse. Hessey was more involved with business matters than his partners, but he remained a generous friend to Keats and contributed with Taylor to the expenses of the final trip to Italy.

HUNT, JAMES HENRY LEIGH (1784–1870). Poet, co-founder, and editor of the *Examiner*. Sentenced to prison with his brother John for libelling the Prince Regent in the paper in 1813, he became a hero to Keats even before they met in 1816. Hunt showed Keats's poetry to Hazlitt and other literary people, and published it in the *Examiner*. Although Keats often resisted his literary advice, and sometimes shrank from his vanity and affectation, the friendship held over the course of Keats's life and introduced him to a vibrant social and intellectual environment. Their association in the 'Cockney School' provided the focus of the attacks on Keats in the conservative press.

JEFFERY, MARY-ANN (1798–?) and Sarah (?). Daughters of the Teignmouth family with whom Tom, first with George, and then with Keats, stayed in 1818. Editors before Gittings sometimes made the mistake of thinking there were three sisters because Sarah was also known as Fanny. There is a tradition that Mary-Ann was in love with Keats. Her poem 'Si deseris pereo' is addressed to him.

KEATS, FRANCES MARY (Fanny) (1803–89). The youngest of the Keats siblings, she was given a restrictive upbringing by her guardian Richard Abbey. In 1816 she was sent to a boarding-school in Walthamstow, which she left two years later. Abbey tried to limit her contact with Keats, but they developed a close and caring relationship. When she came of age in 1824, Dilke forced Abbey to make over her portion of her grandmother's estate. She married the Spanish novelist Valentin Llanos in 1826.

KEATS, GEORGE (1797–1841). After leaving the Enfield school, George worked for a time at Abbey's firm. He left in 1816 after a quarrel. Before emigrating to America in the summer of 1818, he lived with Keats and Tom in London. He had married Georgiana Wylie not long before they left for the Birkbeck settlement in Illinois. Disappointed with what they found there, they moved on to Kentucky, where George suffered a business setback after investing with the naturalist Audubon. Later they moved to Louisville, where George eventually became a respected citizen. In 1820 he was forced to return to Britain to seek financial help. He does not seem to have been aware of how difficult it was for Keats to help him financially, but the result was some resentment on Keats's part, and this feeling seems to have ended the marvellous journal letters that had crossed the Atlantic over 1818–19.

KEATS, GEORGIANA AUGUSTA WYLIE (1799?–1879). Daughter of a junior army officer, she married George Keats in the spring of 1818 and left for America with him soon afterwards. Keats seems to have admired her spirited independence, and his letters suggest that he felt able to relax in her company. She remarried in 1843, two years after her husband's death.

KEATS, THOMAS (1799–1818). Tom worked with George for a short time at Abbey's firm after leaving school, but the consumption that was to prove fatal forced him to leave. He visited France with George in 1817. In early 1818 he convalesced in Teignmouth, nursed by each of his brothers in turn. He returned with Keats to London in the spring. After a slow and painful illness, through which Keats nursed him, he died on 1 December.

REYNOLDS, JOHN HAMILTON (1794–1852). Originally a clerk in an insurance office, Reynolds briefly tried a literary career before he took up articles with a law firm in November 1817. The decision seems to have been based on a need to secure a reliable enough source of income for him to marry. He had met Keats through Hunt the previous year, and played an important role in extending his circle of friends. Keats was very close to Reynolds's mother and his two sisters Jane (1791–1846) and Marian (1797–1874), until their disapproving comments on their cousin Jane Cox led to a cooling. Reynolds's poetry included *The Naiad* (1817) and a wonderful parody of Wordsworth's *Peter Bell* brought out in April shortly before the original was published. Keats and Reynolds planned a collaborative volume based on Boccaccio. The fruits of the unfulfilled plan were Keats's 'Isabella' and Reynolds's own volume *The Garden of Florence* (1821). He defended Keats in the press against the attacks in the *Quarterly* in October 1818. A close friend who shared many of Keats's literary and political attitudes, their friendship seems to have become more distant after the engagement to Fanny Brawne.

RICE, JAMES (1792–1832?). Rice met Keats through Reynolds. Rice and Reynolds were members with Bailey of a literary society (the Zetosophians). Rice was continually in ill health, but Keats appreciated his cheerful spirits and good sense. He helped pay the expenses of Keats's trip to Italy.

SEVERN, JOSEPH (1793–1879). Keats and George (who became close to him) seem to have met Severn in 1816 when he was struggling to establish himself as a painter. He was also a friend of Haslam, Hunt, Reynolds, and Brown. His *Cave of Despair* painting won a Royal Academy prize in 1818, but his early work was not particularly successful. At Haslam's suggestion he went with Keats to Rome, and nursed him until his death. He stayed on in Rome and eventually became British consul there. He is buried beside Keats. Before and after Keats's death, he created several portraits of the poet.

SHELLEY, PERCY BYSSHE (1792–1822). Radical poet. He met Keats through Hunt, who celebrated them both (and Reynolds) in his 'Young Poets' essay in the *Examiner* of 1 December 1816. His arrival in the Hunt circle seems to have discomforted Keats. Hunt later ascribed these feelings to a sense of social inferiority, but their personalities were not well matched. Shelley invited Keats to stay with him in Italy in 1820 when he learnt of his illness, and mythologized his death in *Adonais*.

TAYLOR, JOHN (1781–1864). The more literary partner in the Taylor and Hessey firm. From 1821 he edited the *London Magazine* with Thomas Hood, and, unknown to Keats, of whose admiration for her he was unaware, he developed a passionate friendship with Isabella Jones.

WOODHOUSE, RICHARD (1788–1834). Scholar and lawyer. He was an adviser to the Taylor and Hessey partnership. Woodhouse admired Keats's poetry, and began collecting memorabilia of the poet from early on. He was a supportive and generous friend during Keats's lifetime.

WYLIE, MRS JAMES. Mother of Georgiana, who lived with her son, Charles, after her daughter went to America. Keats seems to have kept up a warm relationship with them until his death.

INDEX

Numbers in bold indicate the first page of a letter written to the person listed. A reference followed by 'n.' is to the explanatory note for that page.

The Oxford World's Classics Website

www.worldsclassics.co.uk

- Information about new titles
- Explore the full range of Oxford World's Classics
- Links to other literary sites and the main OUP webpage
- Imaginative competitions, with bookish prizes
- Peruse *Compass*, the Oxford World's Classics magazine
- Articles by editors
- Extracts from Introductions
- A forum for discussion and feedback on the series
- Special information for teachers and lecturers

www.worldsclassics.co.uk